WOMEN AND THE MASS MEDIA

Sourcebook for Research and Action

WOMEN AND THE MASS MEDIA

Sourcebook for Research and Action

Matilda Butler, Ph.D.

*Far West Laboratory for
Educational Research and Development,
San Francisco, California*

William Paisley, Ph.D.

*Stanford University,
Palo Alto, California*

With a chapter on Children and Media by Suzanne Pingree, Ph.D., and Robert Hawkins, Ph.D.

*University of Wisconsin,
Madison, Wisconsin*

HUMAN SCIENCES PRESS

72 Fifth Avenue   3 Henrietta Street
NEW YORK, NY 10011 ● LONDON, WC2E 8LU

Copyright © 1980 by Human Sciences Press
72 Fifth Avenue, New York, New York 10011

Printed in the United States of America
1 98765432

Library of Congress Cataloging in Publication Data

Butler, Matilda.
  Women and the mass media.

  Bibliography: p.
  Includes index.
  1. Women's rights—United States.   2. Sex role
in mass-media.   3. Mass media and children.
4. Social action.   5. Sexism—United States.
I. Paisley, William, joint author.   II. Title.
HQ1426.B86   301.41'2   LC 79–16271
ISBN 0–87705–409–6   0–87705–419–3 (pbk.)

PREFACE

The need for this sourcebook arises in our teaching and research on media sexism. Students come to our courses concerned with media "isms"—sexism, racism, and other stereotypes. What they seek is a framework of research and action into which their concern can be translated.

Many of our students and perhaps some readers of this book are journalists. They know that the media are mirrors of the best and worst in society. Column by column and channel by channel, the media are a study in contradictions: courageous and timid, steadfast and vacillating, compassionate and crass. The same newspaper that challenges a president of the United States and wins is sued by its female employees and loses. Objecting where objection is warranted, we nonetheless remember that we became students of the media because of what they do right, not because of what they do wrong.

The topics in this book have been discussed at length in Stanford and Wisconsin courses. Many ideas come from class discussions. The Stanford Organization for Women in Communication has been a forum for discussing problems that women face as media professionals, researchers, and academics.

As we worked with the literature on media sexism in planning our own studies and writing this book, we saw how scattered and inaccessible the earlier studies are. Therefore we have reviewed significant studies as extensively as space permits.

The five sections and twenty chapters of this book have been designed with several uses in mind. The instructor who assigns *Women and the Mass Media* as the core text in a course on women and communication (whether taught with a communication or women's studies focus) will find that the book can be divided into about twenty discussion units. Chapters 1 and 4 are best discussed together in the first substantive meeting of the course. Chapters 2 and 3 form a second discussion unit; an instructor with a background in linguistics or psychology may wish to expand on the theoretical foundations of these chapters or perhaps conduct an experiment in class.

Other chapters form integral discussion units; however, Chapter 12 may be divided into two discussion units because of its length and because of the importance of the employment issue. Class meetings can be devoted to student projects after studying Chapters 10 and 14. That is, content analyses of popular media, with pairs of students check-coding the same content and with the class as a whole spreading itself across a systematic sample of content, will reduce the methodological mystery associated with content analyses reviewed in the book. Similarly, institutional analyses (even if they are only masthead counts of male/female ratios on magazine editorial staffs, although interviews with local media staffers are also possible) will consolidate the propositions covered in Chapters 11 to 14.

Analyses conducted by class members can provide useful findings (see Notes 5 and 36 ff.) in Chapter 12 for reference to four of the numerous class analyses that we review for their findings.

We do not propose a class-conducted audience analysis following Chapter 18 because of the problems of gathering field data within the constraints of a course. However, the class itself could participate in an effects experiment, with random assignment of class members to experimental conditions involving films, television programs, printed materials, etc.

The discussion units and activities just described can be compressed or expanded as necessary to fit either quarter or semester scheduling.

As the supplementary text in a course such as "Mass Media in Society," the book as a whole can serve as a lecture resource while students read a sampling of chapters. Chapters 1 to 4, 6, 9, 10, 12, 16 to 18, and 20 provide a "reader's digest" of the book for this purpose.

Local media action groups and local chapters of national organizations such as NOW can use the book as a resource in media sexism workshops by making one workshop participant responsible for a five- to ten-minute presentation on each chapter. Thereafter, throughout the workshop, that participant can serve as resource person for the particular chapter. Workshops longer than a day or two can use the book more as a course text.

Other users of the book, including media personnel, administrators, legislators, educators, parents, etc., will find that the index crosses the dimensions of content, institution, and audience with the six media (television, radio, magazines, newspapers, books, and films) that are repeatedly discussed. Thus the reader can quickly find studies dealing with each dimension in relation to each medium.

MATILDA BUTLER
WILLIAM PAISLEY
Palo Alto, California

ROBERT HAWKINS
SUZANNE PINGREE
Madison, Wisconsin

ACKNOWLEDGMENTS

Friends and advisers have improved each draft of this book with suggestions for revision and with fugitive materials from their files. There is more than an alphabetical reason for mentioning Donna Allen first; as editor and publisher of *Media Report to Women,* she has documented the current history of women and the media for more than six years. Kathleen Bonk, Audrey Rowe Colom, Douglas Ferguson, Marilyn Fife, Helen Franzwa, George Gerbner, Timothy Haight, Karen Shapiro, William Rivers, and Valerie Wheat are among the many others whose help we gratefully acknowledge.

Both in research and in manuscript production, our good friend M. Violet Lofgren worked tirelessly until every page met her high standards for accuracy and appearance.

Norma Fox, editor in chief of Human Sciences Press, provided guidance in the final revision of the book and exerted gentle pressure toward its completion. Vivian H. Kahane carefully edited the last draft. We appreciate her attention to detail.

Chapter 17, on children and media, is close to us. In writing the book we often thought of Allison, Andy, Edward, Hailey, Kenneth, Paisley, Raymond, and William, four of whom were born during (and contributed to) the book's own long gestation. Children come to media with exuberance and open minds. Do they find what they deserve?

M. B.
W. P.
R. H.
S. P.

CONTENTS

ANTECEDENTS

This book is about sexism in media. What do we mean by sexism? And what are media? Let us begin a glossary of key terms used in this book.

Sexism refers to a set of beliefs, formerly enacted into law and still reinforced by social custom, concerning the appropriate social roles of women and men. In American society, women play a limited (although increasing) range of roles. Many of these roles are subordinate to men's roles (e.g., nurse to doctor, secretary to boss). Reversals in women's and men's roles, although possible and heartening, are rare. Like the domestic roles of wife and mother, women's working roles are circumscribed by beliefs about intellectual and emotional differences between women and men.

As you might expect, biological differences are somewhere in the background of sexist beliefs. Few people would say that a nurse is biologically unfit to be a doctor or that a secretary is biologically unfit to be a boss. However, women's biological role of child*bearing,* itself only a brief episode in their lives, is generalized into the social role of being more responsible than men for child*rearing.* Long-term responsibility for childrearing keeps women away from the training and apprenticeship that desirable working roles require.

Persistent beliefs fulfill their own predictions. If girls and women are told often enough that they are intellectually, emotionally, or biologically inferior to men, some of them will believe what they are told and play the dumb, unstable, or weak role. Given a normal distribution of abilities and other traits among women and men, there will always be cases of competence and incompetence that "confirm" the sexist beliefs held by both sexes.

Sexists beliefs held by both sexes? Many women doubt that the sexes can be or should be equal. Others find that playing the dependent role is comfortable. Still others worry that sexual equality will leave them in limbo, lacking social approval for the dependent role of the past and lacking skills for the independent role of the future.

Actually, dogmatic sexual equality is almost as sexist as dogmatic sexual inequality. To progress beyond "-isms" we must encounter people as individuals, not as groups whose characteristics dictate equal or unequal treatment. Not every man has the ability to play a wide range of social roles; neither does every woman. The long sexist era of human history will be over when we do not notice, except as a point of individual appreciation, whether the individuals who make society function are women or men.

Media (or, more formally, *media of mass communication*) are typographic, photographic, and electronic systems for disseminating messages to many people at the same time. Media account for about half of the daily communication input of the average American. The other half of this comes from direct experience, from listening to other people and observing events. By scripting, producing, and disseminating identical messages to large audiences, media substitute inexpensive one-to-many communication of indirect experience for expensive one-to-one communication of direct experience.

Ranked according to average audience hours per day, the American media are *television, radio, newspapers, magazines, films,* and *books.* Although their use is more age restricted than other media, *phonograph records* and *audiotapes* also belong on this list.

Throughout this century, new media have blurred the distinction between direct and indirect experience. In the case of newspapers and magazines—the media of 1900—the reader's sense of involvement depends on imagination and reading skill. With the introduction of motion pictures, radio and television, a sense of involvement comes easily to the viewer and listener.

Whether you belonged to the film or TV generation as a child, do you remember wondering whether the enchanting or terrifying story you had just seen was real? Children still ponder that question.

If we take away the photographic and electronic media, and return to the typographic media of 1900, we might be less concerned about media sexism. However, the photographic and electronic media are very much with us (almost as much with us, by weekly average, as school and work), and what they disseminate should be called *surrogate direct experience.* The photographic and electronic media have mastered the production of what Daniel Boorstin calls "pseudo-events"—contrived happenings marked by simplicity and stereotypy.[1] Pseudo-events are seductive and memorable in a society where complexity causes "information overload."[2]

Are there practical questions behind this jargon? What do the media pseudo-events tell us and our children about the roles that women and men play in American society? Sometimes it seems that hours of television are devoted to "lessons for dumb housewives" from crisp, knowledgeable, male voice-overs (commercials in which the product is extolled by an unseen speaker). How true is that impression? Sometimes it seems that women are an endangered species on television programs; even when they are not being murdered or brutalized by men, their helplessness raises doubts about their survival. What does an analysis of television programs say about the roles given to women and men? Many women are movers and doers in American society. Do the media tell us about them?

Who are the media decision makers who choose what we see and hear? What are their values? How many of them are women? Do women have a fair chance to work at each level in the media?

What are the effects of media messages on their audiences? What are the effects on children; do they believe and internalize the messages, such as the helplessness of women? What are the effects on adults; in the more than 20,000 commercials that the average adult television viewer sees in a year, does the 500th or the 1000th "lesson for dumb housewives" cause the viewer to doubt that women are capable of self-government?

If the media have been entrusted with great power and are abusing it, what can be done to correct the abuses? Are additional facts needed from research (e.g., from monitoring)? What legal and economic action can be taken? What are some opportunities for "direct action?"

Media sexism raises many questions in our minds, and this book tries to answer them. Some of the answers are not satisfactory, because studies have not been conducted and actions have not been attempted. The last chapter of this book leaves some important questions for you to answer.

Historically, media sexism is influenced by roles that women have played in American society and by the 200-year struggle for women's rights. Chapter 1 reviews the high points and low points of that history.

Conceptually, media sexism is conveyed by linguistic forms and visual images that are fixed in the rituals of reporting, scripting, editing, and producing media messages. Chapters 2 and 3 provide frameworks for thinking about sexism in language and image.

The growth of American media in the past century has been so rapid that each generation of twentieth-century Americans has been born into a different media environment. Chapter 4 discusses the one unchanging fact about American media—that their structure and function change in every decade.

WOMEN'S RIGHTS IN AMERICA

All I ask of our brethren is that they will take their feet from off our necks.[1]

THE 200-YEAR STRUGGLE FOR WOMEN'S RIGHTS IN AMERICA

Equality for women dominates the American civil rights agenda of the 1970s. Two hundred years after Abigail Adams pressed her husband to represent women's rights at the Continental Congress in 1777, those rights are still to be fought for. The Equal Rights Amendment, or ERA, first introduced in Congress in 1923 at the urging of former women suffragists (not "suffragettes," a derisive term coined by the media) was not passed finally by the House of Representative until 1971 and the Senate until 1972. The text of the amendment, "Equality of rights under the law shall not be denied or abridged by the United States or any State on account of sex," is being interpreted by ERA opponents to foreshadow unisex bathrooms and homosexual marriages. In 1979 the amendment still lacks 3 of the 38 state ratifications needed. States seeking to rescind previous ratifications are receiving more publicity than new states seeking to ratify ERA. The granddaughters of suffragists have learned that their rights are slow to be won.

With or without ERA, women's legal, economic, educational, and occupational rights now rest on a decade of remarkable legislation: the Equal Pay Act of 1963, the Civil Rights Act of 1964, the Equal Employment Opportunity Act of 1972, the Education Amendments of 1972, the Equal Credit Opportunity Act of 1974, and comparable acts of the states (16 of which have added equal rights amendments to their own constitutions). However, noncompliance with equal rights laws by businesses, labor unions, educational institutions, etc., creates enforcement problems that federal and state governments have not solved. ERA advocates believe that the amendment will strengthen enforcement of these laws and also invalidate discriminatory laws (e.g., "protective" labor laws) still on the books in many states.

The struggle for women's rights in America has many origins. By the 1830s, two sets of events prepared women to speak on their own behalf. The 1830s were the pioneering decade of women's higher education. Oberlin College, founded in 1833, welcomed both women and men. Mount Holyoke College, founded in 1837, was the first women's college. Women college graduates, although rare for decades, did not remain silent in a society governed by men who, on the average, had completed only primary education.

The 1830s also saw the growth of the abolition movement from a handful of agitators to a national organization. The American Anti-Slavery Society was established in 1833, followed by abolition societies for women, who were excluded from the male societies. For women, the arguments against black oppression and the practice of speaking publicly for an unpopular cause provided both the substance and the skill that served their own movement a few years later. The cadence of an abolition speech can be heard in Sarah Grimke's famous words:

I ask no favors for my sex. . . . All I ask of our brethren is that
they will take their feet from off our necks and permit us to stand
upright on that ground which God destined us to occupy.[2]

The first notable consciousness raising for women's rights
took place in 1840 at the World Anti-Slavery Convention in
London. Women delegates, who had worked as hard and risked
as much as men in the American abolition movement, were
refused seats. The Reverend A. Harvey of Glasgow stated his
conviction that:

. . . if I were to give a vote in favor of females sitting and deliber-
ating in such an assembly as this, . . . I should be acting in
opposition to the plain teaching of the Word of God.[3]

Lucretia Mott and Elizabeth Cady Stanton, rebuffed in
London, decided that a women's rights convention was necessary. They began planning what became the Seneca Falls Convention of 1848. The convention was well attended by men and
women. The Declaration of Principles that was adopted (and
signed by 32 men as well as the women delegates) remained the
women's rights agenda well into the twentieth century.

In a statement before the New York State Legislature in
1860, Elizabeth Cady Stanton drew a parallel between sexism
and racism.

The woman has no name. She is Mrs. Richard Roe or Mrs. John
Doe, just whose Mrs. she may chance to be. . . . Mrs. Roe has
no right to her earnings; she can neither buy nor sell, make
contracts, nor lay up anything that she can call her own. . . . Mrs.
Roe has no legal existence; she has not the best right to her own
person. The husband has the power to restrain and administer
moderate chastisement.[4]

From 1850 to 1865 many feminists subordinated their own
cause to black liberation. The women's movement also suffered
from the neglect of men such as Frederick Douglass, whose

Rochester newspaper had supported the Seneca Falls Convention. Douglass stated that his work for black liberation had to be single minded.

While the Negro is mobbed, beaten, shot, stabbed, hanged, burnt, and is the target of all that is malignant in the North and all that is murderous in the South, his claims may be preferred by me without in any wise exposing myself to the imputation of narrowness or meanness toward the cause of women.[5]

Although Douglass was back in their ranks when the feminists marched in Washington in 1871, the united front against racism and sexism faltered after the Civil War for another reason. Leaders of the women's movement felt they had to oppose the proposed Fourteenth Amendment. Unlike the Constitution itself, the amendment seemed to restrict suffrage to "male citizens twenty-one years of age." Prior to the Fourteenth Amendment, power to grant suffrage to women lay with the states. If the amendment passed, feminists led by Elizabeth Cady Stanton and Susan B. Anthony believed that their efforts to win over state legislatures would be in vain.

Some feminists disagreed with Stanton and Anthony on the timing and strategy of their opposition to the Fourteenth Amendment. As a result, two separate women's suffrage organizations were founded in 1869. The National Woman Suffrage Association, led by Stanton and Anthony, took the more radical positions on suffrage, women's labor, marriage, organized religion, etc. The newspaper of this association, *The Revolution,* examined topics such as the double standard and prostitution under its masthead motto, "Men, their rights and nothing more; women, their rights and nothing less."[6]

The more moderate American Woman Suffrage Association was led by Lucy Stone and her husband, Henry Blackwell. Although the "American," unlike the "National," sought respectability for suffrage by skirting the controversial issues of marriage and religion, it was not a token association. Stone was possibly the first American woman to insist on keeping her birth name in marriage. Blackwell was the founder of the first women's hospital in America and the brother of Elizabeth Blackwell, first American woman physician.

In 1890 the two factions were reunited in the National American Woman Suffrage Association, which then launched the final two decades of the campaign for suffrage. Stanton, Anthony, Stone, and Blackwell did not live to savor the victory of the Nineteenth Amendment or the reorganization of their suffrage association as the League of Women Voters.

Is this how women's suffrage came about? Certainly these associations and their redoubtable leaders forced the issue of women's suffrage on the national consciousness. A women's suffrage amendment was introduced into every session of Congress from 1878 to 1919.

But why was women's suffrage won between 1919 and 1920 instead of many years earlier or later? Not, we think, because of legal, economic, or social necessity, but because of symbolism. Two richly symbolic acts occurred in the 1910s.

The first event was world war. In large measure, women won the right to vote on the assembly lines of wartime factories. A nation of "go-getters"[7] was unimpressed by suffrage arguments as long as women remained at home. However, the sight of women doing "men's work" in the heat, noise, and danger of war industry affected public opinion both in the United States and in England, which extended suffrage to women in 1918.

The second event was female militancy. In 1913 a militant feminist, Alice Paul, founded a radical group that was to focus its efforts entirely on the passage of a federal constitutional amendment. (The National American Woman Suffrage Association worked in the *states*, mounting hundreds of campaigns to place suffrage arguments before the voters, legislatures, and constitutional conventions).[8] Paul's group, the Congressional Union, introduced an unpredictable jeopardy into the congressional delay on a suffrage amendment.

The Congressional Union's hunger strikes, demonstrations, and uninvited visits to Congress were reminiscent of the tactics of the English suffrage organization, the Women's Social and Political Union, prior to 1912. The similarity was not coincidental; Alice Paul had been working with the Women's Social and Political Union in London before returning to the United States. As the Congressional Union progressed to window smashing according to the English plan, American politicians must have wondered when arson and bombing would follow.

Between 1912 and the outbreak of World War I, the activities of English suffragists had escalated from the hunger strikes of 1909. In one historian's summary, the suffragists:

> ... burned and looted and smashed, chalked slogans wherever a stretch of pavement was unwatched by the constabulary eye, burned "Votes for Women" in acid on the putting greens of exclusive golf courses, fired catapults full of stones from the tops of double-decker buses, placed bombs in Liberal strongholds up and down the country, set fire to the Tea Pavilion at Kew and almost every week rallied and marched and spoke, so that London rang with the sound of their voices.[9]

Only World War I saved England from the suffragists.[10] In the United States, not occupied with the war until 1917, the Congressional Union was a symbol of latent violence and disruption. While ostensibly yielding to the demands of the National American Woman Suffrage Association, politicians watched over their shoulders for Congressional Union guerillas.[11]

What do the 1910s tell us about the winning of women's rights? Both in England and in the United States, the key to women's suffrage lay in:

1.   A large and well-disciplined organization.
2.   Eloquent spokespersons.

3. A few friends on the inside.
4. A threatening capacity for "direct action."

The horrors of World War I led to a rejection of social concerns and a retreat into private lives in the 1920s. In countries like England and the United States, many of the most able women and men, exhausted in battle and disillusioned in victory, chose libertine over libertarian as their philosophy. The women's movement dwindled to stalwarts like Alice Paul, who recognized that suffrage was an empty privilege if women did not press for other denied rights.

The 1930s produced a hiatus of another kind. Economic disaster led to suppression of men's rights as well as women's rights. The rise of fascism amid collapsed economies overshadowed the subtler issue of women's rights.

When world war returned, the role of women again became egalitarian by necessity. Short of combat duty, there were few roles that women did not play in the armed services, in war industries, and in domestic occupations from which men had been called away. "Rosie the Riveter" symbolized women's new versatility.

The last women's gesture of World War II patriotism was to vacate jobs on behalf of returning veterans. Women yielded their well-earned positions in the work force more grudgingly in 1945 than in 1918. It took a media campaign on "the feminine mystique" of wifehood and motherhood to get them home again.[12] The "new look" of women's fashions in the early 1950s brought skirts down to decorative rather than functional length.

The redomestication campaign was only briefly successful. As soon as the postwar "baby boom" passed, women left home again. They crowded the colleges, including the graduate and professional schools. They won election to legislatures. They challenged and overcame sex discrimination in field after field. They lobbied and voted for federal and state laws that began to confirm women's legal, economic, educational, and occupational rights for the future.

However, as leaders of the black liberation movement learned earlier, the progress of an oppressed group looks better on paper than in shops, offices, union halls, schoolrooms, and public assemblies. When overt discrimination becomes illegal, it often goes underground in the beliefs of employers, labor leaders, educators, etc. Covert forms of discrimination are traps that spring on women, like blacks, along paths marked by "equal opportunity" signs.

We cannot minimize the progress in women's rights that has been made in all 200 years of the American national experience. Thousands of women and men lent their talents and efforts to the struggle. However, seeing around us the sexism that laws do not defeat, we pace ourselves to think of 2000, not 1980, as a victory year for the women's movement.

INSIGHTFUL PARALLELS BETWEEN RACISM AND SEXISM

In the nineteenth century feminists compared the status of women with that of blacks, and even a black leader like Frederick Douglass accepted the parallel (see page 26). More recently, Swedish sociologist Gunnar Myrdal noted in his study of American racism:

> . . . there are at least two groups of people, besides the Negroes, who are characterized by high social visibility expressed in physical appearance, dress, and patterns of behavior, and who have been "suppressed." We refer to women and children. Their present status, as well as their history and their problems in society, reveal striking similarities to those of the Negroes.[13]

Another social scientist, Helen Mayer Hacker, took up the women's side in a pioneering article, "Women as a Minority Group." Hacker first met the difficulty that many women do not view themselves as members of a minority group. These women were either "those who do not know that they are being discriminated against on a group basis," or "those who acknowledge the propriety of differential treatment on a group basis." Women's insensitivity to discrimination may arise in socialization.

> Militating against a feeling of group identification on the part of women is a differential factor in their socialization. Members of a minority group are frequently socialized within their own groups. . . . The conception of his role by a Negro or a Jew or a second-generation immigrant is greatly dependent upon the definitions offered by members of his own group, on their attitudes and behavior toward him. . . . But only rarely does a woman experience this type of group belongingness. Her interactions with the opposite sex may be as frequent as her relationships with members of her own sex. Women's conceptions of themselves, therefore, spring as much from their intimate relationships with men as with women.[14]

At the heart of Hacker's argument is this schematic presentation of Myrdal's parallels.[15]

Negroes	*Women*
1. *High social visibility*	
a. Skin color, other "racial" characteristics.	a. Secondary sex characteristics.
b. (Sometimes) distinctive dress, bandana, flashy clothes.	b. Distinctive dress, skirts, etc.
2. *Ascribed attributes*	
a. Inferior intelligence, smaller brain, less convoluted, scarcity of geniuses.	a. Ditto.
b. More free in instinctual gratifications. More emotional, "primitive" and childlike. Imagined sexual prowess envied.	b. Irresponsible, inconsistent, emotionally unstable. Lack strong superego. Women as "temptresses."

3. Rationalization of status

a. Thought all right in his place.

b. Myth of contented Negro.

a. Woman's place is in the home.

b. Myth of contented woman—"feminine" woman is happy in subordinate role.

4. Accommodation attitudes

a. Supplicatory whining intonation of voice.

b. Deferential manner.

c. Concealment of real feelings.

d. Outwit "white folks."

e. Careful study of points at which dominant group is susceptible to influence.

f. Fake appeals for directives; show of ignorance.

a. Rising inflection, smiles, laughs, downward glances.

b. Flattering manner.

c. "Feminine wiles."

d. Outwit "menfolk."

e. Ditto.

f. Appearance of helplessness.

5. Discrimination

a. Limitations on education—should fit "place" in society.

b. Confined to traditional jobs—barred from supervisory positions.

c. Competition feared.

d. No family precedents for new aspirations.

e. Deprived of political importance.

f. Social and professional segregation.

g. More vulnerable to criticism.

a. Ditto.

b. Ditto.

c. Ditto.

d. Ditto.

e. Ditto.

f. Ditto.

g. Ditto; for example, conduct in bars.

Hacker goes on to discuss the function or purpose of discrimination.

The sex relations cycle bears important similarities to the race relations cycle. In the wake of the Industrial Revolution, as women acquired industrial, business, and professional skills, they increasingly sought employment in competition with men. Men were quick to perceive them as a rival group.... They excluded women from the trade unions, made contracts with employers to prevent their hiring women, passed laws restricting the employment of married women, caricatured the working woman, and carried on ceaseless propaganda to return women to the home and keep them there.[16]

In 1972 Hacker told the American Psychological Association that progress against sex discrimination was slow and that liberationists

... seek to move the minds of the majority of American women who have no wish to be liberated. It is indeed understandable that older women whose lives have followed the traditional pattern of domesticity have little or nothing to gain from the liberation movement, but rather are threatened by a devaluation of their status as homemakers and mothers.... At this point in their lives attractive options are not open to them. Similarly, unless stirred by a spark of divine discontent, it is difficult to resist the enormous appeal of being given social approval for a dependent, secure status protected from competition.[17]

The media played a dual role in black liberation. After decades of caricaturing blacks, the media became platforms for black leaders. The "status-conferral" function of media elevated Martin Luther King, Malcolm X, and other black leaders to the status of folk heroes.[18] Caricatures of blacks have not disappeared from the media, but progress toward fair presentation is evident in any comparison of media content across decades since the late nineteenth century.

No comparable progress is found in media portrayal of women. The United Nations Commission on the Status of Women noted a parallel between "the endless jokes about mothers-in-law and nagging wives and dumb blondes" and the kindly illiterate 'Uncle Tom' blacks that most producers have now been shamed out of portraying.[19] The UN report identified three aspects of the female stereotype in advertisements.

1. "Women are usually portrayed as unable to think for themselves"; they defer to men to make decisions.
2. "Loss of masculine approval is viewed as a threat"; the advertised products are used to gain approval from men.
3. "According to advertisements, women seem to be obsessed with cleanliness"; they express a "gamut of emotions" in embracing whiteness, brightness, and freshness.[20]

Of course, the public shares responsibility with writers and media producers for these stereotypes of women. The public often rejects nonstereotypic portrayals, at least insofar as television ratings reflect public attitudes. However, media managers do not allow racist attitudes of the public to dictate media portrayals of blacks. Sexist attitudes of the public should not dictate media portrayals of women.

Writers, producers, and media managers may be experiencing "future shock" of a kind. Demands on them to lead, and not to follow public opinion, are growing. They have no special training or motivation for this role. As a management consultant confessed to one feminist writer, "I'm not ready for a woman. But, boy, would I love to get hold of a good Negro."[21]

SEXISM IN LANGUAGE

Womanly: Like or fit for a woman (womanly modesty);
Manly: Having the qualities that a man is supposed to
have; strong, brave, honest, etc.[1]

To Be a Linguistic Variant or to Be Ignored Altogether?

This chapter asks about the forms of sexism in *language.* What are the messages that keep women in their place?

Over thousands of years, the sexual caste system has created a sexist language that no speaker or writer can evade. That "woman," "female," and "she" are variants of the masculine forms becomes clear to children as they learn to read and write. Children learn that neuter nouns are implicitly masculine; variants are required to denote women: "driver," "lady driver"; "doctor," "woman doctor." Exceptions to this rule are stereotypic or unflattering: "nurse," "male nurse"; "prostitute," "male prostitute."

There is an alternative to being a linguistic variant, and that is to be ignored altogether. "Man" as a generic noun denotes both men and women in countless media contexts every day. In compounds such as "manpower" and "chairman" it reinforces the assumption that such persons are males.

Some research supports the hypothesis of "linguistic relativity" that language affects thought by facilitating some linguistic codings of experience and impeding others.[2] For example, on a walk through the forest, a person who knows many of the names of trees, flowers, birds, and animals will recollect the forest differently from a person who knows none of the names. A scientist and poet will recollect the forest according to their respective vocabularies of science and poetry.

The lifelong experience of women is to encounter themselves as linguistic variants or, in a literal sense, nonentities. More and more, women are keeping their own names after marriage, but they cannot obtain fair treatment from language as a whole. Jane Jones wins the skirmish of keeping her own name but loses the battle of identity in messages such as the following.

> Ask any Buick owner. He'll tell you that. . . .

> In choosing between the Ph.D. and Ed.D. programs, an applicant should consider whether his career goals lead him toward research or professional activities.

Once it is understood by users of a language that neuter nouns are implicitly masculine (e.g., "professor" equals "male holding professorial appointment") and that masculine pronouns denote both men and women (e.g., "he" encompasses "she"), the foundation is laid for a more conscious level of linguistic sexism. For example, in a 1974 convention announcement from the Association for Education in Journalism to journalism professors, these teachers of future journalists were told:

SEXISM IN LANGUAGE   37

... if you want double accommodations for yourself and your wife, your registration fee would be $100 ($65 for you as a member and $35 for your wife).[3]

We cite this example because it was written for the journalism profession, but recent examples are easy to find. A new advertisement for minicomputers states that:

... professionals using computer terminals at home have helped their wives organize family budgets, menus, investments, and tax records.[4]

Some sexist phrasings in advertising copy are calculated. Sales loss in the feminist market is more than balanced by sales gain in the nonfeminist market. The minicomputer advertisement does not seem to be based on such a calculation, nor would this rephrasing be less effective:

... professionals and their families use computer terminals to organize family budgets, menus, investments, and tax records.

Attitudes Toward the Status Quo

Sexism in the English language is not deplored by everyone who recognizes it. Otto Jesperson regarded English as "the most positively and expressively masculine" of the languages he knew. He called it "the language of a grown-up man, with very little childish or feminine about it."[5]

A peevish acknowledgment of linguistic sexism has appeared in *Editor and Publisher,* a trade journal for the press. In the "Editorial Workshop," Roy H. Copperud wrote:

Feminists appear to be getting more and more worked up over the tendency to use apparently masculine designations (such as "chairman," "chairmen") in reference to women or to mixed groups. . . . They argue earnestly that applying masculine nouns to women or mixed groups unconsciously reinforces sexism (a new word, by the way). . . .

We are on dangerous ground here, for William Congreve recorded three centuries ago that hell has no fury like a woman scorned, and as we all know this is no less true if she only thinks she has been scorned or even slighted. "He or she" may be asking too much, but the sexless plural ("All who haven't registered should sign their names" instead of "Anyone who hasn't registered should sign his name") is the best way of discretion when possible.[6]

A graceful concession to the need for change appears in Benjamin Spock's 1976 revision of *Baby and Child Care.*

> The main reason for [this revision] is to eliminate the sexist biases of the sort that help to create and perpetuate discrimination against girls and women. Earlier editions referred to the child of indeterminate sex as he. Though this in one sense is only a literary tradition, it, like many other traditions, implies that the masculine sex has some kind of priority.
>
> In discussing the clothes and playthings parents buy their children and the chores they assign them I took it for granted that there should be a deliberate distinction between boys and girls. But this early-childhood differentiation begins in a small way the discriminatory sex stereotyping that ends up in women so often getting the humdrum, subordinate, poorly paid jobs in most industries and professions, and being treated as the second-class sex.[7]

Why does linguistic sexism, although easily recognized, persist in media? Tradition and present context shape the messages that keep women in their place. Tradition is a major factor in journalism training. In journalism textbooks, the subordinate role of women is implicit:

> Managing editors say that a newsman is not worth his salary until he has had some months on the job.

> Only men with views acceptable to the publisher are engaged as editorial writers.

Better journalism requires better journalists—intelligent, educated men with a serious attitude toward their work.

He [a good reporter] is a man. He moves quickly and quietly, asks specific questions, even anticipates events and reactions when it is possible to do so. . . . he is no demigod. He is a reporter on your daily newspaper.

A girl's best chances of employment are in the women's department covering the specialties—society, fashion, food, homemaking, and childraising.[8]

Present context—other messages conveyed by the media—weighs on the writer who seeks to avoid sexist language. The context is monotonously sexist. The following advertising copy is quite typical and worth quoting only because it implies that "anybody who's successful" is a man.

Let's face it. Anybody who's successful at anything spends most of his time in his own particular field. So naturally, there are a lot of other areas he can't possibly know everything about. . . . After all, a man builds up a tidy sum during his lifetime. His home. Savings. Life Insurance. Investments.[9]

Recent research makes useful distinctions among the forms of linguistic sexism. Linguist Robin Lakoff states that

. . . women experience linguistic discrimination in two ways: in the way they are taught to use language, and in the way general language use treats them. Both tend . . . to relegate women to certain subservient functions: that of sex object or servant; and therefore certain lexical items mean one thing applied to men, another to women, a difference that cannot be predicted except with reference to the different roles the sexes play in society.[10]

Such research is in its early stages. Sol Saporta addressed the Modern Language Association on the theme, "A linguist trying to discuss language and sexism is immediately confronted with the absence of the relevant theory." A point made by both Lakoff and Saporta is that linguistic theory alone does not account for the connotations of parallel terms such as "master" and "mistress" or "bachelor" and "spinster." The intrusion of social roles into linguistics leads Saporta to say, " . . . language is to sexism as symptom is to disease."[11]

In linguistic theory, "man" is an unmarked term that denotes both sexes, while "woman" is a marked term that denotes only one sex. Barbara Bate states that women must contend with the ambiguity of unmarked "man" at three levels:

> Socrates is a man. (Linguistic level)
> All men are created equal. (Cognitive level)
> Caution: men at work. (Social level)[12]

Women have no argument with the first assertion; it is entirely accurate. The second assertion is accurate as far as it goes. The third assertion, however, may be entirely inaccurate. The workers may be women. The decline of sexism in employment leaves linguistic sexism exposed. Women cable splicers are working in "manholes" and women "linemen" are cleated to telephone poles.

Until recently, critiques of linguistic sexism have been anecdotal. Research now based on random samples of language helps to define the extent of sexist usage. A recent doctoral dissertation randomly sampled 2028 sentences containing at least one gender noun or pronoun from the *Random House Dictionary of the English Language.* [13] In these sentences, which were created by the dictionary's editors to exemplify usage, masculine nouns and pronouns outnumbered feminine nouns and pronouns by three to one.

It could be argued that masculine nouns and pronouns in dictionaries exemplify generic rather than specific masculine usage; for example, "The average American child watches more than 25,000 hours of television before he reaches the age of 18" instead of "The professor stroked his beard." However, another pronoun sampling of 100,000 words found that 79 percent of the uses of "he" referred to specific male persons and another 13 percent referred to male animals. Only in the remaining 8 percent did the ambiguity of the generic masculine appear.[14] Summarizing this and other studies of pronoun usage, Wendy Martyna stated:

> Not only do we see the word HE far more often than we see SHE but the HE which is so frequent is being used to describe specific males, not human beings in general.[15]

Researchers such as Martyna offer three lines of evidence on the effects of masculine nouns and pronouns on thought. The first line of evidence is humor. If our interpretation of a masculine noun or pronoun is generic, statements such as the following will not seem humorous: "Man, like other mammals, breast-feeds his young." Generally such statements evoke humor, indicating a mental crossover to the specific masculine interpretation.

A second line of evidence comes from listeners or readers who are asked to supply missing pronouns. Martyna conducted a sentence-completion experiment with psychology students, intermixing a few singular sentences with a large number of plural sentences intended to conceal the experiment's true purpose. One-third of the singular sentences were somewhat male related (e.g., "When an engineer is unsure of a calculation, . . ."); one-third were somewhat female related (e.g., "After a nurse has completed training, . . ."); and one-third were neutral (e.g., "When a teenager finishes high school, . . ."). Martyna found significant sex differences in the number of masculine pronouns used by male and female students in all three kinds of singular sentences, with the greatest difference occurring in their completion of the neutral sentences.[16]

A third line of evidence comes from images that the generic masculine evokes in listeners or readers. It is difficult to tap imagery without giving away the basis of one's interest and biasing what is said, but Joseph Schneider and Sally Hacker devised an experiment to tap images without bias. They instructed students in sociology classes to collect illustrations for a hypothetical sociology text, of which the students received only the table of contents. There were, in fact, two tables of contents, differing only in the masculine versus neutral reference of two chapters ("Urban Man" versus "Urban Life," "Economic man" versus "Economic Life"). Schneider and Hacker hypothesized that chapter headings with masculine references would evoke more male images and cause more male illustrations to be submitted. Other chapter headings that did not differ for the two randomly chosen groups of students would serve as controls.

Illustrations featuring only males were submitted by 64 percent of those who received the masculine form of the table of contents and by 50 percent of those who received the neutral form. Analyzed by chapter, the difference was statistically significant only for the test chapters.[17]

Experiments like this clarify the crossover between the generic and specific interpretations of masculine nouns and pronouns. Well beyond chance probability, the generic masculine excludes women in the listener's or reader's thought.

Gender-fair terms of reference are gradually displacing sexist language, both for the generic person and for women and men in specific roles. The example set by a best-selling author such as Benjamin Spock is a powerful impetus for change, as are publishers' guidelines for textbooks. A recent survey of university faculty, conducted at the University of Oregon by Barbara Bate, indicates the willingness of men as well as women to accept new terms and to give up favorite old terms.[18]

Bate's survey provide two useful sets of findings: (1) which alternative new terms were most acceptable, and (2) which terms, old and new, produced different responses among women and men on the Oregon faculty. The most common term of reference for the generic person ("a person . . . he") was acceptable to 50 percent of the respondents, with no difference in acceptability between women and men. The alternative term "he or she" was acceptable to 80 percent of the respondents overall and was slightly more acceptable to men than to women. The alternative term "s/he" was acceptable to only 20 percent overall; more women than men favored it. The alternative term "a person . . . they" was acceptable to 30 percent overall, with no sex difference.

The role term "college boy" was acceptable to only 15 percent of the respondents overall, and these respondents were entirely female; no male faculty member accepted "boy." The complementary term "college girl" was acceptable to 40 percent overall, with no sex difference. Thus, even in the language of well-educated persons such as university faculty members, "girl" continues to refer to postadolescents while "boy" does not.

Two sets of specific role terms were tested. The term "poet" was acceptable as a generic reference to all respondents. Alternative terms that could refer to women who write poetry —"woman poet," "poetess," and "lady poet"—were acceptable to 55, 25, and 10 percent overall, but acceptance among women was only 40, 20, and 0 percent.

The role term "chairman" was acceptable to 70 percent of the respondents overall, including 60 percent of the women and 80 percent of the men.

In general, gender-fair terms were well accepted, implying that further change will follow as linguistic habits are overcome. Terms that emphasize an unnecessary difference (e.g., "woman poet") were less acceptable, particularly to women.

LANGUAGE *OF* WOMEN AS WELL AS LANGUAGE *ABOUT* WOMEN

Sexism in the language *of* women (e.g., language imputed to women in media portrayals) has not been studied as extensively as sexism in language *about* women. Nine linguistic features are thought to characterize the language of women:

1. Women have a large stock of words related to their specific interests, generally relegated to them as "woman's work": *Magenta, shirr, dart* (in sewing), and so on.
2. "Empty" adjectives like *divine, charming, cute. . . .*
3. Question intonation where we might expect declaratives: for instance tag questions ("It's so hot, isn't it?"). . . .
4. The use of hedges of various kinds. Women . . . are socialized to believe that asserting themselves strongly isn't nice or ladylike. . . .
5. Related to this is the use of the intensive "so. . . ." Here we have an attempt to hedge on one's strong feelings, as though to say, I feel strongly about this—but I dare not make it clear *how* strong. . . .
6. Hypercorrect grammar; women are not supposed to talk rough. . . .
7. Superpolite forms; women are supposed to speak more politely than men. . . . Women don't use off-color or indelicate expressions; women are the experts at euphemism. . . .
8. Women don't tell jokes. . . . It is axiomatic in middle-class American society that, first, women can't tell jokes—they are bound to ruin the punch line, they mix up the order of things, and so on. . . .
9. Women speak in italics, and the more ladylike and feminine you are, the more in italics you are supposed to speak.[19]

A study by Cheris Kramer shows that these linguistic expectations are borne out in the dialogue of women and men in *New Yorker* cartoons and the Sunday comic strips. In the 152 *New Yorker* cartoons, women used weaker, more restricted language; they used fewer exclamations and curse words; and they did not discuss topics such as finance or politics. The 56 Sunday comics confirmed these differences.[20]

A study of *Reader's Digest* humor by Philip Zimbardo and Wendy Meadow contributes to this vein of research on linguistic sexism. Over the many years of *Reader's Digest* anecdotes encompassed in the study, women are the most frequent butt of humor. Women's expressions are the "humorous" aspects of many anecdotes.[21]

Linguistic sexism is not one problem but many, and all are socially ramified. Sol Saporta concluded his address to the Modern Language Association with the question, "Given the data, then, is language sexist or are people sexist or is society sexist? The probable answer, regrettably, is all three."[22]

3

SEXISM IN IMAGE

Behavior depends on the image.[1]

THE IMAGE: CHILD OF EXPERIENCE AND PARENT OF KNOWLEDGE

Language is a diffuse form of media sexism that reminds women of their subordination but does not tell them what role to play or how to play it. *Images* are focused forms of media sexism. Year after year, the media return to their limited stock of images of women—commercial prop, intellectual inferior, hapless dependent, butt of humor, meddler in men's affairs, etc. Because advertisers believe that women's bodies sell products, many images are entirely visual. Little is communicated about women in these images beyond the carefully styled hair, the cosmeticized smile and, of course, the postured body. Other stereotypes not to the contrary, women in commercials are not talkative. Male voice-overs extol products. Only in the closing seconds of commercials are women allowed to say, "I was so relieved when they gave back my Clorox"or "No more ring around the collar, dear."

Media images of real and fictional women are vivid portrayals of a limited range of life-styles. These images have more presence in American homes than many relatives or neighbors.

In the age of electronic media, "image" has come to mean a packaging of impressions. However, images have a more basic role in perception and cognition than the Madison Avenue conceptions. Before there were media, there were images of people, places, times. Human knowledge has always originated in images.

The concept of image used in this book derives from Kenneth Boulding's *The Image.* The following excerpt from *The Image* deals with the relationship of images and knowledge.

> As I sit at my desk, I know where I am. I see before me a window; beyond that some trees . . . the rooftops which mark the town of Palo Alto . . . the bare golden hills of the Hamilton range. I know, however, more than I see. Behind me, although I am not looking in that direction, I know there is a window . . . beyond that the Coast Range . . . the Pacific Ocean. Looking ahead of me again, I know that beyond the mountains that close my present horizon there is a broad valley; beyond that a still higher range of mountains . . . and other mountains, range upon range, until we come to the Rockies; beyond that the Great Plains and the Mississippi . . . The Alleghenies . . . the eastern seaboard . . . the Atlantic Ocean . . . Europe . . . and Asia. I know, furthermore that if I go far enough I will come back to where I am now . . .
>
> What I have been talking about is knowledge. Knowledge, perhaps, is not a good word for this. Perhaps one would rather say my "Image" of the world. Knowledge has an implication of validity, of truth. What I am talking about is what I believe to be true; my subjective knowledge. It is this Image that largely governs my behavior.[2]

Boulding speaks of the growth of a child's images.

> In infancy the world is a house and, perhaps, a few streets or a park. As the child grows his image of the world expands. He sees himself in a town, a country, on a planet. He finds himself in an

increasingly complex web of personal relationships. Every time a message reaches him his image is likely to be changed in some degree by it, and as his image is changed his behavior patterns will be changed likewise.[3]

Everything that comes to our attention through our senses has the potential of forming an image. Why do some percepts form significant images, while others are forgotten? The question is relevant if we are to understand why some *media* percepts form significant images while others do not. Perception theories offer several explanations, such as the following.

1. *Learning Theory.* Some percepts are subject to more exposures or "trials" than others. Exposures may be associated with positive or negative reinforcements in some form.
2. *Need Theory.* Regardless of the number of exposures or reinforcements, some percepts form significant images because they relate to a person's needs. Percepts relating to food, sex, security, play, etc., have a high probability of forming significant images.
3. *Gestalt Theory.* Features of the percept itself may determine the significance of the image it forms. "Goodness of form," "wholeness," and other features of the percept affect the resulting memory trace.

The importance of perception theory is not that one theory is more correct than others. We can combine the theories and say that a percept is likely to form a significant image if it is exposed repeatedly, if it satisfies a need in the perceiver, and if it has "good form."

MEDIA IMAGES

Media images compete well with direct images in these respects. A media image may be exposed hundreds of times a year to the same audience. Media images may cater to several audience needs, particularly the quadrumvirate of food, sex, security, and play. Finally, because of "iconic" properties that Marshall McLuhan and others have pointed out, media images often have "good form"; for example, the low resolution of halftone and television causes attention to focus on simple outlines, on the essence of form.[4]

The vividness of media images has been apparent at least since Orson Welles' broadcast of "The War of the Worlds" in 1938.[5] Audiences perceive in the media a surrogate reality that satisfies various needs.

There is no sharp boundary between the fictional world of entertainment and the nonfictional world conveyed by news programs, documentaries, etc. Daniel Boorstin, in his book on comtemporary American culture, *The Image,* states that public demand for novelty causes the media to report "pseudo-events" as news. Pseudo-events are preferred over spontaneous events for six reasons.

1. Pseudo-events are more dramatic; . . .
2. Pseudo-events, being planned for dissemination, are easier to disseminate and to make vivid; . . .
3. Pseudo-events can be repeated at will, and thus their impression can be reinforced;
4. Pseudo-events cost money to create; hence somebody has an interest in disseminating, magnifying, advertising, and extolling them as events worth watching and believing;
5. Pseudo-events, being planned for intelligibility, are more intelligible and hence more reassuring; . . .
6. Pseudo-events are more sociable, more conversable, and more convenient to witness.[6]

ELUSIVE IMAGES OF SOCIAL REALITY

Images of physical reality can be processed by the perceiver in terms of a few attributes such as shape, size, weight, and color. If the perceiver is uncertain about such attributes of a physical image, measurements can be taken for verification.

Images of social reality are more elusive. Some social attributes are not verifiable except in the negative range (e.g., the honesty of politicians). It is in social perception that we rely on what Jerome Bruner and others call "categorizing with probabilistic cues."[7] As we move through social environments, we pick up hints about the roles that we and others should play, about what is good for us and them, etc.

Social perception is important to us. When it is done well, it profits us. When it is done poorly, it costs us. In traditional societies, social perception tells children at an early age what their adult roles will be. In modern societies, with more latitude of choice, adults as well as children continuously form images of roles that they might and might not play. Roles that are communicated by simple, repeated, and need-satisfying percepts seem more inevitable to the media audience than roles that are not communicated in this way.

Images of roles affect what we *do* in contrast to images of the self that affect who we *are* in our own eyes. George Miller, Eugene Galanter, and Karl Pribram, in their sequel to Boulding's *The Image*, outline a theory of "planful behavior" based on images. They say:

> . . . the central problem of this book is to explore the relationship between the Image and the Plan. . . .
>
> —A Plan can be learned and so would be part of the Image.
>
> —Knowledge must be incorporated into the Plan, since otherwise it could not provide a basis for guiding behavior. Thus, Images can form part of a Plan.
>
> —Changes in the Plans can be effected only by information drawn from the Images.[8]

Although "image"and "plan" are closely related, the distinction is worth making in the context of media sexism. Images formed from mediated percepts become part of a woman's conception of herself. Mediated percepts of the status and abilities of other women (e.g., stereotypic housewives and girl fridays in television comedies) affect her image of her own status and abilities.

Plans are formed partly from images of the roles that other women play. Never seeing women in some roles and seeing women playing other roles poorly reduces the likelihood that a woman will attempt such roles herself.

We began this chapter by contrasting two embodiments of media sexism—language and image. Language tells a woman that she is an afterthought, a linguistic variant, an etcetera. Images tell her how to regard herself in specific terms. Images shape her plans for her life. Although she may be able to ignore the affronts of language, she probably cannot eliminate media images from her "construction of reality," as the totality of images is described.[9]

It is important to understand media images, both informally through daily contact with the media and formally through techniques such as content analysis, which is described in Chapter 5.

AMERICAN MASS MEDIA

From language to writing: tens of thousands of years. From writing to printing: thousands of years. From printing to films and broadcasting: four hundred years. From the first experiments with television to live television from the moon: fifty years.[1]

With 5 hours per day averaged across the year, media reading/ viewing occupies almost as much of the adult American's day as does working.[2] Newspapers, magazines, and books consume about an hour of daily media time. Radio and television consume the other 4 hours. In the average American household, television sets are used more than 6 hours a day during the winter months, less during the summer. Members of the household are a constantly changing audience in front of the 1.6 sets that the average household possesses. Averaged across the life cycle from school days to retirement, media occupy more of an American's waking hours than any other activity.

GROWTH OF AMERICAN MEDIA

As surprising as the ubiquity of American media today is their growth in the past century. In 1870 the only "mass" medium was the *newspaper.* In that year, an average of 2.6 million newspapers circulated each day to the 7.6 million households. Roughly one household in three received a daily newspaper. In 1900, an average of 15 million newspapers circulated each day to 16 million households. Almost every household received a daily newspaper. Thanks to circulation-building gimmicks invented by publishers like Joseph Pulitzer, in 1910 circulation reached 1.36 newspapers per household, the highest level in American history.

Throughout this century, newspaper circulation per household has declined from the 1910 level. In 1950 it was 1.24 newspapers per household; in 1970 it was 0.99. Since 1973, each year's circulation per household has been the lowest in the century.[3]

Media researchers talk of *displacement* when a medium loses its audience in a growing population. Newspapers were undoubtedly displaced after 1910. The steepest decline in circulation occurred between 1930 and 1940, when economic depression and radio made newspapers less affordable and necessary.

Magazines have been a part of the American scene since 1741, when Bradford's *American Review* and Franklin's *General Magazine and Historical Chronicle* were launched in the same week in February. Magazines became a mass medium in the twentieth century with the introduction of photographic halftones and color printing, but even today the monthly circulation of newspapers, about 2 billion, greatly exceeds the monthly circulation of magazines, about 350 million.

Beginning with nickelodeons in the first years after 1900, *films* attracted huge audiences. By 1920, the nation's 26 million households accounted for nearly 40 million film attendances weekly. Peak attendance was reached in 1930, when 30 million households accounted for 90 million attendances weekly. Economic depression, the war, and the rise of television thereafter kept the public from neighborhood theaters, which closed by the thousands. From 3.0 weekly attendances per household in 1930, the decline in film's popularity was precipitous: down to

1.4 weekly attendances in 1950, then down to 0.2 weekly attendances in 1970.

However, film studios did not follow neighborhood theaters into oblivion. According to "McLuhan's principle" on the succession of media, television *encapsulated* film.[4] Although the number of theater films produced in the United States dropped from 400 in 1945 to 200 in 1960, in those years Hollywood shifted much of its production capacity to film for television.

On a worldwide scale, *radio* grew from a pre-1914 curiosity to *the* mass medium of the twentieth century. Radio's universal appeal is understandable: receiving equipment was inexpensive from the outset; literacy was not required; listening did not conflict with household tasks.

In the United States, only 1 household in 100 possessed a radio receiver in 1920. Radio stations and receiving sets diffused together in the following decade. In 1922 alone, 500 stations, many of them converted amateur transmitters, began broadcasting.

Between 1920 and 1930 the number of radio receivers in the United States increased 40 times over, to 13 million. Every second household possessed one. The balance of one receiver per household was passed in 1936 and, by 1940, about half of all households possessed two receivers.

After 1945 radio diffused not as a family medium like the newpaper (one copy in the living room), but as a personal medium like the magazine (copies to suit personal taste throughout the house). The average household possessed five receivers in 1970, and sales continued at the rate of 15 million receivers per year.

Television was a well-publicized experimental medium by 1930, but its acceptance was slow for two decades. World War II slowed its diffusion. Even by 1948 only 1 household in 40 possessed a television receiver. The number of receivers then doubled, on the average, each year from 1948 to 1953, when more than half of all households possessed one of the 32 million receivers.

Television passed the balance of one receiver per household in 1960, just as color receivers reached the market. As late as 1965 color receivers comprised only 7 percent of all television receivers in use but, by 1970, they dominated receiver sales and were 34 percent of all receivers in use. Continuing into the 1970s, about 1 household in 10 purchased a color receiver each year (6 to 8 million annual sales).

WHO PAYS FOR MEDIA?

Each person in the average household, by reading/viewing media about 5 hours per day, generates revenue for the business offices. In the mid-1970s, revenues of the media and related industries exceed $30 billion annually. Directly and indirectly each household spends about $400 annually for media products (newpapers, magazines, books, films) and related equipment (television and radio receivers, phonograph records, tapes, and playback devices).[5]

Although the consumer supports all media either through the costs of media products or through costs added by advertising to other commodities, a distinction is made between circulation revenues and advertising revenues at the media business offices. Consumers are the direct source of one-third of the $30+ billion total revenues of the media. They are the indirect source of the two-thirds of total revenues derived from advertising.

Advertising revenues can be divided between national and local advertising campaigns. About $8 billion, or 58 percent of total advertising revenues, is spent on local campaigns.

Television exemplifies a pattern found in major media: advertising expenditure is concentrated in the largest corporations. In 1974, the 50 leading television advertisers provided almost half ($2.2 billion) of television's $4.9 billion advertising revenues. At the top of the list, Proctor and Gamble spent $234 million on television advertising. Below the top 50, thousands of other corporations provided the other $2.7 billion of television advertising revenues.[6]

THREE FRAMEWORKS FOR STUDYING THE MEDIA

Institutions as important as the media must be studied within multiple frameworks to answer questions of social theory and public policy. Sexism focuses attention first on media *content,* since it is content that shapes audiences' surrogate reality. *Content analysis* provides an initial framework for studying the media.

However, analyzing media content for sexism is like analyzing river water for pollution. Questions are raised upstream and downstream from the point of analysis. How did pollution *enter* the river? What are the *effects* of pollution on users of the river water? By analogy, conditions by which sexism *enters* media content and *effects* of sexism on audiences are as important to know as the sexist content itself.

Conditions by which sexism enters media content belong to an *institutional analysis* framework. Media in the United States are profit-making corporations with boards of directors, bureaucratized divisions, goal conflicts between "creative" and "business" personnel, and a siege mentality with respect to government regulation. Content is determined by an interaction of forces within these organizations. Institutional analysis identifies some of the forces and their interactions.

Institutional analyses take several forms. Case studies of individual organizations are common, as are surveys that reflect conditions across sectors of the industry. Studies focus on economic variables, power variables, structure variables, role variables, etc. All of these variables bear on institutional sexism.

Effects analysis or, in the larger sense, *audience analysis* first characterizes the audience of each medium in terms of demographic variables such as sex, race, age, educational background, occupation, income, etc. A second aspect of audience analysis focuses on knowledge variables; that is, what do audiences learn from their exposure to media?

The third and most difficult aspect of audience analysis focuses on belief and action variables; that is, how do audiences believe and act differently because of their exposure to media? Because media reach individuals in the context of their families, neighbors, work groups, etc., it is rarely possible to show direct effects of media content on beliefs and actions. Research on media effects is ambiguous, but important questions of theory and policy attract researchers to this aspect of audience analysis.

In the following sections of this book, the three frameworks of content analysis, institutional analysis, and audience analysis structure reviews of media sexism studies from which indications for research and action are drawn.

2

SEXISM IN MEDIA CONTENT

Social researchers have long been attracted to the media as mirrors of society because of the openness and permanance of the media record. Content is pivotal; it is a social artifact in itself, and it reflects on institutional and audience variables that we want to know more about than we can find out directly.

Content analysis consists of procedures for making our everyday observations of media content more systematic. Like surveys and other tools of social research, content analyses follow certain rules (e.g., of definition and sampling) and adhere to certain criteria (e.g., of reliability and validity). Chapter 5 briefly discusses how the method of content analysis developed and how it is used today.

Chapters 6 to 9 tell about the portrayal of women in television, radio, magazines, newspapers, books, and film. Propositional summaries at the end of each chapter help to clarify patterns of portrayal that are consistent across media and over time.

Chapter 10 describes and illustrates a "consciousness scale" for analyzing media sexism.

HOW MEDIA CONTENT IS STUDIED

> Communication content is so rich with human experience, and
> its causes and effects so varied, that no single system of substan-
> tive categories can be devised. . . .[1]

Content analyses of media sexism serve applied and theoretical
goals. Each goal requires a different system of categories and a
different sample of content.

Applied analyses lead to FCC petitions to deny the renewal
applications of broadcasters who persist in sexist programming.
They lead to boycotts of manufacturers whose advertisements
belittle women. They lead to suits against school boards over
the use of sexist textbooks. They lead to the production of
nonsexist media materials.

Theoretical analyses relate media content to beliefs and
behaviors of people. Sexism and other "-isms" arise in insecurity;[2] that is, if another person can be regarded as inferior to you
and me because of sex, race, IQ, etc., we have gained an easy
superiority. The dynamics of prejudice need to be understood
so that sexism, when it becomes unfashionable, will not be
replaced by another "-ism."

Content analyses also chart "trends in the composition and structure of mass-produced systems of messages that define life in urbanized societies."[3] These "cultural indicators," as they are called, show that women have been depicted in different social roles in each decade of this century.

CONTENT ANALYSIS DEFINED

The best-known definition of content analysis was proposed by Bernard Berelson in 1952.

> Content analysis is a research technique for the objective, systematic, and quantitative description of the manifest content of communication.[4]

In addition to *content* (text and pictures) and *technique* (a repeatable procedure involving skill), this definition stresses *system* (a set of rules or relationships) and *objectivity* (suspension of personal values in judgment). Analyses of debatable points should also be *quantitative* and focus on *manifest* content (i.e., nothing read between the lines).

CONTENT ANALYSIS DEFENDED

If media sexism is blatant enough to rouse public groups to protest, why is a technique such as content analysis needed? There are several answers to this question, including:

- *One* offensive advertisement or program may be a fluke; *5* indicates a tendency; *10* indicates a policy (choose your own indicative levels).
- Some forms of media sexism are *low key;* you do not notice

them until a monitoring technique directs you to (e.g., what was the male-to-female ratio of voice-over commercials in your most recent day of television viewing?).

- Perception is *selective;* without the rigor of a technique such as content analysis, we may see what we expect to see or wish to see.

Recently one of us spoke in a conference on Women and the Media in Los Angeles. The fact that men narrate about 90 percent of all voice-over commercials was mentioned. At the end of the session, a member of the audience came forward and said, "Your data must be wrong. A friend of mine narrates voice-overs and she's in constant demand." One swallow doth not a summer, nor our friends a sample, make.

QUANTITATIVE VERSUS QUALITATIVE ANALYSIS

As early as 1920, Walter Lippmann and Charles Merz analyzed over 1000 issues of the *New York Times* published between 1917 and 1920 to assess the *Times'* coverage of the Russian Revolution.[5] This is the earliest case we have found of content analysis used for *media performance* assessment. Recent assessments of media performance (e.g., *The News Twisters* and *Women in the Wasteland Fight Back*[6]) are also descended from studies conducted in the 1930s by Susan Kingsbury and Hornell Hart under the title, "Measuring the Ethics of American Newspapers."[7]

Media performance is best studied *quantitatively* so that the analyst has data to marshal when conclusions are disputed. *Qualitative* studies may provide insights as the "latent significance" of content is uncovered. However, where one person finds latent significance, another person may find nothing. Such qualitative findings are not trusted in assessments of media performance.

Qualitative analysis has a strong role in *media socialization* research (e.g., the classic "Happy Housewife Heroine" chapter in *The Feminine Mystique*).[8] Socialization studies draw on media content, but their purpose is to reflect the values of a society as transmitted from one generation to the next or from majority group to minority group.

A century ago and less, children were exposed to few socialization influences apart from their parents, school, church, and peers. In that simpler communication environment, one of the most influential socializers was the *McGuffey Reader.* During an era when the U.S. population grew from 17 million (1840) to 63 million (1890), more than 120 million *McGuffey Readers* were sold.[9]

In our electronic era, television is the children's McGuffey. No other medium and scarcely any person holds their attention for so many hours each week. Whereas William Holmes McGuffey transmitted what he believed were positive values, the commercial interests behind television programming have created a bazaar of positive and negative values that children may not have the wisdom to choose among.

ANALYSIS OF VISUAL "LANGUAGE"

A number of years ago one of us (Paisley) wrote:

> Content analysis . . . has grown on a foundation of words. The word is a comfortable unit of analysis; we can analyze individual words or combine them in phrases, sentences, or paragraphs. [In contrast,] visual records are seldom divided into small natural units. . . . [10]

Still pictures as well as motion pictures have a fluidity, a lack of internal boundaries and markers, that makes them difficult to analyze. Concepts of visual positioning and nonverbal com-

munication have been well understood since the current literature on these subjects began with Edward Hall's *The Silent
Language* in 1959.[11] However, only a few procedures have been
developed for the analysis of visual media such as news photographs, advertising illustrations, films, and television programs.[12]

The most provocative analysis of sex roles in visual media
is Erving Goffman's "gender advertisements."[13] Goffman contends that the carefully posed models and carefully selected
settings of advertisements create a pseudo-reality that is "better
than real." Advertising images are planned to be striking and
memorable; studies show that they are both. Goffman's analysis
of nearly 400 familiar advertisements makes it clear that gender
differences in function and status not only carry over from the
real world to the advertisement world but may find their purest
expression there. Advertisements possess what may be called
"iconic" properties or "good form" (following Gestalt theory)
for two reasons, according to Goffman.

> First, ads . . . are intentionally choreographed to be unambigu-
> ous. . . . Second, scenes contrived for photographing . . . can be
> shot from any angle that the cameraman chooses, the subjects
> themselves splayed out to allow an unobstructed view; these are
> two liberties that a person viewing a live scene cannot take.[14]

Most content analyses of media sexism up through 1978
have focused on verbal content, sometimes in conjunction with
a synopsis (but rarely an analysis) of the characters and setting
of the visual content. The analyst is often frustrated by this
approach; significant nuances of function and status are noted
but not analyzed in the visual content. What is needed in future
analyses is an equal emphasis on verbal and visual content.
Progress in visual content analysis involves procedures (e.g., for
recording and coding visual content) and theories (e.g., of the
syntax of visual "language").[15]

CONTENT ANALYSIS PROCEDURES

There are common procedures to be followed whether a content analysis is applied or theoretical, quantitative or qualitative, verbal or visual. With the availability of book-length treatments of content analysis, we need only present some of the questions that you should ask before accepting the conclusions of a content analysis.[16]

How is the research problem formulated? The problem should correspond to findings that content can produce. For example, "trends in media portrayal of women" is a content analysis problem, whereas "producers' intentions in depicting women as helpless" and "effects on children of seeing women depicted as helpless" are not.

Are variables defined in a reasonable way? A media performance study, *The News Twisters,* was criticized because it defined "bias" in a limited way.

> While Efron found a blatant anti-Nixon, pro-Humphrey bias on all networks . . . , the present study indicates a remarkably similar treatment of Nixon and Humphrey. . . . We found that the time the candidates spent speaking before the camera [uncoded by Efron] overshadows the amount of reporter commentary.[17]

Studies of media sexism often update previous studies. In these cases the previous definitions of variables should be continued in new studies so that findings can cumulate. Sometimes the previous definitions are found to be defective. Even so, it is important to use them again in conjunction with better definitions to provide one point in time that is common to both the old and the new measurements.

Content analyses involve not only *content* variables but also *context* variables (who wrote the content, when and where did it appear, etc.). An example of a poorly defined *context* variable comes from a 1976 study, "Who Writes Children's Books?", by W. Bernard Lukenbill.[18] To gauge the social class of authors of children's books, Lukenbill used "the occupational-prestige levels of their fathers (for men and unmarried women) or their husbands (for married women)." In other words, the authors had no social class of their own; it was conferred on them by a male relative. If someone updates this study in a few years, both Lukenbill's definition of social class and a nonsexist definition should be used to complete one data series and to begin another data series.

Does the extent of the content sample, across time and media, correspond to the extent of the problem? The power of content analysis lies in comparisons that are possible across time and media. Thanks to the permanence of print media, samples of print content can be drawn from previous decades or even previous centuries if the problem calls for findings across time. Samples of print content can also be gathered from around the world for the same day, as was done in Wilbur Schramm's *One Day in the World's Press.* [19]

The impermanence of broadcast media has made content analysis difficult until now. To draw samples of broadcast content across stations and hours of the day, it has been necessary to schedule monitors in morning, afternoon, and evening shifts. Recently, however, broadcast content has been sampled through recordings regulated by automatic timers, so that the actual content analysis can take place in a single session, when the day's tape is complete.

Media content is too rich for samples to encompass a large fraction of the millions of words and images produced each day. Small samples are required; as a corollary, the small samples must be representative of the majority of content that cannot be included. Procedures have been developed for compiling "composite weeks" of media content by randomly sampling editions, pages, broadcast hours, etc., across many weeks until a 7-day period is represented. Media that appear less frequently, such as magazines and books, can be sampled into "composite months" and "composite years."

Does the content analysis meet the triple test of reliability, validity, and utility? Our goals in analyzing media content cannot be achieved unless other persons (policymakers, media managers, researchers, etc.) agree that the analyses are well conducted. During the 50 years that content analysis has served as a tool of media research, three tests of a well-conducted analysis have evolved.

Reliability is the test of consistent measurement. When two or more persons apply the same categories to the same content, their findings should agree within limits set by the complexity of the analysis. Agreement of 80 percent may be acceptable for a complex analysis (e.g., role dominance in television dramas). Agreement of 90 percent or higher should be obtained in a simple analysis (e.g., sex of product representatives in television commercials).

Testing reliability is a nuisance. The content analyst must arrange for some of the measurements to be repeated by another person. But consider the alternative. If one of us conducts a private analysis, who can judge the credibility of the findings?

Classically, *validity* is tested against reality. For example, if a person's ability to succeed at a job is measured by paper and pencil questions, the validity of the paper and pencil questions is tested by the person's actual performance on the job.

The reality criterion is vague in many important measurements. We test creativity, personality, and a host of other traits without fully knowing how valid the measurements are. In such cases we look for *independent* measures of the same traits, and we validate one measure by its *convergence* with other measures.

Whether a variable is easily validated has little to do with its importance. "Obscenity" is an important variable whose measures are difficult to validate. As we work on this book, the media are debating whether it is obscene for pornographic films to show children engaged in sexual activities. One group's measure of obscenity is rejected by another group as too restrictive or permissive. Yet obscenity cannot be dismissed as an important variable in media content.

Utility is the test of cost benefit. The utility questions are:

What are the findings good for? What decision is affected by them? What will we do differently, either in practice or in research, because of the new findings?

Deliberate balancing of the reliability, validity, and utility criteria is necessary because content analysis does not come in standardized packages. Bernard Berelson, the first major writer on content analysis, deserves to have the last word on this subject.

> Because of the relative availability of the raw material, many sins have been committed in the name of content analysis. . . . At the same time, however, the method has produced a number of useful studies which combine original ideas with sound, careful documentation. . . . Content analysis, as a method, has no magical properties—you rarely get out of it more than you put in, and sometimes you get less. In the last analysis, there is no substitute for a good idea.[20]

TELEVISION AND RADIO

Woman. . . .
We insult her every day on TV
And wonder why she has no guts or confidence.[1]

Media portrayal of women has been a concern of the women's movement since the 1960s. Early criticism focused on commercials like "Fly me—I'm Barbara." Advertisers felt that women were overly sensitive to "unintended" connotations in individual advertisements.

Women understood the spirit in which advertisements were singled out for criticism. Each advertisement was more than an affront in itself; it symbolized the use of women as commercial props. Nor did women misread the sexual message in many advertisements. Soon after National Airlines launched its sales-boosting advertising campaign, a film entitled *Fly Me* was making the rounds of pornographic theaters.

Most systematic analyses of media images of women have been conducted since 1970. In this chapter and the three that follow, we review all major studies, including early ones beginning in 1935 for motion pictures, 1944 for radio, 1946 for children's textbooks, 1949 for magazines, 1954 for television, and 1957 for newspapers. Many studies reviewed in these chapters are unpublished; they came to us as photocopied reports. Because readers may have difficulty obtaining unpublished reports, we err on the side of presenting too many rather than too few findings.

TELEVISION COMMERCIALS

Television is the most pervasive medium. Children in their preschool years watch about 24 hours a week. Older children and adults spend even more time with television. By the time a student finishes high school, she or he has seen more than 350,000 commercials. What do these commercials say about women and men?

The studies reviewed in this section document five aspects of commercials: voice-overs (offscreen narrators), roles, activities, settings, and the ages of women and men. Following a propositional summary of findings in each of these categories, we present details of the studies.

Proposition 6.1: Almost All Commercials with Voice-Overs *Are Spoken and Sung by Men.*

Between 1972 and 1978, at least 11 studies reported the percentage of female and male voice-overs. Across these years there has been little change in the general pattern of many male voices and few female voices. The earliest study, conducted by the National Organization for Women (NOW) and published as *Women in the Wasteland Fight Back,* showed that men provided 93 percent of the voice-overs and women only 7 percent.[2] The other 10 studies support this finding.[3] One unique study was conducted by the Screen Actors Guild. They made a distinction between spoken and sung voice-overs and found that 93 percent of the spoken parts and 71 percent of the sung parts used male voices.[4]

Each of the voice-over studies was conducted by different researchers sampling different commercials in different years. Yet they agree that the voice of authority that tells us what to buy is male. Overall, the studies indicate that about 90 percent of the voice-overs are male and only 10 percent are female.

Proposition 6.2: Commercials Show Men in More Roles than Women and More Often Show Women in Family Roles.

Five studies provide evidence on the *number* and *kinds* of roles that women and men portray. The finding by Dominick and Rauch that commercials show women in considerably fewer roles than men (18 roles for women and 43 roles for men[5]) has been confirmed by the research group known as Women on Words and Images (21 roles for women and 40 roles for men[6]). The most common role for a woman is that of family member—wife, mother, grandmother, or daughter. Data from five studies show that an average of 60 percent of the women are shown in family roles while only 18 percent of the men are shown in comparable roles.[7] Closely related is the finding that men are more often shown as employed than women (67 percent of those employed were males[8]). Men are also given the high-status jobs (60 percent of the men and 14 percent of the women had high-status jobs[9]).

Proposition 6.3: Commercials Show Women Doing Activities in the Home and Show Men as Beneficiaries of These Activities.

Women are often shown doing housework or being concerned with their physical appearance. Summing the results of several studies, we find that about 38 percent of the women and only 11 percent of the men are involved in cleaning, washing, and cooking.[10] Women on Words and Images found that nine women and one man did the cooking on the set of commercials they monitored.[11] When not occupied with domestic chores, women are shown striving to improve their physical appearance.[12] But what about men? Men are the beneficiaries of women's activities. They eat the food, wear the laundry, enjoy their homes and their wives' appearance, and are nursed back to health.[13]

Proposition 6.4: The Settings of Commercials Show Women Inside the Home and Men Outside the Home.

Findings concerning the settings of commercials complete the pattern. Women work inside the home and men work outside. According to three studies, approximately 43 percent of the women and 18 percent of the men are shown working in the home and 32 percent of the women and 63 percent of the men are shown working outside.[14]

Proposition 6.5: Women in Commercials Are Shown as Younger than Men.

Contrary to the statistical fact that more than 50 percent of American women are over 40 years old, television commercials show only about 25 percent of the women as over 40. Although the average age of women in the population is somewhat higher than that of men, television reverses this fact and shows about 45 percent of the men as over 40.[15] For example, Alice Courtney and Thomas Whipple found that 16 percent of the women and 44 percent of the men in the commercials they monitored were over 40.[16] Our society has long emphasized youthfulness, but it is women in the 1970s who must forever be young. Television reinforces this in two ways: actresses are young, and they sell the concept of youthful appearance in products such as Oil of Olay and Liquid Ivory Soap. Television tells women that they should be young and offers them many ways to imitate the image they see.

The studies that led to these five propositions will now be described. In each case we have tried to include when and where the study was conducted, how many commercials were monitored, and any additional interesting findings. For clarity, we sometimes regroup categories and compute new percentages. Although some readers may wish to turn to the source documents for complete information, we have tried to provide enough detail so that these synopses can take the place of the original studies.

STUDIES OF COMMERCIALS. The landmark study of television using quantitative content analysis was published in 1972 as *Women in the Wasteland Fight Back.* This research was sponsored by the Washington, D.C., chapter of NOW. Although some might contest the findings on the grounds that the coders were feminists, the findings have been verified by every study conducted since. NOW monitored WRC-TV during a composite week and used the data as evidence in a petition to the FCC to deny renewal of the station's license. Selected findings appear here, and others appear in the section on television programming.

During the chosen week, monitors coded 2750 commercials broadcast from 7 to 1 A.M. They found women and men portrayed differently in several ways. Among those appearing as *product representatives* (person speaking for product), women were shown in 13 roles while men were shown in 23 roles. Similarly, among all *other persons* in the commercials, women were shown in 18 roles while men were shown in 30. Women serving as product representatives were more frequent in the 7 A.M. to 4:30 P.M. time block (54 percent women and 46 percent men) than in the 4:30 P.M. to 1 A.M. time block (33 percent women and 67 percent men).

What activities did these women and men perform? Among the product representatives, the women were busier than the men, since 49 percent of the women were shown performing some task while only 26 percent of the men were shown doing anything. Furthermore, 33 percent of the women were shown doing domestic chores as compared with only 7 percent of the men. This last finding was also supported among nonproduct representatives; 43 percent of these women and only 15 percent of these men were involved in domestic chores.[17]

NOW was responsible for a second early study of television commercials. The New York chapter monitored 1241 commercials over an 18-month period. Judith Hennessee and Joan Nicholson found that men were shown as beneficiaries in 54 percent of the food commercials and 81 percent of the cleaning commercials. The commercials portrayed women in various ways.

1. Twenty-three percent showed women as housekeepers.
2. Forty-three percent showed women as household workers.
3. Thirty-eight percent showed women as adjuncts to men.
4. Thirty-four percent showed women as dependent on men.
5. Twenty-four percent showed women as submissive.
6. Seventeen percent showed women as unintelligent.
7. Seventeen percent showed women as sex objects.[18]

A third study from this early period was conducted at Queens University by Joseph Dominick and Gail Rauch. Monitoring 986 prime-time commercials broadcast during a composite week, they found that 75 percent of the commercials featuring women were for kitchen and bathroom products. Women were portrayed as younger than men; 71 percent of the women and only 43 percent of the men were between 20 and 35 years. Among those under 35:

1. Fifty-six percent of the women and 14 percent of the men were shown in family roles.
2. Thirty-eight percent of the women and 14 percent of the men were shown in the home;

3. Nineteen percent of the women and 44 percent of the men were shown outdoors.[19]

Alice Courtney and Thomas Whipple analyzed data from 434 commercials using product representatives that were aired in Toronto in early 1973. Results from Toronto indicate:

1. Fifty-six percent of the women and 12 percent of the men were shown in family roles.
2. Thirty-two percent of the women and 9 percent of the men were shown actually using the product.
3. Thirty-one percent of the women and 53 percent of the men made product claims.

Forty-two percent of product representatives shown from 1 to 3 P.M. were men, and 65 percent of product representatives shown from 8 to 10 P.M. were men.[20]

The Screen Actors Guild monitored a random sample of commercials submitted for the 1973 Clio Awards. In 340 commercials 63 percent of the onscreen speaking principals and 60 percent of the onscreen nonspeaking principals were men.[21]

Women on Words and Images published their study of prime-time television as *Channeling Children.* In the 214 commercials viewed during an analysis of 16 dramatic shows, they found that 23 women and 1 man were attending to appearance; 0 women and 8 men were sick or being cared for; and 23 women and 4 men were doing housework.[22]

William O'Donnell and Karen O'Donnell analyzed 367 commercials. In examining the product representatives, they found that 81 percent of the women and 36 percent of the men were portrayed with domestic products, while 19 percent of the women and 64 percent of the men were portrayed with non-domestic products.[23]

Jeanne Marecek and her colleagues found similar segregation of women. They monitored 1168 commercials over a 3-year period to determine changes in the portrayal of women and found that women who were shown as the onscreen expert (the offscreen expert is the voice-over) were primarily associated with the traditional feminine tasks of cooking, cleaning, etc. This pattern became stronger over the 3 years, with 66 percent of the women representing these products in 1972 and 82 percent of the women speaking for them in 1974.[24] Looking at all commercials, the authors found that the male voice-over continues to "get the last word." Although more women were in this category over time, it seems that they perform this role primarily for the appropriate female products.[25]

Katherine Cirksena and Matilda Butler analyzed more than 1000 commercials in 1977. Of the 960 where a single product is identified and where either a male or a female is the major character, they found:

1. Forty-nine percent of the women were shown in household advertisements, 0 percent in alcohol advertisements, 2 percent in vehicle advertisements, 11 percent in cosmetics advertisements, 7 percent in business advertisements, 15 percent in personal hygiene advertisements, and 17 percent in others.
2. Forty-two percent of the men were shown in household advertisements, 5 percent in alcohol advertisements, 10 percent in vehicle advertisements, 2 percent in cosmetics advertisements, 15 percent in business advertisements, 6 percent in personal hygiene advertisements, and 19 percent in others.

Cirksena and Butler note that considerably stronger differences are found within product types. For instance, 61 percent of the household advertisements portray a woman as the main character, 90 percent of the alcohol advertisements portray a man, 77 percent of the vehicle advertisements portray a man, 88 percent of the cosmetics advisements portray a woman, 62 percent of the business advertisements portray a man, and 77 percent of the hygiene advertisements portray a woman.[26]

COMMERCIALS DIRECTED AT CHILDREN. Commercials broadcast during children's programming were monitored in four studies that document two important aspects of the commercials children see on Saturday mornings: roles portrayed by women and men and the relative presence of women and men. The first of these points extends Proposition 6.2 to include commercials during children's programming. The second point, however, calls for a new proposition.

Proposition 6.6: In Commercials during Children's Programming, Women and Girls Are Seen Less Often than Men and Boys.

When a little girl watches television on Saturday morning, she may wonder about her place in the world. Not only is she not seen at all in the exciting action commercials, she is not seen very much in any of the commercials. Two studies found that women and girls were about 34 percent of all characters in commercials while men and boys were about 66 percent.[27] Other studies analyzing the relative presence of girls and boys alone or together in commercials show that boys and men are much more visible than girls and women.[28]

STUDIES OF COMMERCIALS DURING CHILDREN'S PROGRAMMING. An early study of commercials shown during Saturday morning children's programming was conducted by Earle Barcus for Action for Children's Television. He monitored 406 commercials during 2 months in Boston and found that 49 percent showed men and boys only while 16 percent showed women and girls only. Commercials aimed at girls emphasized beauty and popularity; commercials aimed at boys emphasized size, power, noise, and speed.[29]

Charlotte O'Kelly reviewed commercials shown during 7 hours of children's programming. Forty-five percent of the males versus 29 percent of the females shown were adults. Adult males were shown in 17 different roles versus 7 roles for adult females. Thirty-four percent of the adult females versus 14 percent of the adult males were shown in family roles.[30]

Cornell Chulay and Sara Francis analyzed 294 Saturday morning commercials. Seventy-nine percent of the single voice-overs were spoken by men. Thirty-five percent of the commercials showed boys, while 10 percent showed girls. Chulay and Francis found that 53 percent of the girls and only 2 percent of the boys were shown in family roles. Among four types of products, there was a substantial difference in the percentage of girls or boys shown using them.

1. No girls were shown in advertisements for cars and planes; 27 percent were shown with games, 27 percent with food, and 26 percent with dolls.
2. Forty-seven percent of the boys were shown in advertisements for cars and planes, 36 percent were shown with games, and none were shown with food or dolls.[31]

In the most current study of children's commercials available to us, Armando Valdez found that:

1. Ninety-one percent of the voice-overs were male.
2. Fifty-four percent of the product representatives were male (18 percent female and 27 percent equal male/female).
3. Sixty-six percent of the lead characters in dramatized commercials were male (22 percent female and 12 percent equal male/female).
4. Of the major characters other than the lead character, 41 percent were male (21 percent female and 38 percent equal male/female).[32]

TELEVISION PROGRAMS

There have been at least 18 studies of television programs. Most of these monitoring projects have focused on soap operas and prime-time dramas, but there are also studies of quiz shows, news shows, and public affairs programs. Although we present detailed findings from each of these studies, we look first at three issues that are addressed in many studies: relative appearance, employment, and marital status.

Proposition 6.7: In Television Programs, Women Are Seen Less than Men.

Thirteen studies document the relative appearance of women and men in television programs. Over the 20-year period of these studies, the appearance of women has become less frequent. For instance, in a 1954 study conducted by Dallas Smythe, men were 66 percent of the characters and women were 34 percent.[33] Herbert Northcutt, John Seggar, and James Hinton report in 1975 that 79 percent of the white characters were men and 90 percent of the black characters were men.[34] Across all studies, men were about 72 percent of the characters and women were only 28 percent.[35] In soap operas, we see more women, although they are still outnumbered by men. Three studies showed that about 53 percent of soap opera characters are men and 47 percent are women.[36]

Proposition 6.8: In Television Programs, Men Are More Often Employed than Women and Have Higher-Status Jobs.

Six studies investigated the portrayal of working women and men. Three of them found that about 79 percent of those shown employed are men and only 21 percent are women.[37] Three other studies looked at the percentage of all male and female characters who are shown working and found that approximately 75 percent of the men and 44 percent of the women are shown employed.[38]

A second finding relates to the *kinds* of occupations held by these working women and men on television. Although slightly different codes were used in the studies, we can say that on the average, 40 percent of the men are shown as professional or technical staff, 18 percent are shown as managers, and 17 percent are shown as policemen or law enforcement personnel. On the average, women are shown as professional and technical staff (33 percent), secretaries (18 percent), managers (14 percent), and nurses (12 percent).[39] Census data indicate than men are actually much more likely to be craftsmen and operatives than professionals or managers and that women are more likely to be secretaries and operatives than professionals or managers.[40] These studies of television show that the distortion between media occupations and real occupations is exaggerated in favor of men.

Proposition 6.9: In Television Programs, Marital Status *Is Known More Often for Women than for Men.*

Television emphasizes the importance of knowing the marital status of women. Assuming that our interactions with others may sometimes require us to know if they are married or single, we should need this information as frequently for men as for women. However, in the world of television drama, we are told the marital status of about 70 percent of the women and only about 43 percent of the men.[41] A study of soap operas confirms this finding but indicates that the marital status of both women and men is even more important to the plots of the afternoon soaps. We are told the marital status of 85 percent of the women and 73 percent of the men.[42]

STUDIES OF PROGRAMS. In the synopses of studies that follow, you will find details that could not be summarized in the propositions. Since we could not reproduce all the findings of each study, we have selected findings that most clearly show the portrayal of women and men.

Dallas Smythe published one of the earliest analyses of women and men on television, based on 86 drama programs broadcast in New York in 1953. The males among the 476 characters were shown as older than the women (average of 36 years for men and 33 years for women). Whereas male and female "heroes" averaged 34 versus 29 years of age, male and female "villains" averaged 42 versus 47 years. Non-American female heroes were as potent and active as American male heroes, but American female heroes were not as potent or active. Overall, male villains were less stereotyped than female villains.[43]

A decade later, Melvin DeFleur published one of the few other pre-1970 analyses of women and men on television. He monitored 250 half-hour periods from 3:30 to 11 P.M. on weekdays and from 10 A.M. to 11 P.M. on weekends. His data on television occupations seen in an Indiana community were compared with actual employment data for Indiana.

1. Men were shown primarily as managers (33 percent), professionals/technicians (30 percent), and service workers (14 percent), while census data reported that men were primarily employed as operatives (24 percent) and craftsmen (21 percent).
2. Women were shown primarily as professionals/technicians (37 percent), clerical workers (29 percent), and household workers (11 percent), while census data reported that women were primarily employed as clerical workers (30 percent), operatives (17 percent), and service workers (15 percent).[44]

George Gerbner summarized the sex of 240 characters in 1967 and 307 in 1969. In five types of programs, males were:

1. Fifty-three percent (1967) and 59 percent (1969) of those in feature films.
2. Seventy-three percent (1967) and 78 percent (1969) of those in comedies.
3. Eighty-six percent (1967) and 87 percent (1969) of those in crimes/westerns/adventures;

4. Seventy-nine percent (1967) and 71 percent (1969) of those in other dramas.
5. Ninety percent (both 1967 and 1969) of those in cartoons.[45]

In an update of this study, Gerbner found little change in the overall percentage of women and men. For family hour, late evening, and weekend daytime children's programs, men were 77 percent of the characters between 1967 and 1975.[46]

Women in the Wasteland Fight Back reports on the presentation of women and men in soap operas, quiz shows, prime-time dramatic shows, and public-affairs programs.

In *soap operas:*

1. Fifty percent of the women versus 16 percent of the men were shown in family roles.
2. Forty-seven percent of the women versus 88 percent of the men were identified with jobs.
3. Ten percent of the women versus 25 percent of the men were involved in single-sex conversations.
4. Twenty-three percent of the advisers in advice-giving situations were women and 77 percent were men.

In *quiz shows:*

1. One hundred percent of the moderators were men.
2. Forty-five percent of the female participants and 90 percent of the male participants were identified with jobs.
3. Forty-eight percent of the women and 20 percent of the men were under 30 years of age.

In *prime-time dramatic shows:*

1. Twenty-one percent of those shown employed were women and 79 percent were men.
2. Fourteen percent of the employed women and 57 percent

of the employed men were shown in high-status occupations.
3. Eighty-five percent of the women and 60 percent of the men were under 40 years of age.

In *public-affairs programs:*

1. Twenty percent of the moderators were women and 71 percent were men.
2. Twenty-three percent of the guests and panelists were women and 77 percent were men.
3. Sixty-two percent of the women and 81 percent of the men were identified with jobs.

In the two program types that feature "real people"—quiz shows and public-affairs programs—a total of 45 female roles and 67 male roles were shown.[47]

Natan Katzman published results of monitoring four weekly episodes of 14 soap operas. Among the 371 characters, he found that women were primarily identified as housewives (33 percent) and nurses/secretaries (29 percent). Men were primarily identified as doctors, lawyers, and businessmen (60 percent).[48]

Mildred Downing monitored 300 episodes of 15 soap operas. Among the 256 characters:

1. Men were shown as older than women.
2. Men were shown primarily as professionals (58 percent), managers, (10 percent), and law enforcement personnel (10 percent), while census data reported that men were primarily employed as craftsmen (20 percent), operatives (18 percent), and professionals/technicians (14 percent).
3. Women were shown primarily as housewives (30 percent), professionals (19 percent), and clerical employees (9 percent), while census data reported that women were primar-

ily employed as clerical workers (34 percent), service workers (22 percent), and professionals/technicians (15 percent). (Housewife is not listed as an occupation in the census.)[49]

Nancy Tedesco analyzed a sample of 1969 to 1972 noncartoon, prime-time network dramatic programs. For the 775 characters, she found:

1. Forty percent of the women and 64 percent of the men were shown employed.
2. Employed men were shown primarily as professionals (32 percent), law enforcement personnel (20 percent), and managers (18 percent).
3. Employed women were shown primarily as professionals (43 percent), clerical workers (17 percent), and managers (17 percent).
4. Men were more powerful, smart, rational, tall, and stable.
5. Women were more attractive, sociable, warm, and peaceful.[50]

Joseph Turow analyzed pecking orders on 12 hours of soap operas and 12 hours of prime-time programs. Only directives given by one sex to the other were included. He found for the 117 characters in *soap operas:*

1. Fifty-six percent of the directives were given by males.
2. Forty-six percent of the directives involved "feminine" subjects such as love and personal problems, 4 percent involved "masculine" subjects such as government and business, and 60 percent involved "neutral" subjects such as simple requests to close a door or buy a newspaper.
3. Women gave most of the directives involving "feminine" subjects, while men gave most of the directives involving "neutral" subjects.

For the 105 characters in *prime-time dramas:*

4. Seventy percent of the directives were given by males.
5. Seventeen percent of the directives involved "feminine" subjects, 33 percent involved "masculine" subjects, and 30 percent involved "neutral" subjects.[51]

Jean McNeil monitored 43 prime-time programs broadcast during a composite week in March 1973. She recorded occupational information for 279 characters and found that 72 percent of the men versus 44 percent of the women were shown employed. Employed women were shown primarily as clerical workers (18 percent), nurses (10 percent), artists (10 percent), academic personnel (10 percent), and managers (10 percent). Employed men were shown primarily as law enforcement personnel (30 percent), managers (13 percent), and doctors (10 percent). Sixty percent of the women versus 36 percent of the men worked under supervision. Among men, the ratio of professional to personal (e.g., justice versus romance) interaction was nearly equal. Among women, personal interaction was five times as common as professional interaction.[52]

The Screen Actor's Guild monitored a month of prime-time programs on the ABC, CBS, and NBC stations in Los Angeles. They found a particularly youthful portrayal of women. Specifically, men outnumbered women five to one in the over 35 category.[53]

The Sacramento, California, branch of AAUW reported on coverage of women in television news. Ninety percent of 5353 straight news stories were about men, and 84 percent of 1668 news features were about men.[54]

Women on Words and Images monitored the 16 top-rated, prime-time shows aired in 1 week between 7:30 and 9:30 P.M. The programs included adventure shows such as "Cannon" and "Hawaii Five-O" and situation comedies such as "Maud" and "Mary Tyler Moore." This 2-hour time period was chosen because it represents a major viewing time for children as well as for adults. For the 142 characters, they found:

1. Fifteen percent of those in adventure shows were women.
2. Forty-five percent of those in comedies were women.
3. For the eight shows with families, women were 25 percent of the wage earners.
4. Across all programs, 18 percent of the women and 22 percent of the men were explicitly shown in competent behaviors, while 20 percent of the women and only 9 percent of the men were explicitly shown in incompetent behaviors.
5. Thirty-three percent of the women and 42 percent of the men were shown in positive behaviors (e.g., bravery, supportiveness, humor).[55]

Judith Lemon studied dominance patterns in four comedies and four crime dramas and found that 23 percent of the comedies and 47 percent of the crime dramas showed men dominating women. Only 13 percent of the comedies and 6 percent of the crime dramas showed women dominating men. In comedies, interactions within the family were dominated more by men (19 percent) than by women (15 percent). Also in comedies, interactions outside the family were dominated more often by men (27 percent) than by women (12 percent). Not only were interactions involving masculine content dominated more often by men (55 versus 39 percent), but interactions involving feminine content were also dominated by men (20 versus 18 percent).[56]

Caroline Isber and Muriel Cantor authored *The Report of the Task Force on Women in Public Broadcasting.* They monitored a week of programming distributed by the Public Broadcasting Service, including general adult programming, drama, and children's programming. In *general adult programming,* they found that women were only 9 percent of the announcers; 28 percent of the women versus 56 percent of the men discussed issues of public importance. In examining the occupations of women and men appearing in these programs, Isber and Cantor created three categories: female occupation, male occupation, and neutral occupation. An occupation was classified as female if women represent 60 percent of those employed in that job. A male occupation has 60 percent men employed in it. A neutral occupation has 40 to 60 percent males and females. For the women seen in the general adult programming, 62 percent had female occupations and 32 percent had neutral occupations. For the men, 76 percent had male occupations and 24 percent had neutral occupations.

For *drama,* women were 20 percent of the characters in "Theater in America" and 55 percent of the characters in "Upstairs, Downstairs." Only 5 percent of the women actively participated in the programs for more than 5 minutes, while 11 percent of the men did. Similarly, women (44 percent) were more likely to participate for less than 30 seconds than men (19 percent).[57]

John Seggar and Penny Wheeler analyzed 250 half-hour television segments. Their random sample was limited to programs that showed people in modern settings and were broadcast between 3:30 and 11 P.M. on weekdays and between 10 A.M. and 11 P.M. on weekends. Among 1930 characters seen during February and March 1971:

1. The five most frequent occupations for white females were secretary (15 percent), nurse (15 percent), stage dancer (8 percent), maid (6 percent), and model (5 percent).
2. The five most frequent occupations for white males were physician (8 percent), policeman (8 percent), musician (5 percent), serviceman (5 percent), and government diplomat (4 percent).
3. The five most frequent occupations account for 49 percent of the white females and 30 percent of the white males.
4. The five most frequent occupations for black females were nurse (30 percent), stage dancer (15 percent), musician (5 percent), government diplomat (5 percent), lawyer (5 percent), and secretary (5 percent).
5. The five most frequent occupations for black males were

government diplomat (19 percent), musician (14 percent), policeman (10 percent), guard (10 percent), and serviceman (5 percent).

6. The five most frequent occupations account for 65 percent of the black females and 58 percent of the black males.[58]

Two years later, Herbert Northcott, John Seggar, and James Hinton expanded the Seggar and Wheeler study. They monitored 96 half-hour program segments in April 1971 and 120 half-hour segments in February 1973. Little change was evident across the 2 years. Women represented 2 percent more of the white American characters and 7 percent fewer of the black American characters in 1973 than in 1971. Occupations of blacks and whites, males and females remained constant within a few percentage points from 1971 to 1973.[59]

A 1976 study of soap operas indicated that changing the topics women and men discuss does not alter the interaction patterns. For example, a conversation concerning abortion or drugs is just as likely to have the man giving directives as a conversation concerning romance. Sherry Finz and Judith Waters chose three soap operas—"The Guiding Light," "The Doctors," and "General Hospital"—to monitor every day for 2 weeks. Each scene in which there were four or more verbal remarks was coded. Although there were some differences among the soaps ("The Doctors" was the most progressive), all three contained stereotypic verbal behavior patterns. Women were more nurturant, displayed more avoidant behavior, and expressed more hopelessness than men. Men gave more directives than women. When the authors examined the settings of conversations between same or different sex pairs, they found that 12 percent of the male/male conversations took place in the home and 75 percent took place in the office, while 50 percent of the female/female conversations took place in the home and only 17 percent took place in the office. Most of the female/male conversations took place in the home (47 percent in the home and 25 percent in the office). In spite of widely acclaimed changes in soap operas, women are still shown in traditional interaction patterns.[60]

Programming in the late 1970s has not been systematically analyzed yet. Joel Segal, senior vice president of the Ted Bates advertising agency, reports of the 1978 to 1979 season: "The theme will be dopey broads and handsome men."[61] FCC Commissioner Margita White refers to the new types of programs as sexploitative. She says, " 'Titillation Sweepstakes.' 'Jiggly Programming.' 'Cheesecake.' Call it what you will. Television executives refer to it as 'T— and A— Programming'...."[62] *Time* subtitled its review of the fall 1978 season "Comedy, sci-fi and girls, girls, girls...."[63] Pilots exist for possible series such as "California Girls," "Cheerleaders," "She," "Legs," "The Three Wives of David Wheeler," etc. In moving away from violent programs, the networks have returned to programs that cast women as sex objects.

CHILDREN'S PROGRAMS.   Seven studies of children's television programs document that young viewers see many more boys and men than girls and women. Evidence that Proposition 6.7 also holds for programming designed for children is found in these studies. They indicate that about 75 percent of the characters are boys/men and only 25 percent are girls/-women.[64]

Proposition 6.10: Television Programs for Children Show Men in More Roles than Women and Show Women More Often in Family Roles.

Two of the studies of children's television programs focused on the roles shown in programs. They found that women were shown in about 7 roles, men in about 49.[65] Furthermore, many more women are portrayed in family roles (25 percent) than men (6 percent).[66] The little girl watching television learns that women are expected to be housewives and nurses. The little boy watching television comes to expect his future wife to stay home or be employed as a subordinate in a helping profession.

STUDIES OF CHILDREN'S PROGRAMS. Studies of programs for children have monitored public television programs like "Sesame Street" and "Mr. Rogers" and Saturday morning commercial television programs like "Josie and the Pussycats" and "Fat Albert." Several writers have drawn attention to sex role stereotyping on "Sesame Street."[67] An analysis by Carolyn Cathey-Colvert of one episode (number 189) showed that 69 percent of all character appearances were men and that 88 percent of character appearances with dialogue were men. Eighty percent of narrators were men and 86 percent of dialogue was spoken by men.[68] These early findings were substantiated by Caroline Isber and Muriel Cantor in their later study.[69]

Heidi Hoffman reported data in *Women in the Wasteland Fight Back* from dramatic/live-action children's shows, educational children's shows, and cartoon shows. She found:

1. Fifty-five percent of the hosts on educational programs were women.
2. Thirty-five percent of the guests on educational programs were girls/women.
3. Female guests were entertainers or seekers of information, while male guests were experts or authorities.
4. Nineteen percent of the cartoon characters with speaking parts were girls/women;
5. Eighty-eight percent of the girls/women and 60 percent of the boys/men in cartoons were shown as "good".
6. Fifty percent of the girls/women and 14 percent of the boys/men in cartoons were shown as acted on.
7. Twelve percent of the girls/women and 57 percent of the boys/men in cartoons initiated action.[70]

Linda Jean Busby studied 20 half-hour Saturday morning cartoons broadcast in the 1972 to 1973 season. She found:

1. Male characters were shown in 42 roles versus 9 for female characters.

2. Male characters were shown as adventuresome, knowledgeable, independent, aggressive, sturdy, and bold; female characters were shown as romantic, submissive, emotional, fragile, timid, and patient.[71]

Michele Long and Rita Simon analyzed 22 Saturday morning, late afternoon, and early evening children's programs that had at least one adult female character. Each program was monitored five times in 1972. Reporting only on female characters, they found:

1. Twenty-four percent were leading characters.
2. Fifty-eight percent were married.
3. Seventy-eight percent of the married women had one or more children.
4. Seven percent of the married women were employed outside the home (38 percent of married women were employed according to the 1970 census).
5. Sixty percent of the unmarried women worked.
6. Eighty-eight percent of all women were attractive (tall, thin, nicely dressed).[72]

Long and Simon draw this composite picture of women seen in the 22 programs.

> Women are portrayed primarily in comic roles or as wives and mothers in a family context. . . . [It is rare that] married women work outside their homes, and of the single women and widows who do, only two occupy positions of prestige in the society. But even those two play their particular roles so as to appear subservient, dependent, and less rational than their male counterparts. . . . Women never appear to occupy positions of authority either at home or on the job. They are usually portrayed as silly, over-emotional, and dependent on husbands or boyfriends. . . . [Women] are concerned with their own appearance, and those of their families and homes. Their bodies are subject to evalu-

ation and approval by men. . . . All of the unmarried women spend much of their time trying to attract a man. . . . The overall image is the traditional one that women are dependent and perform expressive and socio-emotional roles within a family context. All of the women are portrayed as housewives, secretaries, quasi-secretaries; none as doctors professors, or executives. Women are referred to as girls, while men are men unless they are in fact boys. . . . The young people to whom these shows are largely or primarily aimed are not likely to gain any new insights into the new roles and perceptions that many women have of themselves or want for their daughters.[73]

Sarah Sternglanz and Lisa Servin analyzed 147 characters who appeared in three episodes of 10 popular half-hour children's programs. Only programs with at least one female character were included. Men were shown in more total activities than women. Men were shown as aggressive, constructive, succorant; they were often rewarded for their actions. Women were shown as deferent; they were often punished for their actions. Seventy-three percent of the men versus 96 percent of the women were characterized as "good."[74]

Isber and Cantor found that 69 percent of 1115 characters in six series of children's programs were men. Seventy-eight percent of the characters on "Sesame Street" were men, 74 percent on "Mr. Rogers," 69 percent on "Electric Company" and "Villa Alegre," 53 percent on "Zoom," and 49 percent on "Carrascolendas." Twenty-six percent of the men versus 16 percent of the women had occupations.[75]

In 1978, the National Advisory Council on Women's Educational Programs released its study of television programs that are supported by the Office of Education. Women on Words and Images conducted the study and report specific instances that indicate that we do not yet have gender-fair programs. They found that "Sesame Street" continues to emphasize males over females. The lack of sensitivity is found both in the programming and in the official goals of the program. Specifically, "Sesame Street" lists its goal of addressing the role of women under the area of "the child and his world." In one episode of "Infinity Factory," there were seven males and two females in occupational roles. All the portrayals were stereotypic with one female shown as a mother with a baby carriage and the other female shown wiping a store counter. In a third series, "Rebop," males were shown in all of the seven occupations in the monitored episode.[76]

RADIO

Radio had the misfortune of being eclipsed by television in the 1950s when content analyses of media began to be conducted on a large scale. Faced with the difficulties of analyzing electronic content, analysts chose to spend their energies on the newer and more debated medium. Therefore we have no current data on the portrayals of women and men on radio.

In the 1970s many radio stations are indulging audience nostalgia by rebroadcasting serials of the 1930s and 1940s. By this quirk of programming, audiences once again listen to serials that were studied in 1941 by Rudolf Arnheim.[77] In a sample of 596 episodes from 43 serials, Arnheim focused particularly on characters who "create trouble" and who "suffer from problems."

Of those who create trouble:

1. Twenty-four percent of the women and 20 percent of the men are shown as "good."
2. Twenty-four percent of the women and 36 percent of the men are shown as "bad."
3. Forty-one percent of the women and 39 percent of the men are shown as "weak."

Of those who suffer from problems:

4. Sixty-nine percent of the women and 59 percent of the men are shown as "good."

5. Four percent of the women and 5 percent of the men are shown as "bad."
6. Twenty percent of the women and 33 percent of the men are shown as "weak."[78]

Comparable categories have not been analyzed in television serials (soap operas), but our impression is that the radio serials created a "democracy of misery." You can see that women and men scarcely differ in Arnheim's percentages. Neither sex has the corner on goodness, badness, or weakness.

PROPOSITIONAL SUMMARY

Proposition 6.1:   Almost all commercials with *voice-overs* are spoken and sung by men.

Proposition 6.2:   Commercials show men in more *roles* than women and more often show women in *family roles*.

Proposition 6.3:   Commercials show women *doing activities* in the home and show men as *beneficiaries* of these activities.

Proposition 6.4:   The *settings* of commercials show women *inside* the home and men *outside* the home.

Proposition 6.5:   Women in commercials are shown as *younger* than men.

Proposition 6.6:   In commercials during children's programming, women and girls are *seen* less than men and boys.

Proposition 6.7:   In television programs, women are *seen* less than men.

Proposition 6.8:   In television programs, men are more often *employed* than women and have *higher-status jobs*.

Proposition 6.9:   In television programs, *marital status* is known more often for women than for men.

Proposition 6.10: Television programs for children show men in *more roles* than women and show women more often in *family roles.*

MAGAZINES AND NEWSPAPERS

The [women's] section is still a dumping ground for anything the male editors consider a woman's story. So we get all the serious news stories about Equal Rights Amendments, rape-law changes, back-pay lawsuits, etc., back among the girdle ads. . . .[1]

Magazines and newspapers arrive regularly at millions of American homes. Unlike the electronic media, whose images are lost when receivers are turned off, these print media stay around the home to be picked up by more than one reader and by the same reader more than once. Moment for moment, magazines and newspapers may not grip attention as television does, but print media have long-term effects on readers.

What do we know about the words and images presented in print media? After noting in Chapter 6 the extensive current research on television and the absence of current research on radio, we can say that research on magazines and newspapers falls in between.

MAGAZINE ADVERTISEMENTS

Advertisements in magazines have been studied more extensively than other aspects of the print media. Because several researchers have replicated a landmark 1971 study, we have reliable data on advertising portrayals of women and men at work and in other roles.

Proposition 7.1: Magazine Advertisements Show More Men than Women as Employed *and Show Men in* Higher-Status Occupations.

In 1971, Alice Courtney and Sarah Lockeretz published a study of advertisements in eight general audience magazines.[2] Parts of this study were replicated by Louis Wagner and Janis Banos in 1973 and by James Culley and Rex Bennett in 1974.[3] The findings of these studies permit two generalizations. First, about 22 percent of the women and about 49 percent of the men are shown émployed. Second, men are shown in higher-status occupations. Across all the studies, about 3 percent of the women and 21 percent of the men were shown in executive positions. On the other hand, more women (about 46 percent) than men (about 21 percent) were shown as professional entertainers/athletes.[4]

These conclusions are supported by more recent studies by Harold W. Fox and by Ahmed Belkaoui and Janice Belkaoui. In an analysis of 15 magazines, Fox found that 24 percent of the women and 52 percent of the men were shown in business roles. A greater percentage of the men (14 percent) than the women (2 percent) were portrayed as high-level business executives or professionals. Belkaoui and Belkaoui looked at the roles of women and men in advertisements from 1958, 1970, and 1972. There was some increase in the percentage of women shown working outside the home; however, women continued to be shown as unemployed or in low-income jobs.[5]

Proposition 7.2: Magazine Advertisements Show Men in Recreational *Roles and Women in* Decorative *roles.*

The Courtney and Lockeretz study, its two replications, and the Fox study also examined nonworking roles of characters in magazine advertisements. The three categories were family role, recreational role, and decorative role. In general, the studies showed little difference between the percentages of women and men in family roles (about 26 percent). However, more women than men (about 33 percent versus 17 percent) were shown in decorative roles, while more men than women (about 58 percent versus 42 percent) were shown in recreational roles.[6]

STUDIES OF MAGAZINE ADVERTISEMENTS.   Alice Courtney and Sarah Lockeretz examined 312 advertisements in the April 18, 1970 issues of eight general magazines *(Life, Look, Newsweek, The New Yorker, Reader's Digest, Saturday Review, Time, and U.S. News and World Report)*. In the advertisements that showed one or more adults, 9 percent of the women and 45 percent of the men were shown employed. Of those shown employed:

1. None of the women and 19 percent of the men were executives and professionals.
2. Twenty-five percent of the women and 9 percent of the men were white-collar workers.
3. Seventeen percent of the women and 40 percent of the men were blue-collar workers.
4. None of the women and 12 percent of the men were soldiers and police.
5. Fifty-eight percent of the women and 20 percent of the men were entertainers and athletes.

Of those shown in nonworking roles:

6. Twenty-three percent of the women and 22 percent of the men were shown in family roles.
7. Forty-six percent of the women and 56 percent of the men were shown in recreational roles.
8. Thirty-one percent of the women and 22 percent of the men were shown in decorative roles.[7]

Courtney and Lockeretz also found that 40 percent of the advertisements showed men only, while 26 percent showed women only. Men were seen most often in advertisements for institutions, entertainment, industrial products, banks, cigarettes, and alcoholic beverages. Women were seen most often in advertisements for food, cleaning products, beauty products, and drugs.[8]

Two years later, Louis Wagner and Janis Banos studied advertisements in eight general magazines, including seven studied by Courtney and Lockeretz (a different magazine was substituted for one that had ceased publication). Wagner and Banos present information only for the women shown in the advertisements, and evaluation of changes over time is difficult without comparative data for men. Some of the Wagner and Banos findings, with comparable Courtney and Lockeretz findings in parentheses, are:

1. Twenty-one percent of the women were employed (CL: 9 percent).
2. Four percent of the employed women were executives/-professionals (CL: 0 percent).
3. Sixty-one percent were white-collar workers (CL: 25 percent).
4. Twelve percent were blue-collar workers (CL: 17 percent).
5. Twenty-three percent were entertainers and athletes (CL: 58 percent).

Of women shown in nonworking roles:

6. Eight percent were shown in family roles (CL: 23 percent).
7. Thirty-six percent were shown in recreational roles (CL: 46 percent).
8. Fifty-six percent were shown in decorative roles (CL: 31 percent).[9]

Eileen McGinley wanted to see if contrasting types of magazines portray women and men differently. In other words, assuming that advertisers create advertisements to raise interest among the readers of each magazine, what differences are there in the way the sexes are presented? McGinley analyzed advertisements in 36 issues of *Ladies' Home Journal* and *Esquire* from 1962, 1967, and 1972. The 1503 advertisements were coded using categories established by Dominick and Rauch and discussed in the previous chapter. McGinley found that fewer than 10 percent of the men in *Esquire* were shown in family roles, while 24 percent of the women were portrayed this way. In *Ladies' Home Journal*, 42 percent of the men and 68 percent of the women were shown in family roles. The activities of the sexes as well as their roles were different in the two magazines. In *Esquire*, men were shown playing sports (15 percent) or working (10 percent), while women were shown in more passive activities of eating and drinking (13 percent) and listening and watching (9 percent). *Ladies' Home Journal* showed men eating (20 percent) and playing sports (8 percent) and women engaging in domestic activities such as cleaning and cooking (22 percent) and eating and drinking (9 percent).[10]

This study also supports the conclusion from television studies that women are more likely to be shown in the home and men are more likely to be shown outdoors. McGinley found in *Esquire* that men were outdoors in 35 percent of the advertisements while women were outdoors in 26 percent. In *Ladies' Home Journal* men were shown in the home in 39 percent of the advertisements and women were shown in the home in 47 percent.[11]

Donald Sexton and Phyllis Haberman analyzed 1827 advertisements that appeared in 12 issues of five general magazines in 1950 to 1951, 1960 to 1961, and 1970 to 1971. Trends are discussed in six product areas.

In cigarette advertisements:

1. Women were shown as models and public personalities in 1950 to 1951; they were shown as social companions in 1960 to 1961 and 1970 to 1971.
2. The number of advertisements showing more men than women increased over both decades.
3. Women were increasingly shown as decorative over both decades.

In beverage advertisements:

4. Women were decreasingly shown as housewives/mothers over both decades.

In automobile advertisements:

5. Most women were shown as social companions in both decades.
6. Fewer than 10 percent of women were shown in nontraditional roles.
7. Women were increasingly shown as decorative over both decades.

In home appliance advertisements:

8. Women were decreasingly shown as housewives/mothers over both decades.
9. Almost no women were shown in nontraditional roles,

In office equipment advertisements:

10. Sixty percent showed women as employees.
11. Almost no women were shown in nontraditional roles.

In airline advertisements:

12. Women were increasingly shown as employees over both decades.

13. Women were increasingly shown as alluring over both decades.

More than 30 percent of cigarette, beverage, automobile, and airline advertisements showed women as alluring.[12]

In 1975, James Culley and Rex Bennett replicated the Courtney and Lockeretz study using the same general magazines for 1970 and 1974. *Life* and *Look* were excluded, since they had ceased publication. Coding differences and the absence of two magazines account for discrepancies between the Courtney and Lockeretz 1970 data and the Culley and Bennett 1970 data. Culley and Bennett found an increase in the percentage of women shown employed in 1970 (24 percent) and 1974 (33 percent) and a similar increase in the percentage of men employed in 1970 (48 percent) and 1974 (54 percent). Of those shown employed, they found:

1. None of the women in 1970 and 8 percent in 1974 were shown as high-level business executives, while 13 percent of the men in 1970 and 30 percent in 1974 were shown in this status.
2. Sixty-one percent of the women in 1970 and 42 percent in 1974 were shown as professionals, including entertainers and athletes, while 26 percent of the men in 1970 and 16 percent in 1974 were portrayed this way.
3. Twenty-two percent of the women in 1970 and 36 percent in 1974 were shown as blue-collar workers, while 21 percent of the men in 1970 and 13 percent in 1974 were blue-collar workers.
4. None of the women in either year were soldiers or police, while 9 percent of the men in 1970 and 16 percent in 1974 were.

Over the 4 years, 8 percent more women and 17 percent more men were shown as business executives, 19 percent fewer women and 10 percent fewer men were shown as professionals/

entertainers/athletes, and 14 percent more women and 8 percent fewer men were shown as blue-collar workers.[13]

Finally, Culley and Bennett report that men were seen most often in advertisements for alcoholic beverages, cars, cigarettes, entertainment media, industrial products, institutions, and travel in both 1970 and 1974. Women were seen most often in advertisements for clothing, food products, and home appliances in both years.[14]

Harold W. Fox analyzed 410 characters in 250 advertisements from 15 magazines.[15] His content codes corresponded with those used by Courtney and Lockeretz and Wagner and Banos, although the list of magazines did not. He found that 52 percent of these characters were male and 48 percent were female. Of those shown in business roles (52 percent of the males and 24 percent of the females):

1. None of the women were shown as high-level business executives, while 8 percent of the men were shown in this status.
2. Thirty-three percent of the women were shown as professionals, including entertainers and athletes, while 58 percent of the men were portrayed this way.
3. Sixty-seven percent of the women and 8 percent of the men were shown in nonprofessional and white-collar positions.
4. None of the women and 23 percent of the men were shown as blue-collar workers.
5. None of the women and 3 percent of the men were shown as soldiers or police.[16]

Thus the evidence of past studies of the portrayal of women and men in magazine advertisements indicates that men are presented in more roles, in more employment-related roles, and in higher-status positions. You will find exceptions to this rule in current issues of general magazines. Corporations that have felt the sting of sex-discrimination suits (e.g., AT&T, Bank of America) now show women working in nonstereotypic, blue-collar occupations and in management. Advertisers of travel services (e.g., United Airlines, Hyatt Hotels) show women as business travelers. Advertisers that serve the executive market (e.g., New York Life Insurance Company, *Business Week* magazine) provide creditable and credible glimpses of female executives.

If we could award a "nonsexist advertiser of the year" citation, it might go to Dewar's Whiskey, whose "Dewar's Profiles" have featured women in roles such as symphony conductor, rough-river guide, physicist, and ecologist. Prominently displayed on the back covers of general magazines, the profiles have undoubtedly altered some public images of "women's work."

MAGAZINE ARTICLES AND SHORT STORIES

Studies of articles and short stories have examined themes, social norms, types of occupations, and attitudes toward working in men's and women's magazines. The last of these variables has been included in most of the studies, and findings permit this proposition.

Proposition 7.3: In Magazine Articles and Short Stories, Few Women Work; Those Who Do Quit Upon Marriage or the Birth of a Child.

Five studies document this proposition. Helen Franzwa sampled issues of women's magazines from 1940 to 1970 and found few married women who worked. Most women portrayed as working were using their job as a means of finding a man to marry. Upon marriage all but 9 percent left their jobs. In only one story was there a mother who worked because she had been left by her husband. She "severely damaged" her son's understanding of personal relationships.[17]

Margaret Lefkowitz examined women's magazine short

stories between 1957 and 1967 and reached the same conclusions as Franzwa; few women were shown pursuing careers, and those who did were portrayed as unwomanly. The typical heroine was attractive, married, between 26 and 35 years of age, middle class, love oriented, and a housewife.[18]

Another multiple-year study was done by Judy Morelock and Suzanne Kurth. They looked at roles of women in women's magazines between 1956 and 1970. Analyzing the theme of employment of women, they found that twice as many articles were unfavorable as were favorable.[19] A study by Mary Hatch and David Hatch in the mid-1950s indicated that articles dealing with married women who work generally emphasized some form of conflict.[20]

Cornelia Butler Flora examined fiction in working- and middle-class women's magazines in the United States and Latin America. She found that most jobs were viewed as a step toward getting a husband. Across both samples, few women (about 15 percent) continued working after marriage, and all middle-class heroines quit after getting pregnant. Six percent of the working-class women were portrayed as working even though they were married and had children.[21] The details of these and other studies follow.

STUDIES OF MAGAZINE ARTICLES AND SHORT STORIES.   Patricke Johns-Heine and Hans Gerth published an early study of women and men in five magazines from 1921 to 1940. The majority of male characters were over 30, while the majority of female characters were under 30. More stories emphasized love themes in a magazine such as *Ladies' Home Journal* than in a magazine like *Country Gentleman;* the converse was true of success themes.

Johns-Heine and Gerth commented on themes in women's magazines:

> One may impute that the function of such themes is the systematic magnification of the woman's traditional role precisely in

contrast to her publicly changing role. Acclaim of the model
lady, wife, and mother remains dominant in the face of current
competing claims.[22]

Mary Hatch and David Hatch examined three magazines
published for working women. During 1956 to 1957, they found
35 articles dealing with the problems of working married
women. They report:

1. Eighty-eight percent dealt with some form of conflict.
2. Seventy-four percent of the conflict articles dealt with career/home conflict.
3. Thirty percent of career/home conflict articles suggested part-time work as the solution,
4. Thirteen percent of career/home conflict articles suggested that problems solve themselves because the working woman is a happy efficient woman.
5. Nine percent of the career/home conflict articles suggested waiting for careers until the children are grown. (Hatch and Hatch present this as the "unprejudiced" solution.)[23]

Peter Clarke and Virginia Esposito studied the motivational themes in 19 magazine articles on working found in three
popular women's magazines in 1963 to 1964. Stating that most
vocations were esoteric (oceanography, political staff work,
television research, filmmaking), Clarke and Esposito report for
the 453 motivational statements that:

1. Twenty-six percent concerned achievement (advancement, competition).
2. Nineteen percent concerned power (influence, advice).
3. Seventeen percent concerned affiliation (people).
4. Twelve percent concerned cognitive need (information, ideas).
5. Eleven percent concerned diffuse energy (adventure, action).

6. Ten percent concerned terminal values (work schedule).
7. Five percent concerned feminine mystique (marriage and career).
8. Affiliation and power were the two themes used jointly most often.

In keeping with the philosophy of such research in the mid-1960s, Clarke and Esposito say that the findings show "discrimination against feminine interests." They say that stories should emphasize affiliation instead of achievement.[24]

Margaret Lefkowitz examined the role of the heroine in *Ladies' Home Journal, McCall's* and *Good Housekeeping* fiction in 1957 and 1967. Her findings show:

1. Careers decreased over the time period, with 9 percent of the women working in 1957 and 4 percent working in 1967.
2. Those with careers were portrayed as unwomanly and as threatening to the marriages of nonworking women,
3. Marriages became happier over the decade, with 81 percent happy in 1957 and 93 percent happy in 1967.[25]

Another study encompassing multiple years was conducted by Judy Morelock and Suzanne Kurth. They analyzed nonfiction articles from March and October issues of *McCall's, Ladies' Home Journal*, and *Good Housekeeping* for 1956 to 1970. They were primarily interested in how employment and marriage were portrayed. They found that almost all of the articles discussing the working mother (15 out of 17) were unfavorable.[26]

In all, 31 articles dealt with employment for women. Twenty-six percent were favorable, 52 percent were unfavorable, and 23 percent were mixed. Even though the 1966 to 1970 period saw a more equal presentation of viewpoints, Morelock and Kurth comment that the 46 percent of the readers who work were not well represented in these magazines.[27]

Morelock and Kurth examined the portrayal of marriage

to see if the "traditional" marriage or the "equalitarian" marriage was favored in these magazines. Here, the findings are somewhat more promising, with traditional marriages (in which the woman does everything, even if she works) decreasing over time and equalitarian marriages increasing. However, over the 15-year period, 55 percent of the articles emphasized the traditional marriage, 12 percent presented the equalitarian marriage and 33 percent had elements of both.[28]

Cornelia Butler Flora made comparisons not over time, but across cultures. She analyzed 202 fiction stories drawn from working-class and middle-class women's magazines of the United States and Latin America. The U.S. sample consisted of *True Story* and *Modern Romances* (the two largest- circulation, working-class magazines) and *Redbook* and *Cosmopolitan* (large-circulation, middle-class magazines with readers in the same age category as the first two magazines). The Latin American sample consisted of *Corin Tellado*, *Novelas de Amor*, and *Tu y Yo* (three *fotonovelas* appealing to working women) and *Vanidades* and *Cromos* (two middle-class women's magazines). Flora found that female dependence was more often shown as desirable (41 percent of the stories) than undesirable (20 percent) for the U.S. magazines. Furthermore, dependence was more likely to be shown as desirable for middle-class than for working-class women. In the Latin American magazines, there was an even sharper contrast, with 8 percent presenting dependence as undesirable and 57 percent as desirable. The differences by class were in the same direction as the U.S. sample, but not as great. Male dependence was seldom mentioned in the stories (71 percent never mentioned it) and, when discussed, was presented only as undesirable.[29]

Flora found that few women in the stories continue to work after marriage, although U.S. magazines were more likely to portray the working wife than Latin American magazines (26 percent versus 5 percent). She found little difference by class, with slightly more working-class wives continuing employment in the U.S. stories and slightly more middle-class wives continuing employment in the Latin American sample. But for those few who stay in the labor force after marriage, a pregnancy ends their employed status.[30]

Helen Franzwa studied the occupations of 155 major female characters in the fiction of "two randomly selected issues per year (selected at five- year intervals) of *Ladies' Home Journal*, *McCall's*, and *Good Housekeeping* between the years 1940 and 1970." She found for the 41 percent who were shown as working women:

1. Fifty-one percent were in low-status jobs (secretaries, clerks, and servants).
2. Thirty-eight percent were in middle-status jobs (teachers, nurses, stewardesses, writers, commercial artists).
3. Eleven percent were in high-status jobs (college professors, geologists, museum directors).
4. Three percent were married.[31]

Most women who worked were looking for a husband and intended to quit after marriage. Those who continued to work either had lost their husbands or had unhappy marriages. Fourteen stories specifically featured the theme that married women do not work. Contrasting her research with that of Clarke and Esposito, Franzwa commented that magazines need to broaden the occupational horizons of women instead of restricting them to the roles of wife and mother.[32]

Gale Stolz and her colleagues also studied magazines from 1940 to 1970. Examinations of several women's magazines and general magazines indicated that the proportion of female authors has always been low. Within the stories, the proportion of women shown as housewives has slightly increased; the proportion of married women shown working outside the home has always been low.[33]

Dwayne Smith and Marc Matre analyzed the social norms of 48 romance magazine stories and 27 adventure magazine stories. These magazines, read primarily by blue-collar families, socialize female readers of romance and male readers of adventure to different norms. Percentaging only on stories in which particular norms were either upheld or rejected, the following differences were found between romance and adventure stories.

1. Role segregation between the sexes: both romance and adventure stories rejected (77 percent and 57 percent),
2. Premarital and extramarital sex: romance stories rejected (76 percent); adventure stories upheld (100 percent),
3. Marriage as a primary goal in life: both romance and adventure stories upheld (89 percent and 64 percent),
4. Stern punishment for illegal acts: romance stories rejected (55 percent); adventure stories upheld (71 percent),
5. Perception of individuals as helpless in a hostile environment: romance stories upheld (94 percent); adventure stories rejected (94 percent),
6. Orientation to stability and security: romance stories upheld (97 percent); adventure stories rejected (85 percent).[34]

In addition, Smith and Matre found that 40 percent of the adventure stories did not present a female character, but only 2 percent of the romance stories did not present a male character. Both women and men were more often portrayed as aggressive in adventure stories (69 percent and 96 percent) than in romance stories (15 percent and 33 percent). Women were more often portrayed as passive in romance stories (39 percent) than in adventure stories (19 percent), but men were seldom portrayed as passive in either (0 percent and 6 percent).[35]

Carole Ruth Newkirk studied the roles of women as portrayed in the nonfiction of *Mademoiselle*, *Redbook*, and *Ms*. She drew a random sample of articles that represented 35 percent of the possible articles. She coded the stories into four major types: domestic, nondomestic, self-identity, and social activist. For 1972 to 1974, Newkirk found:

1. *Mademoiselle* had 2, *Redbook* had 9, and *Ms.* had no articles featuring women in domestic roles.
2. *Mademoiselle* had 9, *Redbook* had 10, and *Ms.* had 37 articles featuring women in nondomestic roles. In these articles, *Mademoiselle* had 8, *Redbook* had 2, and *Ms.* had 9 articles featuring women as professionals or managers.
3. *Mademoiselle* had 6, *Redbook* had 10, and *Ms.* had 8 articles featuring women in the self-identity roles (pursuing own goals).
4. Together *Mademoiselle* and *Redbook* had 5 and *Ms.* had 32 articles featuring women as social activists.[36]

Newkirk concludes that although over time more women are being shown in nondomestic roles, these magazines still do not provide a balanced view of women.

Charles Lazer and S. Dier selected 213 short stories from *Atlantic Monthly* and *Saturday Evening Post* for the 12-month period preceding the census years of 1940 to 1970. Because the *Post* did not publish in 1969, stories were chosen from 1968. Of the 2828 short story characters, 28 percent were women and 62 percent were men. These percentages did not significantly change over time. Approximately 25 percent of the women and 63 percent of the men were portrayed as working. When Lazer and Dier compare these members of the fictional labor force with census figures, they find that women are underrepresented in all years. Between 1940 and 1970, women increased from 25 percent to 38 percent of the actual work force.[37] In *Saturday Evening Post*, women decreased from 17 percent to 12 percent. In *Atlantic Monthly*, women increased from 15 percent to 21 percent, but fell behind actual increases in the work force. As is true with the occupational portrayals on television, the characters in these magazines are overrepresented in some categories. For instance, using 1970 data:[38]

1. In fiction (F), women are overrepresented according to census (C) figures as professionals (33 percent F and 16

percent C), private household workers (13 percent F and 4 percent C), and service workers (28 percent F and 17 percent C).

2. Women are underrepresented as clerical workers (13 percent F and 33 percent C) and operatives (3 percent F and 13 percent C).

3. Men are overrepresented as professionals (23 percent F and 14 percent C), managers/administrators (34 percent F and 11 percent C), and service workers (18 percent F and 8 percent C).

4. Men are underrepresented as clerical workers (2 percent F and 8 percent C), sales workers (2 percent F and 7 percent C), craftsmen (5 percent F and 21 percent C), and operatives (2 percent F and 20 percent C).

Apart from these studies of the roles that women play in magazine articles and fiction, we know little about magazine content insofar as it addresses women's issues. However we recently took advantage of the unusual coverage of the Equal Rights Amendment that appeared in more than 30 women's magazines during the 1976 bicentennial year thanks to *Redbook* editor Sey Chassler, who persuaded other editors that ERA deserved more attention, pro or con, in their magazines.[39]

We were able to obtain 28 of the magazines involved in the cooperative coverage of ERA. Most of the magazines (75 percent) presented information on ERA in articles. In others, letters to the editors (14 percent) and editorials (11 percent) were used as forums for ERA coverage.

Amount of ERA coverage in the 28 magazines can be expressed two ways. First, the number of pages devoted to ERA indicates the amount of editorial effort invested in ERA coverage. Second, the number of ERA pages expressed as a percentage of total editorial pages in each magazine corrects for differences in length among magazines.

In terms of pages, the most extensive ERA coverage appeared in *Ms., New Dawn, Playgirl*, and *Redbook* (each five pages or more), followed by *Family Circle*, *Girl Talk*, and *McCall's* (each three or four pages), followed by *American Girl*, *Co-Ed*, *Ladies' Home Journal*, *Mademoiselle*, and *Woman's Day* (each two pages). Lagging in this set are *Bride's*, *Cosmopolitan*, *Daytime TV*, *Glamour*, *Good Housekeeping*, *Harper's Bazaar*, *Modern Bride*, *New Woman*, *Parents*, *Viva*, and *Vogue* (each one page). The least coverage (less than one page) appeared in *Seventeen*, *True Confessions*, *True Experiences*, *True Story*, and *Women Sports*.

The rank order of magazines changes only slightly when coverage is expressed as a percentage of total editorial space. In descending order, *Ms.*, *Girl Talk*, *Playgirl*, *New Dawn*, *American Girl*, *Co-Ed*, and *Ladies' Home Journal* each devoted 5 percent or more total editorial space to ERA. At the bottom of the list, *True Confessions*, *True Experience*, and *True Story* each devoted less than 0.5 percent of total editorial space to ERA.

One reason why the "confession" magazines provided so little coverage of ERA is the inflexibility of their content. There is almost no way, except for a planted letter to the editor, that these magazines can introduce content other than the "confession" stories. For example, the magazine with the least coverage, *True Confessions*, published only a 100-word letter that begins:

> My husband is always making remarks about Women's Lib. He thinks all it means is burning bras and using the same public restrooms. I've tried to tell him that's not so, but I wish I had some *real* information about equal rights for women. . . .

True Confessions "answered" this letter by printing the text of the Equal Rights Amendment.

In spite of write-in campaigns by ERA opponents, most of the articles (73 percent) favored ERA. Some (14 percent) remained neutral, some (11 percent) presented both pro and con arguments. Only one (3 percent) was anti-ERA, and it was followed by a pro-ERA article. Overall, no magazine took an anti-ERA stand.

What ERA-related issues did the magazines choose to discuss? Most often mentioned was employment, which accounted for 25 percent of all issue references. In the discussion of employment, 86 percent of the points made were pro-ERA

Divorce accounted for 24 percent of all issue references; points made were 87 percent pro-ERA. Marriage and military draft each accounted for 13 percent of all issue references; 82 percent and 81 percent of the points made were pro-ERA.

Comprising the other 25 percent of all issue references were seven issues: unisex bathrooms, homosexual marriages, education, rape, credit, abortion, and day care. On the average, 84 percent of the points made concerning these issues were pro-ERA.

We next question how this coverage of ERA fits into the overall pattern of magazine coverage of equal rights for women. According to the *Reader's Guide to Periodical Literature*, which indexes magazine content from 1890, the first article on equal rights appeared in 1922, a year before ERA was introduced in Congress. Grouping the years between 1922 and 1976 into 5-year periods, we find 32 articles on equal rights in the earliest period and 166 in the most recent period. Magazine coverage of equal rights meshes well with historical trends. There was less coverage during the 1930s (47 articles) than the 1920s (62 articles), and there was considerably more coverage during the 1940s (92 articles) than the 1950s (41 articles). By the second half of the 1960s, coverage of equal rights rose to a new level (102 articles) that was then surpassed by the first half of the 1970s (166 articles).

Looking specifically at articles that mention ERA in their titles, we find only two for 1970. The trend of a few ERA articles per year continues until 1975 and 1976, when it jumps to 21 articles and 28 articles.

One other study helps to indicate the range of studies still to be conducted. This one concerns media roles of women and men in relation to heart disease. June M. Fisher and Noreen Z. Janus examined the messages that women find in *Ladies' Home Journal*, *Reader's Digest*, and *Time*. Although heart disease is the major killer of women over 50, the 198 articles they analyzed focused on men. For instance, men and heart disease was mentioned in 94 percent of the articles, while women and heart disease was mentioned in 33 percent of the articles. Looking for articles that mention heart disease and only one sex, Fisher and Janus found that 67 percent mentioned men and 6 percent mentioned women. Perhaps more striking were the messages indicating that women could prevent or ameliorate men's heart diseases. Rarely is a man portrayed in an auxiliary role to a women.[40]

These studies of the content of magazines are useful in helping us to understand how social values, norms, and expectations are communicated. When you next look at a magazine, ask yourself how fair the content is to women. Judge whether women are shown only in traditional roles or whether the magazine opens new doors and raises new possibilities for women and girls.

NEWSPAPER ADVERTISEMENTS

We find only two studies of the portrayal of women in newspaper advertising; since each is quite different, it is not possible to form propositions from them. The first study, conducted in the 1950s, analyzed movie advertisements. The second is a 1976 study of products and target audiences for advertisements in four major newspapers.

David White, Robert Albert, and R. Allen Seegar analyzed advertisements of 970 films appearing in three large-circulation newspapers from 1935 to 1955. Data from the prewar, wartime, and postwar periods shows that 9 percent of the prewar advertisements, 27 percent of the wartime advertisements, and 30 percent of the postwar advertisements used "sexy" photographs of women. Of advertisements mentioning marriage, 38 percent implied that marriage was desirable for women and undesirable for men; 19 percent implied that it was desirable for both; 15 percent implied that it was undesirable for both; and 12 percent implied that it was desirable for men but did not mention women.[41]

Susan Miller analyzed advertisements appearing in the *New York Times*, the *Washington Post*, the *Chicago Tribune*, and the *Los Angeles Times* in 4 weeks from the months of January, April, July, and October 1965 and again in 1975. Over the 10-year period, the number of advertisements per page in the women's/life-style sections and the type of products did not change. However, there was a change in the percentage directed primarily to women. Averaged across four newspapers, there was a 10 percent decrease in the percentage of advertisements directed to women (from 56 to 46 percent) and a corresponding increase in the percentage of advertisements directed to both women and men. There continue to be few advertisements for men in this section of the paper.[42]

NEWSPAPER ARTICLES

There have been two kinds of studies of newspaper content. One examines ways in which newspapers are dominated by the male point of view and the other examines what is happening to the "women's section." We can form two propositions from these studies.

Proposition 7.4: Newspapers Are Written Primarily By and About Men.

The Northern Virginia chapter of NOW's study of nine newspapers in Washington, D.C., and Virginia, as well as Susan Miller's study of photographs in the *Washington Post* and the

Los Angeles Times support the proposition that newspapers tell us more about men than about women. Findings from the first study include the percentage of stories reported by men (more than 90 percent) and the percentage of male obituaries (more than 80 percent).[43] Findings from Miller's study indicate that most photographs show men. Women appear in photographs when they are wives of famous men or socialites/celebrities.[44]

Proposition 7.5: The New Women's/Life-style Sections Represent Only a Slight Improvement in Coverage of Issues That Concern Women.

Zena Beth Guenin and Susan Miller both found that the traditional columns of advice, marital news, club news, etc., are less likely to be found in the redesigned women's sections than in the traditional sections. However, most of the leftover space has been given to entertainment content. Because the new sections are smaller than the old sections, readers find the same amount or less coverage of life-style and consumer issues than they did 10 years ago. In general, the new and old sections carry equal coverage of issues such as aging, children, and education. Miller contends that "in some instances, the changes have been for the worse."[45]

STUDIES OF NEWSPAPER CONTENT. The Northern Virginia chapter of NOW monitored nine Washington, D.C., and Virginia newspapers. Based on daily observations for 3 months in the summer of 1972 and 1 month in the winter of 1973, their findings for the *Washington Post* include:

1. Ninety-four percent of the front page stories were reported by men.
2. Ninety-four percent of the columns on the editorial page were written by men.
3. Eighty-two percent of the obituaries were male.

4. Seventy-five percent of stories on the first page of "Style" (formerly the women's section) were written by men.

For all nine newspapers including the *Post* they found that:

1. Metropolitan papers were more likely to substitute "girl" for "woman" than suburban papers.
2. Hard news about women often appeared on the women's pages, not in the appropriate news section.
3. Metropolitan papers appointed men as editors of redesigned women's sections, and male columnists were added.
4. Editorial writers were primarily men.
5. Business pages gave women little, but fair, treatment.[46]

Susan Miller analyzed news photographs appearing in every eighth issue of the *Washington Post* and the *Los Angeles Times* for a year from mid-1973 to mid-1974. Of the 3661 photographs, she found that 30 percent of the photographs showed women and 81 percent showed men (11 percent of the photographs showed both sexes). Looking at sections of the newspaper, she found even higher percentages of men on the front page (90 percent), the inside news section (86 percent), the business section (94 percent), and the sports section (95 percent). Only in the entertainment section (78 percent men) and the life-style section (50 percent men) was there less than a 40 percent difference.[47]

Miller also found that in the 4047 separate appearances of women and men, men were shown as professionals (28 percent), public officials (24 percent), sports figures (23 percent), entertainers (10 percent), and socialites/celebrities (6 percent) while women were shown as wives (23 percent), socialites/celebrities (18 percent), professionals (16 percent), entertainers (14 percent), and as subjects of human interest (11 percent).[48]

Zena Beth Guenin analyzed women's sections in three newspapers with traditional sections and three newspapers with redesigned sections. For eight issues of each newspaper that appeared during April 1973, she found:

1. Twenty-one percent of the redesigned sections versus 66 percent of the traditional sections contained traditional content (advice columns, astrology, beauty, marital news, clubs, etc.).
2. Twenty-two percent of both the redesigned and traditional sections contained coverage of adolescence, aging, children, consumerism, economics, education, etc.
3. Thirty-eight percent of the redesigned sections versus 1 percent of the traditional sections contained entertainment stories.
4. The women's rights movement was covered in 2 percent of the content of the redesigned sections and none of the traditional sections.[49]

Susan Miller later examined changes over 10 years in the women's/life-style sections of four major newspapers. This study, mentioned briefly in the section on newspaper advertising, dealt with subject matter (e.g., life-style, consumer issues, entertainment), story focus (about women, men, or both), and photographs (of women, men, or both) for 1965 and 1975. Averaging across all four newspapers, Miller found that between 1965 and 1975:

1. Life-style stories (e.g., work, personal relationships, child rearing) increased from 8 percent to 16 percent.
2. Consumer stories (e.g., health, environment, finances) increased from 5 percent to 12 percent.
3. Social stories (e.g., social events, engagements) decreased from 49 percent to 20 percent.
4. Entertainment/arts stories (e.g., reviews, artists, performances) increased from 11 percent to 23 percent.
5. There was little change in coverage of food or fashion.[50]

In 1975 there were half as many stories about women as in 1965 (16 percent versus 31 percent), three times as many stories about men (7 percent versus 2 percent), and 10 percent more about both (77 percent versus 67 percent).[51]

Miller concludes that redesign of the women's/life-style sections have been primarily window dressing, with little change in subject matter, focus of stories, photographs, and advertisements. Changes that have occurred (e.g., fewer stories of social news and more of entertainment) are not necessarily responsive to the needs of women.[52]

Leo Bogart addressed the Associated Press managing editors in late 1977 to report on his findings from a national probability sampling of adults. The readership study was partially described in terms of recommendations. One of these stated:

> Talk to the changed interests of women readers. . . . we're still running six or seven times as much special interest material for men as for women.[53]

These studies of newspapers make it clear that most of the newspaper is written by and about men. The women's/life-style sections, where women might expect to find coverage of issues that concern them, continue to divert more than inform. In an effort to broaden the appeal of these sections, editors have settled on the common denominator of entertainment coverage.

PROPOSITIONAL SUMMARY

Proposition 7.1: Magazine advertisements show more men than women as *employed* and show men in *higher status occupations*.

Proposition 7.2: Magazine advertisements show men in *recreational* roles and women in *decorative* roles.

Proposition 7.3: In magazine articles and short stories, few women *work*; those who do quit upon marriage or the birth of a child.

Proposition 7.4: Newspapers are written primarily *by* and *about* men.

Proposition 7.5: The new *women's/life-style sections* represent only a slight improvement in coverage of issues that concern women.

8

BOOKS

One of the prime functions of literature and poetry is to make
some sense out of the chaos in which human beings live. . . .
[Children's books] give girls even more to overcome by constantly belittling them.[1]

This chapter examines the portrayal of women and men, girls
and boys in literature for adults and children. Many excellent
studies of children's books are the basis of several propositions.
However, studies of adult literature are difficult to summarize
because they probe portrayals by individual authors or themes
that involve women in a few books, and this forms a casual
sample by time period or genre. Because of the diversity of
literature, authors and themes are rarely analyzed from a common perspective.

ADULT BOOKS/TEXTBOOKS

Our review finds imagination and insight in studies such
as these:

1. Natalie Shainess' discussion of women in literature who provide clues for psychotherapy.[2]
2. Kate Millet's analysis of patriarchal and countersexual revolutionary bias in stories by four writers.[3]
3. Wendy Martin's discussion of archetypes of fallen women and women imprisoned by a false sense of duty to love and marriage.[4]
4. Dolores Schmidt's discussion of "bitches" in literature—frustrated, dissatisfied, man-eating females.[5]
5. Judith Gustafson's contrasting view of "bitches"—women struggling for self-identity.[6]
6. Susan Cornellion's review of women in literature from a feminist perspective (women as heroines, invisible woman).[7]
7. Michele Murray's presentation of little-known literature to illustrate how women have been portrayed (little girl, virgin, independent woman, wife, mother, old maid, unattainable other).[8]
8. Lucy Schwartz's discussion of women in the novels of Madame de Souza (approved women were young and innocent, disapproved women were independent and intelligent).[9]
9. Natalie Holtzman's analysis of newswomen in novels (capable and independent, yet needing a man and children for feminine fulfillment).[10]
10. Charlotte Goodman's discussion of novels portraying farm women as idealized wife and mother figures, as strong figures, and as defeated figures.[11]

One unusual study of adult literature was conducted by Don Smith. He analyzed every fifth "adults only" paperback available on newsstands and in regular bookstores in eight communities in five states. Among the 3108 main characters in 428 pornographic novels published between 1968 and 1974, he found few differences in the proportions of women and men (54 percent were women and 46 percent were men) or in their marital status (48 percent of the women and 54 percent of the men were married). However, he found differences in their ages (64 percent of the women and 46 percent of the men were under 30), their occupations (4 percent of the women and 55 percent of the men were in professional/executive/white-collar positions), and their sexual orientation (77 percent of the women and 94 percent of the men were heterosexual, 16 percent of the women and 5 percent of the men were bisexual, and 7 percent of the women and 1 percent of the men were homosexual). Smith says that men were not physically described, with the exception of their genitals, while women were described "down to the last dimple."[12]

UNIVERSITY TEXTBOOKS. The portrayal of women in sociology, gynecology, and psychology textbooks has been studied. Each study had a different focus, and the set of studies does not permit generalization about college and university textbooks.

Betty Kirchner analyzed 10 introductory sociology textbooks randomly chosen from *Books in Print.* Fifty percent did not index a reference to women; 20 percent mentioned occupational wage differentials, but did not quantify the differential; and 50 percent characterized the contemporary American family as egalitarian.[13]

Diana Scully and Pauline Bart analyzed 27 general gynecology texts published since 1943 that are still in use. Dividing the books into a pre-Kinsey, 1943 to 1952 period (6 books); a post-Kinsey/pre-Masters and Johnson, 1953 to 1962 period (9 books), and a post-Masters and Johnson, 1963 to 1972 period (12 books), Scully and Bart report the following omissions and misconceptions.

1. Thirty-three percent of the books in the pre-Kinsey period, 11 percent in the post-Kinsey period, and 25 percent in the post-Masters and Johnson period do not index female sexuality.

2. Twenty-five percent of the books indexing female sexuality

in the pre-Kinsey period, 62 percent in the post-Kinsey period, and 67 percent in the post-Masters and Johnson period discuss sex primarily as an urge for reproduction.

3. Fifty percent of the books indexing female sexuality in the pre-Kinsey period, 62 percent in the post-Kinsey period, and 89 percent in the post-Masters and Johnson period discuss the male's stronger sex drive.

4. Twenty-five percent of the books indexing female sexuality in the pre-Kinsey period, 37 percent in the post-Kinsey period, and 33 percent in the post-Masters and Johnson period describe women as typically frigid.

5. Thirty-three percent of the books in the pre-Kinsey period, 56 percent in the post-Kinsey period, and 66 percent in the post-Masters and Johnson period do not index orgasm (clitoral/vaginal).

6. Nine percent of the books indexing orgasm in the pre-Kinsey period, 75 percent in the post-Kinsey period, and 50 percent in the post-Masters and Johnson period characterize vaginal orgasm as the mature response.[14]

Janice Birk, Linda Brooks, Joseph Juhasz, Linda Barbanel, Michele Herman, Robert Seltzer, and Sandra Tangri on the American Psychological Association's Task Force on Issues of Sexual Bias in Graduate Education analyzed the 11 most frequently used psychological textbooks. They found:

1. Fifty-eight percent of the sample passages were devoted to men, while 5 percent were devoted to women;

2. Fifteen percent of those described in charts and graphs were men, 6 percent were women, 6 percent were mixed groups, and 39 were neither (34 percent were animals).

3. Seventy-seven percent of those acknowledged in the preface were men; men acknowledged in the preface were thanked for criticism (47 percent) and contributions (41 percent), while women acknowledged in the preface were thanked

for typing (44 percent), criticism (21 percent), and editorial comments (19 percent).

4. In nine texts having subject indexes, 99 percent of the human references were to men.
5. In four texts using the convention of listing full names for women and initials for men, 94 percent of the author references were men.
6. In one text where the percentage of female authors cited was 20 percent, the actual percentage of female authors in the field was determined to be 35 percent.
7. Men were described in more vocational, family, and other roles than women.
8. Men had more personality and demographic descriptions but fewer physical descriptors than women.[15]

CHILDREN'S BOOKS/TEXTBOOKS

There has been continuing concern with children's books and textbooks since the civil rights movement was reborn in the 1950s. Even to the casual observer, it was clear that most of the characters in these books were white. Rarely did a child see a black, Chicano, or Oriental face in school readers. In the late 1960s, researchers began to investigate how girls/women and boys/men are characterized in these books. Studies now document the relative *presence* of each sex in the *text, pictures,* and *titles*, the sex of *authors,* the number of *occupations* shown for each sex, and the *themes* associated with each sex.

Proposition 8.1: Children's Literature Features More Male Characters than Female Characters in Text.

There have been so many studies of children's literature that only a sample can be reviewed in this chapter. Of the 19 studies we examined, 8 tabulated the percentage of female and male characters. Some studies counted only main characters and others counted all characters, but their results agree. Approximately 75 percent are boys/men and 25 percent are girls/women.[16] Some studies have analyzed books over many years, providing an awareness of the patterns of female and male character presentation from the 1900s to the 1970s. For example, Suzanne Czaplinski analyzed the characters in leading roles in Lewis Carroll Book Shelf Award books that were chosen between 1941 and 1972 but written between 1900 and 1972. She found that male characters were 100 percent of all characters from 1900 to 1929, 83 percent from 1930 to 1939, 29 percent from 1940 to 1949, 42 percent from 1950 to 1959, 80 percent from 1960 to 1969, and 100 percent from 1970 to 1972.[17] Other studies have been comprehensive. For instance, Gwyneth Britton and Margaret Lumpkin analyzed 16,176 stories from 49 series by 26 publishers. They found that these 1976 stories continue to show males four times as frequently as females.[18]

Proposition 8.2: Children's Literature Shows More Male Characters than Female Characters in Pictures.

Seven studies analyzed pictures in children's books and found that about 75 percent show boys/men and about 25 percent show girls/women.[19] In a sample of children's books displayed in bookstores and libraries, 80 percent of the pictures showed boys/men.[20] An analysis of the 80 winners and runners-up of the Caldecott Award between 1950 and 1970 showed the following percentages of pictured characters who were boys/men: 54 percent from 1951 to 1955, 59 percent from 1956 to 1960, 65 percent from 1961 to 1965, and 74 percent from 1966 to 1970.[21]

Proposition 8.3: Children's Literature Names More Male Characters than Female Characters in Titles.

When researchers analyze titles that mention one sex or the other, they find that more than 75 percent refer to boys/-

men.[22] One study was conducted by Lenore Weitzman, Deborah Eifler, Elizabeth Rada, and Catherine Ross, who documented this pattern for the 33 Caldecott winners since 1938 (27 percent female and 73 percent male), the 18 Caldecott winners and runners-up since 1967 (11 percent female and 89 percent male), the 28 best-selling Little Golden Books (31 percent female and 69 percent male), and the 49 Newberry winners since 1922 (23 percent female and 77 percent male).[23]

Proposition 8.4: More Than Half of the Authors of Children's Books Are Women.

The actual percentage of female and male authors varies somewhat by year and by type of book. Diane Graebner's analysis of elementary reading textbooks showed more women in the 1961 to 1963 period (89 percent) than in the 1969 to 1971 period (66 percent).[24] The Weitzman et al. study of Caldecott winners indicates that more women were writing books in the pre-1967 period (48 percent) than in the post-1967 period (33 percent).[25] Susan Wiik found that junior high school literature anthologies were written primarily by men (84 percent),[26] while W. Bernard Lukenbill noted that 68 percent of authors listed in a reference book about children's authors (*Something About the Author*) were women.[27]

Some studies assert that women are more positive than men in their portrayal of women. For example, Susan Wiik found that 3 percent of the male authors and 20 percent of the female authors portrayed women in nonstereotypic roles.[28]

Proposition 8.5: In Children's Literature, Male Characters Are Shown in More Occupations than Female Characters.

Four studies examined the occupations of the characters in children's books. The findings are quite consistent. Men are shown in about four times as many occupations as women.[29] One study was conducted by the research group known as Women on Words and Images. They analyzed 34 elementary readers published by 14 companies between 1964 and 1971 and found that, on the average, men were shown in 24 occupations while women were shown in 5. However, they counted 147 *different* occupations for men and only 26 for women.[30]. The most extensive study was conducted by Gwyneth Britton and Margaret Lumpkin. After examining 49 textbook series, they found that in some cases the discrepancy was as great as 20 males to 1 female in career assignments.[31]

Proposition 8.6: In Children's Literature, There Is Adherence to "Male Themes" and "Female Themes."

The themes of achievement, aggression, activity, independence, ingenuity, industry, strength, creative helpfulness, acquisition, and adventure are primarily associated with boys/men. The themes of harm avoidance, rejection avoidance, nurturance, passivity, dependence, goal constriction, and humiliation are primarily associated in stories with girls/women. Three interesting studies that investigated characterization themes were conducted by Irvine Child, Elmer Potter, and Estelle Levine, by Diane Graebner, and by Women on Words and Images. Their studies and others of interest follow.[32]

STUDIES OF CHILDREN'S LITERATURE   A pioneering study of children's textbooks was conducted by Irvine Child, Elmer Potter, and Estelle Levine in 1946. They analyzed 914 stories containing 3409 thema from 30 major third-grade readers and found that 72 percent of all thema within single-sex groups involved boys and men. Each sex was associated with certain thema more often than their overall numbers would predict. Boys/men were often associated with achievement, activity, and cognizance thema. Girls/women were often associated with nurturance, affiliation, elation, order, embarrassment avoidance, blame avoidance, and rejection thema.[33]

Few other studies provided detail on portrayals in children's textbooks until the rise of feminism. Since the late 1960s, many studies have appeared. Those included here illustrate the variety of studies and the consensus of findings.

During the early feminist concern, Jamie Frisof analyzed five social studies textbooks published between 1962 and 1969 for grades one to three. She found that men were shown in over 100 different occupations, while women were shown in fewer than 30. Only men were shown as leaders of organizations, while only women were shown as volunteers. Family decisions (timing of vacations, places to live, etc.) revolved around the father. All first-named authors of the texts were men.[34]

Buford Stefflre examined the portrayal of several thousand adult women and men in more than 60 elementary school readers from six publishers; he found that 19 percent of the women and 87 percent of the men were employed. Comparing the percentage of women in the stories with census data, Stefflre found too low a percentage of married working women (39 percent in stories versus 60 percent in census data), too many working women shown as professionals and managers (63 percent in stories and 17 percent in census data), including teachers (33 percent in stories and 7 percent in census data), too few working women in clerical and sales jobs (13 percent in stories and 38 percent in census data), and too few as processors and machine operators (3 percent in stories and 22 percent in census data). Those shown as service workers are proportionate to their presence in the work force (18 percent in stories and 21 percent in census data).[35]

Aileen Nilson analyzed 58 picture books used by children's literature teachers at Eastern Michigan University. Eighty-four percent of the books portraying women showed them wearing aprons. Pictures of women not wearing aprons included a nun, a queen, an Indian squaw, and a mother on an outing with her children.[36]

Marjorie U'Ren reviewed 30 elementary school textbooks adopted or recommended for use in California. Boys/men accounted for 75 percent of the main characters, 80 percent of the story space, and 85 percent of the illustrations. In general, boys were achievers and girls were helpers; many boys received public acclaim for their achievements, but only two girls did. Stories featuring boys often had no girls, but stories featuring girls almost always had boys. As for adult characters, only 4 percent of the stories with adult main characters portrayed a woman. Many men, versus one woman, were shown to have ambition. Many men were shown as professionals; only one woman was shown as a professional, and she was a scientist working under a male supervisor.[37]

Karen DeCrow analyzed social studies books and readers published by 10 companies for students in kindergarten through third grade. In these books, working women were shown as teachers and nurses and were always single. Men were always shown working full time; they made family decisions and did "masculine" chores (gardening, taking out the garbage); women did "feminine" chores (cooking, washing, caring for baby). Elder children were boys and younger children were girls.[38]

In an analysis of fairy tales, Marcia Lieberman found that physical characteristics of men were not important, but that women were always beautiful if sought after and ugly if wicked. In the fairy tales, as in later texts, elder children were boys and younger children were girls.[39]

Diane Graebner analyzed 554 stories in elementary reading textbooks published between 1961 and 1963 and between 1969 and 1971 to determine changes over time. In these stories, published by two major companies, boys/men comprised 71 percent of the main characters in the early period and 75 percent in the later period. Using these percentages as reference points, Graebner found that men/boys were:

1. Extremely unlikely to be shown in passive activities (52 percent less than expected in the early period and 49 percent less in the later period).
2. Unlikely to be associated with themes of dependence (34

percent less in the early period and 26 percent less in the later period).

Over this decade, the percentage of female authors declined from 89 percent to 66 percent, and the percentage of female illustrators declined from 36 percent to 28 percent.[40]

Suzanne Czaplinski analyzed 32 Caldecott Award books from 1941 to 1972, 32 picture books chosen for the Lewis Carroll Book Shelf Award from 1958 to 1972, and 3 picture books on the best-seller list of the *New York Times Book Review of Children's Books* in November, 1971. Her findings about main characters in all three groups of books are presented in the text and notes of Proposition 8.1. Her findings about illustrations show that boys/men are 52 percent of persons dipicted in the Caldecott books, 82 percent in the Carroll books, and 85 percent in the *New York Times* books. Between 1900 and 1972, the portrayal of men/boys in the illustrations of the Carroll Award books show that between 1900 and 1929, male characters were 87 percent of persons depicted; between 1930 and 1939, male characters were 85 percent; between 1940 and 1949, male characters were 72 percent; between 1950 and 1959, male characters were 39 percent; between 1960 and 1969, male characters were 80 percent; and between 1970 and 1972, male characters were 70 percent.

Czaplinski measured activities using three scales of strength that ranged from 10 (great strength) to 1 (no strength). Male physical activities had an average strength of 5.3; female physical activities had an average strength of 3.4. Male intellectual activities had a strength of 7.3; female intellectual activities had a strength of 5.3. Male emotional activities had a strength of 6.7; female emotional activities had a strength of 3.8.[41]

Women on Words and Images analyzed 34 elementary readers published by 15 companies between 1964 and 1971. For the 2760 stories, they found:

1. Seventy-two percent of the stories about children featured boys.
2. Seventy-five percent of the stories about adults featured men.
3. Seventy percent of the stories about animals featured male animals.
4. Seventy-nine percent of the folk fantasies featured boys/-men.
5. Eighty-six percent of the biographies featured boys/men.

The research team also examined dominant themes in the boy- and girl-centered stories. Remembering that only 28 percent of these stories featured female characters, we find that they are underrepresented in the themes of reward (17 percent), cleverness (20 percent), bravery (20 percent), problem solving (22 percent), and adventure (24 percent). They are represented in three themes—creative helpfulness, apprenticeship, and altruism—about as often as would be expected (25, 26, and 29 percent, respectively). They are overrepresented in the themes of incompetence (54 percent), routine helpfulness (56 percent), rehearsal for domesticity (77 percent), passivity (86 percent), and victimization/humiliation (91 percent).[42]

Jennifer MacLeod and Sandra Siverman analyzed the major senior high school U.S. government textbook distributed by each of eight major publishers. They found:

1. Ninety-nine percent of the quotations were by men.
2. Ninety-seven percent of those mentioned in the index were men.
3. Thirteen percent of the illustrations of voters showed only women, 32 percent showed only men, and 55 percent showed both sexes.
4. No illustrations of juries showed only women, 38 percent showed only men, and 62 percent showed both sexes.
5. Thirty-one percent of the cartoons showed unfavorable

stereotypes of women and 6 percent showed unfavorable stereotypes of men.

6. One percent of the pictorial chapter headings showed only women, 61 percent showed only men, and 33 percent showed both sexes.

7. Two percent of the illustrations of judges showed women, and 98 percent showed men.

8. Eight percent of the illustrations of attorneys showed women, and 92 percent showed men.

9. Six percent of all illustrations showed only women, 63 percent showed only men, and 31 percent showed both sexes.

In addition, 62 percent of the discussion of suffrage in these books dealt with black male suffrage (Fifteenth Amendment), and 38 percent dealt with female suffrage (Nineteenth Amendment).[43]

Additional research that supports the conclusions of these other studies has been conducted by Janice Pottker,[44] Winifred Tom Jay,[45] and Janice Law Trecker.[46] Pottker analyzed 20 elementary school readers for the personal characteristics and occupations of girls/women. The textbook presentation of occupations was compared with census data. Jay analyzed the second-, fourth-, and sixth-grade editions of mathematics textbooks of four publishers and found that 46 of the 49 famous individuals shown were males, 86 of the 104 occupations portrayed males, and only two roles for males and two roles for females were nonstereotypic. An interesting aspect of Jay's study was the analysis of textbook pages by parents and by students as to the gender-related interest in a sample of items. With a 91 percent agreement between the two groups, he found that 71 percent of the 160 items were classified as neutral, 14 percent as masculine, and 6 percent as feminine. Trecker conducted a qualitative analysis of 13 U.S. history high school textbooks and discusses the conclusions that a high school student would draw about women in America.

As early as 1972, publishers began to react to the pressure to change the stereotypic portrayals of their textbooks. Scott, Foresman and Company was the first to issue guidelines to authors that would help to eliminate sex-role stereotyping in future books. Other publishers soon followed suit. It is tempting to believe that recent textbooks have been corrected for bias and that it is no longer necessary to monitor the portrayals of women and men. However, a study by Tara Brown makes it clear that revised and updated materials reflect some changes but primarily show women and men in traditional roles.[47]

Brown analyzed 432 first-, second-, and third-grade stories from 106 readers of 10 textbooks series that were adopted by California in 1977. These textbooks should be among the best available, since they were thought to satisfy the 1973 West Supplement to the California Education Code that prohibits sexist portrayals of women in state-purchased materials.[48] Brown compared her findings with those from a 1972 study of 270 stories also for first through third graders in California.[49] The same research methods were used in both studies. This allows us to look at change over the 5- year period when publishers and educators were becoming aware of the sexist portrayals of women and men.

Brown found considerable consistency between the stories being read in 1972 and the stories being read in 1977. Of the four locations where adults were shown—home, outdoors, school, and business—males were also twice as likely as females to be shown in business settings, while females were almost four times as likely as males to be shown in schools. Specifically, of those adults teaching, 82 were females and 18 were males. Change in the portrayal of women is best characterized as some movement from home and outdoor locations to business locations. Although the stereotypes are not as rigid in 1977 as in 1972, they still persist.

Brown's study causes us to conclude that bias is more subtle than it once was. There are still some of the obvious problems, such as the underrepresentation of females among the textbook characters (39 percent in both 1972 and 1977). The appearance of a few women in nontraditional roles should be applauded, but it should not lead us to believe there is an accurate or a nonbiased portrayal of women in textbooks.

A thorough review, tentatively titled *Biases Against Minorities and Females in Textbooks: A Review of the Literature* is being developed by the U.S. Commission on Civil Rights. The report is scheduled to be available in 1979 and should help to consolidate what is known about textbook bias, including the extent and impact of the bias.

COMIC STRIPS AND COMIC BOOKS

COMIC STRIPS AND COMIC BOOKS. Comics have long been the most widely read form of children's literature, and comic characters also appear on Saturday morning television and in scholastic publications. Four studies of the comics indicate how women and men are portrayed. The first study, conducted by Gerhart Saenger in 1955, analyzed 156 comic strips that appeared in nine New York City newspapers during October 1950.[50]

Saenger divided comic strips into three types—domestic, adventure, and comedy. Single men in adventure strips were strong, brave, and intelligent, aggressive, etc. Married men in domestic strips were weak, frightened, unintelligent, passive, etc. In addition:

1. Eighteen percent of the single women and 73 percent of the married women versus 72 percent of the single men and 17 percent of the married men were aggressive.
2. Six percent of the single women and 4 percent of the married women versus 7 percent of the single men and 19 percent of the married men were helpless.
3. Sixteen percent of the single women and 49 percent of the

married women versus 80 percent of the single men and 31 percent of the married men were intelligent.

4. Fourteen percent of the single women and 50 percent of the married women versus single men and 50 percent of the married men were taller than their partners.[51]

Gloria Steinem analyzed the themes of the original *Wonder Woman*. Created by William Marston in 1941, *Wonder Woman* was counter to the violence of other comic books. *Wonder Woman* valued human life, used violence only in self-defense, emphasized the worth of women, and converted "misled females" to self-reliance and self-respect.

When William Marston died in 1947, *Wonder Woman* was taken over by other writers. By 1968, she had been stripped of her original strengths and was voicing conventional "womanly" values.[52]

Betty Chmaj discussed the relation of the women's movement to comic books. Noting that comics reflect cultural attitudes, she wrote:

1. Valkyrie was introduced in the December 1970 issues of *Avengers* as a villain who tricked the superheroines into helping her temporarily defeat the avengers.
2. Valkyrie took her position of "up against the wall, male chauvinist pigs" as a "personal revenge inspired by her love for a man."
3. By 1973, Valkyrie had been transformed into a heroine who apologized to men whenever she seemed outspoken.
4. Women in comics are usually shown as supporting, not independent, characters.
5. Women in comics often wonder "in secret whether the men really want them."[53]

Caren Boyle and Billie Wahlstrom also analyzed comic books and found that 75 percent of the characters were male. Sixty percent of the female characters were shown as victims.

Eighty-four percent of the male characters versus 5 percent of the female characters were shown in heroic roles.[54]

PROPOSITIONAL SUMMARY

Proposition 8.1: Children's literature features more male characters than female characters in *text*.

Proposition 8.2: Children's literature shows more male characters than female characters in *pictures*.

Proposition 8.3: Children's literature names more male characters than female characters in *titles*.

Proposition 8.4: More than half of the *authors* of children's books are women.

Proposition 8.5: In children's literature, male characters are shown in more *occupations* than female characters.

Proposition 8.6: In children's literature, there is adherence to "male *themes*" and "female *themes*."

FILM

[The film industry] is giving women the same treatment it gave blacks for the half-century after *Birth of a Nation:* a kick in the face or a cold shoulder.[1]

In the 1930s and 1940s, the new tool of content analysis was used in several *quantitative* studies of film. Two of these, by Edgar Dale and Dorothy Jones, provided rich detail on the portrayal of women and men.[2] For a quarter-century thereafter, few film studies were conducted.

Feminist concern led to several *qualitative* studies of film in the 1970s. Molly Haskell, Joan Mellen, Marjorie Rosen, and others drew on well-known films in each decade of the twentieth century.[3]

Three recent quantitative film studies by Judith Gustafson, Lee Israel, and Midge Kovacs confirm the conclusion of Haskell, Mellen, and Rosen that the 1960s and at least the early 1970s were the nadir of women's portrayal in film.[4]

Proposition 9.1: From the Early Days of Film Until the Present, the Number and Significance of Roles *Played by Women Have Declined.*

Lacking quantitative studies of the early years of film, we must characterize the 1910s and 1920s with reference to individuals and the rise of the star system. Sarah Bernhardt brought her unparalleled stage reputation to film in *Queen Elizabeth* (1912). Lillian Gish and Mae Marsh, hardworking veterans of Biograph one- and two-reelers, became stars in *Birth of a Nation* (1915). Mary Pickford, Constance Talmadge, Norma Talmadge, Beverly Bayne, Theda Bara, Fannie Ward, Louise Lovely, Mary Astor, Claire Windsor, and Pauline Frederick were just a few of the other actresses whose names were well known to the public around 1920. Most leading men were eclipsed by these women until Westerns and gangster films began to replace the exotic diversity of earlier films in the 1920s and 1930s.[5]

When quantitative studies caught up with film around 1930, men comprised 66 percent of the leading characters.[6] By the early 1940s, men were 67 percent of the leading characters.[7] After a quarter-century hiatus in this kind of film study, the late 1960s and early 1970s showed that men had taken over 80 percent of all roles and 90 percent of speaking roles.[8]

Proposition 9.2: Films Have Mirrored and, Because of Their Popularity, Also Reinforced Stereotypes *of Women Held in Each Decade.*

Several film researchers have tried to typify the roles offered to women in each decade. One researcher aptly states that in the 1920s female film characters had sex without children but, by the late 1930s they were having children without sex; also, female film characters of the 1950s were "about sex, but without sex."[9] The most abrupt change in the portrayal of

women occurred at the end of the 1940s, when feminine auton-
omy personified by actresses such as Katherine Hepburn gave
way to domesticity personified by Doris Day and to breast
fetishism personified by Marilyn Monroe.

STUDIES OF FILM.   Edgar Dale conducted the first quantitative content analysis of motion pictures from 1929 to 1931. A
random sample of 115 films showed that:

1. Sixty-six percent of the leading characters were male.
2. Fifty-one percent of the heroes and heroines were male.
3. Seventy-percent of the villains and villainesses were male.
4. One percent of the male characters versus 41 percent of the
    female characters had no occupation.

A detailed analysis of 40 of the 115 pictures showed that:

1. Nineteen percent of all men versus 62 percent of all women
    were under the age of 26.
2. Twenty-one percent of the heroes versus 92 percent of the
    heroines were under the age of 26.
3. None of the villains versus 43 percent of the villainesses
    were under the age of 26.
4. Seventeen percent of the men versus none of the women did
    not reveal their marital status.[10]

The second major quantitative analysis of motion pictures
was conducted by Dorothy Jones. She analyzed 100 films released in 1941 and 1942 and found that 67 percent of all leading
characters were men. Sixty-four percent of the men versus 79
percent of the women regarded love as a main value; 11 percent
of the men versus 33 percent of the women viewed love as their
only "want."[11]

Martha Wolfenstein and Nathan Leites analyzed 67 Holly-
wood-produced movies that appeared between September 1945

and September 1946. The following facts were among their findings.

1. Men were shown as professionals and women were shown as unemployed.
2. In contrast with film vamps of the 1920s, women in the 1940s were portrayed as good bad girls (seemingly dangerous women with pure hearts).
3. Eighty percent of films focusing on the love/hate problems of a man had a good bad girl as the main female character.
4. In 50 percent of the films, the good bad girl successfully opposed a bad girl.[12]

Joseph Baunoch and Betty Chmaj discuss four types of star roles that women played from the 1930s to the 1970s.

1. The Pillar of Virtue has four subtypes: the Sweet Young Thing, the Perfect Wife, the Gracious Lady, and Mother/ Mammy/Mom/Ma.
    (a) The Sweet Young Thing is Janet Gaynor in *State Fair,* Shirley Temple in *Rebecca of Sunnybrook Farm,* June Allyson in *Little Women,* Doris Day in *Pillow Talk,* and Julie Andrews in *Mary Poppins.*
    (b) The Perfect Wife is Myrna Loy in *Cheaper by the Dozen,* June Allyson in *Executive Suite,* and Eva Marie Saint in *A Hatful of Rain.*
    (c) The Gracious Lady is Irene Dunne in *Anna and the King of Siam,* Greer Garson in *Mrs. Miniver,* and Deborah Kerr in *Tea and Sympathy.*
    (d) Mother/Mammy/Mom/Ma is Fay Bainter in *Mother Carey's Chickens,* Hattie McDaniel in *Gone with the Wind,* and Jane Darwell in *The Daughter of Rosie O'Grady.*
2. The Glamour Girl has four subtypes: the Femme Fatale, the Sex Goddess, the Showgirl, and the Cool Beauty.

(a) The Femme Fatale is Marlene Dietrich in *Blond Venus*, Rita Hayworth in *Salome*, Hedy Lamarr in *The Female Animal*, and Ava Gardner in *The Barefoot Contessa*.

(b) The Sex Goddess is Mae West In *I'm No Angel*, Jean Harlow in *Bombshell*, Lana Turner in *Ziegfeld Girl*, Marilyn Monroe in *Bus Stop*, and Raquel Welch in *Myra Breckinridge*.

(c) The Showgirl is Ruby Keeler in *Footlight Parade*, Alice Faye in *Lillian Russell*, and Betty Grable in *Coney Island*.

(d) The Cool Beauty is Constance Bennett in *Our Betters*, Gene Tierney in *Laura*, Alexis Smith in *The Woman in White*, and Grace Kelly in *The Swan*.

3. The Emotive Woman has three subtypes: the Long-Suffering Lady, the Vixen, and the Sexually Frustrated Neurotic.

(a) The Long-Suffering Lady is Greta Garbo in *Romance*, Bette Davis in *Dark Victory*, Barbara Stanwyck in *Stella Dallas*, and Katherine Hepburn in *The Lion in Winter*.

(b) The Vixen is Bette Davis in *Of Human Bondage*, Joan Crawford in *Queen Bee*, Barbara Stanwyck in *Baby Face*, Susan Hayward in *I Can Get it For You Wholesale*, and Elizabeth Taylor in *Cat on a Hot Tin Roof*.

(c) The Sexually Frustrated Neurotic is Miriam Hopkins in *The Old Maid*, Agnes Moorhead in *Since You Went Away*, and Rosalind Russell in *Picnic*.

4. The Independent Woman has five subtypes: the Career Woman, the Regular Gal, the Durable Dame, the Brassy Modern, and the Liberated Modern.

(a) The Career Woman is Jean Arthur in *More Than a Secretary*, Katherine Hepburn in *Woman of the Year*, Claudette Colbert in *She Married Her Boss*, and Rosalind Russell in *A Woman of Distinction*.

(b) The Regular Gal is Joan Blondell in *He Was Her Man* and Ginger Rogers in *Lucky Partners*.

(c)   The Durable Dame is Marie Dressler in *Tugboat Annie,* Marjorie Main in *Friendly Persuasion,* and Bette Davis in *Pocketful of Miracles.*

(d)   The Brassy Modern is Ethel Merman in *Call Me Madam,* Betty Hutton in *Annie Get Your Gun,* and Barbra Streisand in *Funny Girl.*

(e)   The Liberated Modern is Jane Fonda in *Klute,* Julie Christie in *Darling,* Faye Dunaway in *Lovers,* and Glenda Jackson in *Women in Love.* [13]

Judith Gustafson analyzed the top 10 money-making movie stars each year from 1932 to 1971. She found that men were 51 percent of the top stars in the 1930s, 76 percent in the 1940s, 81 percent in the 1950s, 72 percent in the 1960s, and 90 percent for the first 2 years of the 1970s.[14] Omitting the 1970s from the calculation, the increase per decade in men among the top stars is 7 percent.

Qualitative analyses of motion pictures have continued in the 1970s. Joan Mellen discusses 4 decades of the portrayal of women. In the 1940s, women were shown as autonomous career women striving to achieve their aspirations (Katherine Hepburn, Joan Crawford, Irene Dunne, Barbara Stanwyck, Bette Davis). In the 1950s, women were shown "as simpering, dependent hysterics or as undulating sexual manikins" (Marilyn Monroe). In the 1960s, women were shown as remaining outside the safety of marriage and finding "devastating loneliness and despair" (Karen Black). In the 1970s, women are shown as "shrill and unfulfilled, while the bourgeois family and established values are refurbished" (Barbra Streisand). Also in the 1970s, women in pornography films are shown as "lecherous whore(s) of endless appetite and sexual ingenuity" (Linda Lovelace).[15]

Molly Haskell describes a variety of roles in each decade since the 1920s and reports these emphases.

1.   In the 1920s, women expressed their own lust and sexuality and had sex without children.

2. Until the Production Code of 1933 to 1934, women had "sexual desire without being freaks, villains, or even necessarily Europeans."

3. In the late 1930s, women expressed love and romance and had children without sex, but there was "the sense of equality and mutuality between romantic leads."

4. In the 1940s, some women left their pedestals and became cheap, soulless characters; others played the superwoman role.

5. In the 1950s, "breast fetishism" was the vogue, and women were "about sex, but without sex."

6. In the 1960s and early 1970s, directors moved from "covert misogyny" and "kindly indifference" toward women to "violent abuse and brutalization." Women are "less intelligent, less sensual, less humorous, and altogether less extraordinary" than in any other period of motion films. In the 1960s and early 1970s, the ideal woman is "a girl, an ingenue, a mail-order cover girl." There is "less need for exciting and interesting women; any bouncing nymphet whose curves look good in catsup would do."

Haskell summarizes the current situation as follows.

[The film industry] is giving women the same treatment that it gave blacks for the half-century after *Birth of a Nation:* a kick in the face or a cold shoulder. And whether it is tokenism or the "final solution," it is, as minorities everywhere have discovered, no solution at all.[16]

Marjorie Rosen has traced the image of women in motion pictures from 1910 to the 1970s.

1. From 1910 to 1919, women were often shown as children, repressing sexuality and denying womanhood.

2. In the 1920s, "movies glorified women who were young, beautiful, highly moral, and ready to drop job and glitter

for a good man"; "the sound of babies, not applause, would fill her ears and satisfy her ego."

3. In the early 1930s, "depression movies focused on women living by their wits." In the late 1930s, women were shown as "meddlesome and manipulative."

4. In the early 1940s, "bitchiness and frivolity on the screen gave place to female strength; strength and love and support between mother and daughter, woman and woman." In the late 1940s, some women were shown with overt sexuality.

5. In the 1950s, movies were "reaffirming male dominance and female subservience"; women were shown "trapping men" and "preparing for the wedding"; movies showed women as breasts and buttocks, again idealizing women who were "pretty, amusing, and childish."

6. In the 1960s, movies emphasized "Will she or won't she?" Women were often shown as waifs with little-boy bodies ("an almost violent reaction to the breasts-and-buttocks fetishes of the Monroe period").

7. In the 1970s, some movies showed women "getting gang-banged"; other movies showed women in sensationalized lesbian roles. Few movies showed women with dignity, and many movies did not show women at all.[17]

Howard Haymes applied Simone de Beauvoir's five literary prototypes to films. In the 1950s, Haymes says, some women were treated brutally because of their sexuality; other women, who seemed to be self-activators, were punished by death or destruction. Some women were shown "as a guide to divine existence," but it was the men who ascended. Some women were shown "as a guide to beauty, truth and poetry," but it was the men who took action. Some women were shown as equal with men, but it was the men who proved themselves.[18]

Lee Israel analyzed almost 200 films made from 1968 to 1974 and found that 98 to 99 percent of the films were written, produced, and/or directed by men. Eighty percent of all roles were male, and 90 percent of the speaking roles were male.

Men were shown as older than women; men up to the age of 60 were shown as resourceful and powerful; girls up to the age of 19 "spoke very little and screwed quite a lot"; women between 20 and 30 had important roles; women over 30 (few in number) were shown as flawed (drunken, mentally tortured). Men were often seen with other men, but women were rarely seen with other women. Women "functioned most effectively when motivated by sexual frustration"; they spent 10 percent of their time enjoying orgasms and rape.[19]

Midge Kovacs and others of the NOW Image of Women in Films Task Force analyzed the 25 films distributed by Paramount Pictures during 1974 and 1975. They found that 56 percent of the films featured male leads, while only 20 percent of the films featured female leads.[20]

The strength of these studies is their long view of the portrayal of women in films since the 1910s. Women were important in the star system from 1910 to the 1920s. Women under contract to the large studios, were given important roles in as many as four movies a year. Their sexuality was treated openly and with respect. In the 1930s, particularly after the Production Code was adopted, women began to be shown in submissive roles. The 1940s saw two types of portrayals. During the war years, women were shown as independent and self-assured. After the war, women were shown in the home, often suffering from physical or mental disabilities that made them incapable of coping. In the 1950s, films reaffirmed women's domesticity while showing tantalizing glimpses of women who were not "the marrying kind." Films reflected some of the new feminist consciousness of the 1960s, but women who chose alternatives to marriage and motherhood were shown as lonely and unfulfilled.

The early 1970s saw the culmination of the trend of brutalization of women that began in the late 1960s. In the later 1970s, films offer stronger roles for women (e.g., *Looking for*

Mr. Goodbar, starring Tuesday Weld and Diane Keaton; *Three Women,* starring Sissy Spacek, Shelley Duvall, and Janice Rule; *Julia,* starring Jane Fonda and Vanessa Redgrave; and *Turning Point,* starring Anne Bancroft and Shirley MacLaine). These are promising signs, but it is too early in the new cycle of films to determine if women are making a comeback in films and are no longer "an endangered species."[21]

PROPOSITIONAL SUMMARY

Proposition 9.1:   From the early days of films until the present, the number and significance of *roles* played by women have declined.

Proposition 9.2:   Films have mirrored and, because of their popularity, also reinforced *stereotypes* of women held in each decade.

THE CONSCIOUSNESS SCALE

Look in a mirror. If you are a woman, what do you see? A woman waxing a floor? Feeding children? Spraying her hair? Scribbling on a steno pad? Gazing at a man with mixed reverence and awe? The simple mirrors that hang over bureaus and on the backs of closet doors only tell superficial physical things about ourselves. The real-life mirrors are the media. . .[1]

Most of the content analyses described in the previous chapters relied on frequency counts to tell us how many women and men are cast in productions, shown as employed outside the home, have speaking parts, serve as narrators, give directives, etc. Our next concern is to move from these *tabulations* of images to the *levels,* or intensities, of feminine roles that the images portray.

To do this, we have developed a *consciousness* scale that classifies media images of women in five ordered consciousness levels. *Level I* can be characterized as "put her down." In blatant examples of this women are portrayed as sex objects, in subtle examples they are portrayed as props or decorations. *Level II* can be described as "keep her in her place." Women illustrating this level are primarily found in the home or in traditional working roles. *Level III* is "give her two places." These women have careers but also manage the home and family. *Level IV* is "acknowledge that she is equal." Women and men are shown as equally competent in the same roles. *Level V* is "recognize that she (and he) is nonstereotypic." Women and men are able to be superior according to their own talents, interests, and motivations, not according to their sex.

The examples that follow illustrate the five consciousness levels more fully. We have used different media to show that the levels apply to newspapers, magazines, and films as well as to television. However, we have not illustrated each level with material from all media. At the conclusion of the chapter, we present results of two studies that have more systematically applied the consciousness scale to media content.

CONSCIOUSNESS LEVEL I

A pretty blond woman in a micro-mini skirt sits at her desk polishing her nails as four worried men try to arouse her interest in some calculating machines. Says the copy: "Our new line of calculators goes through its final ordeal. The dumb blond test."[2]

These consciousness levels correspond to stereotypes in the belief systems of writers, editors, producers, etc. Level I ("put her down") images include the dumb blond (situation comedies and ads), the sex object (*Playboy* and other breast/buttock magazines), and the whimpering victim (television crime dramas and detective magazines).

Level I in Television

Television images often "put her down." The Silva Thin cigarette advertisement was noteworthy enough to have been discussed in *Advertising Age*. The main character is described as:

... the epitome of the modern-male-on-the-prowl who picks his women the way you'd pick your hors d'oeuvre off a smorgasbord table; they are merely to satisfy his momentary appetite. He is obnoxious, arrogant and quite possibly incurably selfish. ... Women (an important market for this cigaret) especially dig the scene of "The Impossible Cigaret." Psychologically, they seem to feel right at home with the situations. They quite willingly put themselves in the place of the suffering heroine. The makers of this campaign demonstrate a shrewd insight into the emotional makeup of today's woman. ... Ignoring practically every rule of etiquette, he summarily puts his girlfriend in her place, and exactly where so many would unconsciously like to be.[3]

The article compares the probable success of Silva Thins with that of Virginia Slims:

Our guess is that the appeal of Virginia Slims—which claims that its cigaret is made for women to permit them to assert their independence at last—will not be as successful as that of "The Impossible Cigaret."

The television "Fly Me" campaign for National Airlines illustrated the use of language to give Level I connotations to otherwise wholesome photographs of flight attendants. The campaign was considered so successful (National's increase in passenger traffic led the industry by 11 percent in its first year) that Continental Airlines started a similar campaign based on the slogan "We really move our tail for you." Continental executives, while insisting that the slogan is not sexist, initiated a rejoinder-of-the-month award for the stewardess who best squelches the passenger who asks her to "move your tail."[4]

The importance of their appearance is emphasized to women from the time they begin watching television in their preschool years. The study *The Image of the Female Child on Saturday Morning Television Commercials* shows that the role of model is presented second only to the role of wife/mother. Cornell Chulay and Sara Francis say:

The Barbie Vanity Case Commercial typifies this observation when the little girl closes by saying, "It's all like being grown up." In other words, TV is also indoctrinating the female child into accepting the role of a sex object.[5]

Level I in Magazines

Research on Level I material in *general* magazines indicates that there is little blatant use of nude bodies or references to sexual activity. However, the same research shows a subtle sexism in which women serve decorative functions only. These data are drawn from advertisements in *Life, Newsweek, The New Yorker, Saturday Review, Time, U.S. News and World Report,* and *Reader's Digest.*[6]

Examples of women as decorations are found by opening any general magazine and reading the advertisements. Women wear bikinis on the beaches of Hawaii and Mexico. They drape themselves on the front seats of cars. In a 1976 National Cash Register advertisement, a woman in a long, white, evening gown decorated a room that featured computers. Often the adornment borders on explicit sexuality. Amphora's Black Cavendish's pipe tobacco was advertised in 1977 by a man with his arms around a woman and the caption "For the man who gets what he wants." Faberge's 1975 Tigress Cologne advertisement presented a woman in striped leotards as "Tigress. Because men are such animals."

Blatant Level I imagery is found in *Playboy, Penthouse, Oui,* etc. The editorial policies of these magazines state concisely how they view themselves and the women who make them profitable. *Penthouse* policy reads: "A magazine edited for the sophisticated male reader . . . Its editorial scope ranges from outspoken contemporary comment to photographic essays of beautiful women."[7] *Oui* is: "A magazine edited especially for worldly, sophisticated young Americans . . . Editorial spectrum includes humor, interviews . . . lovely girls."[8] *Playboy* is: "A magazine of entertainment offering . . . picture stories of pretty girls."[9]

Although we are focusing on Level I presentations of women in the media, note that women's sex magazines (e.g. *Playgirl*) treat men as sex objects and should be criticized on the same grounds as men's sex magazines.

Many professional magazines and journals carry Level I advertisements. A review of advertisements in November 1973 engineering journals found that women were used as sex objects in many advertisements. Examples included a full-page nude with the caption, "Product X doesn't lie down under pressure"; a naked woman wearing a shield over her torso and the caption, "Protection for vital parts"; and two women in ruffled panties saying, "He tried to tell me he was an expert on smooth bottoms."[10] These advertisements were so offensive to women who might be working in engineering and related fields that we were curious to learn if the situation had improved by the time this chapter was being written in 1978. We reviewed a number of engineering journals in the Stanford University Library and can report that women have "advanced" from sex object to decoration. The most notable fact about the 1978 advertisements, however, was the absence of women either as demonstrators or as users of products.

Advertisements in medical journals use women's bodies to attract attention. In one of the more bizarre examples, drug companies use nudes as background figures for lists of indications and contraindications, the former appear in the genital and breast areas, and the latter appear around armpits, toes, etc.

Level I in Film

Writers such as Sharon Smith, Lee Israel, Marjorie Rosen, and Molly Haskell have studied the image of women in film. Rosen states that the movie industry shows women as a "Popcorn Venus, a delectable but insubstantial hybrid of cultural distortions."[11] Israel anticipates that anthropologists of the future, using films of the 1968 to 1974 period, will infer that

American women never produced films themselves, represented only 20 percent of the population, died after the age of 30, never developed friendships with other women, spent 10 percent of their time having orgasms, and enjoyed rape.[12] Smith summarizes this less-than-person image of women: "Women provide trouble, sexual interludes for male characters, or are not present at all."[13]

The most detailed review of film's image of women is found in Haskell's book *From Reverence to Rape*. After describing the film roles that women played from the 1920s through the 1950s, she wrote:

> Whores, quasi-whores, jilted mistresses, emotional cripples, drunks, daffy ingenues, Lolitas, kooks, sex-starved spinsters, psychotics. Icebergs, zombies and ball breakers. That's what little girls of the sixties and seventies are made of.[14]

By 1977, Haskell found little change for the better. She commented that the two female stars most sought after by Hollywood, Tatum O'Neal and Jodie Foster, have a combined age of 27. These teenyboppers differ from their predecessors, Mary Pickford and Shirley Temple, in their sexual precocity and gutter language. Producers and dirctors have found a way to have female characters without having to deal with women.[15]

CONSCIOUSNESS LEVEL II

> Soon I will have found some girl that I adore.
> ... While I sit around, my love can scrub the floor.
> ... On a moonlight night she'll cook me onion soup.
> Kiddies are romantic,
> And if we don't fight, we soon will have a troupe.[16]

> Keep a woman in subjection and the only way a man will feel safe is to keep her "barefoot and pregnant." If she has nothing

to do except undignified and repetitive labor, a woman will want baby after baby as the only escape to something else.[17]

Level II ("keep her in her place") acknowledges the traditional strength and capacity of women, but only in traditional roles. Women are shown functioning well as wives, mothers, secretaries, clerks, teachers, and nurses. Negative Level II images show women struggling with roles that are "beyond them" (executives, doctors, editors, etc.) and in which they develop "unwomanly" traits.

Lucy Komisar acknowledges the skill of advertisers and media producers in "selling" Level II images to women:

In a country where the low status of maids probably cannot be matched . . .it is an amazing feat of hocus-pocus worthy of Tom Sawyer and Phineas T. Barnum to lovingly declare that domestic labor is the true vocation of women wearing wedding bands.[18]

Advertising agencies see women in ways that account for their adherence to Level II images:

She likes to watch television and she does not enjoy reading a great deal. She is most easily reached through television and the simple, down-to-earth magazines. She finds her satisfaction within a rather small world and the center of this world is her home.[19]

The six winners of the American Advertising Federation's 1974 Advertising Woman of the Year award voiced similar feelings about what kinds of images are appropriate. A few of their comments follow.

Our research has proven that a big part of women's satisfaction comes from being wives and mothers. I see no sense in ramming liberation down their throats. (Jacqueline DaCosta)

Personally, I don't feel any resentment toward "chauvinistic" advertisers, perhaps because I'm not looking for chauvinism. (Janet B. Covington)

Successful marketers understand what most women want. Frankly, most women are not interested in careers but in affairs of the family and home. (Shirley Young)[20]

As we review Level II media content, we should keep in mind that, in fact, women are involved in many jobs/roles/activities. The media show women primarily in the home, greatly concerned with the sight and smell of their bathrooms and kitchens, waiting for "The Man From Glad" or "Mr. Muscle" to solve their household problems.

One study of television commercials reports that "nearly all ads show women inside the home, 43 percent of the time as adjuncts to men."[21] Another study of commercials presented during Saturday morning children's television programs showed women in the role of mother/housewife 58 percent of the time. Males were shown as fathers/husbands only 2 percent of the time.[22]

Alice Courtney and Thomas Whipple reviewed four studies of commercials and found that women and men are portrayed differently as product representatives. Women are shown *using* the product; men only *demonstrate* the product. Courtney and Wipple conclude that "women, for the most part, continue to clean house, launder, cook and serve meals, while the men give the orders and advice and eat the meals."[23]

Women also learn their place by seeing where they are not present. Women rarely make major purchases such as cars. Television commercials often show the man of the family arriving home with a new car; the woman shows surprise and delight, as if she had not participated in selecting the car. Only for major purchases thought to affect home decor, such as television sets, does the woman join the man at the time of purchase.

Role learning begins early in childhood, when many hours are spent watching television. Pamela Cheles-Miller questions the effects of stereotypic television commercial roles on children's perceptions.

For the most part, the roles of husband and wife depicted on TV commercials are caricatures which most adults can recognize and discount. But children interested in learning the "correct" behaviors to attribute to these important roles may not be able to discriminate as well."[24]

A trite but enduring television soap opera device to keep the woman in her place is to occupy her with pregnancies. Ellen Peck describes the transformation of yesterday's bunnies into today's rabbits.

Susan, in "As the World Turns," is pregnant. . . Susan in "Days of Our Lives" is also pregnant, as are Kate in "Love of Life," Mrs. Donovan in "Love of Life," Ann Jones in "Bright Promise," Kathy in "The Doctors," Alice in "Another World," Chris Cameron in "Where the Heart Is," and Iris in "Love is a Many-Splendored Thing."[25]

Gloria Scott Kinzer adds a demographic footnote.

Sudsville heroines give rise to a birthrate on afternoon TV that is eight times as high as the U.S. birthrate as a whole, and higher than the birthrate of any underdeveloped nation in the world. . . . This frantic rabbitlike reproduction underscores the pronatalist attitude of TV writers. . . .[26]

When you turn on your television set, only moments pass before Level II themes appear. In 1979, we noted that Gerber baby foods were always fed to babies by mothers, Dreft laundry detergent was used by mothers, Yuban coffee was fixed and served by women, Nestle's hot cocoa was made by mothers, and Chicken of the Sea tuna was prepared by mothers. The Charmin advertisement reinforced the belief that women *shop* and men *work* at grocery stores.

Level II in Magazines

Advertisements socialize girls to roles that will be expected of them as women. For example, the caption under a picture of mother and daughter asks, "What are little girls really made of?" and goes on to say:

> Notice how she's right there ready to help when you're making cookies? She's even beginning to take an active interest in sewing and housework. And, would you believe, helping with the dishes? Well, it's not all pretend and playing house, Mom. Your little girl is growing up before your very eyes. She wants to know how everything's done. So teach her all you can now. These are the years that'll help make her the kind of woman . . . housewife . . . mother, she'll soon become.[27]

Magazines are primers of the Level II image. *Ingenue* pushes teenage girls toward the wife/mother role with advertisements for engagement rings, pictures of romantic couples, suggestions for trapping the man, etc. *Glamour* emphasizes the importance of what the man thinks ("How Five Groovy Men Would Make You Over Into Their Dream Girls"). Magazines published for classroom use are similar. *Co-Ed* says: "Our magazine is written and edited for teenage girls. Its editorial content includes fashion and beauty, home furnishings and decoration, home management and equipment, foods and nutrition, parties and entertainment, finance and family living, child care and careers."[28] The categories make it clear that the role of homemaker is major and multifaceted, while the role of career woman is minor and singlefaceted.

Teenage magazines tell girls that the homemaker role will be exciting and fulfilling. Advertisements in general magazines convey a more honest image of the one member of the family who stays home each day to wash the dishes and clothes, dust furniture, scrub floors, make beds, cook meals, care for babies, etc. Comparing images in their teenage magazines and general magazines, girls may suspect that the princess, once kissed and wed, turns into a frog.

The 1975 to 1978 Birds Eye Combinations advertisements reminded the woman that she is the family cook, although not a very good one. The advertisements promised that the husband (never the wife) will pay attention to vegetables that are prepared by Birds Eye. The 1979 Lysol Spray advertisements dwelled on the theme that women stay home (with an occasional trip to a public restroom or motel, where Lysol Spray is needed) and work on ridding the home of all germs.

Healthknit showed the woman primarily concerned with taking care of her husband, including buying his underwear; under the title "When a woman loves a man," the text of a 1974 ad read:

> What pleases your man? Isn't it those little inconsequential things which only you can do? Like cooking his favorite dinner, asking about a problem or just making sure he has what he needs.[29]

A 1978 Jockey advertisement had a similar theme. It emphasized that a woman should be as careful in choosing her man's underwear as she is in choosing her own. In general, these Level II advertisements show that women do things for men like cook, clean, and purchase their underwear. Men do things for women like purchase a car or a diamond.

CONSCIOUSNESS LEVEL III

> I have nothing against a woman [as vice-president] just so she can cook and get home on time.[30]

Level III ("give her two places") represents the consciousness of many "progressive" media images of women. Level III images liberate the woman from the home only to the extent of making her responsible for both home and office. Since the media project few images of men performing housework in a two-career family, it is women who must achieve the impossible —working a full day while managing home, husband, and children before and after work.

Level III thinking is evident in some writings of the women's movement. Part-time work is advocated, with the assumption that women always have full home responsibilities as the first claim on their time. Rita Ricardo Campbell, member of the Citizens Advisory Council on the Status of Women, expresses this assumption. After quoting a 1968 Swedish government report to the United Nations that emphasized the need to educate men to share household and child-rearing responsibilities so that women can achieve equality in business, she says:

> I simply do not believe that many American men will accept the role implied in the above, at least not within the next ten years. Thus I opt for more part-time careers as a life style.[31]

Campbell's choice is in many ways a nonchoice. Part-time careers give rise to the myth of limited commitment, which allows men to say that women should not have responsible jobs because they are not serious about working.

There is pressure on the woman who wants a career to continue her full responsibilities at home. She has been socialized from childhood to take care of the home and everyone in it. As an adult, she is aware that most of her friends devote full time to the home. It is difficult to ignore the years of training and the continuing social pressure. Even in the 1970s, Level III is a radical position for many women to consider. For example, a 1976 television advertisement for Yardley Soap showed a women vacuuming while her husband reads. The voice-over told us that the woman works in an office in the daytime and at home in the evening. In a rare moment of relaxation, she treats herself to a Yardley bath. Similarly, a 1974 advertisement for a school of interior design had the caption, "Thelma Turkel. Wife, mother, and Interior Decorator." The text continued:

> A growing number of women are leading successful double lives. Thelma Turkel is one of them. She spends most of her day cooking, cleaning, chauffeuring, and looking after her family in a lovely suburban town.

But for two or three precious hours she lives in another world, enjoying all the excitement and rewards of a career in Interior Decorating.[32]

Level III took on a negative cast in a *McCall's* questionnaire for women who work. The introductory paragraph emphasized how difficult it is to have a job and take care of family and home. Three questions asked about disadvantages associated with working, additional costs because of the job, and areas of home and family life that suffer. There were no questions about benefits from working. The most positive response a woman could make is that there are no disadvantages and that nothing suffers.[33]

Women as people who *sometimes* work outside the home but *always* work in the home are the target audience of *Sphere,* the Betty Crocker magazine for:

... modern homemakers, including working wives and mothers, who need and want a source of inspiration ... It is intended to provide interest, inspiration and nourishment for those who consider the home as the center of their world, by concentrating on better living at home.[34]

CONSCIOUSNESS LEVEL IV

Ad Scene: Woman and man, each holding briefcase and New York Life Insurance Company policy.

Caption: For women who are equal partners—equal life insurance.

Level IV ("acknowledge that she is fully equal") is so rare among media images of women as to be hypothetical in many details. With the exception of Margaret Mead, Joan Sutherland, Barbara Walters, Billie Jean King, Barbara Jordan, and a few others, media protrayals of famous women emphasize sexiness, wifeliness, or motherliness. Entertainment images of women at Level IV appear only in short-lived programs such as "Adam's

Rib" (1973 to 1974 season) and "Kate McShane" (1975 to 1976 season).

Level IV in Television

When it terminated in 1977 after 7 years, "Mary Tyler Moore" was the longest-running show featuring a woman as a professional. Mary Richards was producer of a television news program. However, she often made the coffee, picked up donuts for her boss, and performed other functions of a woman office worker. In one episode Mary discovered that the previous producer, a man, earned $50 more per week for the same work. Mary complained and was eventually given a raise, but "equal pay for equal work" lost to "you don't have a family to support."

The circumstances of Mary Richards' life and work were contrived to keep issues of sexual equality in the background. Unlike her co-workers Murray Slaughter and Ted Baxter, Mary was unmarried. She did not have to juggle her career and family responsibilities. Moreover, the WJM newsroom had no visible secretaries; even the executive producer, Lou Grant, did without one. Mary was never shown relating to other women in her own department. In spite of these limitations, "Mary Tyler Moore" presented a new image of American women. Lance Morrow, in a 1977 *Time* essay, wrote a farewell to "Our Mary." He said:

> In its gentle way, the show changed television's image of women. During the pleistocene era of "Ozzie and Harriet" or "Donna Reed," the women, in skirts curiously bouffant for housework, had to make their witticisms in or near the kitchen, lest the chocolate-chip cookies burn. . . . In "MTM" Mary Richards—Moore's character—gave a humanely plausible version of American women . . . She was single, independent, pursued her career, was interested in men but not in an obsessive, husband-trapping way. Many women in the audience felt happier with themselves because of her.[35]

In the 1976 to 1977 season Bernadette Peters played Charley, a Washington photographer, in "All's Fair." Charley held her own with Richard, the columnist with whom she was having an affair, but Washington's male chauvinism cropped up in every episode. She seemed to realize that her relative equality with men was related to the fact that she was no man's wife, and refused Richard's proposals of marriage.

There was no example of a married, Level IV, career woman, with or without children, in 1977 to 1979 television entertainment.

Level IV in Magazines

A 1974 Bulova Accutron advertisement almost made Level IV. A woman with briefcase in hand is entering a conference room. Other women and men are already gathered, waiting for her. The advertisement said, "An unreliable watch can make you unreliable. Your watch has done you in again. And everybody's fed up with your excuses." The woman was shown as a professional, but she is not quite competent.

A 1976 Bulova advertisement was better. It showed the clasped hands of a woman and a man, each wearing an Accutron. The caption was, "Equal Pay. Equal Time."

Advertisers are beginning to realize the economic potential of the fact that women assume many responsibilities outside their traditional sphere. A 1975 advertisement from the Rite Autotronics Corporation stated, "You don't need the man in your life to tune the car in your life"; a book on do-it-yourself tune-ups was offered. Sears, which was a NOW target for several years because of alleged discrimination in hiring and promotion, mounted a 1975 advertising campaign that showed women selling stoves, servicing cars, and making home repairs. The advertisments were captioned, "We don't separate the women from the men."

Dewar's Whiskey advertisements do show women as equals. For example, the 1975 Dewar's profile of Eve Queler, conductor, described her professional life without mentioning her favorite recipes.

Delta Airlines and American Airlines advertisements also treat women as professionals, in contrast to airline advertisements that do not. In a continuing campaign, one Delta advertisement says:

> Delta is an airline run by professionals. Like Barbara O'Hanlon, Reservations Sales Agent. She knows all about schedules, fares, ticketing and routing . . . When she makes your reservation, she doesn't just use her computer. She uses her head.

Mary Grace Ritter, American Airlines reservation agent, says:

> I know why I'll never be replaced by a computer . . . when any customer has a problem, or when a family's taking a trip and they need advice—that's when no computer can do what I do best.

Litigation and research by women led American Telephone and Telegraph to adopt new practices in hiring and advertising. For instance, one AT&T advertisement showed a telephone installer on a pole; the caption read:

> The phone company wants more installers like Alana MacFarlane. Alana MacFarlane is a 20-year-old from San Rafael, California. She's one of our first women telephone installers. She won't be the last.

These advertisements provide new "images of potentiality" for women.

A 1978 Advertising Council advertisement for Savings Bonds told one story of equality. The picture and text described Molly Pitcher, who fought side by side with her husband and became a heroine of the American Revolution. This type of advertisement helps to document the importance of women and men in our history.

Level IV in Newspapers

A 1975 Honda Civic newspaper advertisement was an imaginative example of Level IV equality. On the left side of the page we saw a man standing next to his car. Beneath him was a list of 15 reasons why a *man* purchases the Honda Civic. On the right side of the page we saw a woman standing next to her car. The 15 reasons why a *woman* purchases the Honda Civic were the same. The two persons were treated as equals, "masculine" reasons were not attributed to the man or "feminine" reasons to the woman.

CONSCIOUSNESS LEVEL V

> I'm lookin' for a man to wash my clothes,
> Iron my shirts, and blow my nose;
> Sweep the floor and wax the kitchen
> While I sit playin' guitar and bitchin' . . .[36]

Level V, topping the consciousness scale, is nonstereotypic. *Individual* women and men are viewed as superior to each other in some respects and inferior in other respects. The dogmatism of Level IV ("women must be equal to men") is unnecessary, because individuals are not judged by their sex. Level V is included because the consciousness scale logically requires it, not because there are many Level V images in the media. In 1979, there were two types of Level V presentation—the *role reversal* and the *unusual role*. The unusual role shows the woman in an occupation or situation usually reserved for men, such as lawyer or doctor, and shows the man in an occupation or situation usually reserved for women, such as homemaker or nurse. Eventually we hope to find women and men in so many overlapping roles that media presentations of a man cooking dinner or a woman filing a law brief will be *nonstereotypic* and *usual*.

Level V in Television

Aetna Life Insurance Company advertisements were among the first to show women nonstereotypically. In 1975, the company sponsored the television special "Babe," the story of Mildred (Babe) Didrikson. All of the program's commercials portrayed women as individuals, valued for their abilities (even the Little Leaguer who easily holds her own with the boys). In the 1978 to 1979 television season, several examples of Level V presentations appeared. Lemon Pledge showed a man proud of his ability to polish household furniture. A similar Windex advertisement showed a man polishing kitchen surfaces when his wife returned home from work; "body language" told us that the kitchen is his territory and that he is pleased with its appearance. In a Duncan Hines advertisement, a woman was typing her college term paper when her teenage son came in for a snack; the son then baked a Duncan Hines cake. Campbell's Soup has received favorable publicity for its advertisement that showed a man preparing dinner ("At first it was strange, coming home to the range, but I've got a working wife . . .")

Level V in Magazines

In the single picture and few words of a magazine advertisement, it is difficult to say that a woman is being shown as superior to a man in particular respects. One good example, however, is a 1975 ad for Piper Aircraft Corporation. The picture of a woman in the pilot seat was captioned, "Are men really better pilots than women?" The text told us:

> Not according to the figures. And not according to the facts . . .
> On any one of those points a woman is equal to a man—if not superior. So when you come right down to it, there's no reason

in the world why a woman can't be equally adept at flying an airplane. Maybe even better.

A 1976 Dewar's profile described Sheryl Handler, "urban and natural resource analyst," who "has a unique ability to mobilize experts in many different fields to attack the problems of people from areas as diverse as small New England towns and large Asian cities." She said of herself:

> My feminine instinct to shelter and nurture contributes to my professional perspective. Instinct, as much as analysis, is required to rationalize the use of natural resources with economic growth.

This advertisement is an unusual example of Level V consciousness. Not all women would be effective resource analysts, but Handler attributed *her* effectiveness partly to her sex.

Magazine Level V advertisements in 1977 are exemplified by the United Airlines "You're the boss" campaign which showed a woman as a business executive, and the Delaware Management Company's campaign which showed a busy executive who has DMC invest her money in mutual funds.

In 1978 the O.B. series showed women in occupational roles such as ice skating instructor, scuba diving instructor, and flag woman. Gulf showed women such as Adrian Mills, tanker program analyst, and Debbie Hawk, computer technician, as fully competent in their occupational role. And Miller encouraged women to work for them in areas such as sales, marketing, engineering, and production management.

APPLYING THE CONSCIOUSNESS SCALE TO ADVERTISEMENTS

Suzanne Pingree, Robert Hawkins, Matilda Butler, and William Paisley applied the consciousness scale to advertisements in *Ms., Time, Newsweek,* and *Playboy.* To be included, advertisements had to show a woman and occupy at least one-sixth of a magazine page. Ten advertisements from each magazine were randomly sampled from all issues in each month for 1 year (July 1973 to June 1974). For the 447 advertisements, there was 97 percent agreement among coders. Some of the findings were:

1. Twenty-seven percent of all advertisements were Level I ("put her down").
2. Forty-eight percent of all advertisements were Level II ("keep her in her place").
3. Four percent of all advertisements were Level III ("give her two places").
4. Nineteen percent of all advertisements were Level IV ("full equality").
5. Two percent of all advertisements were Level V ("individuality").
6. Fifty-four percent of advertisements in *Playboy* showed females at Level I.
7. Fifty-five percent of advertisements in *Time* and 60 percent of advertisements in *Newsweek* showed females at Level II.
8. Forty percent of advertisements in *Ms.* showed females at Levels IV and V, but another 40 percent showed females at Level II.[37]

The study shows that analysts can reliably apply the consciousness scale to profile the consciousness levels of advertisements appearing in various magazines. Somewhat surprising is the high percentage of Level II women shown in *Ms.* This finding helps us to realize how pervasive the stereotype is that women are primarily homemakers.

Pingree et al. extended the consciousness scale to men's roles. Level I for men shows them as two-dimensional sex objects or decorations. Examples are frequently found in advertisements for cigarettes. For instance, Camel, Winston, and Salem Longs all feature rugged, sexy, outdoor men. Level II shows men primarily working outside the home, performing "masculine" chores at home, or being waited on. A Gala II commercial showing Tennessee Ernie Ford barbequeing ribs outdoors, a Glad commercial showing the son taking out the garbage, and a Chef Boyardee Ravioli commercial showing husband and son being served dinner all exemplify Level II men. Level III shows men helping competently at home (including child care and cooking) but functioning primarily as breadwinners. Level III men are not found frequently in the media. However, a Dove detergent commercial showing the husband and children "helping" with the dishes and a Downey Fabric Softener commercial showing the husband helping to put away towels exemplify Level III men. Level IV "equality" and Level V "individuality" already encompass men, as discussed on pages 160–166.

Suzanne Pingree, Robert Hawkins, and Michele Waldinger analyzed 8 hours of videotaped commercials representing the three networks across 7 days during a week in March 1975. Results indicate that both women and men are overwhelmingly shown in Level II images. Only 20 percent of the women and 7 percent of the men were shown at other than Level II. Half of these women (10 percent) were shown at Level I, less than 1 percent of the non-Level II men were shown at Level I. Seven percent of the men were shown at Levels III and IV, as were 9 percent of the women. No one was coded as Level V.[38]

The consciousness scale provides a method for examining media portrayals of women and men that anyone can use. The examples in this chapter help you to define the five consciousness levels for both sexes. It may be difficult for you, as it was for us, to find comparable portrayals of women and men at each level. For example, we expected to find that *Playgirl* "puts him down" just as *Playboy* "puts her down." However, whereas in *Playboy* nude women strike poses of languid inactivity, in *Playgirl* nude men are photographed in activities such as swimming and reading. In *Playboy* nude women advertise products. In *Playgirl* it is also nude women, not nude men, who advertise products. In *Playboy* women discuss their sex lives. In *Playgirl* men discuss their careers. We are oversimplifying the contrast between *Playgirl* and *Playboy* for the sake of illustration but, in fact, it is difficult to say that both sets of "playmates" receive the same Level I portrayal.

The consciousness scale may raise as many questions as it answers, but that is not all bad.

INSTITUTIONAL SEXISM IN THE MEDIA

It was not a contemporary feminist, but Susan B. Anthony, who said:

> Just as long as newspapers and magazines are controlled by men, every woman upon them must write articles which are reflections of men's ideas. As long as that continues, women's ideas and deepest convictions will never get before the public.[1]

An industry that generates annual revenues in excess of $30 billion can be expected to respond defensively to criticism and cautiously to proposals for change. Historically, media organizations have been about as sexist as other business organizations their size. They have resisted and evaded antidiscrimination laws. Where affirmative action programs have been established for lower staff positions, the executive suite and the boardroom have been kept as masculine as the most evasive interpretation of the law permits.

Media organizations could not be more central to the issue of sexism in society if they were selling sexism directly to the public, for that is exactly what they do. Other business organizations sell their refrigerators, automobiles, and toothpaste with sexist symbolism when it profits them to do so. But the products of media organizations are symbols *per se*. Media managers are merchants of symbols, and many of them believe that sexist symbols are the fastest-moving line.

Institutional media sexism is embodied in personnel, policies, practices, and products. Chapter 11 describes the use of surveys and case studies to gather data on these four facets of media organizations.

Chapter 12 deals with employment of women in media organizations—their hiring, compensation, promotion, and utilization. Women have a long way to go in the industry that invented the slogan, "You've come a long way, baby."

Chapter 13 investigates the editorial and advertising decisions that encourage or tolerate sexism. Such decisions are not part of the open record. We must infer the decision factors from glimpses of editorial and advertising strategies.

The present generation of media managers may not be capable of reducing institutional sexism or media sexism very much. For the sake of argument let us assume that they run the shop only as they were taught. What about the generation of media managers now in training? Chapter 14 asks the question this way: can the next generation of media managers rise above the sexism of their current training in journalism and communication schools?

HOW MEDIA INSTITUTIONS ARE STUDIED

As long as there has been human communication, there have been persons, organizations, and places that have served as centers as the input and output of information.[1]

Media content in the United States and other capitalist nations differs strikingly from media content in socialist nations and in third-world nations. Similar but smaller differences exist between nations in the same bloc. These differences in media *content* reflect economic, political, organizational, and other factors that shape media *institutions.* That is, what the media *say* reflects what the media *are.*

Arrangements for human communication have been with us since antiquity. Troubadours in the Middle Ages and poster walls in modern China exemplify the diversity of such arrangements. They also show that arrangements for communication may have other functions, such as entertaining and decorating.

THINKING OF THE MEDIA AS INSTITUTIONS

Today's media differ from earlier communication arrangements in their size, technological complexity, and economic significance. Above all, in the words of George Gerbner, they are "new social organizations . . . in the special domain of institutionalized public acculturation."[2]

To understand media treatment of women, blacks, civil rights legislation, corporation taxes, labor unions, copyright, or any other issue, we must understand how the media as institutions are affected by the issue. That is, *institutional* analysis interprets the findings of *content* analysis.

Also note that the media are corporate employers of more than 2 million persons in the United States. With a work force in the millions and revenue in the billions, the media are a match for other institutions in our society, including the federal government.

Institutional studies of media are conducted (1) to interpret trends or differences in media content, and (2) to explain how the media's policies and practices come about and are carried out.

What are the important dimensions of institutional analysis? Gerbner describes six types of "constraints . . . affecting decision-making in mass communications," which we describe more simply here.

1. *Client relationships* with investors, advertisers, and other groups supplying capital and operating costs.
2. *Patron relationships* with audiences, who must be cultivated to strengthen the media's position vis-à-vis clients.
3. *Logistical requirements* related to resources, personnel, facilities, etc.
4. *Leverage,* or pressure exerted on media or clients by third parties through boycotts, strikes, legislation, etc.
5. *Legal requirements* pertaining to media as businesses and licensed carriers.

6. *Supervisory relationships,* internal to each institution, that affect what the media produce.[3]

The media operate in the context of other institutions that finance, regulate, and pressure their operation. These external forces are felt even by a small-town weekly newspaper with 1000 subscribers. As the scale of media operation grows to serve audiences in the tens of millions, the external forces are felt intensely.

Internally, media institutions may be studied in terms of personnel, policies, practices, and products. *Personnel* are recruited, hired, utilized, compensated, promoted, etc. *Policies* are based on profit-making or public-service assumptions and also on laissez-faire or "social responsibility" beliefs about the role of media in society.[4] *Practices* consist of technological requirements of production and "tricks of the trade." *Products* have attributes of quality, quantity, marketability, etc.

DEEP VERSUS BROAD INSTITUTIONAL ANALYSIS

All research offers the choice of depth versus breadth. In institutional analysis, deep and broad are two distinct traditions.

Deep analyses focus on individual organizations, such as the *New York Times* in Gay Talese's *The Kingdom and the Power* and CBS in Robert Metz's *CBS: Reflections in a Bloodshot Eye.*[5] These anecdotal studies are insightful but often err in imputing decisions to rivalries in the executive suite instead of to balance sheets in the business office.

Transitional between deep and broad is a study such as William Rivers' *The Opinionmakers.*[6] This account of the Washington press corps describes encounters between government agencies and correspondents. Without losing perspective in the activities of a single organization, Rivers generalizes about conflicts in media/government relations.

Broad institutional studies, which combine economic, political, and technological perspectives, are exemplified by Ben Bagdikian's *The Information Machines.*[7] In addition to telling the history of the American news system, *The Information Machines* forecasts developments in communication technology through 1995. Technological forecasting is needed in institutional analysis, which would otherwise propose future policies for past media. The media are fast-moving targets; to propose progressive policies for them in the future, we need to know where they will be at the time.

Institutional studies contrast with each other in objectives, definitions of variables, data collection procedures, and interpretations of data. Objectives are primary. Unlike content analysis, for which data come in fixed bundles, institutional analysis can be almost any form of research for which its objectives call, from the deepest case study to the broadest survey.

ILLUSTRATIVE INSTITUTIONAL ANALYSES

Values and Decisions of Media Personnel

In 1955 Warren Breed interviewed executives and staff members of middle-sized daily newspapers.[8] He was concerned with "social control in the news room" (i.e., how newspaper staff learn to conform to the values of editors and publishers).

Breed found that sanctions against nonconforming staff were subtle. Staff are rarely fired; clauses in American Newspaper Guild contracts limit causes of firing. However, staff fear that they will be reassigned from good outside beats to obituaries. Staff also fear that they will not move up the ladder unless they "think like executives."

Daniel Garvey updated Breed's study in *Social Control in the Television Newsroom.*[9] As you might expect, moving the news operation from print to broadcast media does not change the values of executives or the pressures on staff to conform to those values.

David Manning White initiated a related stream of research with "The Gatekeeper."[10] Gatekeeping studies focus on individual stories in the daily news flow: who has formal or informal power to affect the news flow, and how are different news topics affected?

Fred Friendly's important book, *Due to Circumstances Beyond Our Control,* is a gatekeeping study.[11] It describes events surrounding the CBS decision not to broadcast the February 1966 Senate Foreign Relations Committee hearings on Viet Nam, a decision that led Friendly to resign as president of CBS News. Although media critics reacted strongly to this incident, it was a simple clash of values between news staff and business staff, since the hearings yielded to profitable reruns of "I Love Lucy" and "The Real McCoys."

Trends in Media Ownership

According to Raymond Nixon, a concentration of newspaper ownership has been taking place in the United States.[12] Several factors account for the trend: (1) the formation of newspaper chains; (2) the elimination of multiple daily newspapers in cities of less than 50,000; and (3) the corporate merger but separate publication of daily newspapers in cities larger than 50,000.

In real or imagined influence, television stations now overshadow newspapers, and media researchers are concerned about the effects of group ownership of television stations. Herbert Howard reported that 71 percent of television stations in the 100 largest TV markets, which contain 87 percent of the nation's TV households, are licensed to group owners.[13] Group ownership of stations in these markets crossed the 50 percent level in the mid-1950s, then increased 10 percent per decade into the 1970s.

Herbert Howard also studied the joint ownership of newspapers and television stations.[14] In the 100 largest markets, 34 percent of all VHF stations were owned by or affiliated with newspapers in 1973. In some cases, multimedia ownership involves more than one city, which is regarded as less of a threat to competition than multimedia ownership within a single city. Focusing attention on a single-city ownership, we find that 20 percent of all VHF stations were owned or affiliated with newspapers in the 100 largest markets in 1973.

A New Focus

Writing this book a decade ago, we might have omitted a section on institutional analysis. In recent years it has become clear that media organizations must be studied to understand internal and external factors that affect their performance. An era of institutional analysis of the media has begun. It will certainly continue until the media become more responsive to the public interest.

INSTITUTIONAL ANALYSIS PROCEDURES

Institutional analysis is not a single technique; we cannot outline institutional analysis procedures as simply as content analysis procedures (Chapter 5). However, all research techniques have some procedures and criteria in common. You should ask the following questions before accepting the conclusions of an institutional analysis.

Is a single organization described in depth or are several organizations (perhaps an entire industry) described in breadth? Case study techniques provide deep information on individual organizations; surveys provide broad information on any number of organizations that can be contacted. Records analysis is intermediate between these extremes; the records of an organization can be analyzed in a deep study of that organization alone or in a broad study of several organizations.

Are variables defined in a reasonable way? The dimensions of institutional analysis—personnel, policies, practices, and products—seem to be clear without definition. At a second level of analysis, however, a variable such as "utilization of personnel" is not at all clear. If a media organization wishes to mislead the FCC or the EEOC about its utilization of women, it can create fictitious job titles. Researchers have become skeptical about the validity of utilization data reported by stations to the FCC on Form 395; every year there are more managers and fewer secretaries as women "progress" in television.[15]

Is the sample of times, media, organizations, persons, events, etc., as extensive as the conclusion that is being drawn? To sustain a complaint of sex discrimination in employment against a media organization, data from several years and from several personnel categories must be compiled to establish the discriminatory pattern. That is, even though the study focuses on a single organization, two kinds of sampling (time sampling and personnel category sampling) are required to fulfill the objectives of the study.

It is often easier to sample in support of a theoretical conclusion than an applied conclusion. For example, using the procedure known as network analysis, we can show that women in media management have a different and smaller set of contacts than men at the same levels (as a consequence of home responsibilities versus after-work recreation, etc.). Even casual samples of women in media organizations support this conclusion. In contrast, an applied conclusion of discrimination on the part of a media organization draws critical attention to the sampling plan that was employed.

If the objectives of an institutional analysis are theoretical, nonrandom sampling plans are often adequate. If the objectives are applied, random sampling is usually necessary to counter the charge of research bias.

Does the study meet tests of reliability, validity, and utility? In institutional analysis, we often use "informants" to describe the organizations in which they work. An example of an informant-based study is *Rooms With No View,* compiled by the Media Women's Association.[16] Even if informants seem to be unbiased in their descriptions, the *reliability* question is whether other persons who have equal or greater knowledge of the organizations would describe them in the same way.

When standard questions have been used in a survey of organizations, reliability depends on the respondents' understanding of the questions. When organizational records are being analyzed, reliability depends on the accuracy of the records, the consistency of definitions employed over time, etc.

In institutional analysis, the *validity* question is whether each variable measures the aspect of an organization that it is supposed to measure. Where, for example, does the power lie within an organization? To test validity, it may be necessary to "triangulate" on several independent measures. This is the criterion of convergence, previously discussed on page 66.

By convention and by regulation, some facts of media organizations are disclosed in their own products (e.g., editorial mastheads) and reports (e.g., FCC Form 395). These indicators are useful alternatives to expensive new data, but they may lack validity. Doubts about the validity of Form 395 reports are mentioned on page 189. Another example of invalid indicators involves women's names on the mastheads of women's magazines. Over the years, male staff writers on these magazines have sometimes adopted female pseudonyms. The proportion of women's names on the masthead is therefore not a valid indicator of the female proportion of the editorial staff.

As is true of content analysis, the *utility* of an institutional analysis depends on what the findings are good for, relative to their cost. Institutional analysis is more costly than content analysis; findings must justify the higher cost.

12

EMPLOYMENT

Title VII of the Civil Rights Act of 1964, as amended by the Equal Employment Opportunity Act of 1972. Title VII prohibits discrimination in employment in Federal, State and local government, and in the private sector on the basis of race, color, religion, sex, or national origin. Enforcement of Title VII in the private sector . . . is generally within the province of the Equal Employment Opportunity Commission (EEOC).[1]

Part 2 of this book examined media content. Stereotypic presentation of women raises the obvious question. Why? Why is media content not just a reflection but an intensification of sexism in American society? This question requires us to examine the media as institutions. Is media content more or less sexist than the institutions that create it?

This chapter reviews available evidence on numbers, salaries, promotions, and assignments of women and men in the media. We ask you to forgive what may seem like repetitions of these data as we look at the employment of women in television, radio, magazine, newspaper, film, and book industries. Only when the detail of discrimination against women in the media is fully documented can we evaluate alternatives for change.

HIRING

Hiring of media personnel is regulated by Title VII of the Civil Rights Act of 1964, as amended by the Equal Employment Opportunity Act of 1972. The intent of the law is clear. Employers are not to discriminate on the basis of sex. Public radio and television stations are also covered by Title IX of the Education Act Amendments of 1972. These stations were notified in 1974 that:

> Public broadcasting stations which are applicants for or recipients of such Federal financial assistance are subject to the provisions of Title IX and should review their activities to ensure non-discrimination on the basis of sex in employment practices and the delivery of broadcast services.[2]

Proposition 12.1: Men Are More Likely than Women to Be Media Managers.

Some employment data exist for each of the media. Annual figures for commercial television have been released by the Communications Office of the United Church of Christ since 1972. Across the years, men are about 76 percent of all employees and about 90 percent of those in the top four job levels (officials and managers, professionals, technicians, sales workers). Figures for public television indicated that women fare somewhat better (about 30 percent of all employees), but that the top three job levels (public television does not have sales personnel) are still predominantly staffed by men (about 82 percent).[3]

Data for public radio indicate that although there are differences at each level, women are about 21 percent of the professionals. They are 82 percent of the business managers but none of the engineers.[4]

Data from magazines come from their own editorial listings and from testimony of women in the industry. Approximately 75 percent of all editorships are held by men.[5] However, there are major differences according to type of magazine.

Men are even more numerous on newspaper staffs. Combining data from six major papers, we find that men are about 87 percent of the editors/managers/officials.[6]

Film continues to be controlled almost entirely by men. Across a variety of positions (actors, directors, producers, writers, etc.), about 95 percent of the staff are men.[7]

Book publishing has more female staff than any other media. Approximately 36 percent of the industry's editors, vice presidents, and professionals are women.[8] The record is better in small publishing houses, worse in large houses.

Grouping all the media together (commercial and public television and radio, magazines, newspapers, films, and books), we find that men hold almost 80 percent of the desirable positions (e.g., reporters, editors, writers). The studies summarized here provide detail that supports this conclusion.

STUDIES OF TELEVISION EMPLOYMENT.   Until the 1970s, there were only sketchy records of employment in the broadcasting industry. Lawrence Lichty and Joseph Ripley provided early estimates of numbers of women and men in television and radio. They say that of 80,000 full-time employees in 1966, approximately 75 percent were males and 25 percent were females.[9]

With the rise of the women's movement, more detailed figures have been compiled and published. In 1970 Lucy Komisar found it difficult to compile data for a New York City statement on the status of women in media because only the *New York Times* and WNBC-TV were willing to release statistics. Other industry sources declined to comment. With the help of several women in the industry, however, Komisar was able to compile the following unofficial record.

NBC Television has about 45 male reporters, two reporters are women. There are over 100 male writers and ten women. Of more than 20 announcers, none are women. . . . There are over 350 men managers and executives; under 20 are women. There is one woman producer.

ABC-TV has a President (male), 2 Vice Presidents (male), a News Manager (male), 2 Assistant News Managers (male), a News Director (male), an Executive Producer (male), 2 Producers (male), 7 Associate Producers (male), 7 Assignment Editors (male), 2 Directors (male), 2 writers (one male, one female), 44 correspondents and reporters (42 male, 2 female) and 6 desk assistants (all male). There are also 2 production assistants (female) and 4 secretaries (you guess). All in all, 75 professional men and three women.

On to CBS, where there are over 300 men in top management and two (count 'em) women. . . . there is one National Editor (male), one International Editor (male), one Executive Editor (male), 5 Executive Producers (male), 20 to 25 Producers (2 women), 25 to 30 Associate Producers (2 women), 11 writers (one woman), 35 to 40 correspondents and reporters (2 women), a dozen desk assistants (one woman). The assignment editors, directors, production assistants, etc. are all men.[10]

Without reproducing all the detail in Komisar's report, it is worth noting that in 1970 the five television stations in New York City owned by multistation corporations (CBS, NBC, etc.) employed a minimum of 110 women and men on their production staffs. Of these, 16 (14 percent) were women.

In June 1969, the Federal Communications Commission issued guidelines to all licensed stations on the necessity of providing equal employment opportunities. The FCC wrote:

Each station shall . . . (4) Conduct a continuing campaign to exclude every form of prejudice or discrimination based upon race, color, religion, national origin or sex, from the station's personnel policies and practices and working conditions. (5) Conduct continuing review of job structure and employment practices and adopt positive recruitment, training, job design, and other measures needed in order to insure genuine equality of opportunity to participate fully in all organizational units,

occupations, and levels of responsibility in the station.... (c)...
applicants for renewal of license who have not previously done
so, shall file with the Commission programs designed to provide
equal employment opportunities for Negroes, Orientals, American Indians, Spanish-surnamed Americans, and women....[11]

In 1971 each station was required to file its first Annual
Employment Report (Form 395). Beginning in 1972, after sub-
mission of the second employment reports, Ralph Jennings, at
the Office of Communication, United Church of Christ, began
an annual reporting and summarization of the employment of
women and minorities in television stations.

When Jennings issued his first report on television stations,
he found that for the 609 stations reporting data for both years,
there had been no increase between 1971 and 1972 in the percentage of full-time female employees (22 percent); there were
no women in management in 317 stations (52 percent of stations); and there were no women in professional jobs in 211
stations (35 percent). In addition, 52 stations employed fewer
women as officials and managers in 1972 than in 1971. Another
106 stations employed fewer women in professional job categories in 1972 than in 1971. In the 609 stations reporting in 1972,
only 10 percent of the 5515 full-time officials and managers
were females and 13 percent of the 7925 full-time professional
employees were females.[12]

The Jennings and Tillyer report issued by the United
Church of Christ in 1973 accounted for the 584 commercial
television stations that had filed reports for all 3 years. In these
stations, "the proportion of women [among full-time em-
ployees] rose to 23 percent in 1973, from 22 percent in 1972 and
1971." The proportion of women among those employed full
time in the upper four job categories (officials and managers,
professionals, technicans, sales workers) increased from 6 percent in 1971 to 9 percent in 1973. The report also states: "Although only two stations employed no women full time, 86 (14
percent) had no women employees in the upper four job catego-

ries and 58 (9 percent) employed women only in office and clerical positions."

The report dealt separately with public stations, where women fare better than at commercial stations. "Women accounted for 1432 (30 percent) of full-time employees in 1973. The proportion of women in full-time employment in 1972 was 29 percent and in 1971, it was 28 percent." The proportion of women among those employed full time in the upper three job categories (public stations do not have sales staffs) increased from 15 percent in 1971 to 17 percent in 1973. Ten stations (8 percent of the 127 public stations) "reported no women on their full-time staffs and 25 (20 percent) reported none in the upper three job categories. Twelve stations (10 percent) employed women only in office and clerical positions."[13]

By 1974, the Jennings and Jefferson report showed that the proportion of women among those employed full time in the 613 commercial stations filing reports across all years increased another percentage point to 24 percent. The proportion of women among those employed full time in the upper four job categories increased to 11 percent. Among all 647 stations reporting in 1974, 6 stations (1 percent) had no women on their full-time staffs and 70 (11 percent) had no women employees in the upper four job categories.

The 1974 report also showed that the proportion of women among those employed full time by public stations increased from 28 percent in 1971 to 31 percent in 1974. The proportion of women among those in the top three job categories increased from 15 percent in 1971 to 19 percent in 1974. "Eight stations (6 percent) had no women on their full-time staffs and 21 (16 percent) reported none in the upper three job categories."[14]

The Jennings and Jefferson report for 1975 showed a continuation of earlier trends. In the 639 commercial stations with reports for earlier years, the proportion of women among those employed full time increased to 25 percent by 1975. This is an increase of three percentage points in 4 years. The proportion of women among those employed full time in the upper four job categories increased to 13 percent. This is seven percentage points above the 1971 level. "Eleven of the stations (2 percent) employ no women full time, and 63 (10 percent) have none in the upper four job categories."

Figures for the public stations again indicated greater employment of women than in the commercial stations. "Women held 32 percent of all full-time jobs at public stations in 1975." This is four percentage points greater than in 1971. The number of women employed full time in the upper three job categories was 21 percent, an increase of seven percentage points above the 1971 level. "Twenty-one stations (12 percent) had no women on their full-time staffs and 34 (19 percent) reported none in the upper three job categories." The comparable 1971 figures were 8 percent with no women at all and 20 percent with no women in the upper three job categories.[15]

Jennings urged caution in accepting the industry-generated statistics.

In previous studies, we have pointed out the need for job classifications that describe actual positions in broadcasting. The generic titles currently in use by the FCC are subject to widespread misinterpretation. . . .

For example, the data suggests that women in clerical posts are being given paper promotions with impressive titles that station managements can report to the FCC. The proportion of women employees in full time office and clerical jobs has purportedly dropped 18.3 percent since 1971, from 76.8 percent to 58.5 percent of the work force. In the same period, women in the upper level management, professional, technical and sales job categories are reported to have increased from 19.5 percent to 38.5 percent of the work force.

The suspicion that much of this improvement in the status of women is fictitious arises from the fact that between 1971 and 1975 the number of office and clerical work positions reported dropped by 509. In the same period 1,302 new positions were reportedly established for officials and managers. It seems improbable that this greatly increased corps of management personnel can function with reduced clerical support.[16]

The figures for 1976 showed a continuation of the "five-year-long practice of making paper promotions of women and minorities."[17] Based on data supplied by stations, 78 percent of all jobs are classified as managerial, professional, technical, or sales. Statistics from the broadcast industry in the past and from other industries have indicated that there are one or more support staff members for every upper-level employee. Ralph Jennings and Allan Walters point out that, if we accept the current broadcasting figures as true, there are three upper-level employees for every support staff member. The stations have created more than 6000 upper-level jobs since 1971 while doing away with more than 3000 lower-level jobs. With specific reference to women, the report says that their employment status has been distorted. The broadcasters' data indicate "that the number of women in full-time clerical posts has dropped 22 percent since 1971, from 77 percent to 55 percent of full-time women employees. In the same period, women in upper-level management, professional, technical and sales jobs are reported to have increased from 19 percent to 42 percent of all women employees."[18] Statistical sleight of hand makes it difficult to assess the progress of women in television. However, even accepting the broadcasters' data, at the end of 1976 men were 82 percent of the officials/managers, 77 percent of the professionals, 95 percent of the technicians, and 84 percent of the sales staff.[19]

Caroline Isber and Muriel Cantor coauthored the *Report of the Task Force on Women in Public Broadcasting.* Using employment statistics of CPB licensees for fiscal year 1974, they found that women held 30 percent of all jobs in television stations and 29 percent of full-time jobs. Community stations were the most likely to have female employees. At these stations women had 35 percent of the full-time positions and 38 percent of the part-time positions. Following is the percentage of women among those employed in managerial positions in public television stations for 1974.

General manager, 3 percent.

Station manger, 2 percent.

Operations manager, 7 percent.

Program manager, 13 percent.

Production manager, 5 percent.

Business manager, 45 percent.

Chief engineer, 9 percent.

These women represent 9 percent of all persons employed in managerial positions.[20]

The Report of the Canadian Broadcasting Corporation Task Force on the Status of Women, entitled *Women in the CBC,* examined opportunities for women and men in the CBC as of mid-1974. Studying a staff of 10,445, of whom 25 percent were women, the Task Force found that women were 8 percent of management in 1974 (3 percent higher than in 1970) and 15 percent of the producers (also 3 percent higher than in 1970).

Most CBC employees were occupationally segregated. The report notes that 5185 employees were in eight "men's jobs"— job categories filled by more than 90 percent men. These include technicians, announcers, and television production assistants. In the four "women's jobs" (secretaries, script assistants, etc.) there were 1061 employees. Four of the men's positions employed no women; none of the women's positions lacked male employees. In "integrated jobs" in which both sexes held at least 10 percent of the positions, 2795 were employed as clerks, producers, news editors, etc. According to a more stringent criterion of integration, such as 20 percent of women and men in the same positions, only four positions were "integrated." These were clerks, computer operators, designers, and radio producers.[21]

The staffing of daytime television serials has recently been studied. Mildred Downing reports that 40 percent of the 38 serial writers are women and that only 5 of these women are creators or head writers. Women are 20 percent of the producers.[22]

The Media Women's Association (MWA) book, *Rooms With No View,* edited by Ethel Strainchamps, presents anecdotal and statistical evidence on the status of women in the media.[23] For example, women at CBS are 51 percent of the work force. They are:

• Twenty-four percent of the news staff.
• Ten percent of the news staff when 100 percent sex-segregated jobs are excluded (e.g., secretary and director).
• Five percent of the film editors.
• One percent of the film crew.
• Seventeen percent of the producers.
• Six percent of the highest-ranking employees.

Women at ABC are 25 percent of the work force. Excluding secretarial positions, women are:

• Twenty-five percent of the associate producers.
• Nineteen percent of the full producers.
• Eleven percent of the television correspondents.

Women at National Educational Television are:

• Twenty-two percent of the producers.
• None of the vice presidents, department directors, executive producers, or directors.

In 1977, the California Commission on the Status of Women released the results of hearings held in 1975 on women and the media. Two of the testimonies are of particular interest, because they provide some information on employment in television. Alice Backes, chairperson of the National Women's Committee of the American Federation of Television and Radio Artists, reports the figures compiled by Barbara Walters and originally reported in the documentary "Of Women and Men." Women are 6 percent (4) of the correspondents at ABC, 10 percent (7) at CBS, and 8 percent (6) at NBC.[24]

Barbara Searles, chairperson of the Directors Guild of America's Women's Committee, notes that women are 2 percent of DGA's membership. Since most television and film work takes place on the West Coast, Searles analyzed the female director/members there. She contends that the 21 women (1.5 percent of the membership) direct even less than 1.5 percent of the shows and films. More than half (11) try to support themselves by being directors. All are unable to do so and work as assistants, stage managers, writer producers, etc. About another quarter (6) of the women have second careers to support them (5 are actresses and 1 is a script supervisor). A seventh (3) have not directed in 20 years. One woman finally left the West Coast. Searles also speaks of her personal experiences with discrimination. Although she was director of "The Nation's Future" for NBC-TV in New York, she has been unable to get directing jobs on the West Coast. She has turned to writing (one documentary won an award for KNBC), but she is never allowed to direct. When she wrote a documentary on women's rights, she again requested to direct the program. The station program director told her, "No woman could direct this film. No woman could be objective."[25]

Much detailed information on hiring, salary, promotion, and assignment policies and practices has been collected by women for litigation. Other data have been provided by federal EEOC investigators who have access to files not open to individuals or organized groups of women. Aspects of these cases will be described in later sections of this chapter. New affirmative action programs and cash settlements that resulted from suits against NBC and *Reader's Digest* are reported in Chapter 20.

HIRING IN RADIO.   In 1972, Barbara Patterson of WFCR-FM, Amherst, Massachusetts, and Elaine Prostak of WBFO-

FM, Buffalo, New York, surveyed public radio stations. Their findings showed that women employed full time in 103 public radio stations were 14 percent of management and 16 percent of on-the-air performers. Among part-time workers, women were 2 percent of management and again 16 percent of on-the-air performers.[26]

In 1974, the Corporation for Public Broadcasting conducted a survey of the employment of women and minorities in CPB-qualified public radio stations. As reported to the Communications Subcommittee of the House Interstate and Foreign Commerce Committee, the data showed that women, although 11 percent of upper management in 1972, were only 9 percent in 1974. However, women gained ground in professional and technical positions between 1972, when they were 20 percent, and 1974, when they were 26 percent. The numbers of women in management are disheartening, since 80 percent of the stations have affirmative action plans and more than 70 percent of the stations are licensed to universities and hence are subject to their affirmative action policies.[27]

Caroline Isber and Muriel Cantor found the following percentages of women employed in managerial positions in CPB radio stations for 1974.

- Four percent of the general managers.
- Twelve percent of the station managers.
- Nineteen percent of the operations managers.
- Seventeen percent of the program managers.
- Five percent of the production managers.
- Eighty-two percent of the business managers.
- None of the chief engineers.

Women occupying these positions represent 12 percent of all managers, whereas they are 26 percent of all radio station employees. In public radio's leadership organization, National Public Radio, women are 25 percent of the directors.[28]

HIRING IN MAGAZINES. Lucy Komisar (1970) found that women were 25 percent of the managers of magazines in New York City and 55 percent of the professionals. Komisar's figures for *Life* magazine illustrate the general pattern.

> The 6 top editors are men, 10 Assistant Managing Editors are men, 1 is a woman—the Chief of Research; 12 Senior Editors are men, 2 are women; 8 staff writers are men, 2 are women; 31 photographers are men, 1 is a woman; 9 in the photographic department are women; 15 Associate Editors are men, 1 is a woman; 8 Assistant Editors (researchers) are men, 15 are women; 5 reporters (researchers) are men, 23 are women; 2 copy readers are men, 9 are women; 15 layout staff are men, 1 is a woman; 12 bureau desk staff are men, 9 are women; and all 36 correspondents of the Time-Life News Service are men.

In these positions at Life, women were 31 percent of the staff.[29]

Rooms With No View has chapters discussing 18 well-known magazines. Employment figures, based primarily on the magazines' own disclosure of positions, are given for the following seven magazines.[30]

- Seventeen percent of the editors at *Family Circle* are women.
- Sixty percent of the editors at *Good Housekeeping* are women.
- Twenty-five percent of the top editors at *Ladies' Home Journal* are women.
- Twelve percent of the editors at *The New Yorker* are women.
- None of the editors at *Newsweek* are women.
- Four percent of the editors at *Reader's Digest* are women.
- Seventy percent of the editors at *Redbook* are women.

Descriptions of employment at these magazines make it clear that number counting is not enough. For example, the senior editorships at *Redbook* are held by men, even though women are 70 percent of the editors.

Sarah Seaver, in a study of magazine editors for the Women's Institute for Freedom of the Press, checked the names of editors in the 1973 edition of *The Working Press of the Nation.* She found "that 11 percent are women, while 74 percent have men's first names, 13 percent give initials in lieu of a first name, and 2 percent have names used for both sexes. . . ." Women were most likely to edit technical magazines that have small circulations. Men edit the well-known women's and news magazines. Only 1 of the 25 listed news magazines was edited by a woman.[31]

Most employment figures for individual magazines have been compiled for EEOC complaints. Media women filed a complaint with the EEOC against *Newsweek* magazine in 1970. The complaint reported the following numbers of women on the editoral staff: "One woman writer out of 52; 12 women reporters out of 76; one male researcher out of 35."[32] Five months later the complaint was withdrawn and a "Memorandum of Understanding" was signed. Although nonspecific, the agreement indicated *Newsweek's* intention to be less discriminatory in hiring and promotions.[33]

A second complaint was filed with the EEOC in 1972, when women at *Newsweek* felt that no real changes had taken place since the signing of the agreement. As a result of this action, management met with the women and formulated a set of goals and a timetable. By 1973, the second complaint was withdrawn and another "Memorandum of Understanding" was signed. During the interim:

> The number of women writers at *Newsweek* then began to increase, rising from 1 to 13, and *Newsweek* hired its first woman columnist. A woman has now been appointed chief of a domestic bureau, and the number of women domestic and foreign bureau correspondents has risen from 8 to 11.

> In addition, 8 men have been integrated into the research staff, which with one exception had been an all-female category.[34]

The second agreement specified that by the end of 1974, 33 percent of the writers would be women, no major editorial department would be without a woman writer for more than 6 consecutive months, and at least one of the seven major editorial divisions be headed by a woman by the end of 1975.[35]

In 1977, four studies were conducted at Stanford University to examine the pattern of women and men on the editorial staffs of various magazines. Issues were sampled from every 5-year period from 1945 to 1975. Each provided a final update by gathering data from 1977. Only their 1977 data are included here. Elaine Levin studied all editorial positions (including editors, associate editors, department editors, and assistant editors) for *Business Week, Changing Times, Fortune, Journal of Finance,* and *Nation's Business.* She found, on the average, that 83 percent of the editors were men and 17 percent were women. *Fortune* had the largest percentage of women (39 percent) and the *Journal of Finance* had the smallest percentage (4 percent).[36]

Julie Flores examined the top editorial positions (no category lower than associate editor) for the three major news magazines, *Time, Newsweek,* and *U.S. News and World Report.* On the average, 84 percent of these positions were occupied by men and 16 percent by women.[37]

John Durham studied four analytic magazines, *Harper's, Atlantic Monthly, Saturday Review,* and *Scientific American.* He found that 61 percent of all staff listed on the mastheads were men. Looking just at the top positions, he found that 82 percent were occupied by men. Since there were fewer women than men, Durham notes that 8 percent of the women versus 22 percent of the men were in top positions.[38]

Cynthia Ellwood did a comparative study across four types of magazines, women's, popular, news, and business. Included in her analysis were executive and managing editors, their assistants, and editorial heads of departments. For women's magazines, Ellwood examined the mastheads of *Ladies'*

Home Journal, McCall's, and *Good Housekeeping.* She found, on the average, that 33 percent of the positions were occupied by men. Although *Ladies' Home Journal* and *McCall's* were similar in the percentage of men (13 percent and 25 percent, respectively), *Good Housekeeping* had considerably more men in these top positions (62 percent). Ellwood's analysis of popular magazines originally included *Life, Look,* and *Reader's Digest.* However, for the 1977 period, only *Reader's Digest* was still publishing. She found that 76 percent of its editorial positions were occupied by men. For newsmagazines, she included *Newsweek, Time,* and *U.S. News and World Report.* Men held 88 percent of the editorial positions. For a sample of business magazines, she studied *Fortune, Business Week,* and *Nation's Business.* On the average, 93 percent of the editorial positions were filled by men. Across all four types of magazines, including the women's magazines where there are larger number of women, Ellwood found that 73 percent of the major editorships went to men.[39]

HIRING IN NEWSPAPERS.   Lucy Komisar reported findings from the EEOC's 1968 investigation of newspapers and women in New York City. Women at that time were 5 percent of the officials and managers and 10 percent of the professional staffs of major New York City newspapers. Komisar took a 1970 look and found:

> The *New York Post* has a dozen women among 55 reporters, no women among 17 on rewrite, one woman among 14 on the copy desk and only men as Executive Editor, Managing Editors, City Editors, Assistant City Editors. There are 4 men and one woman in the Financial News Dept., 7 men and 7 women in the Features Department (that includes 5 women in women's news and one female editorial assistant) and there are 10 male photographers.
>
> The *Daily News* has a total of about 400 editorial employees, including reporters, editors and photographers. There are 35 women reporters, but all but 9 are in women's news. Of the nine, one is a feature writer and two are new trainees. There are three women editors: women's news, society and television.

And one woman photographer out of 50.

The *New York Times* has a total of 485 editors, reporters, foreign correspondents and copy editors. Of these, 53 are women and 432 are men. (Even the society editor is a man!) One of the foreign correspondents is a woman.[40]

By 1972 women were 10 percent of the editors, reporters, copyreaders, and desk people at the *New York Times,* 18 percent at the *Washington Post,* 24 percent at the *San Francisco Chronicle,* and 12 percent at the *Los Angeles Times.*[41]

The Northern Virginia chapter of NOW monitored nine Washington, D.C. area newspapers in 1972 and again in 1973, finding that:

On both metropolitan newspapers (*Washington Post* and *The Evening Star/News*) all top editorial positions were filled by men. Males edited Style and Portfolio. Nearly all editorial writers and editorial columnists were men.

Out of a total of 222 *Star News* employees classified as editorial (including copy persons and dictationists), 65 were female. Three women were employed as news editors, but all were assistant editors working under men.

Suburban newspapers tended to have more female employees.[42]

During the 1970s, individual women have made breakthroughs in the newspaper business. Carol Sutton was the first woman to be managing editor of a major U.S. newspaper, the *Louisville Courier-Journal.* Christy Bulkeley was the first woman to be in complete control of a Gannett Group (54 dailies) newspaper, the *Saratoga Springs Saratogian.* In 1976, she became the publisher of the larger-circulation *Commercial-News* in Danville, Illinois. Women have forced newspapers to establish equitable hiring programs. Lawsuits helping to bring about these changes were filed against newspapers such as the *Washington Post, Newsday, New York Times, Sacramento Bee, New Haven Register,* and *St. Louis Post Dispatch.*

In the *Washington Post* case, employment figures were compiled by women of the *Post* in 1972. They reported:

> The 10 managing editors at the *Washington Post* are all men. The 9 news desk editors are all men. The 9 more desk editors in finance and other special sections of the paper are all men. Of the metropolitan, national, and foreign desk editors, there are 3 women and 50 men. Of critics in the Style section, which includes what was once the women's section, 7 are men and 1, who is part-time, a woman. Of the metropolitan reporting staff there are 8 women and 43 men.
>
> Two years ago the percentage of women at the *Post* was 15 percent. Today it is 13.6 percent, compared to 39.8 percent women in the nation's professional and technical work force.
>
> Yet 44 percent of the graduates from journalism schools are women, and 40 percent of the applicants for jobs at the *Post* are women.[43]

In June 1974, the EEOC made a determination in this case. The following data were reported by the EEOC for June 1972 to May 1973.

- None of the editorial writers and cartoonists were women.
- Seven percent of the editors, bureau chiefs, and art directors were women.
- Eleven percent of the artists/photographers were women.
- Eighteen percent of the assistant editors and directors were women.
- Nineteen percent of the reporters, columnists, and critics were women.

The *Post* provided EEOC with the following list of employees holding management level positions.

- None of the production management were women.
- Seventeen percent of general management were women.
- Twelve percent of news and editorial management were women.
- Nineteen percent of commercial management were women.

The EEOC Determination stated:

> Thus, the evidence on managerial employees indicates that females occupy 13 percent of the managerial positions, but 6 of the female managers (24 percent of the total female managers) supervise an overwhelmingly female unit. In addition, there are no females in production management. In the commercial departments where females constitute 41 percent of the total employees, they constitute only 19 percent of the managers. Based on the statistical evidence and in the absence of any legitimate explanation for the small proportion of females in managerial positions it is reasonable to infer that Respondent restricts females as a class from managerial positions because of their sex in violation of Title VII.[44]

In December 1973, 40 women reporters and editors at *Newsday* filed charges of discrimination with the EEOC. Employment statistics were released by *Newsday* as an appendix to their proposed affirmative action plan. *Newsday* wrote:

> On January 1, 1969, there were 140 reporters, writers, and editors on the news staff. Of this number, 28 (20 percent) were women. . . . On January 1, 1974, there were 183 reporters, writers and editors on the news staff, of whom 39 (21.3 percent) were women.
>
> On January 1, 1969, there were 15 managers in the editorial department. All were male. By January 1, 1972, the number of managers had reached 22, and all but one were male. On January 1, 1974, there were 27 managers in the editorial department, and two of them were women.
>
> There has never been a woman reporter in the sports department at *Newsday*. . . . There is currently one woman photographer among the 31 staff members in the photography department (3.2 percent). . . . the art staff on January 1, 1974, consists of 18 men and 1 woman.[45]

Finding it impossible to make progress in negotiations with *Newsday*, four women filed suit in 1974 in the U.S. District Court for the Eastern District of New York. The brief stated:

> *Newsday* has limited most of its top-level influential and supervisory job titles solely to men, including those of Publisher, Editor, Managing Editor, Associate Editor, Bureau Chief, Critic, Columnist, and Foreman.
>
> *Newsday* virtually has limited to men its officerships and top-ranking positions appearing on the *Newsday* masthead. . . . Not until January 1974 did *Newsday* promote a woman to the position of Viewpoints Editor, now the only position of the 33 appearing on the masthead held by a woman, and the only Senior Editorship held by a woman.
>
> *Newsday's* middle-management positions are held by men, with a few women in token positions. As an example, of the 21 *Newsday* employees holding the title of Manager, only three are women and these three are "office" managers with mainly clerical duties.
>
> *Newsday* employs no women in most of its important, prestigious, highly visible and highly paid jobs in the Editorial Department. For example, as of September, 1974, *Newsday* employed no female Managing Editors, no female day or night City Editors in Nassau or Suffolk, no female Bureau Chiefs, no female Special Writers or Reporters on the National Desk, and no female Photography or Sports Editors.[46]

In early 1975, *Newsday* released the reports of its first year of affirmative action in employment. The goals show it will take the newspaper 14 years to provide equal opportunities for women. As of January 1975, men were 89 percent of the managers, 80 percent of the news staff, 100 percent of the sports staff, 93 percent of the photography staff, and 91 percent of the arts staff.[47]

More recently, the EEOC has issued its Determination of *Newsday's* practices and has found it discriminatory in job classification, promotion, and in the hiring in noneditorial positions. Findings were based on data from the third year of the newspaper's affirmative action plan. For instance, EEOC noted that in the Editorial Department "the higher titles and positions . . . are filled by males." Of the 76 reporters, 71 percent are males. In the Circulation Department, 92 percent are males. In the Administration Department, "The record shows that there are 35 persons on the Executive Payrolls; they are all males."[48]

In November 1974, six women sued the *New York Times.* Approximately 1 year later, the U.S. District Court ordered that the *Times* release salary information from its computer tapes. In February 1977, the suit was granted a class action status. One year later, analysis of the computer tapes was submitted to the Federal District Court. Although most findings focus on salaries, the report notes that women are 41 percent of the editors and reporters in the United States. However, they are only 16 percent of the editors and reporters at the *Times.* [49]

In examining the directing editors of newspapers with a daily circulation of at least 40,000, Dorothy Jurney found that 97 percent were male.[50]

The wire services provide employment for large numbers of journalists. How do women fare at Associated Press and United Press International? The story is mixed and probably changing faster than it can be captured. Lucy Komisar's 1970 figures show:

> At the Associated Press, with a total of 3,300 employees around the world, there are no women in management positions and no women heading any of the 38 domestic or 60 foreign bureaus. . . . In New York City, there are 7 women out of 52 editors and reporters.
>
> United Press International is more of the same. At the national headquarters in New York, there are 10 executive officers, all men. There are 25 domestic news editors that are men; one is a woman (you're right: women's news). There are 5 men in the International News Department, one in International Features, 12 managers and editors of the Newspictures Department, the category of auditor, labor relations and communications.
>
> UPI has a television news department in New York City. There are 5 male executives and managers, 9 male cameramen, soundmen, electricians; 2 male reporters and one woman; 7 male desk editors, 2 male film editors and one woman; 5 male librarians. . . . There are 8 clerks, secretaries, production assistants—feminine gender.[51]

Two years later, *Time* reported that women are 11 percent of Associated Press's nationwide news staff of 1050 and that women are 9 percent of United Press International's news staff of 900.[52]

Another picture of the wire services is presented by two women in *Rooms With No View*. A status report on the Associated Press indicates that a few additional women have been employed. By 1973 the sports department had 1 woman writer and the general desk had 4 female desk staff out of 24. In the New York Bureau, women are one-third of the reporters. In spite of this progress, the author of the AP status report believes that much of the ground gained by women in New York had been abandoned by males who no longer want a New York assignment where life is expensive and dangerous. For the same pay, a position in Denver or Phoenix is considered more desirable.[53]

The author who describes United Press International makes many positive statements. For example UPI changed its slogan of "A UPI man is at the scene" to "UPI is at the scene" in an effort to be nonsexist. Women are 15 percent of the news staff. Women hold some supervisory positions. In 1973, seven small bureaus were headed by women. A woman runs the business desk at the world headquarters. Women hold positions such as women's news editor, family news editor, assistant news features editor, and national radio news editor. Women on the UPI staff abroad have reported from Viet Nam, France, China, England, and other countries. Women at UPI report from many national locations, including statehouses, the White House, and the Supreme Court. However, few women are found in supervisory and executive positions.[54]

In 1973, the Wire Service Guild charged the Associated Press (AP) with discrimination against its female and minority members. When the EEOC had prepared their initial findings, AP asked that nothing be released until the conclusion of its negotiations with the union. Negotiations took place between February and June 1977. An unsatisfactory outcome caused the

EEOC to begin a second investigation in August 1977. In May 1978, the EEOC found that AP did discriminate by not recruiting, hiring, and promoting women. In addition, AP did not hire minorities as newspeople. EEOC data for the end of 1977 shows that males are 100 percent of the assistant bureau chiefs, 98 percent of the bureau chiefs, 97 percent of the correspondents, 90 percent of the news editors, and 85 percent of the news people.[55]

Although there are no overall hiring statistics available for Reuters News Agency, there is a recent settlement between Marsha Dubrow and Reuters. In February 1978, with the assistance of the New York Division of Human Rights, the two parties agreed that Dubrow would receive $6000 in back pay and would be promoted to the job category of reporter/editor retroactive to January 1, 1976.[56]

HIRING IN FILM.   Motion pictures are the most male dominated of the media. June 1974 membership figures for the Motion Picture Academy of Arts and Sciences show that men are:

- Eighty-nine percent of the actors/actresses.
- One hundred percent of the cinematographers.
- Ninety-nine percent of the directors.
- Ninety-eight percent of the executives.
- Ninety-nine percent of the producers.
- Ninety-two percent of the writers.
- Eighty-nine percent of the editors.
- Ninety percent of the art directors.
- Ninety-four percent of all members.[57]

Women are far less than 1 percent of the members of the Producers' Guild (8 out of 3068). They are 1 percent of the members of the Directors' Guild (23 out of 2366) and 5 percent of the members of the Writers' Guild (148 out of 2976).[58]

In 1975 some film companies were prodded to review their record on the employment of women. Columbia Pictures Industries agreed to compile statistics on women and minorities provided that Barbara Brusco, a stockholder, would withdraw her resolution prepared for the Annual Stockholders Meeting. At the same time a proxy for Barbara Brusco presented a resolution at the Annual Stockholders Meeting of Paramount Pictures Corporation. The resolution, which called on Paramount officials to provide information on the employment of women and minorities, to end discrimination against women, and to present women more positively, was defeated.

The absence of women in the motion picture industry is the focus of a class action discrimination suit filed with the EEOC by the San Fernando Valley chapter of NOW against Universal City Studios and affiliates, International Alliance of Theatrical Stage Employees and Motion Picture Machine Operators. The suit contends that Universal City Studios, as the largest motion picture studio complex, has a record of underemployment of women and minorities. IATSE and locals were included in the suit, because many of the locals exclude women and others admit only token numbers. Inability to join a union effectively bars women from working in many film occupations.[59]

The Association of Cinematograph and Television Technicians in England has reported on the extent of discrimination against women in film and television production and in the film laboratories. In the film production branch, women are 12 percent of the members, while 20 years ago they were 17 percent of the members. In 20 out of more than 60 grades, there are no women; only two grades have no men.

> The apparent distribution of women through the 40 remaining grades is misleading, for women have not made serious inroads into the male preserves. About a third of the women are continuity girls or production secretaries/assistants; another third are editors and assistant editors; and the remaining third scattered mainly in the pre-production grades (e.g., casting director) or post-production (e.g., negative cutting). Just as there are hardly any women involved specifically in processing film in labs, so there are hardly any involved in actually producing or shooting the film. . . . There has only been a handful of women sound

recordists and assistant cameramen. There are none in lighting. ... [t]he proportion of women directors, producers and producer/directors is about 6 percent.... The proportion of women editors is under 10 percent, though the proportion of women assistant editors is about 18 percent.[60]

HIRING IN PUBLISHING COMPANIES.   Lucy Komisar's data on women in book publishing companies show:

> Women are 18 percent of the officials and managers in book publishing and 42 percent of the professionals. This includes the women who work in children's books and text books where many are concentrated. And women who are copy editors. The prestigious editorial jobs are held by men.[61]

Although complete data were not available, the Women's National Book Association estimated in 1971 that women were 60 percent of the work force in the book industry. Their membership study reports on several aspects of sex discrimination in the industry and will be discussed later in this chapter.[62]

Information compiled by the Media Women's Association indicates that the publishing companies are changing. Women are visible from clerical levels through middle management. Women are rarely found in upper-management positions. However, many of the small companies tolerate, even if they do not actively encourage, women wanting to advance. Some of the individual reports show:[63]

- Forty-four percent of the editors at Doubleday are women.
- Thirty-eight percent of the top eight editors at Bantam Books are women, but only 9 percent of the vice presidents are women.
- Fifty-two percent of the decision-making positions at Farrar, Straus and Giroux are filled by women, although only three women are in editorial positions.

HIRING IN PUBLIC RELATIONS.   Although not a medium *per se,* public relations is a related field of employment for women. Sondra K. Gorney has reviewed recent progress of women in that field. After citing examples of individual women who have been promoted to management positions or have opened their own firms, she discusses the results of a telephone survey of leading public relations agencies. She reports slow but promising progress.

> For instance, in 1970, the largest of the agencies, Hill and Knowlton, had a total of 114 professionals, of whom only 19 were women. Today, they have 125 professionals, 29 of them women. . . .
>
> The next largest firm, Burson-Marsteller, reported that 20 percent of their executives nationally are now female. One is an executive vice president, and four are vice presidents.
>
> In 1971, Harshe-Rotman & Druck had five women holding the title of vice president or better out of a total of 15 such titles. Today they have six women vice presidents out of a total of 20; two of them senior VPs and one the director of the Houston Office. . . .
>
> The best record may possibly be Ruder and Finn's. In 1971, they had eight women with the title of VP or better out of a total of 27 such titles. Their last report indicated they now have 23 women VPs as against 14 men VPs working for Ruder and Finn Incorporated. Two of the women are senior VPs, as are ten of the men.[64]

SALARIES

The principle of equal pay for equal work was established during World War I, when large numbers of women entered "male" occupations for the first time. The National War Labor Board enforced a policy of "no wage discrimination against women on the grounds of sex." In those early years of women in the work force, two states, Michigan and Montana, passed equal pay laws. Ten additional states passed equal pay laws during World War II, when women came back to the work force. In 1963, the federal Equal Pay Act amended the Fair Labor Standards Act to prohibit salary discrimination on the basis of sex. By the mid-1970s only five states had neither an equal pay law nor a fair employment practices law to cover sex discrimination in private employment.

Unions have played an important role in asserting the principle that a woman and a man holding the same position with the same responsibilities will earn the same salary. For example, contracts negotiated by the Newspaper Guild provide equal salaries for female and male editorial and business office employees of newspapers and newsmagazines. Unions playing this role include:

> Associated Actors and Artists of America (membership of 63,000). (Actors' Equity Association, American Federation of Television and Radio Artists, American Guild of Musical Artists, Screen Actors' Union, Screen Extras' Guild).
>
> National Association of Broadcast Employees and Technicians (8900).
>
> The Newspaper Guild (32,535).
>
> Writers' Guild of America (4300).[65]

However, in spite of equal pay laws and union contracts, many of the salary studies show a lack of equality. Men consistently earn more than women.

Why the difference? First, there is the attitude of management that women need less money than men, since married women are "bringing in a second income for the family" and single women "do not have a family to support." Women are placed at a disadvantage both by management's attitude and by their own training not to be "pushy" in demanding fair pay.

Second, unions and management set lower salary scales for jobs held by women. Reporters for the "women's page" have a lower salary than reporters in general. Since women are traditionally assigned to the women's page, their salary has been lower. However, if a man were assigned to the women's page, union scale would dictate the same minimum salary as a woman. Some of these discriminatory practices are changing, particularly in newspapers. However, there continue to be unions that discriminate against women by turning away women members and by undervaluing "woman's work."

Proposition 12.2: Men in Media Have Higher Salaries than Women.

Salary information is more difficult to obtain than employment information. However, from the data that have been released for various years, it is clear that women receive less pay than men. For example, women employees in public television in the United States earn less than $8000; men earn more than $11,000.[66] Comparable figures for commercial television are not available, but we suspect the situation for women may be worse there. Public television has a better record for hiring women that may also extend to salary scales. Salary levels of women and men in public radio are almost identical to those in public television. In newspapers, there continues to be pay inequality, although the unions are beginning to reduce the differentials. Since 1974 the Newspaper Guild has sought to establish parity for women and men, but it is a slow process. A 1976 study of Capitol Hill correspondents indicated that, on the average, women receive less than $16,000 and men receive more than $23,000.[67] A 1977 study of women's page/life-style editors concludes that the difference in salaries (49 percent of the males earn more than $20,000 versus 23 percent of the females) persists even after possible differences in education, college major, experience, number of subordinates, and size of newspaper have been taken into consideration.[68] In 1978, the Federal District Court heard testimony that the *New York Times* pays males more than $3700 more than women. This difference is attributable to sex discrimination.[69] We have little information on salaries in the magazine industry. Although *Rooms With No View* relates several anecdotes about inequality in pay, it does not provide statistical data.

SALARIES IN TELEVISION. The most extensive documentation of salaries in television comes from American public television and from the Canadian Broadcasting Corporation. One study of salaries for public television in the United States in 1972 showed that female managers earned about $12,000 and male managers earned about $21,000; female engineers earned about $7500 and male engineers earned about $10,500; female directors earned about $10,000 and male directors earned about $11,500; and female on-the-air/performing talent earned about $10,500 and male on-the-air/performing talent earned about $12,000. In 19 out of 23 specified positions, men outearn women. Only for the positions of producer/director, production crew, film director, and manual/custodial is the average salary for a woman higher than the average salary for a man. In addition to being more frequent, salary discrepancies favoring men are also greater than those favoring women. The greatest discrepancy favoring a woman is $3891 for a film director; the greatest discrepancy favoring a man is $7290 for a business manager. When all positions are included, we find that women have an average salary of $7690 and men have an average salary of $10,970.[70]

Caroline Isber and Muriel Cantor reported salary information for full-time employees of public-broadcasting television and joint (television and radio) stations who responded to their mail survey. On the average, women received $8736 in television stations and $10,271 in joint-facility stations; men received $11,916 in television stations and $13,777 in joint facility stations.[71]

Of the 607 public television employees who provided salary figures to Isber and Cantor, 81 percent of the women versus 49 percent of the men earn less than $11,000. Of the 560 employees in joint facilities, 82 percent of the women versus only 37 percent of the men earn less than $11,000 The differences at the top of the scale are just as striking. In public-television stations, 1 percent of the women versus 5 percent of the men earn more than $21,000 annually. In joint facilities, the picture is worse. Only 1 percent of the women versus 11 percent of the men earn more than $21,000.[72]

The report of the CBC Task Force on the Status of Women also documents the different salaries of women and men. The average 1974 CBC salary was $10,100 for women and $13,800 for men. The most telling analysis shows the work histories and salaries of 86 women and men who have worked 30 years or longer for CBC. These careers all started at the bottom, "as a clerk 1 or 2, steno, receptionist, switchboard operator, or office boy." All specialist positions were excluded. The entry requirements for the "women's jobs" were higher than those for the "men's jobs." Women had to have completed high school and have stenographic skills; men often had to have completed only the tenth grade. At first, the difference in requirements paid off for the women. Their average yearly salary was $893, and the men had an average yearly salary of $630. But, in the long run, it paid to be a man. The 34 women in this analysis, with an average seniority of 32.3 years, had increased their salary 15 times over to an average of $13,476. The 52 men with an average seniority of 33.7 years, had increased their salary 30 times to an average of $19,214.[73]

SALARIES IN RADIO.   Radio continues to be an underdocumented medium. There are few studies of radio content and few studies of radio networks or stations as business institutions. Isber and Cantor do report on public radio. They find that, of the full-time employees in public radio who responded to their survey, 45 percent of the women versus 14 percent of the men earned less than $7000. Looking at the upper salary ranges, they find that none of the women versus 8 percent of the men earned more than $17,000. Averaging all salary categories, women earned $7898 and men earned $11,147.[74]

SALARIES IN NEWSPAPERS.   Reports of salaries for newspaper workers come from several sources. As early as 1973, it was stated that the "wage differential between men and women is greater now than it was in 1955 when women earned 63.9

percent of what men were paid. That figure is now 59.4 percent."[75] By 1974, several complaints were filed not only with the EEOC regarding hiring and advancement, but also with the U.S. Department of Labor's Wage and Hour Division regarding pay discrimination. Three of the complaints filed by the Newspaper Guild were against *Foster's Daily Democrat* in Dover, New Hampshire, the *Portland Press Herald* in Portland, Maine, and *Express and Telegram,* also in Portland, on the following grounds.

> The Dover, N.H. complaint accuses the newspaper of paying its society and wire editors, both women, less than it pays reporters. The women's top minimum is $139, compared to $144 for reporters, $157 for news and sports editors and $163 for political, state, and editorial-page editors, all of them men.
>
> In the case of the Portland, Me., papers, the company had refused to eliminate long-standing wage discrimination against the women's page editor and writers, society reporters and cleaning women. The top minimum for women's page editor is $206.25, $234 for reporters. The top for women's page writers is $201.50 and for society reporters $173.75. The top for cleaning women is $141.50, but janitors are paid $162.25.[76]

Marjorie Hunter of the *New York Times* Washington Bureau described the following situation.

> A sex discrimination suit was filed by the women at the *New York Times* about a year ago seeking an affirmative action program. . . .
>
> But one of the appalling discoveries was that there was a $59 a week differential between men and women in what we call Group O—a classification that includes reporters, desk heads, critics and various top level positions. Men were making an average of $59 a week more than women doing the same jobs. After some adjustments, and I was one of the beneficiaries, the differential remains at $54![77]

Hunter also discussed how salary differentials relate to pension differentials at retirement. According to pension fund data, the *Times* has 1048 males who are over 34 years old and have been employed there at least 5 years. Their average salary is $18,761. In the same age and length of service category there are 288 females with an average salary of $14,079. This difference of $4682 each year affects the amount of accrued pension credit.[78]

As noted earlier in this chapter, salary information has been analyzed for the *New York Times* and was submitted to the Federal District Court on February 17, 1978. After examining salary differences that could be attributed to education, amount of experience at the *Times,* amount of job relevant experience, and particular division at the *Times,* there was still an average difference of $3735. In examining just editors/-reporters, it was noted that women earned approximately $4000 less per year than men. Mark Killingsworth, professor of economics at Barnard College states ". . . The amount by which women were paid less than men with the same background—the effect of sex on salary—did not change between the end of 1973 and the end of 1976."[79]

In a separate analysis of the same data, John M. Abowd, lecturer in econometrics at Princeton University, examined the salaries of those who are paid more than the Guild minimum. He found that men earned $5200 more than women with the same characteristics.[80] These analyses indicate that women receive less salary partly because they are hired into lower-paid departments and partly because they receive less of the salary premium that is offered above the Guild required minimum.

The Newspaper Guild represented female employees at the *Washington Post* in their complaint against the paper. Information concerning salaries shows that for those earning $400 a week or more there were:

- None of the women and 74 percent of the men in the position of editor, bureau chief, and art director.
- None of the women and 42 percent of the men in the positions of artist/photographer.
- Sixty-nine percent of the women and 80 percent of the men in the positions of assistant editor, director.

• Thirty-three percent of the women and 60 percent of the men in the positions of reporter, columnist, and critic.

There were no women in the position of editorial writer or cartoonist, but all of the men in that category earned more than $400 a week. Combining categories, 39 percent of the women versus 67 percent of the men earned $400 or more a week. Citing these figures and others, EEOC determined that the *Washington Post* discriminated against women employees in salaries.[81]

Progress in eliminating one form of inequality in salaries has been made in contracts recently negotiated by the Newspaper Guild. The Guild has announced its intention to eliminate salary differences between women's news reporters/editors and other reporters/editors. On February 1, 1974, there were 23 Guild newspapers with pay differentials ranging from $80 per week lower for women to $4 per week lower. On the average, women received $45 less per week than men; this is about $2300 a year.[82]

In 1974, the International Executive Board of the Newspaper Guild sent a policy statement to all locals informing them that they could sign a contract that perpetuates pay differentials only if the employer is notified that legal procedings against salary discrimination will be initiated upon signing. The following progress was reported in *The Guild Reporter.*

> Parity was achieved in 13 contracts in the most recent round of bargaining and in six the previous round, for a total of 19. Prior to that, lower minimums were eliminated in only eight contracts during the past 12 years.[83]

As of January 1976, the Newspaper Guild's efforts affected dailies in 123 cities and weeklies in 9 cities, 10 wire and news services, 22 magazines, 7 radio and television stations, 14 labor newspapers and services, and 20 other publications. The Guild sets an important standard of reference for the print media.

Won Chang conducted a national survey of women's page editors. Chang sent mail questionnaires to a random sample of

936 women's page editors and received 335 back. Of these, 305 were women and 30 were men. Salary data show that 45 percent of the women versus 3 percent of the men earned $7000 or less. Five percent of the women versus 50 percent of the men earned $17,000 or more.[84]

Recognizing that a variety of factors influence salaries, Chang asked about amount of education and number of years in journalism. Within each education level, men's salaries were still significantly greater than women's salaries. Among those with 6 to 15 years of professional journalism experience and those with more than 21 years of experience, men's salaries were significantly greater than women's. Men who have worked 1 to 5 years and 16 to 20 years in journalism earned more than women working that long, but the difference is not statistically significant.[85]

Because Chang's study had a low response rate and did not control for circulation size of newspaper, Sharyne Merritt and Harriet Gross again studied women's page/life-style editors of daily newspapers. They had responses from 71 percent (171) of those in the over 50,000 circulation group and 58 percent (267) of those in the under 50,000 circulation group. In examining salaries, Merritt and Gross provide data only for the higher-circulation metropolitan papers. They found:[86]

Salary level	Percent women	Percent men
Less than $15,000	38 (49)	13 (4)
$15,000 to $24,999	59 (75)	60 (18)
$25,000 to $49,999	4 (5)	26 (8)

Kathleen Endres interviewed 43 female and 42 male Capitol Hill correspondents. Along with other information, she compiled data on the salaries of these congressionally accredited reporters. She found that the women had a median income of $16,110 compared with $23,530 for the men. On the average, a woman was earning 58 percent of a man's salary. These data compare with 1970 census data on median pay for women reporters/editors of $5530 and for men reporters/editors of $10,620. In 1970, women were earning 52 percent of a man's salary. Endres notes that, according to a 1928 nationwide survey of correspondents, women earned an average of $29.50 a week versus $39.50 a week for men. In 1928, women were earning 75 percent of a man's salary.[87]

SALARIES IN BOOK PUBLISHING.   Comparative data on the salaries of women and men in publishing are not available. However, the following information on median salaries of women was compiled as part of a survey conducted by the Women's National Book Association in 1971.

- $12,901 for management.
- $11,001 for school and library promoting.
- $10,001 for advertising.
- $9271 for editorial.
- $8706 for production and design.
- $8376 for administrative assistant.
- $8358 for publicity and promotion.
- $7500 for rights and permissions.
- $7189 for sales.
- $4985 for secretarial.

Across all positions and publishing houses, 33 percent of the women received less than $7500, another 33 percent earned between $7500 and $10,000, 14 percent earned between $10,000 and $12,000, 10 percent earned between $12,000 and $15,000, 6 percent earned between $15,000 and $18,000, and 4 percent earned over $18,000. On the average, women in the book industry received just less than $10,000 in 1971.[88] Although more recent data are not available, these figures provide a baseline for future studies.

PROMOTION

Even without data for all the media, we find a clear pattern of approximately equal percentages of women and men seeking promotions, but greater percentages of men receiving them. The same pattern holds for those who do not seek promotions —a greater percentage of men than women receive them.

Proposition 12.3: Men in Media Are More Likely than Women to Receive Promotions.

PROMOTION IN TELEVISION.   Caroline Isber and Muriel Cantor inquired about employee advancement in their mail questionnaire. For example, they wanted to know if a promotion had ever been requested, if a promotion had ever been received, if a promotion had ever been refused, and if place of employment had ever been changed to bring about a promotion. They also asked two questions to determine the ambition of each respondent: what position would the person like to hold in 5 years and what position did the person think she or he would hold in 5 years.[89]

The Isber and Cantor data show that men in public-television stations are slightly more likely than women to request a promotion. That is, 29 percent of the women and 34 percent of the men had requested a promotion. The major difference is the number of times that men versus women were successful in seeking advancement. Of those requesting promotions, 78 percent of the men versus 54 percent of the women received them.[90]

For joint television radio facilities, the pattern is somewhat different. Women were slightly more likely to request a promotion (35 percent) than were men (31 percent). However, of those requesting a promotion, the men were still more likely to receive them (81 percent versus 73 percent).[91]

What of those not requesting a promotion? Again we find that more men in television (49 percent) and in joint facilities (49 percent) than women in television (32 percent) and in joint facilities (41 percent) received a promotion.[92]

In spite of their limited advancement in public television, women do seek to be promoted. Isber and Cantor wrote:

> Of all the women respondents now in lower levels, 63 percent said they wanted to be promoted to higher positions within five years; 53 percent expressed a desire to rise to middle-level jobs; and 10 percent aspire to top managerial positions within five years.[93]

They pointed out that women wanting to advance within their present levels or wanting to advance after 5 years are not included in these figures.

The CBC Task Force on the Status of Women report discussed number and quality of promotions. It was found that women, who are 25 percent of the total staff, received 27 percent of the promotions and 35 percent of the transfers. However, these women had access to only 24 percent of all jobs while men had access to 92 percent of all jobs. This means that women primarily advance within their own job levels and only infrequently are promoted to more visible and responsible positions.[94]

Relative to total promotions for each sex, men are three times more likely than women to be promoted to manager/specialist, producer, announcer, or news staff.[95]

PROMOTION IN RADIO. The available data on public radio (Isber and Cantor) show that 30 percent of the men and 46 percent of the women have requested a promotion. Of these, 80 percent of the men versus 69 percent of the women have received a promotion. Of those employees not specifically requesting to be promoted, 51 percent of the men versus 35 percent of the women were given a promotion.[96]

PROMOTION IN NEWSPAPERS. As a well-respected newspaper, the *Washington Post* is being watched by other media to see the final outcome of sex-discrimination charges brought against it. The Equal Employment Opportunities Commission stated in its determination of June 19, 1974:

> We therefore conclude that female employees are denied equal promotional opportunities with male employees as part of Respondent's pattern of restricting and limiting females from its higher paying positions.[97]

When the EEOC issued its determination concerning *Newsday,* it reported that in 1975 twice as many males (14) as females (7) were promoted in the Editorial Department. For the first 4 months of 1976, five times as many males (10) as females (2) were promoted in the same department. New titles for males were Sunday news editor, Washington Bureau news editor, night national editor, etc. Both women were given the title of editorial assistant. The EEOC notes that this last title is primarily a clerical position.[98]

When John Abowd analyzed 10 years of salary data from the *New York Times,* he was able to assess the relative promotion patterns of males and females. He found, for instance, that 84 percent of the women versus 70 percent of the men who were in the lower salary groups (1 to 8) in 1965 were still there 10 years later. Among those individuals hired in that 10-year period, 71 percent of the women and 49 percent of the men were still in the lower salary levels in 1974.[99]

It will be important to follow statistical evidence of changing opportunities for women at newspapers. First, we may find more women seeking and obtaining promotions. Later we may find more women entering journalism because they perceive it as a field of opportunity.

ASSIGNMENTS

The term "assignments" makes us think of newspaper and magazine work. Reporters are sent out to cover stories. We wonder whether men are given assignments that make them more visible. Are women sent out just to cover "the women's angle?" Do magazine editors give preferred assignments to men?

When we think of assignments as all utilization of personnel, we note the work of women and men in television and radio. On the news staff, are women less likely to handle general news, international news, etc.? Are women more likely to be shown interviewing a political candidate's wife? In daytime television programming, who are the moderators of quiz and game shows? Who does the voice-overs and who are the product representatives in commercials?

In the case of visible positions, content analysis is a method for determining the status of women employees. Monitoring newspaper/magazine copy and television/radio programs allows us to compare assignments given to women and men. Less-visible positions must be monitored through other data gathering methods (see Chapter 11).

Proposition 12.4: Desirable Assignments *Are Primarily Given to Men.*

Men are in positions of authority in the media and are responsible for making assignments. The studies we review in Part III confirm the high visibility of men in the media. We see men reporting the news on television, although an increasing number of stations have women on the air. Radio lags behind television in utilization of women. Most front-page news stories in newspapers carry male by-lines. Stories reported by women are more frequently placed in the women's/life-style sections.

ASSIGNMENTS IN TELEVISION. In monitoring PBS programs Isber and Cantor found that 91 percent of the adult programs (excluding music and drama) had male narrators/moderators. Of the remaining programs, 4 percent had females and 5 percent had joint male and female narrators/moderators. Primarily, men were assigned to the 27 PBS panels, documentaries, news, interviews, public affairs, and general information programs shown in a typical week.[100]

Television production credits of 26 programs added some information on the utilization of women and men. For example, 100 percent of the directors were men. Of the associate directors, 29 percent were women and 71 percent were men. Of the assistant directors, 40 percent were women and 60 percent were men.[101]

Isber and Cantor provided a third view on utilization of women and men in public television. After categorizing the topics of the 27 information programs, they counted the number of women and men involved in each subject. Women were seen during the discussion of business/economics/law/government (28 percent of all female appearances), education/career planning (16 percent), general information (16 percent), personalities/biographies (14 percent), and art/music/culture (11 percent). Men were seen primarily during the discussion of business/economics/law/government (56 percent of all male appearances), general human interest (13 percent), and environmental sciences (10 percent).[102]

A 1977 report by Vernon Stone documents the changing utilization of women in television news. He sent a mail questionnaire to 415 commercial television stations. Similar information gathered in 1972 allowed Stone to make the comparison that 50 percent of the stations in 1972 versus 86 percent in 1976 reported they had newswomen on the air. Data for 1976 showed:

- Twenty percent of the anchorpersons were women and 20 percent of the other on-the-air reporting was done by women.

- Thirty-five percent of the stations had no anchorwomen, 48 percent had one, 14 percent had two, and 3 percent had three or more, while 3 percent of the stations had no anchormen, 9 percent had one, 25 percent had two and 62 percent had three or more.

Stone also examined the percentage of women and men employed in news who anchor programs and found almost no difference—27 percent of the women and 26 percent of the men were anchors. A higher percentage of women (44 percent) than men (36 percent) were reported to be "other on-the-air" staff.[103]

These data are encouraging but leave us with several questions. Which news shows have anchorwomen—noon news, prime-time news, or late-evening news? In other words, are women more likely than men to be assigned to newscasts with smaller audiences? How much air time is given to these women? What stories do they report?

ASSIGNMENTS IN RADIO. Isber and Cantor presented data for public radio that parallels their study of public television. Thirteen panel, documentary, news, interview, public-affairs, and general information programs were monitored. Eighty percent of the programs had only men as narrators/moderators, 10 percent had only women, and 10 percent had both women and men.[104]

Using the same topics for the 13 radio programs that were used for television programs (see page 000), Isber and Cantor found different utilization of women than men. Women were involved in the discussion of general human interest (37 percent of all female appearances), business/economics/law/government (17 percent), art/music/culture (16 percent), and nonspecific news (13 percent). Men were involved in the discussion of business/economics/law/government (35 percent of all male appearances), art/music/culture (16 percent), general human interest (16 percent), and nonspecific news (16 percent).[105]

Vernon Stone also reported information from a sample of 330 commercial radio stations. He found that although there had been changes between 1972 and 1976, newswomen were on the air in fewer than 50 percent of the stations. In 1972, newswomen were on the air at 15 percent of the stations and, in 1976, they were on the air at 49 percent. Stone reported:

- Fifteen percent of the newscasters were women and 18 percent of on-the-air field reporters were women.
- Sixty-three percent of the stations had no female newscasters, 3 percent had one, and 5 percent had two or more, 8 percent of the stations had no male newscasters, 24 percent had one, and 68 percent had two or more.

Stone found that 55 percent of the women and 82 percent of the men employed in radio news are newscasters. In addition, 51 percent of the women and 62 percent of the men do "other on-the-air reporting." Although radio underutilizes women, "radio is on its way to the point where news staffs without women on the air seem old-fashioned and incomplete."[106]

ASSIGNMENTS IN MAGAZINES.   Systematic data are not available on staff assignments of magazines. From a case study of the *Ladies' Home Journal*, we know the pattern for one magazine. Others of this genre may have the same pattern. Over a 15-month period, 47 percent of the by-lines were by women and 53 percent were by men. These percentages are somewhat deceptive, since they do not take into account the use of female pseudonyms by male authors. Furthermore, there are women's topics and men's topics. Only infrequently do men write about cooking, clothes, or health. Male by-lines are overrepresented among articles and short stories.[107]

A 1977 study by Jeannie Farley of the 39 women's magazines that covered ERA during the summer of 1976 showed that 72 percent of the by-lines were women's names. The magazines ranged from a low of 31 percent in *Woman's Day* to a high of 100 percent in *Glamour*.[108]

ASSIGNMENTS IN NEWSPAPERS. By the time of the 1972 political conventions, women were well aware of sex bias in newspaper assignments. Ellen Goodman reported in the *Boston Globe* on the many female delegates at the Democratic National Convention and the few female journalists assigned to cover the convention. She wrote that 94 percent of the Associated Press national staff were men and that the situation was similar at UPI. In general, women were assigned to cover only the "women's side."[109]

Coverage of the Republican National Convention was also assigned primarily to men. For example, the *Boston Globe* sent 6 men and 1 woman. *Newsday* sent 8 men and 1 woman (secretary at the Washington Bureau). Associated Press had a news staff of 39 men and 8 women. On the Republican National Committee's press relations staff, men were given major assignments and women were assigned to "women's activities," "the National Federation of Republican Women" and "youth."[110]

The *Washington Post* has resisted efforts to determine if there is sex discrimination in their story assignments. The *Post* wrote to the EEOC:

> The First Amendment bars government from regulating, and from inquiring into, how a newspaper performs its editorial functions. The giving of individual reportorial assignments is protected by the First Amendment.[111]

The Commission did not accept this position. Although it had to work without adequate information on how story assignments are made and who makes them, it wrote:

> The Commission has no interest in attempting to regulate Respondent's editorial policies or functions nor in attempting to dictate who should be assigned what stories. Job assignments, however, are clearly a condition of employment and this Commission is authorized to investigate allegations regarding disparate job assignments based on sex.
>
> A major circumstance involved in this allegation is that the entire process of determining assignments is apparently accomplished by an all-male staff in a highly subjective and essentially

non-reviewable manner. The Commission views with skepticism the treatment that females can receive from males in such circumstances.

... We therefore conclude that in the totality of circumstances presented in this case that there is reasonable cause to believe that female reporters are denied equal consideration with male reporters for story assignments on the city and suburban desks.[112]

The assignment practices of other newspapers have also been challenged. In the complaint filed against *Newsday*, discrimination was alleged in many areas of employment, including story assignments. The complainants monitored four sections of the paper to determine whether women and men were equally likely to be assigned to cover stories. Over 6 months they found:

- Twelve percent of the assignments in the five-column news pages were given to women.
- Eight percent of the assignments in the Upfront section were given to women.
- Three percent of the assignments in the International/National/State sections were given to women.
- Thirty-one percent of the assignments in the Long Island section were given to women.[113]

Assignment will continue to be a thorny issue for some time. In the aggregate it becomes clear that women do not receive a fair share of good assignments.

ATTITUDES/INTERPERSONAL EXPERIENCES

Federal and state law can attempt to regulate policies and practices that bring about sex discrimination, but the law will be undermined as long as women are regarded, by men and even by themselves, as "the weaker sex."

Proposition 12.5: Sexist Beliefs *of Male Managers Work Against the Acceptance of Women in the Media.*

Many male managers have stereotypic beliefs about the kinds of work that women can do and about the right of women to earn equal salaries. Because men believe that women are more at home with typewriters and switchboards than cameras and lights, they do not consider women for the better-paying positions. Because men believe that women's income is secondary, they attempt to pay women less than men in the same positions. Because men value aggressiveness above other qualities and because they believe that only men are aggressive, they are less likely to consider women when managerial positions are open. The following studies show the extent of these beliefs and how they affect the employment of women and men.

STUDIES OF BELIEFS/INTERPERSONAL EXPERIENCES. The beliefs expressed by respondents in the study of the Corporation for Public Broadcasting often did not match the data on hiring and promotion but, at other times, the respondents were quite candid. Following are excerpts from the Isber and Cantor report.

It was found that though most men interviewed professed an open attitude toward the employment of women, the responses to questions indicate that this open attitude is not often translated into hiring and promotion practices. For instance, when asked who had been hired recently at the managerial levels, most men answered with male names. Several male managers said they could not find qualified women for the higher level positions. The few executive women interviewed said the opposite; they had no problem finding qualified females.

. . . a male executive vice president admitted the following, "We have underpaid women in producer roles because we know that perhaps it has been a second job and that their husbands have other jobs. With the job market as it is today, perhaps we can give this person a little less because we want to save as much as we can in terms of budget."[114]

Another way beliefs work against women is that valued characteristics are stereotypically male. Isber and Cantor found that personnel managers look for "drive, aggressiveness, imagination, and self-starting ability" and believe that only men have these characteristics.

In 1974, the Canadian Broadcasting Corporation's Task Force on the Status of Women interviewed male managers across Canada and found many similar beliefs. Four generalizations emerged:

1. *Women Are Not Career Oriented.* This attitude was expressed in various ways: "They have no aspirations.", "Women are happy where they are.", "They just want 9:00 to 5:00 jobs so they can get home to their families.", "They are not willing to take the initiative to improve themselves.", "Women are immobile.", "Women don't really work for money."[115]

2. *Women Are Less Suited Than Men for Many Kinds of Jobs.* This attitude was found among the male managers who said: "They don't have the qualifications;" "It's a bad investment to promote a woman; she's liable to get married, have a baby and quit;" "Women are sick and away much more than men;" "Women are unable to do strenuous physical work;" "A woman couldn't climb up a ladder with those lights;" "Women can't stand cold temperatures; can you imagine one at the top of Mount Orford taping a ski race?"[116]

3. *Women Are Better Suited for Some Jobs.* Interviews revealed this attitude in these comments: "They are better with their hands;" "Women are much more suited than men for switchboard operators, because of their nimble hands;" "They have the manual dexterity it takes for typing; men don't;" I wouldn't mind having a woman in my department (technical), if I could get a position that combined tape editing and typing;" "Women don't mind repeti-

tive jobs;" "She can last better at a job that tends to monotony; she's used to thinking about other things while she does the housework;" "Men are born wanting a life of challenge; women are not born with this want, and that's why they are happy to be just secretaries."[117]

4. *Women Are Overly Emotional and Generally Troublesome.* Although this attitude was expressed in various ways, it was typified by one supervisor who said: "I have a lot of women working for me, and they're quite good. But they cry so much." When women were interviewed, they presented a different perspective. One said: "If a woman cries —usually through sheer frustration with the impossibility of getting through to her boss—she's unstable and a nuisance. If a man shouts, he's a gutsy guy."[118]

Using available data when possible and undertaking research when necessary, the CBC Task Force on the Status of Women found little truth in any of the commonly held beliefs about women. Yet these beliefs affect the hiring and promotion of women and the daily experiences of women who work for men in the media.

Ever since the rise of radio, broadcasters have believed that women cannot be announcers because of their voices. Many men continue to believe this, although fewer are expressing it publicly. In one publicized case, General Manager Fred Gage of WNOR-FM (Norfolk, Virginia) relied on what he called "the consensus of broadcasters" when he moved women to secretarial work after a decline in his ratings. He said: "Females and males alike would rather hear a male voice on the radio. . . . 'A woman's destiny is tied to a man.' "[119]

This chapter has indicated the difficulty of determining the actual status of women in media organizations. There probably are more women in television this year than in 1971, but the figures have been so distorted that we cannot gauge real progress. The print media are not required by law to release employment information, so we rely on public records such as mastheads and listings in directories like *The Working Press of the Nation.*

Much apparent improvement in the status of women in media is just that—appearance. For example, women who were previously listed as researchers at some of the large news magazines have received titles that reflect the work they have been doing all along. In another example, many women who are listed as secretaries and receive secretarial wages do a substantial amount of programming and production work. It is a just recognition of their work if they are retitled assistant producers, but there is no assurance that their status in the organization or their salary has improved. These are some considerations in evaluating future information against the information in this chapter. If there seems to be an improvement for women, be sure to look for alternative explanations.

PROPOSITIONAL SUMMARY

Proposition 12.1:   Men are more likely than women to be media *managers.*

Proposition 12.2:   Men in media have higher *salaries* than women.

Proposition 12.3:   Men in media are more likely than women to receive *promotions.*

Proposition 12.4:   Desirable *assignments* are primarily given to men.

Proposition 12.5:   Sexist *beliefs* of male managers work against the acceptance of women in the media.

13

DECISIONS AFFECTING PORTRAYAL

The vast majority of American women . . . seem content with their roles as wife, mother, and housekeeper. And that, of course, is exactly the female image portrayed on TV.[1]

No one knows, except anecdotally, how and why media managers and advertisers choose the images of women and men that were documented in Chapters 6 to 10. Studies of editorial and advertising decision making are important if we are to change the media.

Proposition 13.1: Media Portrayals of Women and Men Are Generally the Result of Informal Rather than Formal Policies.

Each media organization has formal policies that govern the content of its product; sexism rarely arises in these policies. The following data are anecdotal, but they indicate the importance of informal policies and lines of influence among personnel.

Editorial Decisions

Control of news flow in the media is one form of decision-making. Warren Breed's study, "Social Control in the Newsroom," is an excellent example of the kinds of studies that can be done.[2] However, no studies have specifically focused on decisions that affect the images of women and men. It is necessary to piece together the evidence that does exist.

Perhaps the best-known "case" in this area is described by Fred Friendly in his book, *Due to Circumstances Beyond Our Control.*[3] When Friendly, as president of the CBS News Division, wanted to interrupt the regular afternoon broadcasting to cover the Senate Foreign Relations Committee hearings on the Viet Nam war, he was told by CBS management that housewives would not be interested and that the schedule was to remain uninterrupted. That decision was not the result of a formal policy. It was based on the beliefs of male executives that women would prefer reruns of "I Love Lucy" to world events.

In 1977, three studies provided some evidence on the different editorial decisions that women and men make. Jack Orwant and Muriel Cantor explored a hypothetical situation in which undergraduate students in a communication course rated women's and men's interest in nine news categories. They found that although both sexes attributed stereotyped interests to women and men (e.g., sports to men and cooking to women), female students were less influenced by traditional sex roles than male students.[4] Extrapolating to real situations, this suggests that women, as editors, will make decisions that are less based on stereotyping than men.

By asking male and female editors and a few reporters on six newspapers to rate the acceptability of 48 hypothetical news leads, S. Scott Whitlow studied the selection bias of 17 female and 19 male gatekeepers. The news items combined sex of the news principal (one-half were about women and one-half were about men), social/occupational role of news principal (one-half were traditional and one-half were nontraditional), extent of conflict (one-half had low physical or intellectual conflict and one-half had high conflict), and proximity of story (one-third were local, one-third were national, and one-third were international). Whitlow found five patterns of decision behaviors. For three of these patterns, the sex-related facet of the story was significant. In one pattern, the gatekeepers gave low priority to items with women as the news principal. In a second, gatekeepers rejected items with women in both traditional and nontraditional roles. In the third, gatekeepers assigned low priority to items showing either men or women in nontraditional roles. Stories with high conflict were consistently given higher priority ratings. For only one of the three patterns was there a difference in the number of women and men endorsing the decisions. Seven of the eight gatekeepers who rejected items with women in both traditional and nontraditional roles were men. These same gatekeepers expressed the attitude that women should be primarily restricted to reporting on female-oriented news.[5]

As described in the previous chapter, Sharyne Merritt and Harriet Gross surveyed the editors of women's page/life-style sections. They provided information on sex differences only for the 171 editors (response rate of 71 percent) from the large-circulation newspapers, because few of the men were women's page/life-style editors on small-circulation newspapers. They found that 79 percent of the men versus 34 percent of the women were from papers with a circulation of more than 50,000. In response to the question, "What *is* the most important goal of your section?":

- Seventy-eight percent of the men and 73 percent of the women stated the traditional focus.
- Eighteen percent of the men and 6 percent of the women stated the leisure focus.
- Four percent of the men and 21 percent of the women stated the social change focus.

When asked, "What *should be* the most important goal of your section?":

- Sixty-eight percent of the men and 51 percent of the women stated the traditional focus.
- Twenty-five percent of the men and 9 percent of the women stated the leisure focus.
- Seven percent of the men and 40 percent of the women stated the social change focus.[6]

These findings indicate that while a traditional focus is supported by both women and men, women are already five times as likely as men to emphasize social change and are almost six times as likely as men to believe that social change should be the focus of the women's page/life-style sections.

Merritt and Gross also asked the editors to indicate how much of their copy they devoted in the previous year to each of five topics. Of particular interest is that the women were more likely than the men (65 percent versus 45 percent) to have given more than 10 percent of their section to coverage of the women's movement.[7]

Considering the scarcity of women as editors and the Merritt and Gross finding that women are more likely to cover the women's movement, Monica Morris' results are hardly surprising. She has conducted one of the few studies of newspaper coverage of the women's movement.[8] Morris studied two general-circulation newspapers in Los Angeles County—*Los Angeles Times* and *Herald Examiner*—from mid-1968 to mid-1969. Noting that the women's movement began to receive limited attention in 1966, Morris expected to find adequate coverage by the 1968 to 1969 period. Defining 30 lines as a story unit, she found that of more than 250,000 units of news, only 26 were devoted to the women's movement. Seven of these units concerned the Los Angeles area, and the other 19 units concerned the rest of the United States.

Publishers as well as editors make decisions that affect the presentation of women. The *New York Times* reported on a face-lifting at *Redbook*.

> The high command of *Redbook* . . . decided some time ago that "The Magazine for Young Mamas" was no longer the appropriate advertising theme for the magazine.
> But what should they use instead?
> "For the new woman" and "for the working woman" were considered and discarded.
> Last week at his offices Carlo Vittorini, tall and youthful-looking president and publisher, revealed the new slogan: "*Redbook,* the Magazine of the New Management."
> In a full-page ad in mid-January headlined "A Manifesto" *Redbook* will explain that while it congratulates "the millions of young women who are now emerging from homebody to somebody," the magazine is evolutionizing right along with them and that "Married or not, working or not, women run their own lives. They're the New Management."[9]

Self-descriptions of editorial policy are provided by many magazines in *Writer's Yearbook.* For example:

> *True Secrets/My Romance/My Confession/Secret Story/Intimate Romances/Intimate Secrets:* likes realistic, identifiable plots and characters in stories that involve . . . emotionally . . . the audience of unsophisticated women with limited education. . . . Stories must be related in the first person singular, preferably from the woman's point of view, employing a conversational tone. We no longer follow the sin, suffer, repent syndrome. Rather, our stories reflect sexual attitudes and behaviors as they exist in our enlightened present day society. We are fairly liberal in our attitude toward sex scenes, but they should not be forced.[10]

> *The Sportswoman:* No women as sex objects.[11]

> *Intimate Story:* First person stories in which the love interest is dominant. . . . We need stories that have strong personal identification for our readers because women read this magazine in order to learn how to solve their own problems.[12]

To counterbalance presentations of women in the media at large and to cover events and issues of concern to women, a group of New York feminists has started a biweekly newspaper, *Majority Report*, with an initial circulation of 20,000. The advertising policy prohibits sexist presentation of women and men, sex advertising, and advertising influence over editorial content.[13] Other publications by and for women are starting all across the United States. *Ms., Womensports,* and *Working Woman* are well-known magazines; *Media Report to Women* and *Spokeswoman* are widely circulated newsletters; and *Signs, Sex Roles,* and *Psychology of Women Quarterly* are important research journals. Each year, the number of publications grows. *Media Report to Women* lists more than 100 feminist publications in its annual directory.

ADVERTISING DECISIONS

Thomas R. Hasket, speaking as an advertising agency executive, responded to the Hennessee and Nicholson analysis of 1241 commercials (see Chapter 6 for a discussion of their findings). He said:

> While feminists are trying to change society, advertisers are trying to appeal to people as they are. . . .
> Advertisers attempt to sell goods and services to real people who exist today in the U.S., not people as NOW wishes they would become. The vast majority of American women . . . seem content with their roles as wife, mother, and housekeeper. And that, of course, is exactly the female image portrayed on TV.
> . . . No advertiser would stay in business very long if he did not aim his commercials at people as they actually are today.[14]

Sheridan Crawford interviewed advertising agency personnel in San Francisco and New York. When asked about his agency's portrayal of women, one advertising man responded:

I assume that most kitchen products are used by women and that men don't give a damn about them, even the bachelors. Since women are the major consumers, the main purpose of such an advertisement is to present a product in an average situation, usually the kitchen, being used by an average type person—the middle class housewife.[15]

Crawford was told by an advertising woman:

I was working on Proctor and Gamble accounts, and I used to have frequent discussions with my creative supervisor. One day I went in and asked him if it bothered him what he was doing to women, not the women in the target audience, but the young ones growing up who receive all the messages and the silent ones too, and he said, "Well somebody would do it and it allows me to have the finest Pre-Columbian art collection in the city—so shut up and go back to the script."[16]

This woman also tried to organize a consciousness-raising group for advertising agency personnel. Before the first meeting, she was told that the group had already met and had decided that "advertising had no responsibility to women, or to anyone. The only responsibility was to the client to sell the product."[17]

Other advertising decisions concern the target audience for a campaign. In the "Business Briefly" section of each weekly issue of *Broadcasting* magazine, major new advertising campaigns are announced. The product, length of campaign, type of campaign, and target audience are described. For example, in a typical issue of *Broadcasting,* 20 new campaigns were announced; all but three listed target audiences.

- Borden chocolate milk targeted to women 18 to 49 and children.
- A&W root beer targeted to women 18 to 49 and teenagers.
- J. S. Filbert Spread 25 targeted to women 18 to 49.
- Hormel bacon and ham targeted to women 25 to 49.

- RJR Foods Hawaiian Punch drink mix targeted to women 25 to 49.
- Larsen vacuum-packed and frozen vegetables targeted to women 25 to 49.
- California and Hawaiian sugar targeted to women 18 to 49.
- Balm Barr skin and hair care products targeted to women 18 to 49.
- National Coal Association public information targeted to adults 18 to 49.
- GTE Sylvania GT-matic color receivers targeted to adults 25 to 49.
- Schick Sun Classic pictures targeted to adults 18 to 49.
- Shulton Old Spice deodorant targeted to men 18 to 49.
- Ziebart International rustproofing product for auto bodies targeted to men 25 to 49.
- Fram oil filter targeted to men 18 to 34.
- Bristol-Myers Sunshine Harvest shampoo targeted to teen-agers.

The details of this listing are supplemented by content analysis of *Broadcasting* magazine for one year. Sampling one issue randomly from each month, we found 180 campaigns with specified target audiences. Forty-one percent of these campaigns were aimed at women, 23 percent at men, 26 percent at adults of both sexes, and 7 percent at children/teenagers.

Which types of products are targeted at women, men, adults, and children/teenagers? Women are the primary target audience for food, household supplies, nonprescription drugs, and vitamins.

- Sixty-nine percent of food products were targeted to women, 2 percent to men, 19 percent to adults, and 10 percent to children/teenagers.
- Ninety-one percent of the household products were targeted to women and 9 percent to men.
- Seventy-five percent of the drugs and vitamins were targeted to women and 25 percent to adults.

Men are the primary target audience for only one product type.

- Eighty-three percent of the automobile and automobile-related products were targeted to men and 17 percent to adults.

The small number of campaigns prevents us from generalizing about other types of products, but three of the four airline campaigns, three of the four insurance campaigns, the one calculator campaign, and the one *Time* campaign were directed to men.

Target-audience data indicate not only whether women or men are assumed to be the consumers, but also which age groups are sought after. The question might be, "Is there purchasing power after 49?" In 145 advertising campaigns specifying age of adult target audience, as announced in the 12 randomly sampled issues of *Broadcasting,* there were few efforts to reach consumers older than 49.

- Three percent of the campaigns were directed to those up to the age of 24.
- Nine percent of the campaigns were directed to those up to the age of 34.
- Seventy percent of the campaigns were directed to those up to the age of 49.
- Eight percent of the campaigns were directed to those up to the age of 54.
- Ten percent of the campaigns were directed to those up to and over the age of 54.

The last category consists primarily of open-ended age targets such as "36 and older," "18 and older," etc. Only three campaigns mentioned adults over 54. Schenley vermouth advertising was targeted to adults between 30 and 55; B. F. Goodrich advertising was targeted to men between 25 and 64; and Pfeiffer salad dressing advertising was targeted to women between

25 and 64. No campaign was targeted to persons older than 64.

Other critical advertising decisions concern which television programs will be sponsored. Almost inevitably these are dollars and cents decisions. Few advertisers can afford to bring costly programs to small audiences. When corporations such as Xerox, Hallmark, Aetna, General Electric, Polaroid, and Mobil sponsor dramatic or documentary "specials," the decision reflects corporate solvency as much as corporate taste.

In the everyday world of television programming, the networks must use profits from daytime programs to make up their losses on prime-time shows.

> A show like "Kojak" costs $250,000 to produce but brings in revenues of only $200,000. To make one week of "Days of Our Lives" costs NBC $170,000; daily advertising revenues are $120,000.[18]

Advertisers buy audiences, not programs. When audience ratings slip, advertisers move their money to shows that are more popular with their target audiences. Most of the programs that have shown women nonstereotypically (e.g., "Adam's Rib," "Fay," "Kate McShane") have succeeded with critics but failed with general audiences. "Mary Tyler Moore" was a longstanding exception to this rule. "All's Fair," "One Day at a Time," "Phyllis," "Feather and Father Gang," and "Rockford Files" have been popular programs with nonstereotypic portrayals of women. Charley, Ann, Phyllis, Feather, and Beth (Rockford's much needed attorney) all work and manage their own lives.

"Woman Alive!," the public television series first seen in 1975, sought funding for over 2 years. During that time more than 100 foundations, corporations, and other funding sources were approached. Finally, "Woman Alive!" was funded by the Corporation for Public Broadcasting and produced in collaboration with *Ms.* magazine. The Corporation for Public Broadcasting agreed in 1976 to provide up to $554,000 for a second season of "Woman Alive!" With the new money the series was able to expand to a 1-hour format.

The Advertising Council is another organization that has considerable influence over media presentation of women. Approximately 80 percent of public-service announcements are distributed by the Council. When NOW sought support from the Council in 1971, the request was rejected on the grounds that NOW was too political. Later this decision was reversed and, in June 1973, the campaign, "Womanpower. It's too good to waste." was launched.

Another Advertising Council campaign illustrates that old stereotypes of women can move to new settings. In the opening scene of a public-service announcement, a woman is shown working in her office. The voice-over tells of her competence in her job, then asks if she is prepared for emergencies. As her wastebasket catches fire and she fumbles with a fire extinguisher, a man rushes in to douse the fire.

Media managers and advertisers work under great pressure. Deadlines, budgets, and competition occupy their working hours. In the past, one of their genuine pleasures has been "the club," which for some is a mahogany-walled male preserve and for others is the corner saloon. In the legends of their fraternity, maleness is clever and exploitative; femaleness is stupid but receptive. To many of these men, accepting women as equals on the job is more than a professional gesture; it is their reconsideration of the role of women in society. When John Mitchell said of the *Washington Post* publisher that "Katie Graham is going to get her tits caught in a big fat wringer," he was echoing a value system that affects media and advertising decisions every day.

PROPOSITIONAL SUMMARY

Proposition 13.1:   Media portrayals affecting women are generally the result of *informal* rather than formal *policies.*

TRAINING

Both professionally and personally, women are suspect. It seems we must be better students than men and more womanly than non-student females.[1]

Inequality in media employment (see Chapter 12) and inequality resulting from editorial/advertising decisions about the portrayal of women (see Chapter 13) are obvious. Social values, often hidden from analysis, are the bedrock of inequality. Outcroppings of these values are found in policies and practices that affect the training of media personnel.

Only recently has attention focused on training as the cause and possible cure of some of the problems that women face in the media. In 1972 the Association for Education in Journalism (AEJ) established its Ad Hoc Committee on the Status of Women in Journalism Education. In 1976, in consideration of the long-term problems with which it had to deal Status of Women became a regular committee of AEJ. In 1974 the International Communication Association (ICA) established its own Ad Hoc Committee on the Status of Women in Communication. Both committees have been concerned with opportunities for women students, course content, hiring of women for faculty positions, salary differentials, and other forms of discrimination that women face in academic journalism and communication.

Concern with training stems from the belief that the way people are trained in college affects their later options. In the past, many more men than women have studied journalism, using textbooks that depicted journalism implicitly and often explicitly as a male province. Later, as media managers, these students have preferred to hire men and to pay better salaries to men.

Proposition 14.1: Women Students Are Not Admitted to Academic Programs Equally with Men, Have Few Role Models, Receive Inadequate Counseling, and Study from Biased Textbooks.

The training of media personnel has only begun to be studied. The available information indicates that the experiences men are likely to have had are valued above the experiences of women in the admissions process. Traditionally, a male high school student interested in journalism has been urged to work for the local newspaper as copyboy or gofer. A female high school student with the same interest is urged to do well in school and write in her spare time. When applying to a school of journalism, the newspaper experience gives the male student an advantage over the female student.

Both women and men have few female role models in journalism. Therefore, it is difficult for female students to imagine themselves as successful professionals and for male students to learn how to interact with professional women. With faculties composed largely of men, female students must seek counseling from men. Many male professors believe that female students are not serious about careers and therefore give them different advice from male students.

Finally, the area of textbooks, although understudied, suggests that many of the perceptions female and male students have about the field of journalism may come from sexist textbooks. With slow turnover in journalism textbooks, it takes a long time to get rid of stereotypes of women and men.

ADMISSIONS

Several studies of admissions show that male attributes are regarded as more desirable in professional training programs, so women must often be brighter than men to be admitted.[2]

What happens to women admitted to college? Government statistics show that, by graduation, women are 40 percent of those in communication, 46 percent of those in journalism, 24 percent of those in radio and television, and 36 percent of those in advertising.[3] There is more attrition of female than male students at each degree level, as follows.

- Women receive 40 percent of the B.A.s, 39 percent of the M.A.s, and 25 percent of the Ph.D.s in communication (general).
- Women receive 46 percent of the B.A.s, 37 percent of the M.A.s, and none of the Ph.D.s in journalism.
- Women receive 24 percent of the B.A.s, 29 percent of the M.A.s, and none of the Ph.D.s in radio and television.
- Women receive 36 percent of the B.A.s and 20 percent of the M.A.s in advertising (no Ph.D.s offered).[4]

Matilda Butler, Suzanne Pingree, and William Paisley have studied attrition of women students from undergraduate through doctoral programs, contending that:

Mass communication schools cannot redress the imbalance of women and men on their faculties unless a larger percentage of women in the undergraduate pool complete doctoral study. To the extent that fewer women are *admitted* to doctoral study than their proportion among qualified applicants would predict, departments must counter sex discrimination in admissions. To the extent that fewer women *apply* for graduate study than their proportion in the undergraduate pool would predict, departments must counter sex-role socialization influences.[5]

The field of journalism has lacked female role models since it began. Roberta Applegate noted that:

[In 1929], two Helens—Hostetter and Patterson—stuck together for moral support whenever they attended conventions of journalism educators. At the start, they didn't have much trouble finding each other because frequently they were the only women college faculty members present.[6]

By 1964 the picture was not much better.

Fewer than 10 percent of the AEJ (Association for Education in Journalism) membership—7.5 percent to be exact—is made up of women faculty members. Just nine of these women attended the 1964 convention at the University of Texas.[7]

Ramona Rush reported that the 1970 to 1971 membership rolls of AEJ listed 131 women. This was 11 percent of the membership at the time.[8] By 1977, women were 17 percent of the AEJ membership.[9] This percentage is somewhat inflated by the inclusion of student members. In any case, the percentage of women in AEJ has increased by less than 10 percent in 13 years.

TEXTBOOKS

Two studies of journalism textbooks were conducted at the University of Michigan. Judy Hansen found few references to women in journalism history textbooks.[10] Her work was extended by Marion Marzolf in the book *Up From the Footnote: Women in Journalism*.[11]

A second study, conducted by Roberta Evans and Ellen Meyer, cites numerous examples of sexism in journalism textbooks.[12] In particular, textbooks that teach journalistic writing imply that men "do" while women "appear." It is not surprising that reporters describe appearance more often for women than for men, since a textbook once taught them to write this lead.

> Pretty in skirts and pert in slacks—that's Mildred Miller, size 12, mezzo-soprano with the Metropolitan Opera Co.[13]

INTERNSHIPS

Many students participate in journalism internship programs. Traditionally, female students have difficulty obtaining internships. When they do, their routine assignment is the women's page. Male students, on the other hand, often rotate through several departments of a newspaper or magazine. The varied experiences of the male students pay off during the transition from college to media employment.

ATTITUDES/INTERPERSONAL EXPERIENCES

Survey comments from students and teachers in communication/journalism departments illustrate how women feel about their interaction with professors and male students.

> Women are not considered "serious scholars."

> Women are not recognized as professionals. Instead we are treated as "wife on leave" or "mother on leave."

> I feel isolated in my department, where socialization is for males only.

> Women are often told cute "in" jokes about chauvinism and sexism.

Male graduate students are asked to consider the Ph.D. program; female graduate students are asked when they intend to start a family.

Insufficient attention is given to women graduate students in many institutions. Male professors have either paternalistic or exploitative attitudes toward women students.[14]

Similar comments were made in a survey reported by Ramona Rush.

Both professionally and personally, women are suspect. It seems we must be better students than men and more womanly than non-student females.

I feel that I am assumed to be dumb (because I'm female and look young) and must prove myself to be competent. Men, on the other hand, are automatically assumed to be competent unless proven stupid.[15]

The survey of women in the International Communication Association led to a "Bill of Rights for Women in Communication" that was adopted by the Committee on the Status of Women in Communication and affirmed by ICA's board of directors.[16] The points are:

1. *Women Students in Communications Have a Right to Nonsexist Career Counseling in High School and College.* Their "sincerity" in choosing a career is not a legitimate counseling issue. Social role expectation and sex discrimination in particular careers are issues that should be discussed thoughtfully with women students, not used to discourage and disqualify them.

2. *Women Students Have a Right to Be Admitted to Academic Programs According to Their Abilities and Prior Experiences.* Women's scores on SAT, GRE, and other tests should not be discounted "because they are good test-takers." Admission quotas should not be applied either in favor of women or against them but, like other professional minorities,

women should not find themselves isolated in programs that cater to majority students.

3. *Women Students Have a Right to Learning Experiences that Realistically and Effectively Prepare Them for Their Careers.* Sexism in textbooks, even at the graduate level, the absence of women faculty members to serve as "role models," exclusion of women students from the "old boy network" of tips and good advice—these are minor issues individually, but their cumulative effect (as Eric Sevareid said in another context) is one of "being nibbled to death by ducks."

4. *Women Graduates Have a Right to Nonsexist Placement Assistance.* The question,"Will your husband accept a move like that?" is no more (and no less) appropriate than "Will your wife accept a move like that?" The statement "If I recommend you, I want your assurance that you'll stay with them long enough to make it worth their while" is made to women students but not to men students, even though men exhibit less job stability than women.

5. *Women have a Right to Enter Professional Employment at the Same Levels as Men with Comparable Training and to Be Eligible for Promotion on the Same Schedule of Progress.* One of the best-documented facts of discrimination against women in communication are the positions for which they are hired and the promotion opportunities that are open to them, relative to men with comparable training. In schools and departments of communication across the country, women are appointed as lecturers and instructors, while men are appointed as assistant professors and higher. Few women are full professors of communication; fewer still direct a school or department of communication. Statistical analyses show that most women in communication are appointed to positions at the bottom of the ladder and remain in these positions, while men are appointed initially to higher positions and move up thereafter.

6. *Women Have a Right to "Equal Pay for Equal Work."* In

this regard women in business and media seem to fare worse than women in academic institutions and government, where pay scales are more determined by position, training, and experience. Additionally, women's income should never be regarded as less necessary than men's income, particularly as a rationale for paying women less for the same work.

7. *Women Have a Right to Participate in the Field's Research and Production Ventures on an Equal Footing with Men.* Women experience great difficulty in securing organizational support for their own research and production ventures. In the case of federal funding for research, their proposals are subject to double jeopardy: lack of support from their own organization and disapproval by "old boy" federal review panels.

8. *Women Have a Right to Serve in the Positions of Influence and Leadership in Their Field, Commensurate with Their Abilities and Accomplishments.* Appointments to commissions and task forces, elections to officerships and boards of professional associations, and other forms of professional recognition are seldom accorded to women. Women need to believe that their abilities and accomplishments will be recognized in these ways in order to escape the self-fulfilling prophecy that positions of influence and leadership are controlled by men and are not worth striving for.

If training of media personnel were responsive to these eight points, it would not be long before institutional policies and practices in the media would also be responsive to them.

Because college training has often left women unprepared for management responsibility in the media, there have been a few efforts to establish special training sessions/programs for women in midcareer. For example, CBS has two such programs. One consists of in-house sessions to develop management skills in women and to help male managers to accept and work with women as equals. In the other program, women are chosen to attend the Harvard School of Business prior to advancement at CBS.

Business management and, to a lesser extent, media management have called in outside consulting teams to conduct workshops on discrimination and stereotyping. Two books that can be used in planning and carrying out in-house sessions are Alice Sargent's *Beyond Sex Roles* and Jean Baker Miller's *Toward a New Psychology of Women*.[17]

PROPOSITIONAL SUMMARY

Proposition 14.1:   Women students are not *admitted* to academic programs equally with men, have few *role models*, receive inadequate *counseling*, and study from biased *textbooks*.

4

SEXISM AND MEDIA AUDIENCES

Are women, who account for more than half of all media audience-hours, up in arms about sexism? As far as we can tell, most are not. Perhaps, like the fish that is the last to know that it lives in a wet environment, women see the media as mirrors that reflect the social sexism with which they have always lived. It is true that women cannot see a true image of themselves in the media, but how often and where—at home, in school, on the job, or in social gatherings—do they ever see themselves reflected as the competent persons they know they are?

There are virtually no studies of audience reactions to media sexism. However, other studies have uncovered interesting facts about media audiences, female and male, young and old. Some theories of the effects of sex-role stereotyping on media audiences have been proposed. This field of research is ripe but, since the studies have not been conducted, we can only describe their foundation in what is already known about audiences.

Chapter 15 describes the variety of methods that have been used to study media audiences, their demography, and their content preferences. Chapters 16 and 18 both focus on adult audiences, the former on demography and content preferences, the latter on effects. Chapter 17 raises one of the most important questions in this book: what are the possible effects of media sexism on children?

HOW MEDIA AUDIENCES ARE STUDIED

Questionnaires and interviews are probably the most flexible and generally useful devices we have for gathering information. . . . [Yet] there are a number of research conditions in which the sole use of the interview or questionnaire leaves unanswerable rival explanations.[1]

American media consumption approaches 400 billion hours per year. How is the individual average of 1800 hours divided among television, radio, newspapers, magazines, films, books, etc.? What are our programming and editorial preferences within each medium? Who consumes 2400 hours of media per year and who consumes only 1200 hours? How do the media affect our knowledge, beliefs, and actions?

We date scientific audience analysis from W. W. Charter's study, *Motion Pictures and Youth.* Approximately 4000 children, adolescents, and young adults participated in this ambitious project to measure the effects of film viewing on young audiences. Films chosen for classroom showings included *Birth of a Nation* (race prejudice), *All Quiet on the Western Front* (war), *Big House* (punishment of criminals), and 10 others.

Before and after measures proved that "the attitude of children toward a social value can be measurably changed by one exposure to a picture."[2]

Paul Lazarsfeld conducted pioneering studies of the radio audience at Princeton University in the mid-1930s. After moving to Columbia University, he initiated an important series of audience studies, voting studies, and diffusion studies. A study of the 1940 presidential election campaign led Lazarsfeld's group to propose a "two-step flow theory" to account for "opinion leaders" who relay messages from mass media to other persons.[3]

Studies of print media audiences also date from the 1930s. Lazarsfeld and Rowena Wyant investigated magazine readership in 90 cities.[4] In 1940 Lazarsfeld published *Radio and the Printed Page,* which included an ingenious experiment that tested the comparative utility of newspapers and radio broadcasts to their audiences.[5]

In 1947 the National Association of Broadcasters sponsored a national study of media audiences. The National Opinion Research Center in Chicago gathered data on media use from a sample of 3529 adults. Lazarsfeld and Patricia Kendall reported findings from this NAB-NORC survey in their book, *Radio Listening in America.* [6]

Newspapers were omitted from the 1947 NAB-NORC survey, but they were studied in 1949 by Wilbur Schramm and David Manning White.[7] A probability sample of 746 newspaper readers was drawn in a middle-sized Illinois city. Reader age, education, sex, and economic status were tabulated against sections of the newspaper read, including news stories, human interest features, society features, editorials, sports, pictorial matter, political cartoons, and comics. Reading of news stories was found to increase with age, education, and economic status.

Such studies made audience analysis academically respectable; the advent of television made it commercially profitable. The objectives of television audience measurement are simple enough—determine who is viewing television during each time period of the day—but no simple data collection method meets the objectives. A.C. Nielsen's television attachments called Audimeters are the best-known measurement method, but national and local rating services use various methods, including telephone coincidental and telephone recall surveys, personal interviews, and diaries.

Print media require audience measurement for the same reasons as broadcast media: to substantiate circulation claims made to advertisers. The best-known rating service for print media is the Audit Bureau of Circulation which, for 6 decades, has provided the basic service of circulation audit and has recently begun to provide advertisers with detailed market profiles.

The Audit Bureau's service to newspapers is complemented by the W.R. Simmons Associates' service to magazines. The Simmons Magazine Audience Reports provide demographic tabulations of the audiences of more than 50 national magazines. As the attention of these researchers shifts from gross totals to demographic and even psychographic (attitude, trait) analyses of media audiences, we reach a computerized extreme in the 26 volumes of the *Target Group Index,* published by the Axiom Market Research Bureau.[8]

Do these various services use careful research or hocus-pocus? Most of us have heard criticisms of the Audimeter method and of Nielsen's small sample. What is not generally understood is the *convergent validation* data available to advertisers, broadcasters, and publishers. The results of telephone coincidental and telephone recall surveys, personal interviews, and diary studies are reviewed with careful attention to convergence.

Larger sums of money are spent on ratings than on all other audience analyses combined. It is useful to know how the rating services draw their samples, gather data, and perform analyses.

ILLUSTRATIVE AUDIENCE ANALYSES

A Rating Service Study

The detailed methods of the rating services are regarded as trade secrets. However, the following study was described by Harold Israel and John Robinson of W.R. Simmons Associates because it was included in the report of the Surgeon General's Committee on Television and Social Behavior.[9]

The Simmons' *1970 Study of Selective Markets and the Media Reaching Them* was based on a stratified national probability sample of 15,322 adults. Standard Metropolitan Statistical Areas (SMSAs) and nonmetropolitan counties in the contiguous 48 states were stratified to take account of geography, population, rate of population change, income, and race. Eighty-eight SMSAs and 70 nonmetropolitan counties were then selected from the strata to become primary sampling units (PSUs).

Within each of the 158 PSUs, census tracts and untracted divisions were stratified according to family incomes as tabulated by the census. Four income strata were created. Census tracts and untracted divisions were then selected from each stratum, with probabilities proportionate to population.

Within the secondary sampling units (SSUs) of census tracts and untracted divisions, blocks were randomly selected with probabilities proportionate to population. A total of 937 blocks comprised the tertiary sampling units (TSUs).

The care with which households were then selected is indicated by this excerpt from Israel and Robinson's report.

> All housing units within the boundaries of each interviewing area were prelisted in advance of any interviewing in accordance with detailed instructions which required the interviewer to account for all structures within cluster boundaries and to indicate whether or not each structure contained any living quarters. . . .
> Specific housing units (designated in terms of page-and-line

numbers on the applicable prelisting forms) were selected in the New York office by trained sampling personnel using a random procedure.[10]

To minimize bias in selecting respondents within households, each sampled household was predesignated for an interview with either a woman or a man. A selection table printed on each questionnaire randomized the final selection without giving the interviewer any latitude to choose a respondent who might be more congenial or accessible than the randomly selected one.

This sampling procedure has been described in detail to show that ratings are obtained systematically. Some rating services are more competent than others, but ratings are not hocus-pocus.

Television in Our Lives

Wilbur Schramm, Jack Lyle, and Edwin Parker studied children as a television audience.[11] Ten U.S. and Canadian communities provided 5991 children, 1958 parents, and hundreds of teachers, school officials, and other adults as respondents in fieldwork that spanned 3 years. A particularly interesting comparison was possible between "Radiotown" and "Teletown," two communities in Canada that were similar in most respects in 1959 except for the unavailability of television in Radiotown.

The focus of the Schramm et al. study was not exposure *per se,* but the effect of television exposure on children in both their intellectual and emotional development. Schramm et al. found that television had a spectacular effect on children's use of leisure time but less effect on their lives otherwise. When television was introduced, children somehow adapted their leisure time to accommodate as much as 3 to 4 hours of television per day.

Television accelerates learning among young children.

Schramm et al. found that preschool children who watched television entered school with vocabularies about a grade higher than children who did did not watch. However, among children a few years older, incidental learning occurred less. Among teenage children with high mental ability, those who watched television did *less* well in school than those who did not watch.

The landmark study of adult television use was conducted in 1960 by Gary Steiner and was published as *The People Look at Television* in 1963.[12] Steiner found that the "average American viewer" spends hours each day with television but does not regard the medium in any extreme manner—neither extremely good nor extremely bad nor extremely interesting nor extremely dull. Steiner asked the rhetorical question, "How critical can a viewer be when viewing time is a high proportion of total (evening) broadcast time?"

Perhaps the most interesting finding in *The People Look at Television* was the ambivalence of middle-class respondents toward their belief that television should inform and their behavior of tuning out public affairs in favor of crime and comedy. A common response among viewers was that television wastes too much of their time. However, they stopped short of pulling the plug.

Use of Other Media

Matilda Butler Rees and William Paisley used data from California communities to analyze media use.[13] Variables represented respondents' *life cycle* (age and sex), *life-style* (education, occupation, income, etc.), and relevant *attitudes* (achievement motivation, perception of practical education in the media, etc.). The statistical procedure of multiple regression was used to determine how much variation in the use of media could be accounted for by a respondent's life cycle, life-style, and attitudes. In the following list, the strongest predicter of each media use is shown together with the multiple correlation of the media use with the set of predictors.

- Newspaper reading (income, .36).
- Magazine reading (education, .48).
- News magazine reading (education, .34).
- Book reading (education, .36).
- Nonfiction book reading (achievement motivation, .25).
- Television information programming (perception of practical education in the media, .27).
- Radio information programming (age, .33).

Case Studies of Media Audiences

Surveys of media audiences provide the broad view that tells us *which* media appeal to each group in the population. Audience research also takes the form of case studies that focus on reasons *why* each medium has its following. For example, Bernard Berelson used the occasion of a New York City newspaper strike to study the effects of the strike on newspaper readers.[14]

Berelson's 60 respondents, stratified by economic level, were interviewed about their normal use of newspapers and the effects of the strike on their lives. Some reasons why the respondents regularly read newspapers were predictable.

1. For information about and interpretation of public affairs.
2. As a tool for daily living.
3. For respite.
4. For social prestige (gatekeeping function).
5. For vicarious social contact.

What interested Berelson more than these reasons was the "ritualistic and near-compulsive character of newspaper reading" that the strike brought into clear focus. Berelson found that newspaper readers scheduled their time around the newspaper. It was read before, during, and after meals; while traveling to work; and at several other regular times during the day. "Something that had filled a place in [people's] lives was gone, and the adjustment to the new state of affairs was difficult to make."[15]

AUDIENCE ANALYSIS PROCEDURES

The studies mentioned in this chapter show that audience analysis has been an active field of media research since the 1930s. With the spectacular growth in the number and influence of rating services in the television era, audience analysis procedures have become more standardized. As Gary Steiner pointed out, rating services relieve us of the task of answering some of the standard questions.[16] However, we may need nonstandard procedures to answer nonstandard questions. The following points assume that ratings (audience exposure to media content) are not our primary concern.

Is the Question Researchable?

Media researchers live with the knowledge that many important questions are not researchable in the context of:

- The research budget that can be justified.
- The length of time that the answer can be deferred.
- The researcher's prerogative in controlling the media exposure of audiences.

For example, a long-term study of effects (e.g., of sexist content on children) requires an unrealistically favorable context of budget, time, and researcher's prerogative.

A question may also be unresearchable because of its subjectivity. A question such as "What is the effect of television on popular taste?" requires a judgment of "popular taste." It cannot be answered directly from data.

What Is the Range of Data-Gathering Procedures?

The studies mentioned in this chapter report data from experiments, surveys, and case studies. Even apart from the rating services, which spend millions of dollars on field studies each year, the survey is the most common audience analysis tool. Although experiments are more powerful in answering cause and effect questions, they are possible only when the researcher can control media exposure or when some chance condition of media availability creates "experimental" and "control" samples. Case studies are conducted when detail is needed on a small number of persons, families, etc.

The extract at the beginning of this chapter comes from the book *Unobtrusive Measures,* by Eugene Webb, Donald Campbell, Richard Schwartz, and Lee Sechrest.[17] The theme of *Unobtrusive Measures* is not that surveys and other "obtrusive" measures should be replaced by unobtrusive measures, but that *every* measure contains bias. The use of multiple measures leads to a convergence test of validity.

What are some alternatives to experiments, surveys, and case studies? Webb et al. describe three broad categories.

- Physical traces, indications of what people have been doing.
- Records, both the "running record" (e.g., government files) and the "episodic and private record" (e.g., personal letters).
- Observation, both simple observation and staged (e.g., candid camera) observation.

As an example of a trace measure, Webb et al. reported that a Chicago automobile dealer checked the frequencies to which car radios were tuned when the cars were brought in for servicing. More than 50,000 dials a year were checked, with less than 20 percent duplication. The most popular radio stations were then selected to carry the dealership's commercials.[18]

Media audiences are represented in many records that are readily obtained. For example, subscription lists can be purchased from magazine publishers, cable television operators, etc. The private record can be sampled in the mailbags of popular television shows, in letters to the editors in newspapers and magazines, etc.[19]

Observation is useful when media audiences assemble in public places. An observer can gauge reactions to films and television programs by watching audiences in theaters and in bars.

However, unobtrusive measures are seldom powerful enough to be used alone. They are best used to supplement direct measures.

Does the Study Meet Tests of Reliability, Validity, and Utility?

Many kinds of *unreliability* trouble audience analyses. An imaginative researcher can build a reliability test into the field-work plan. Steiner obtained the data for *The People Look at Television* from two independent survey organizations, Elmo Roper Associates and the National Opinion Research Center, each of which collected half of the 2498 cases. Since these organizations have their own procedures for sampling and interviewing, consistency of findings between them is a rigorous test of reliability.

Steiner's gamble on independent half-samples paid off. The Roper and NORC findings were consistent within a narrow range of random difference. For example, Roper and NORC percentages for three typical questions were:[20]

Which medium is most entertaining?
- Television (Roper, 67 percent; NORC, 69 percent).
- Magazines (Roper, 9 percent; NORC, 8 percent).
- Newspapers (Roper, 12 percent; NORC, 14 percent).
- Radio (Roper, 10 percent; NORC, 9 percent).
- Don't know (Roper, 2 percent; NORC, 1 percent).

Which medium gives the most complete news coverage?
- Television (Roper, 18 percent; NORC, 21 percent).
- Magazines (Roper, 3 percent; NORC, 4 percent).
- Newspapers (Roper, 58 percent; NORC, 60 percent).

- Radio (Roper, 20 percent; NORC, 15 percent).
- Don't know (Roper, 1 percent; NORC, 1 percent).

Which medium gives you the clearest understanding of the candidates and issues in national elections?

- Television (Roper, 41 percent; NORC, 43 percent).
- Magazines (Roper, 10 percent; NORC, 10 percent).
- Newspapers (Roper, 36 percent; NORC, 36 percent).
- Radio (Roper, 6 percent; NORC, 5 percent).
- Don't know (Roper, 8 percent; NORC, 7 percent).

One source of *invalidity* in audience analysis is the respondent's wish to impress the interviewer. All variables studied in audience analyses—media use, beliefs, behaviors, and demography—are bound up in the respondent's self-concept. There is a probability, verified in some cases, that the respondent will report what she or he thinks the interviewer would be pleased to hear, regardless of the facts.

In the classroom example of this problem and how to combat it, one person from a team of researchers conducts a home interview on magazine reading. The other person, dressed in overalls, appears at the respondent's back door to collect paper for recycling. Where the interviewer has been told that the respondent reads *Vogue* and the *Atlantic Monthly*, the "recycling collector" may find *True Confessions* and *Argosy*. The deception committed in this procedure makes us wary of it, but it helps us to remember the validity problems of ego-involved self-report.

Utility aspects of an audience analysis require careful thought. Household interviews have reached a unit cost of $40 to $50 within rigorous sampling plans (less within casual sampling plans). The high cost of a large-sample audience survey must be balanced by high reliability, validity, and relevance to the research question.

16

COMPOSITION OF MEDIA
AUDIENCES

Television could be greatly improved by getting more educational and having better type plays. . . . I like good high-class mystery and adventure—not just kid stuff. . . . I'd like to see more national and international events on TV. Incidentally, I want to watch the fights now, do you mind?[1]

Media content is monotonously stereotypic in its portrayals of women and men. Women are passive and dependent. Men are aggressive and independent. Media organizations that produce these stereotypic portrayals are controlled by men. Very few of the thousands of media publishers, producers, editors, etc., are women. The information presented earlier in this book is like a playbill for the theater of the mass media. We know the plot, the cast, and the producers. However, we have not described the audience. Who are they? Which media do they use and how often? What effect does it have on them? The first two questions are answered in this chapter. The difficult question of effect is explored in the following two chapters on children and on adults.

TELEVISION AUDIENCES

Proposition 16.1: Women Watch More Television *than Men.*

In a review of the television viewing of women and men, it is easy to forget that the hours they spend watching television are a *substantial* part of each week. Excluding hours spent sleeping, women spend approximately 1 hour out of every 4 hours of each day watching television. Men, not far behind, spend about 1 hour out of every 5 hours of each day watching television.[2]

HOW MUCH TELEVISION IS WATCHED AND WHO WATCHES IT? Rating services such as American Research Bureau, C.E. Hooper, Pulse, and others monitor program viewing. The findings of these studies determine which programs will be continued, how much advertisers will be charged to sponsor programs, and which programs advertisers will choose to sponsor.

A.C. Nielsen is probably the best-known rating service. In addition to providing ratings on specific programs, Nielsen monitors a household's total use of television. Nielsen figures for 1976 and 1977 show that women continue to be the heaviest users of television. Women spend 31 hours per week with television, versus 25 hours for men, 22 hours for teenagers, and 26 hours for children. Much of the difference is explained by women's weekday viewing. Women spend 6 hours per week while men spend 2.5 hours per week watching between 10 A.M. and 4:30 P.M. on weekdays. However, women also watch more television than men during prime time (11 hours versus 10 hours).[3]

This viewing pattern changes for working women, who view 27 percent less television than nonworking women. Most of the working woman's viewing (over 53 percent) is during prime-time and late-night hours, while only 12 percent of her viewing is during daytime hours. In comparison, 24 percent of the nonworking woman's viewing is during daytime hours.[4]

A.C. Nielsen reports the percentage of female and male

viewers across three age groups and five viewing periods. In general, women and men have similar viewing patterns during prime time (8 P.M. to 11 P.M.), late afternoons (4:30 P.M. to 7:30 P.M.), weekend daytime (7 A.M. to 1 P.M. and 1 P.M. to 7 P.M.), and late night (11 P.M. to 1 A.M.). Only during weekday daytime (10 A.M. to 4:30 P.M.) do we find a difference, with women as the primary audience.[5]

Nielsen's data further show that women's viewing increases with age from 29 hours per week in the 18 to 24 age group to 35 hours per week in the 55 and older age group. Men's viewing also increases with age from 20 hours per week in the 18 to 24 age group to 32 hours in the 55 and older age group. Across the life cycle, men view an average of 5 hours for every 6 hours viewed by women in the same age group.[6]

If we are to gauge the audience effects of a medium as diverse in its content as television, we must be more specific about the time periods in which female and male viewing is concentrated. Across the life cycle, women do about 33 percent of their viewing during prime-time, 14 percent during late-afternoon, 19 percent during weekday daytime, 9 percent during late-night, and 7 percent during weekday daytime hours. Men do about 37 percent of their viewing during prime-time, 14 percent during the late-afternoon, 9 percent during weekday daytime, 10 percent during weekend daytime, and 11 percent during late-night hours. The greatest sex difference in viewing occurs in the young (18 to 24) age group, in which women do much more of their total viewing during weekday daytime hours (21 percent) than men (8 percent). Older men, including those who are retired, do 12 percent of their total viewing during weekday daytime hours, in comparison with 20 percent for older women.[7]

Proposition 16.2: Women and Men Prefer Different Types of Television Programming.

Although studies reported in this section show similar programming preferences, we find three differences. First, women prefer comedies, and men prefer sports and television movies. Preferences for a particular year are, of course, limited by the available programs. During the 1975 season, Nielsen data showed that women preferred programs that featured women, such as "Mary Tyler Moore," "Rhoda," and "Phyllis"; men preferred programs that featured men, such as the "Six Million Dollar Man" and "Sanford and Son." The one program most frequently watched by both sexes that year, "All in the Family," had both female and male major characters.[8] In the 1977 season many of these programs had been replaced. More of the programs feature women and men.

The second difference is that women are less likely to watch violent programs;[9] however, this preference may be explained by the strong male orientation of violent programs of past seasons such as "Starsky and Hutch" and "Streets of San Francisco."

The third difference is that more men than women watch the early-evening news. This "preference" may be explained by circumstances (women are more likely to be preparing dinner).[10]

WHAT TYPES OF TELEVISION PROGRAMS ARE WATCHED? The most recent extensive study of the television audience was conducted by Robert Bower.[11] Bower repeated many of the questions asked by Gary Steiner and reported in *The People Look at Television* a decade earlier. Bower's book provides data from the Steiner 1960 study and from his own 1970 follow-up study. Some of the data reflect on viewing preferences and will be discussed here. Other data tell us about audience attitudes and will be reported later.

Bower found in 1970, as was true in 1960, that women and men have many viewing preferences in common. Some differences that do exist are small. For example, more men (41 percent) than women (38 percent) watch educational television once a week, more women (28 percent) than men (22 percent) watch comedy variety/shows, more men (13 percent) than women (6 percent) watch sports, and more men (22 percent) than women (19 percent) watch movies.[12]

Other differences were reported by Nielsen in 1978. He listed the 15 most popular programs viewed by women and men during the October to December 1977 season. Women preferred "Laverne and Shirley" (25 percent), "Happy Days" (23 percent), "Three's Company" (22 percent), "All in the Family" (21 percent), "Alice" (20 percent), "60 Minutes" (20 percent), "NBC Monday Night Movie" (20 percent), "Little House on the Prairie" (19 percent), "Charlie's Angels" (18 percent), "Rhoda" (18 percent), "On Our Own" (18 percent), "The Waltons" (18 percent), "Eight is Enough" (18 percent), "Family" (17 percent), and "Big Event" (17 percent). The favorite programs of men were "NFL Monday Night Football" (21 percent), "60 Minutes" (20 percent), "Laverne and Shirley" (19 percent), "Happy Days" (19 percent), "All in the Family" (18 percent), "Alice" (17 percent), "ABC Sunday Night Movie" (17 percent), "Three's Company" (17 percent), "On Our Own" (16 percent), "Big Event" (16 percent), "Six Million Dollar Man" (16 percent), "Rhoda" (15 percent), "Charlie's Angels" (15 percent), "M*A*S*H" (15 percent), and "NBC Saturday Night Movie" (14 percent).[13] Some programs appear on both lists, but there is a contrast. Women are oriented to programs that feature women and families; men are oriented to programs, including sports and movies, that feature men.

One reason why the female and male preference lists are as similar as they are may be the continuing popularity of family instead of individual viewing. Even in 1970, when 31 percent of all TV households had multiple sets, most prime-time viewing was done with other members of the family. There was 94 percent joint viewing among one-set families, 80 percent joint viewing among two-set families, and 66 percent joint viewing among three-set families. Husbands and wives watched television together 72 percent of the time in one-set families and 60 percent of the time in multiset families.[14]

When television viewers are wife and husband, 53 percent

of the decisions of what programs to watch are made jointly. Husbands alone make the decision 28 percent of the time, and wives alone make the decision 18 percent of the time. When parents and children watch television together, 42 percent of the decisions are made by the group, 27 percent are made by the father alone, 10 percent are made by the mother alone, and 17 percent are made by the children.[15]

One difference between women and men in their use of television is that women are more likely to *plan* what will be watched. Bower found that although there was no difference in the percentage of women or men who were high planners among those with a grade school education (20 percent of the women and 19 percent of the men), there were significant differences in the percentage of women and men who were high planners among those with a high school education (34 percent of the women and 24 percent of the men) and those with a college education (41 percent of the women and 30 percent of the men).[16]

Another difference between women and men is the viewing of soap operas. Natan Katzman provided 1970 data on the audiences of these programs. He reported that 71 percent of the audience were women, chiefly in the age groups of 18 to 34 and 50 and older.

The number of soap opera viewer hours has grown over the years. In 1955, there were approximately 10 million viewer-hours per day; 15 years later this had increased to more than 50 million viewer-hours per day.[17]

According to Nielsen data used by Katzman, a disproportionate number of the audience are Southerners. A fourth of the U.S. population lives in the South, and yet a third of the soap opera viewers are Southerners. Three factors that correlate with soap opera viewing are most likely to be found in the South: viewers are more likely to live in smaller counties, to have less education, and to have lower incomes than nonviewers. [18]

Observers of the soap opera scene believe that current estimates of the soap opera audience are too low. For instance,

Rose Goldsen states that the audience includes large numbers of mothers with small children, and that at least 15 million children are regular viewers of soap operas. Most audience analyses do not include these children.[19]

Viewer preferences for violent programming have been extensively studied. Harold Israel and John Robinson analyzed data that were collected by W.R. Simmons and Associates from 1968 to 1970. These data, from diaries of television viewing of a national probability sample, provided a profile of "violence viewers." Israel and Robinson's study showed that women were less likely to watch violent programs than men. Among women, race (nonwhite) was the best predictor of violence viewing. In addition, more violent programs were seen by women who did not graduate from high school, whose incomes were less than $8,000, and who were over 50. The same predictors accounted for violence viewing among men, but in the rank order of age, income, education, and race.[20]

Israel and Robinson next analyzed viewing of news. They reported that women were less likely than men to watch one of the national news programs (22 percent versus 25 percent).[21] Women in the 25 to 34 age group were least likely to watch news programs. Israel and Robinson noted that these are "the years when family responsibilities apparently reach a peak leaving little time for keeping up with the news."[22]

Or is it the case that women are less oriented to news and public affairs programming? Israel and Robinson put this question to the test. Among women who reported watching the early-evening news, 62 percent, averaged across the three networks, said they paid full attention to the broadcasts. The comparable coverage among men watching the early-evening news was 79 percent. However, an equal percentage (71 percent) of women and men who watched public-affairs programs scheduled during less busy hours of the day ("60 Minutes," "Meet the Press," and "Face the Nation") said that they paid full attention to the broadcasts. It is more likely, therefore, that women "tune out" the early-evening news because they are busy, not because they lack interest in the news.

Proposition 16.3: In General, Women Are More Approving *of Television than Men, Although They Are More* Critical *of the Presentation of Women.*

Women are more likely than men to say that television adds to their day and that it presents unbiased news. However, women are more critical than men of television's protrayal of women. Both women and men would like to see women portrayed in more roles.

WHAT DOES THE AUDIENCE THINK ABOUT WHAT IT WATCHES?

Steiner's 1960 study and Bower's 1970 study tell us a great deal about the attitudes of women and men toward television. Steiner found that more women than men attributed their enjoyment of the day to television (28 percent of the women versus 22 percent of the men).[23]

In 1960, almost equal percentages of women (55 percent) and men (53 percent) said they usually watch television because "it's such a pleasant way to spend the evening." By 1970, Bower found that women (46 percent) were more likely than men (36 percent) to have positive attitudes toward television when asked the same question.[24]

Women were also more positive about television when asked which "medium presents the fairest, most unbiased news?" Thirty-seven percent of the women and 29 percent of the men named television (21 percent of the women and 24 percent of the men named newspapers). When questioned about the use of media for political information, women (63 percent) were more likely than men (55 percent) to say that television provided "the clearest understanding of the candidates and issues in national elections." Furthermore, women (47 percent) were more likely than men (38 percent) to say that television helped them to choose their candidate in the 1968 elections.[25]

In May 1971, *Good Housekeeping* polled its nationwide Consumer Panel to determine attitudes about television commercials. Toni Robin, an advertising executive, said "TV commercials serve the average woman well by informing her,

entertaining her and stimulating her to be more of a woman."
Slightly more than half the women (53 percent) were in agreement with this policy. Forty percent of the women on the
Consumer Panel felt that commercials were insulting. The attitude of these women is conveyed in a statement by Franchellie
Cadwell, advertising agency president: "The modern woman is
insulted by women-directed commercials and it's time broadcasters realize the days of talking down to her are over."[26]

The *Good Housekeeping* poll also reported that more than
one-third of the respondents found some commercials so insulting that they turned off the television set. Also indicative of
their attitudes is the statement by one-half of the women that
they refused to buy certain products as a way of expressing their
displeasure with the commercials.[27]

Perhaps the largest survey of public attitudes toward television was conducted by the Screen Actor's Guild in 1974.
More than 8700 people responded to a questionnaire printed in
22 daily newspapers throughout the country. An additional
1379 questionnaires were completed in a separate sampling in
Southern California. Since the pattern of responses of the two
groups was similar, all were analyzed together. The responses
came primarily from women (84 percent). Among the findings:

- Sixty-seven percent wanted to see women in positions of
  authority on television.
- Eighty-six percent wanted to see actresses portraying
  women in professions.
- Seventy-three percent wanted to see women as spokespersons for national products.
- Eighty-one percent wanted to see women hosting programs.
- Sixty-three percent wanted to see women in leading roles on
  programs other then comedy, variety, and talk shows.[28]

Some questions on the survey provided information on respondents' attitudes.

- Sixty-six percent believed that television did not encourage young girls to aspire to a useful and meaningful role in society.
- Seventy-two percent believed that sex was overused to sell products.
- Sixty-three percent believed that commercials portrayed women's identity and happiness as dependent on the use of the product.
- Seventy-one percent believed that the relationships and roles on television did not mirror women's life-styles.[29]

Women and men in the sample had contrasting attitudes toward the presentation of women on television. When asked, "Do you like the women you see on TV?", 28 percent of the women and 52 percent of the men responded affirmatively.[30]

A prevailing belief among station managers and network executives is that news should be delivered by a deep-voiced male. This belief was tested by ABC prior to hiring Barbara Walters as the coanchor of its evening news program. ABC surveyed its viewers and found:

- Forty-six percent would prefer a female newscaster.
- Forty-one percent are content with either a male or female newscaster.
- Thirteen percent would prefer a male newscaster.[31]

Magazine Audiences

Proposition 16.4: Women and Men Prefer Different Types of Magazines.

A glance at the magazine rack in any store makes us realize that large numbers of weekly and monthly publications are available. Many are targeted to small and specialized reader-ships. There is virtually no occupational or recreational group in the United States that does not have its own magazine. Regional, ethnic, religious, and age-group magazines add to the variety found on the magazine rack. Some magazines obviously appeal to women. The large category of "women's magazines" includes *Good Housekeeping, Vogue, Seventeen, Ladies' Home Journal, Cosmopolitan, Redbook,* and *True Confessions.* Other magazines, such as *Gentleman's Quarterly, True,* and *Saga,* appeal to men. These groups of magazines are not discussed in this section because their readership is primarily from one sex. Instead, we look at the readership patterns of magazines that are read by both sexes.

Using the *Target Group Index,* we compared the female and male readership of four groups of magazines. Analytic magazines (defined as *Atlantic Monthly, Harper's, Natural History,* and *Esquire*) are read by 3 percent of the women and 5 percent of the men. News magazines (*Time, Newsweek,* and *U.S. News and World Report*) are read by 23 percent of the women and 33 percent of the men. General interest magazines (*Reader's Digest, Parade,* and *Family Weekly*) are read by 63 percent of women and 56 percent of men. Business magazines (*Barron's, Business Week, Forbes,* and *Fortune*) are read by 3 percent of women and 8 percent of men.[32]

The *Target Group Index* also provides information on the relationship between education and the use of print media and electronic media. This relationship exists to a different extent for each sex. For example, 32 percent of women and 37 percent of men with college educations are frequent readers of magazines versus 17 percent of women and 18 percent of men with high school educations. The opposite pattern is found for prime-time television viewing; 15 percent of women and 14 percent of men with college educations versus 21 percent of women and 22 percent of men with high school educations are frequent prime-time viewers.[33]

Although education influences the use of magazines, the reader's sex continues to be the important factor in choosing a magazine. Audience specialization among magazines becomes self-perpetuating. Magazines that represent themselves as "women's magazines" are rarely purchased and read by men; those that represent themselves as "men's magazines" are rarely purchased and read by women.

NEWSPAPER AUDIENCES

Proposition 16.5: Although Women and Men Are Equally Likely to Read Newspapers, They Prefer Different Sections Within Newspapers.

Studies of newspaper readership show that both sexes are about equally likely to be newspaper readers. Sex differences lie in the sections of the newspaper that women and men read. We should not overstate these differences, because they are probably more a reflection of newspaper section stereotypes than the actual topics covered. For example, men are more likely to read the sports sections than women. However, many women are sports fans and would read sports sections if they adequately covered women's sporting events. Renamed women's sections present the opposite problem. Despite newspaper's efforts to include topics (e.g., consumer economics) of interest to both sexes, few men read those sections.

STUDIES OF NEWSPAPER AUDIENCES. According to a W.R. Simmons survey in 1970, 90 percent of both women and men said they had read a newpsper the day before. This similarity holds for many sections of the newspaper in the *Target Group Index* data, which reports that 50 percent of women and 49 percent of men read one newspaper daily and another 14 percent of women and 16 percent of men read two or more daily newspapers. Readership percentages of major sections are:

- Twenty-three percent of women and 33 percent of men read the business/finance section.
- Fifty-four percent of women and 18 percent of men read the women's section.

- Twenty-five percent of women and 52 percent of men read the sports section.
- Forty-three percent of women and 37 percent of men read the entertainment section.

Essentially equal percentages of women and men read the main news section (61 percent), the entertainment section (40 percent), the travel section (22 percent), the classified advertisments (34 percent), and the comics (36 percent). [34]

As newspaper sections change to reflect the multiple roles of women and men, we expect to see different readership patterns.

RADIO AUDIENCES

Proposition 16.6: Women and Men Have Similar Preferences in Radio Programming.

Although each of the other media has shown differences in the content preferences of women and men, radio shows few contrasts. Sports is the only program category in which there is more than a 4 percent spread between the female and male audiences.[35]

STUDIES OF RADIO AUDIENCES. The *Target Group Index* provides detailed information on the radio perferences of each sex. For example:

- Twenty-five percent of women and 26 percent of men listen to news.
- Twenty-six percent of women and 22 percent of men listen to top hits.
- Nineteen percent of women and 19 percent of men listen to country music.

- Fourteen percent of women and 11 percent of men listen to golden oldies.
- Thirteen percent of women and 17 percent of men listen to progressive rock.
- Eight percent of women and 6 percent of men listen to talk shows.
- Four percent of women and 13 percent of men listen to sports.[36]

Factors such as age, education, and family background are probably more important than sex in segmenting the audiences of these different kinds of radio programs, most of which are limited to music.

THE COMPOSITE MEDIA AUDIENCE

Media use was studied by Edwin Parker and William Paisley in two contrasting California communities—San Mateo, a suburb of San Francisco, and Fresno, an agribusiness center of the San Joaquin Valley. Media use by 1869 persons in San Mateo and Fresno showed that variables such as age and education make a difference. However, television viewing cuts across sex, age, and educational groupings to reach most persons in the United States every day. Parker and Paisley found the following differences in above-average television viewing by sex, cross-tabulated by age and education.

1. There was a 17 percent difference in such viewing between women and men (69 percent versus 52 percent) who were under 40 and had not attended college.
2. There was a 5 percent difference in such viewing between women and men (46 percent versus 41 percent) who were under 40 and had attended college.
3. There was a 4 percent difference in such viewing between

women and men (55 percent versus 51 percent) who were 40 and over and had not attended college.

4. There was a 1 percent difference in such viewing between women and men (45 percent versus 46 percent) who were 40 and over and had attended college.[37]

The only strong sex difference in amount of television viewing occurs among younger persons who had not attended college. However, women in this group are an important target audience of nonsexist programming, for which their heavy diet of television creates either barriers or opportunities.

PROPOSITIONAL SUMMARY

Proposition 16.1:   Women watch more *television* than men.

Proposition 16.2:   Women and men prefer different types of television *programming*.

Proposition 16.3:   In general, women are more *approving* of television than men, although they are more *critical* of the presentation of women.

Proposition 16.4:   Women and men prefer different types of *magazines*.

Proposition 16.5:   Although women and men are equally likely to read *newspapers*, they prefer different sections within newspapers.

Proposition 16.6:   Women and men have similar preferences in *radio programming*.

CHILDREN AND MEDIA

Sugar and spice,
   and everything nice;
That's what little girls are made of.

Snakes and snails,
   and puppy-dog tails;
That's what little boys are made of.[1]

Nursery rhymes remind us that sex-role stereotyping has been around much longer than the mass media. The fact that children also face sex bias in media content is not the reason for a separate chapter on children in this book. Children are a special audience for *three* reasons that are of great interest to parents, media managers, and researchers alike.

First, even if our primary concern is for *adult* sex roles—behaviors associated with one's sex or attitudes about the capabilities and proper roles of the sexes—adult behaviors and attitudes do not suddenly materialize on eighteenth or twenty-first birthdays. They are built on many childhood years of

This chapter was written by Suzanne Pingree and Robert Parker Hawkins, University of Wisconsin, Madison.

learning about the world and how it works; sex roles are part of that world. Moreover, childhood is not simply a period of passive learning to be translated into behaviors and attitudes when adulthood later makes them needed. As we will see later in this chapter, even very young children often behave according to their impressions of adult sex roles and are quick to assert their attitudes about what girls and boys can and should do. The implication is that we should study sex-role development in childhood to understand how and why adults are the way they are.

Our second reason for concern with the child audience is also implied by viewing childhood as the formative period for adult sex roles. Depending on one's vantage point, children's openness to new information and influence during these formative years makes them either an audience of special risk to be protected or an audience of special opportunity to be exploited. Seeing children as a target audience provides a rare point of agreement between media managers and social reformers. Of course, media managers see children as consumers; reformers hope to divert children away from sex-role stereotypes before stereotypic thinking becomes too deeply rooted.

The third reason to single out the child audience derives from the first two. If we want to know *whether* and *how* the mass media affect our sex roles and our expectations of others, it makes sense to look first for these effects where we have the best chance of finding them. If television's stereotypic content, for example, affects anyone, surely it affects those who are just forming their impressions of sex roles and are most vulnerable to socialization messages.

SEX ROLES AND SEX DIFFERENCES

In this section, we will first discuss what sex roles and sex differences are and how they appear and change as children grow older; we will then present explanations of how sex roles are acquired. These explanations will provide us with both a reason to expect effects of the media and an important qualification that we will need later.

Proposition 17.1: There Are Few Innate Sex-role Differences Between Girls and Boys.

We all have notions about how different women are from men and girls from boys. It seems to start right at birth, with little girls being more cuddly, fragile, and soft than little boys. Boys are more athletic, independent, assertive, and active, or so the stereotypes say.[2] But is this true? How much difference in behavior really exists between the sexes? This question must be answered before we can consider what, if any, role the media have in teaching us these differences.

According to the most recent summary of psychological research on sex differences, there seem to be very few *real* sex differences. Boys have better visual/spatial ability and greater mathematical ability than girls; girls have better verbal ability and are less aggressive (kicking, hitting, etc.) than boys.[3]

Even though these differences are reliably found in psychological research, they are not very big differences. In fact, it is usually true that boys are more different from each other in their behvaior than they are different from girls as a group, and the same is true for girls. That is, if the number of boys who have different amounts of these four characteristics were plotted against the number of girls, we would probably see about as much overlap as difference. The average or center point of the groups would differ, but it would be obvious that the two sexes are more alike than different.

This fact may be hard for some of us to accept; we *feel* these differences between women and men and we see them every day. Women and men have different jobs, interests, and skills. And, indeed, when we look for more specific differences, such as what kind of job one has or what extracurricular activities one engages in, we find clear and strong sex differences.

Proposition 17.2: Children Develop Sex-role Stereotypic Behaviors *As Young As 3 Years.*

Starting as early as 3 years old, children make toy or occupational choices that reflect the stereotypes—boys like trucks, girls like dolls, boys want to be doctors, girls want to be nurses. Three is very young; it is not surprising to discover that children show more of this kind of stereotyping as they grow older. And there are some interesting facts about the way children develop, as well.

To most of us, sex and sex role are bound up together. But very young children have to learn *both* what sex they are *and* what social role their sex is supposed to play. Most children know whether they are girls or boys by 3 or 4 years, but many do not understand until a few years later that being a girl also means that one will become a woman and that changes in appearance (e.g., long hair versus short, dresses versus pants) or situation cannot change one's sex. Understanding all of these things is called "gender constancy," and it seems to occur in a three-step pattern for both girls and boys: first, knowing what sex one is; second, understanding the link between girl/woman or boy/man; and third, seeing that different appearances or situations do not change one's sex.[4] As will be discussed later, understanding most of this may be important for children who are trying to figure out the sex role their sex is supposed to play.

Children increase their awareness of stereotypically female and male characteristics between kindergarten and second grade, level off for perhaps 2 years, and then again increase so that sixth graders know the traits stereotypically associated with each sex nearly as well as adults. Moreover, both girls and boys know more about what *men* are supposed to do and be like.[5] There is evidence that boys stick more closely to the male sex role than girls do to the female sex role, and this tendency may increase with age.[6] Perhaps it is less awful for a girl to have "masculine" characteristics than for a boy to have "feminine" ones. It is more acceptable to be a tomboy than a sissy.

We do not know much about what happens to children's sex-role stereotypes to produce the rather complete knowledge of sex roles that adults have. It is hard to compare how people of widely different ages answer questions, because they may understand the same question differently. We could assume a gradual, continuous increase in sex-typing until adulthood, but that brings at least two objections to mind. First, there is a distinction to be made between how well one *understands* what the stereotypes are and whether or not one *accepts* the stereotypes. And second, some important things happen during adolescence—such as developing one's own identity and beginning to relate to the opposite sex—that should affect how one accepts a sex-typed view.

Furthermore, full acceptance of sex-role stereotypes may not be conducive to efficient functioning in our society. There is reason to believe that strong acceptance of a sex role, either masculine or feminine, closes off some modes of behavior that may be very effective. People of both sexes who are neither strongly masculine nor strongly feminine but who possess qualities of both sex roles seem to be better able to respond well in a variety of situations.[7]

This transcendence of sex roles, taking the best qualities from each and critically rejecting the stereotypic role that society has laid out, may be a higher level of sex-role development that is similar to higher stages of moral development.[8] The end point of sex-role development is not full acceptance; it is an intelligent weighing of *individual* strengths and weaknesses in the context of what society has to offer. As with other sorts of development, not everyone reaches this final stage.

To summarize, there is not much reason to accept the stereotypes of behavioral and attitudinal differences between women and men, but there are clear social and occupational role differences. Even 3-year-olds understand some of the stereotypes and, although we do not have enough evidence to be sure about age and sex trends, research indicates the following.

- Understanding of gender constancy appears between the ages of 3 and 7 years and seems to develop in an invariant sequence.
- The "masculine"sex role seems to be important to both girls and boys,
- Boys take their role more seriously than girls do theirs.
- Both sexes have a fair grasp of what is appropriate for their sex by middle childhood,
- Developmental changes after middle childhood are more open to speculation, and the degree of final stereotyped behavior may vary.

COMPETING THEORIES. Trying to explain *how* children come to understand and accept sex-role stereotypes is really trying to explain how children organize and build their worlds. Theories that psychologists use to understand how children develop in general can be applied to understanding how children develop sex-role stereotypes. Sex roles are just one part of a culture's system of values and categories for structuring relations that children learn as they develop into functioning adults in their culture.

For sex-role development, as for other types of developmental changes, a controversy has raged for years between "social learning" theories[9] and "cognitive-developmental" theories.[10] Although the arguments are complicated, the basic difference is the degree to which the individual or the environment controls development. Exaggerating the contrast to make the point, social learning theories say that sex-role behaviors and attitudes are pervasive in the child's *environment* and that all that children do is learn what is there. Cognitive-developmental theories hold that individuals construct their *own* views of the world, that the environment is simply a source of raw material. Furthermore, most cognitive-developmental theories argue that the logic of children's thought changes radically as they mature, and that conceptions of sex roles *cannot* be constructed until the child has developed the necessary logic.

SELF-SOCIALIZATION. Gradually, researchers are realizing that this controversy is at least partly a result of each side exaggerating the two theories to show contrasts. The two theories may not be totally different and, where they differ, they may complement each other instead of conflict. In explaining the development of sex roles, particularly specific aspects such as occupational choices and stereotyped expectations of the sexes, the best approach is a combination of the two theories that is labeled "self-socialization."[11]

The basis of self-socialization theory is that we pass through stages of sex-role development that are linked to stages of other kinds of development, notably cognitive and social development. For sex roles, this means that we first develop a "gender identity"—a rudimentary notion of the distinction between female and male—and then begin to infer from available information and experimental pressures what it means to be one sex or the other. Sex-role development thus depends on what one has observed or experienced in the past, on the kinds of new information presented, and on one's ability to think about the new information. Two similar studies illustrate these ideas.

Both studies examined a process integral to both cognitive and social-learning aspects of self-socialization, that of imitating or paying attention to a similar (in this case, same-sex) filmed model. Children who have gender constancy should spend more time imitating or paying attention to a same-sex model. These children have figured out what sex they are and find it satisfying to learn more about their sex and sex role. Similarly, children who have been reinforced for behaving in sex-appropriate ways (measured by how sex-typed they are now) should also be more concerned with the behavior of a same-sex model, since it is this behavior that they are likely to be rewarded for if they imitate it. Both perspectives on the modeling process, then, predict same-sex modeling, the first because children like to organize and learn about the world, and the second because children like to be rewarded.

Ronald Slaby and Karin Frey used gender constancy (an index of cognitive development with respect to sex roles) to look for differences in attention to same or opposite sex models. The cognitive-developmental prediction worked well for 3- to 5-year-old boys: boys who had gender constancy spent more time looking at a male model than boys who lacked gender constancy. Gender constancy did not seem to affect girls' attention to the models.[12] A very similar thing happened in David and Louise Perry's study of sex-typing and imitation of a model by third- and fourth-grade children: the more masculine children (a measure of past reinforcement that led to present behavior) did imitate more of a male model's behavior, but the sex of the model did not matter for feminine children; they imitated either model.[13]

One study of eighth-grade children indicates that girls respond more to same-sex models than boys. Myrna Plost and Marvin Rosen presented a slide show of a woman and a man in two computer-age careers, systems analyst and computer software designer, with half the children seeing the sexes in reversed jobs from the other half. When asked which occupation they would prefer, both girls and boys tended to pick the one held by the same-sex model in their version of the slide show, but this was done by 72 percent of the girls and only 61 percent of the boys. This departure from the two studies just described might be an important age-related change, but it might also be related to the specific situation and materials used here. Perry and Perry, and Slaby and Frey, were dealing with more general things, such as attention or overall imitation, but Plost and Rosen were asking for a very specific occupational preference. While occupational choice is probably an important and interesting topic for eighth graders, females models in professional occupations are very rare. Plost and Rosen report that a 1972 U.S. Office of Education film called *Career Education* contains 150 occupations for men, but only 25 for women, so that the women modeling computer careers were probably extremely noticeable and salient to these eighth-grade girls.[14]

Except for the very specific case of career preference just reported, it looks as if the important same-sex modeling idea does not work very well for girls. For boys, on the other hand, *both* a social-learning approach and a cognitive-developmental approach have merit. *Both* one's cognitive abilities and one's past learning are good predictors of same-sex modeling, at least for boys or children who prefer masculine activities or characteristics. This combination of the two approaches is at the heart of self-socialization theory.

But why does it not work for girls? It probably does, at some level, and what may be going on is that we have not taken enough factors into account. Male models in our society are almost uniformly more powerful and successful (factors that induce modeling) than females, so girls as female children may be faced with a conflict between imitating a similar female model or a powerful and successful male model. The reason that boys accept their stereotyped role more readily than girls may be that sex-role acquisition is easier for boys than for girls in our society. There may be some eventual advantage for girls, however. Having to learn both sex roles may put them in a better position to pick and choose the aspects that they wish to use. At any rate, this explanation of why same-sex modeling is less prevalent for girls illustrates another way in which social-learning and cognitive processes may be combined. It still seems that children learn appropriate behaviors from others but apply their own needs and patterns of thought to this learning. Both these processes have to be fitted into the context of male/-masculine or female/feminine in our society, even though our theories are best suited for explaining the masculine half of humanity.

CHILDREN AS MEDIA USERS

Turning now to the relationship of the media and children's sex roles, we need to examine the child audience. How much do children use different media? Which media and which types of content do children prefer? Do patterns of use and preference change as children grow?

Proposition 17.3: Children Spend Many Hours Each Day with Television and Other Media.

It should come as no surprise to anyone that American children are heavy users of many forms of media, just as American adults are. Two-year-olds ask to have storybooks read to them and spend long periods quietly turning pages, studying pictures, and identifying objects by themselves. After age 6 years, schoolbooks become a major concern, for better or worse, and occupy an important part of children's time. Newspaper reading often begins with comic strips during the early school years and gradually expands to other types of content. Radio is a more important medium to teenagers than to any other age group. And, of course, going to the movies is still a key social event in the lives of teenagers and young adults.[15]

Despite all these other forms of mediated information, entertainment, and opinion, television is *the* medium of American children to an even greater extent than it is for adults. The following information gives some idea how much television children of different ages watch each day and how these amounts changed between 1960 and 1970.

- In 1960, first graders watched 2.3 hours per day, sixth graders watched 2.5 hours per day, and tenth graders watched 2.9 hours per day.[16]
- In 1971, first graders watched 3.5 hours per day, sixth graders watched 4.4 hours per day, and tenth graders watched 4.0 hours per day.[17]

Even though the United States was nearly as saturated with television sets and stations in 1960 as it was 10 years later, children in 1970 watched about 50 percent more televsion—for a total of about 4 hours per weekday. Viewing increases from 3.5 hours per day in the first grade to nearly 4.5 hours by the sixth grade and then decreases (presumably under pressure from increased homework and social life) to 4 hours a day in the tenth grade.

These times are, of course, averages that include some children who watched no television and others who watched 9 hours or more each day. The exact number of hours vary from study to study, depending on whether children or their parents are asked to report the number of hours of television viewing or to check off the shows they watched on a list of programs. But whatever the exact figures, the fact is that children of all ages spend a large part of their waking day watching television. To make these numbers more meaningful, consider that by the time the average American child graduates from high school, she or he has spent more time watching television than attending school, playing, eating, reading, etc. The only activity that has consumed more time than television is sleep, and the difference is not large.

Turning to what children like and what they watch, favorite shows at first are cartoons and other programs made expressly for children, then situation comedies and, finally, adventure and music/variety shows. But even first-grade boys' favorites include more action programs (featuring strong males), while first-grade girls' favorites include many family situation comedies.[18]

On the other hand, although children's favorite programs have something to do with what they actually watch, preference and viewing are not the same thing. Children often watch even when none of their favorites are on, or they bow to family majorities or authorities and watch what others want to watch. Whatever the reason, it is clear that all ages and types of children watch a fairly similar menu of television. Considering the stereotyped nature of television content and the large amount of time children spend with television, we have good cause for concern about the sex roles that children develop.

MEDIA'S CONTRIBUTION TO SEXISM

We now hold several pieces of a puzzle. We know that portrayals of women and men in the media are very stereotyped and limiting (and, for women, often degrading as well) and that these portrayals lag behind social changes that are taking place. We know that children are massively exposed to these stereotyped messages from a variety of media, but especially television. And while we know that sex-role development and stereotyping begins very young and depends on general cognitive sophistication, we also know what children observe is the raw material from which they develop their own ideas.

There is an obvious way to fit these pieces together. Sex-stereotyped media content is attended to by children, learned, and used in constructing their own sex roles. And, since the content is more stereotypic than real life, the effect of the media is to make children more sex-typed than they would otherwise be. In other words, the media act as a drag on changing sex roles.

Proposition 17.4: Media Content Makes Children More Sex-stereotyped.

The problem is that while this is very reasonable, reasonableness is not proof. In logical terms, the three things mentioned that we "know" are necessary but not sufficient conditions for the solution we stated to be true. Instead of fact, our solution is a proposition to be further tested and discarded if necessary.

One might think that the uniformly biased content of the media and the massive exposure of children to it would make testing this proposition easy; surely the effect we are looking for is pervasive, just waiting for us to measure it. Instead, it is a curious fact that either of these conditions make this testing process difficult, and both together present a huge problem. Consider two questions.

1. How do we demonstrate that sexist content increases sexism in its viewers/readers if there is little nonsexist content to produce a different effect?
2. Where do we go to find the unexposed control group (like the viewing/reading group in all respects but this) that would not be affected?

There are no fully satisfactory answers to these questions, but there are two kinds of partial answers, each with its own strengths and weaknesses.

THE EVIDENCE FOR A RELATIONSHIP.   To answer the second question, it is not sufficient to find those few children who do not watch television and compare them with the vast majority who do. It would be no surprise to find this minority different in its sex-role behaviors and attitudes, but it would be implausible to attribute the differences to television, because these children would also be unusual in other important ways. They may come from areas isolated geographically from the mainstream of American life, or they may be extremely poor, or their parents may shelter them from television, perhaps to avoid just the effect in which we are interested. In any case, it could be their isolation, their poverty, or their parents' guidance that is the cause of their different sex roles and not the absence of television in their lives.

If we are willing to state our proposition as, "The *more* one is exposed to stereotyped mass media content, the *more* affected (stereotyped in behaviors and attitudes) one will be," then a compromise answer to the second question is to study a representative sample of the population and compare heavy and light media users. However, finding that heavy media users, on the average, are more traditional than light users is again a necessary but not a sufficient condition for our proposition. Just because the two factors are related in America's child population does not tell us *how* they are related. It could indeed be that media use *causes* children to become more stereotyped. Or it could be that those who are traditional expose themselves more to the media *because* they find it compatible with their goals and values. It could even be that neither of these causes the other. Another factor, such as parent's attitudes, income, or intelligence, could cause children both to be more traditional and to use more media content.

Still, it is some help to know whether the two are related, even if we cannot tell which causes which. After all, if they are *not* related, it is very unlikely that either causes the other. Finding a relationship is a first step in testing the proposition. We can then begin to eliminate other factors that might cause both and so make a direct link more plausible. For example, if the media-stereotyping relationship remains the same both for children whose parents are traditional and for those whose parents are nontraditional, there is one less possible explanation competing with our proposition: it is unlikely that parental attitudes cause both aspects of the relationship.

Because questions about the effects of media sexism are new and because recent work on the similar media violence question[19] makes repetition of the violence studies with sexism substituted less rewarding for researchers, there are few studies to tell us whether reading and viewing sexism are related to traditional behaviors and attitudes. Fortunately, the findings of the few studies that exist are consistent with each other and with the accumulated evidence on television violence and aggression.

Ann Beuf interviewed 63 girls and boys aged 3 to 6 years. Not surprisingly, about 70 percent of the children picked a career stereotypically appropriate for their sex as what they would be when they grew up. However, when Beuf compared the minority of children characterized as "moderate" television viewers with the "heavy" television majority, an interesting difference appeared. Only 50 percent of the moderate viewers picked a sex-stereotyped career for themselves, in contrast to 76 percent of the heavy viewers. Such evidence is not proof of the causal link, but it is consistent with our proposition that stereotyped television content makes children more traditional in their sex-role beliefs.[20]

Terry Freuh and Paul McGhee interviewed kindergarten, second-, fourth-, and sixth-grade children using the IT scale, a measure of traditional sex-role adoption in which children choose masculine or feminine activities for a sex-neutral doll. Heavy television viewers (25 hours or more per week) made more traditional choices than light viewers (10 hours or fewer per week). As a beginning at eliminating other factors that might cause both television viewing and sex-role choices, Freuh and McGhee found that this relationship exists separately from the children's age or sex, although older children and boys were also more traditional.[21]

From these two studies of the everyday behaviors and beliefs of children, we see that viewing a lot of television's sex-stereotyped content is probably *related* to being traditional in one's own sex-role attitudes. However, these two studies tell us little about *why* the relationship exists.

THE EVIDENCE FOR A CAUSAL RELATIONSHIP.   The second compromise view of our proposition approaches the problem through the content instead of the audience. If media portrayals of women and men are uniformly stereotypic, let us estimate what effect these have by presenting children with *nonstereotypic* people. If nonstereotypic presentations can make children less traditional than they are now, or if children who are shown nonstereotypic content are less traditional than those who are shown traditional content, we can argue that stereotyped content has been affecting them all along. Evidence like that would be a powerful illustration of how the media can bring about social change. However, although we could show in these cases that the content caused the different sex roles or attitudes, this is also a compromise proof. By experimentally controlling what children see or read, we introduce some artificiality into the situation. This brings the risk that experimental results might not generalize to real-life situations.

There are studies showing that media presentations can lead to learning and performance of stereotypically sex-linked behaviors, just as they can lead to learning and performing other behaviors. For example, Paulette Fischer and Judith Torney read 5-year-olds a story in which a boy or a girl either solved a puzzle independently or asked for help. When the children worked on the puzzle themselves, both girls and boys who heard a story about an independent model tried longer before requesting help than those who had heard about a dependent model. In this case, the sex of the model did not matter.[22]

More relevant to our question about the effectiveness of nonstereotypic portrayals, Leslie McArthur and Susan Eisen read nursery school children stories about a girl and a boy in which: (1) the girl achieved while the boy stood around and watched or needed help (reverse stereotype); (2) behavior was stereotyped (boy achieved while girl watched); or (3) no achievement-related behavior appeared (control). As predicted, girls were most persistent in a difficult task after a story about a girl achieving, and boys were more persistent after hearing a story about a boy achieving.[23]

From these and other studies like them, it seems that stereotypic and nonstereotypic media models can make a difference in children's behaviors that are commonly linked with one sex or the other. But providing models of specific behaviors will probably not be enough if overall attitudes about limitations on women and men remain untouched. Showing a little girl another little girl solving a difficult puzzle may make a temporary difference in her achievement, but it will probably not persist in the face of a general beliefs that women do not or should not achieve. Obviously we also need to document media effects on children's attitudes and beliefs about the sexes' proper roles.

Charles Atkin and Mark Miller showed 400 second to fifth graders a 15-minute videotape of children's programs (children's news, a cartoon, and multiple commercials). One of the commercials was for eye glasses. Each child saw one of four versions in which a woman was either a judge, a computer programmer, a television technician, or in which the commercial was not inserted. Afterward, as part of a large questionnaire, children were given a list of jobs and asked to mark in which ones they thought women might work. Seeing a woman as a computer programmer or television technician did not seem to make much difference in children's ideas about which jobs women could hold. But seeing a female judge made children more likely to say that a woman could be a judge (51 percent versus 31 percent), with girls and older children more affected. In addition, children who saw the female judge were more likely to think women could be doctors (74 percent versus 60 percent, with no age or sex differences). The evidence from this study is weakened by finding effects only for children who saw a female judge, but we see again that media presentations can affect children's beliefs about women.[24]

Similarly, a study by Suzanne Pingree used television commercials to change children's attitudes about women. Third and eighth graders watched 5 minutes of regular television commercials under the pretext of an advertising effectiveness study. Half the children saw 5 minutes of commercials with women in traditional roles (cooking, cleaning, being beautiful); the other half saw commercials with women in nontraditional roles (golfing, practicing medicine, working as accountants). As part of a postviewing questionnaire, children agreed or disagreed with a number of statements about women and men, such as "women are as smart as men are," "mothers should stay home and take care of their children," and "a woman can do any job a man can do". As one would hope, children who saw the nontraditional women were themselves less traditional in response than those who saw women as housewives and mothers, but the effect was strong only for children who received additional instructions that apparently led them to pay closer attention to the characters in the commercials.[25]

Vicki Flerx, Dorothy Fidler, and Ronald Rogers read 4- and 5-year-olds egalitarian stories in their nursery school for 1 week and found substantial changes in a number of the children's beliefs concerning sex-appropriate behaviors. These changes were more pronounced for the older children, which may mean that the messages were too difficult for 4-year-olds to use.[26]

Where do these findings leave our proposition that media content makes children more sex-stereotyped and traditional? Children who watch more television do appear to be more traditional in their beliefs about women and men, thus establishing one necessary condition for the proposition. The experimental studies just described also show that television and storybooks have the power to alter children's beliefs and behaviors, at least in the classroom or the laboratory. To the extent that conclusions can be drawn from this preliminary evidence, we are led to accept the proposition that stereotypic media content slows change in children's sex-role behaviors and attitudes.

Using Children's Media for Social Change.

Along with the conclusion that the media are a conservative force comes the corollary conclusion that they can be used to teach children nonsexist beliefs and behaviors. In studies such as Pingree,[27] Atkin and Miller,[28] and McArthur and Eisen,[29] nonstereotypic presentations did make inroads into children's stereotypes. However, success in these efforts is not automatic. Some messages affect children while others mysteriously do not; for example, we need to know why Atkin and

Miller's judge commercial was effective and the computer programmer and television technician commercials were not.

The age and sex of the children we are trying to affect are probably crucial in ways that are only partially understood. For example, the attitude improvement reported in Pingree's study was not universal. In contrast to the girls and to third-grade boys, eighth-grade boys were actually more traditional after seeing women as athletes and professionals than after seeing them as housewives and mothers. Unfortunately, this does not seem to be an isolated result. A longer-term program to counter sexism directly in school classrooms was effective for most children, but seemed to make ninth-grade boys even more sexist.[30] Something about this phase in sex-role development for boys, but not for girls, seems to make them react very negatively to nontraditional women. Just why this occurs is a question that will require more reseach, but it is clear that the complications of sex-role development summarized earlier are very relevant to any attempt to change children through the media.

A study by Ronald Drabman, David Hammer, and Gregory Jarvie dramatically illusrates another problem that one can have trying to present children with nonstereotypic media content. First-, third-, and seventh-grade children watched a videotaped visit to the pediatrician's office of Doctor Mary and Nurse David. Instead of asking questions about women's roles in society, the researchers simply asked each child what the names of the doctor and nurse were, using multiple-choice questions. Both first- and fourth-grade children were so convinced that doctors are male and nurses female that they missed the heavily emphasized reversal in the film. The researchers found that:

- Four percent of the first graders chose a woman's name for the doctor and none chose a man's name for the nurse.
- Four percent of the fourth graders chose a woman's name for the doctor and 8 percent chose a man's name for the nurse.

- Seventy-nine percent of the seventh graders chose a woman's name for the doctor and 79 percent chose a man's name for the nurse.
- One week later, on retest, 53 percent of the seventh graders chose a woman's name for the doctor and 53 percent chose a man's name for the nurse.

Even with a clear, nonsterotypic presentation, first and fourth graders changed the facts to fit their own stereotypes. Seventh graders were more open or more perceptive, but they also allowed their stereotypes to reinterpret what they had seen as their memory became less fresh.[31]

Sally Koblinsky, Donna Cruse, and Alan Sugawara found similar although less drastic misperceptions by fifth-grade students. After the children read stories in which the male and female characters displayed an equal number of male and female characteristics, both girls and boys remembered more masculine characteristics of male characters and feminine characteristics of female characters. The children were probably using their sex-role stereotypes to organize information from the stories in memory.[32]

Such studies tell us that children are about as hard to reach through the media as adults. Communication researchers have long recanted their early theory that media messages are comparable to "bullets" that affect everyone in the "target audience."[33] People are skilled in evading the "bullets." With children there are added complexities in their growing ability to understand and their constantly changing beliefs about what is appropriate.

Researchers and reformers should not give up trying to alter media content for children even though their task is difficult. We do know that counterstereotypes can have the desired effect, but we have much to learn about preventing resistance and misperception.

PROPOSITIONAL SUMMARY

Proposition 17.1: There are few innate *sex-role differences* between girls and boys.

Proposition 17.2: Children develop sex-role stereotypic *behaviors* as young as 3 years.

Proposition 17.3: Children spend many *hours* each day with television and other media.

Proposition 17.4: Media content makes children more *sex-stereotyped*.

EFFECTS ON MEDIA AUDIENCES

What toothpaste do you use?
  Gleem.
Why?
  Well, I don't know. But it's not because of the commercials. It's just
  —well, it's just that I can't brush after every meal.[1]

LATENT AND MANIFEST MESSAGES

The previous chapter reviewed evidence that children learn sex-role beliefs and behaviors from the media. Although we cannot separate the effects of media entirely from the effects of parents, peers, and school, indications of media effects on children are found in several studies.

But are we, as adults, also influenced by messages that reach us through the media? We like to believe that we are critical thinkers who are less susceptible to the persuasive intent of the messages. After all, if we do not want to use Crest toothpaste, we will not be persuaded by the commercial. Instead, we may buy Gleem because we think it is the better product. At this point we rise to the advertiser's bait. Large corporations own many product lines and sell competing products within the same line. Proctor and Gamble markets Crest to one group of consumers and Gleem to another group of consumers. They increase their overall sales by segmenting the market for each of the competing products.

Of course, you may not purchase Crest or Gleem. But if you purchase any toothpaste at all, you probably have been persuaded that toothpaste is important for clean teeth, fresh breath, etc. Advertisers plant latent and manifest messages in their copy. The latent message convinces us of a significant need in our lives (e.g., to have "sex appeal"). The manifest message tells us that the advertiser's product satisfies the need.

Research indicates that it is easier to reject the manifest message than the latent message. We can put up our defenses against the manifest message ("No, I don't need a new car this year; my present car still looks new."), but the latent message slips underneath the defenses ("Yes, it is important to have a car that looks new.").

COMPONENTS OF RESPONSE

Many of the images that affect our sex-role beliefs and behaviors are embedded in latent messages. Media researchers delineate three types of message effects—on knowledge, attitude, and behavior. These *components of response,* as they may be called, are differentially affected by messages that differ in source, channel, content, etc. Characteristics of messages interact with characteristics of audiences to increase or diminish effects on knowledge, attitude, and behavior.

The sequence of the components of response (i.e., whether behavior change is preceded by attitude change and attitude change by knowledge change) is studied by media researchers. If a single sequence of responses, such as the commonsensical sequence of knowledge→attitude→behavior, always occurs, we can measure the potential effect of a message by determining how much knowledge change it has produced.

However, other plausible response sequences can be argued. According to dissonance theory, if behavior change can be induced for its own sake, attitude and then knowledge will change to become more consonant with the new behavior.[2] An important variable in the dissonance-theory sequence of behavior→attitude→knowledge is a person's perceived freedom not to comply with the suggested behavior change. A person who perceives no alternative to compliance will suffer no "cognitive dissonance" and require no balancing of attitudes and knowledge. However, a person who perceives that compliance is freely given will be troubled by "cognitive dissonance" to the extent that the new behavior is not consonant with previously held attitudes and knowledge.

Conditions under which each of these response sequences is likely to occur have been explored by Michael Ray.[3] He introduces a third sequence, knowledge→behavior→attitude, as the outcome of "learning without involvement," which is said to result, for example, from exposure to media advertising.

INDIVIDUAL DIFFERENCES

Are people equally persuaded by media messages? Research conducted 2 decades ago indicated that women are more "persuasible" than men.[4] In the 1950s, when the research was underway, the sex difference was interpreted as normal in a society in which boys are raised to be aggressive and demanding and girls are raised to be passive and compliant. Without new research based on samples of adults who have lived through the rebirth of the women's movement, we hesitate to say that marked differences in persuasibility still exist between the sexes.

Each message that is received by an individual is accepted or rejected on the basis of previous experiences that have shaped the individual's cognitive style of response. Some individuals, women as well as men, have had experiences that make them self-reliant and tough-minded with respect to persuasive messages. Other persons, less sure of themselves, are susceptible to messages that allude to their latent needs. As was found in research on the effects of televised violence on children,[5] some individuals can be greatly affected by messages that other individuals hardly notice. Thus the research question should be not "What are the effects of media sexism on *all* of us?", but "What are the effects of media sexism on *any* of us?"

Without proper focus on this question, research is likely to show only bland effects of media sexism on the population at large. Media managers and advertisers say that media mirrors are flawed but harmless. They have used the same argument for years to excuse violence as the resolution of crime and adventure plots. Although the staggering number of televised killings and maimings has been tabulated by researchers, networks have made only cosmetic changes in their violent programs.

Psychological studies of prejudice and dogmatism help us to understand individual differences in response to media sexism. Studies by Theodor Adorno, Else Frenkel-Brunswik, Daniel Levinson, and R. Nevitt Sanford on the authoritarian personality,[6] by Daniel Katz on ego defense,[7] by Arthur Cohen on anxiety reduction,[8] by Gordon Allport and Leo Postman on the psychology of rumor,[9] and by Milton Rokeach on the belief system,[10] among others, provide insight into individual differences. These researchers have all stated, in one way or another, that stereotypic thinking, prejudice, and vulnerability to persuasion are symptoms and consequences of insecurity.

Proposition 18.1: The Media Affect Our Perceptions of the "Real World."

Larry Gross conducted a study of the perceptions of adults in four metropolitan areas.[11] He asked factual questions that focused on differences between the television world and the real world. Respondents who watched 4 hours or more of television per day reflected the television world in their answers; respondents who watched less than 2 hours of television per day gave real-world answers.

The measurement procedure was quite simple. Gross asked respondents to estimate the proportions of professionals, athletes, entertainers, and law enforcement personnel in the work force (note in Chapter 6 that these occupations are greatly overrepresented in television dramas). Heavy television viewers estimated the proportions of these occupations in line with their television experience. Light television viewers estimated the proportions in line with their real-world experience.

Proposition 18.2: Mediated Knowledge Affects Our Behavior.

How do these perceptions affect behavior? By emphasizing some behavior alternatives while ignoring others. If a girl never sees women as physicians and has never learned that women can be physicians, she is not likely to choose medicine as her field of study. If she sees that women do all the cooking, shopping, washing, and cleaning, she will expect to do these chores even if she is working full time outside the home.

Sandra and Daryl Bem conducted a knowledge-behavior study in support of a complaint by the Pittsburgh chapter of NOW against *The Pittsburgh Press.* [12] NOW had charged that sex-segregated help-wanted advertisements were in violation of the Pittsburgh Human Relations Ordinance. In order to show that sex-segregated advertisements "might aid and abet sex discrimination in employment by discouraging female job seekers from applying for jobs listed in the 'Male' column," the Bems asked 52 women at Carnegie-Mellon University to "rate each of thirty-two jobs that had been advertised in Sunday editions of *The Pittsburgh Press.*" Describing the study, Bem and Bem wrote:

Sixteen of the ads had been drawn from the "Male Interest" column and sixteen had been drawn from the "Female Interest" column. Each woman was given a booklet containing all thirty-two ads. She was asked to read each ad and to rate it. . . .

When jobs were segregated and labeled on the basis of sex, as they were in *The Press,* only 46% of the women in this study were as likely to apply for "male interest" jobs as for "female interest" jobs. In other words, a majority of the women did prefer "female interest" jobs. But does this really reflect a true preference on the part of women for so-called "female interest" jobs? No, it does not. For when these same jobs appeared in an integrated alphabetical listing with no reference to sex, fully 81% of the women preferred the "male interest" jobs to the "female interest" jobs.

For example, the job of newspaper reporter fell in popularity from 7th place when it appeared in the integrated listing to 19th place when it was segregated and labeled as a "male interest" job. It seems clear that the newspaper editor who wishes to hire only male reporters—in violation of the law—can place his ad in the "Male Interest" column, secure in the knowledge that this will effectively discourage female applicants. It is in this way that sex-segregated want ads can "aid and abet" discrimination in employment on the basis of sex.[13]

Sensitive to the possible charge that this was a laboratory study and did not address the effects of sex-segregated ads on actual job seekers, the Bems discuss the ways in which their study probably underestimated the effects. They point out that the women rated every advertisement, whether "male interest" or "female interest." In a real job-seeking situation, many women would not look at the "male interest" advertisements. Second, the women in the study only had to rate how willing they would be to apply for each job. It is easier to write down that one is willing to apply for a "male interest" job than it is actually to apply for it. Third, the study used *The Pittsburgh Press*'s modified form of sex-segregated want advertisements (Jobs—Female Interest) instead of the traditional form (Female Help Wanted). Fourth, the disclaimer printed in *The Pittsburgh Press* indicating that employers must consider applicants of either sex occupied 13 percent of the space in the study booklet but less than 1 percent of the space devoted to classified employment advertising in *The Pittsburgh Press.*

Audience effects research is still in its infancy. The ways in which sex-role stereotypes are learned and their impact on knowledge, attitudes, and behavior are largely unknown. However, evidence from available studies indicates that the media do affect our perceptions of others, our perceptions of ourselves, and our behavior.

PROPOSITIONAL SUMMARY

Proposition 18.1: The media affect our *perceptions* of the "real world."

Proposition 18.2: Mediated knowledge affects our *behavior.*

INDICATIONS FOR RESEARCH AND ACTION

Against a dark background, bright figures capture our attention. These are years of rare and often token victories against media sexism. Each victory is savored for future gains that it may presage. These are years when media feminists share stories of women hired in management, of class action suits won, of nonsexist content policies adopted, etc.

If advertisers knew of the word-of-mouth repetition that nonsexist copy receives, they would compose more advertisements like this Inglenook Wines radio commercial (spoken by a proud grandfather).

> A toast to the new baby, the future President of the United States. Here's to Debbie.

Even the token victories do not just happen. Groups and individuals fight for them, sometimes for years. For example, the $2 million class action suit won against NBC in early 1977 by the Women's Committee for Equal Employment Opportunity was filed more than 4 years earlier with the New York City Commission on Civil Rights and the U.S. Equal Employment Opportunity Commission. Since the $2 million is to be shared by more than 2500 women who are past or present NBC employees, the average compensation from the 4-year suit is less than $800.

One thought that this book should leave with you is that media sexism will not go away just because we all object to it. Sexism emerged in American media to serve vested interests, and sexism will remain in American media until the power of the opposition exceeds the power of the vested interests.

What do we, the opposition, have going for us? We have antidiscrimination laws. We have FCC regulations. We have capital (at least the money we can withhold in boycotts of sexist advertisers). We have numbers and energy.

It takes a skillful blend of research and action to mobilize the opposition forces. Laws and regulations cannot be mobilized without evidence. If the evidence is weak, legal support is lost. Economic boycotts succeed only when they are based on a careful analysis of the marketplace. The legion of supporters needed to clinch a campaign are well educated and skeptical of "causes." They want to see the data.

Chapter 19 argues that systematic research on media sexism has hardly begun. Two frameworks are proposed for "unfinished research."

Chapter 20 discusses strategies for legal, economic, and social action against media sexism.

UNFINISHED RESEARCH

Make the data do the work of pressing for action.[1]

In the 1970s, studies of media content, institutions, and audiences are mapping sexism beyond the anecdotal landmarks of the previous decade. However, many areas are still chartless, and all charts more than a few years old must be updated.

Growing interest in the social policy question of how women are treated in and by the media provides support for conducting needed research. Books and journal articles, hearings held by state and local commissions on the status of women, state and national conferences on the progress of American women sponsored by the International Women's Year, the NOW Media Task Force, college courses on women and the media, and similar activities help us to obtain the attention and cooperation that a research program requires.

Unfinished research falls within the categories of *review, prioritization, support,* and *orientation.*

To move beyond *ad hoc* studies whose findings are duplicative and monitoring projects whose methods are weak, we need updated *reviews* of relevant research. This book is a step in that direction. Reviews tell us which studies have useful findings, which studies have rigorous methods, and, best of all, which studies have both.

Research *priorities* need to be drafted, discussed, revised, and implemented. Researchers, media and advertising personnel, and women's action groups should collaborate in all these steps.

Even informal research needs *support* in the form of labor, facilities, and some funds to cover data-gathering costs. Community-based groups, such as the Kalamazoo Committee for Children's Television, have successfully combined volunteer labor with a shoestring budget. This approach will continue to be important in the future. However, more formal research is also required for complaints and petitions to advertisers, media, and federal regulatory agencies. In formal research, funds are needed for the training of interviewers and monitors, for data analysis, and for professional time. It is necessary to work with foundations, federal and state government agencies, and advertising associations.

Finally, our *orientation*—the action context in which we conduct a study—spells the difference between productive and unproductive research. We are influenced by Donald Campbell's *Methods for the Experimenting Society.*

> The experimenting society will be one which vigorously tries out proposed solutions to recurrent problems, which makes hardheaded multidimensional evaluations of the outcomes, and where the remedial effort seems ineffective, goes on to other possible solutions. The focus will be on reality testing and persistence in seeking solutions to problems. The justification of new programs will be in terms of the seriousness of the problem, not in the claim that we can know for certain in advance what therapy will work.[2]

Research on media sexism in an "experimenting society" seeks to match problems with appropriate actions and to ensure that legal, political, economic, or social side effects of the actions do not create new problems. Six phases of research ask these questions.

1. How can media sexism be monitored and measured?
2. What are the actionable aspects of media sexism in a particular case?
3. Considering the legal prerogatives, political support, financial resources, etc., in a particular case, what is the range of actions that can be taken?
4. How can promising actions be tested for effectiveness?
5. For what changes in effective actions (e.g., in strategy, timing, or level of effort) do the results of tests call?
6. What are the long-term effects of actions?

These six phases complete a cycle of research. The sixth phase brings us back to the first phase; monitoring takes over for expensive *ad hoc* studies; other problem areas and appropriate actions are identified.

1. How Can Media Sexism Be Monitored and Measured?

Social accounting through censuses and surveys is a mark of the twentieth century around the world. In the United States, these methods reached a high level of application after the publication of *Social Indicators,* edited by Raymond Bauer, in 1966.[3] The federal government has published several reports based on indicators,[4] and the Russell Sage Foundation has sponsored and published other important reports.[5]

Media indicators of the status and role of women have not been developed. However, Abbott Ferriss set the stage for them in *Indicators of Trends in the Status of American Women* when he wrote about the importance of the media in conveying messages to women and men about their appropriate roles.

Many role ascriptions of the socio-cultural system impinge un-
necessarily upon one's freedom to become an individual with
dignity. . . .

Mass culture and mass communication have also played
their part by stimulating women to try to achieve the nearly
impossible standards of pulchritude portrayed by fashion models. Mass advertising has raised expectations of continuing rewards—diamonds, travel, male adoration, etc.—that in reality
could come to most women only occasionally. . . .[6]

In *Unobstrusive Measures,* a methodological sourcebook,
Eugene Webb, Donald Campbell, Richard Schwartz, and Lee
Sechrest stated that "the media, if carefully selected, can serve
as a mirror of the society's values. . . ."[7] In fact, the media are
more than a mirror; they reflect our values back to us, but they
also transmit values to the next generation.

Proposed projects to monitor sexism in the media have a
parallel in the project conducted by George Gerbner and Larry
Gross at the University of Pennsylvania to monitor violence
indicators in the media.[8] The careful procedures for sampling
media and coding content developed by Gerbner and Gross are
applicable to sexism-monitoring projects. Defensive criticism of
the violence-monitoring project (e.g. "that's just the way
American society is" and the ingenuous converse "everyone
knows that media create a fantasy world") will no doubt be
addressed to sexism monitoring as well.

A further activity of the first phase of research is the
monitoring of hiring, promotion, and assignment of women in
media organizations. Some institutional indicators exist in the
reports produced by the Office of Communications, United
Church of Christ.[9] Other data, such as salary and length of
employment, need to be added. As is true of content indicators,
finding the proportions of women and men who are hired,
promoted, and paid particular salaries can only draw attention
to the problem. However, both content indicators and institutional indicators provide baseline and trend data for assessing
progress over time.

2. What Are the Actionable Aspects of Media Sexism in a Particular Case?

The second phase of research begins with specific problems that have been identified through monitoring. Research that now focuses on particular cases (not broadly, as in monitoring) seeks to clarify the causes of a problem and thereby identify its actionable aspects.

For example, if fewer women are hired as reporters by metropolitan daily newspapers in 1979 than in 1978 or earlier years, we need to know how many men were hired in each year, how large the applicant pools were, and how qualified the applicants were. There are many possible causes: proportionately fewer women than men were hired from their respective applicant pools; proportionately fewer women than men in the applicant pools were qualified; proportionately fewer women than men applied for the positions; proportionately fewer women than men graduated from the "feeder schools" or moved up from small-newspaper apprenticeships, etc.

In the short term, a problem may have few actionable aspects. For example, we can do little if newspapers are reducing their reporting staffs equitably for both sexes to stay within their budgets during a recession.

3. Given Legal Prerogatives, Political Support, Financial Resources, Etc., in a Particular Case, What Is the Range of Actions That Can Be Taken?

Research on possible courses of action is just as important as research on problems and their causes. Despite an American tradition of direct action that dates from the Colonial period and the Boston Tea Party, more long-term progress toward the solution of a problem may result from actions that are not only indirect but also seem to be targeted against the wrong individuals or groups. For example, effective action against sexist advertising may take the form of complaints to local retailers and to federal regulatory agencies, particularly if complaints to advertisers have gone unheeded. Effectve action against biased textbooks may take the form of lobbying with state and local textbook-adoption commissions, particularly in the case of textbook publishers that have not followed the example of other publishers in establishing guidelines for nonsexist writing and portrayal.

Possible courses of action emerge from experience, expert opinion, and brainstorming. Media management and employee groups, women's media groups, advertising agencies, advertisers, and other interested persons can all contribute to the identification of actions that will have the maximum desired effect with minimum side effects. It is important to avoid a "we" and "they" mentality; many of the "they" (e.g., media managers) are as concerned about the problem as "we" are, and they have the perspective of insiders on the probable effects of each action.

Joint action may be required to provide both short-term and long-term solutions to a problem, when the "symptomatic" relief needed in the short term cannot be provided by the "systemic" solution that will be effective in the long term. For example, most of us believe that media sexism will wane as women occupy key management and production positions. According to this belief, the long-term or systemic solution involves hiring, promoting, and assigning women to management and production positions in media organizations. However, the effects of such organizational change on media content may not be evident for years. We also need short-term or symptomatic solutions that involve content guidelines, complaint procedures, economic sanctions, government regulation, etc.

4. HOW CAN ACTIONS BE TESTED FOR EFFECTIVENESS?

A number of actions may be proposed in the third phase of the research sequence. Some of the proposed actions will be more successful than others; the difficulty is that we do not know which ones, nor are resources usually available to test all reasonable actions that may be proposed.

A common shortcoming in this fourth or action-testing phase is early closure on just one alternative action. Testing a single alternative at best provides a finding of success versus failure. Testing multiple alternatives provides a range of choices, from most successful through somewhat successful to least successful. There may also be the finding that two alternatives are successful but in different contexts. Then the adoption of both alternatives, each in its best context, yields a higher success index than a single alternative can.

It is important to test legal, political, economic, and social factors jointly. A classic example of limited testing was the Volstead Act, which passed legal, political, and economic tests but foundered on social acceptance. The goals behind alcohol prohibition (whether we agree with them or not) might have been largely achieved over time by a different approach; in other words, a substantial change that persists over time may be more satisfactory than a total change that is resisted and eventually rejected.

Resistance to the Volstead Act is paralleled today by resistance to anti-sex-discrimination laws. Corporations, universities, and other organizations have shown that such laws can be evaded for long periods of time without penalty. A 1978 determination by the EEOC concerning sex and race discrimination in Associated Press recruiting, hiring, and promoting of news staff (described in more detail in Chapter 12) brings some satisfaction to the Wire Service Guild complainants in the case, but the facts are that the complaint was filed with the EEOC 5 years earlier, in 1973, and more years may pass before the Associated Press actually provides the equal employment opportunity for women and minorities that the Wire Service Guild sought.[10]

Because they can often be evaded, laws and regulations may not be effective actions for long-term or systemic change, although they may be needed for short-term or symptomatic change. If the goals behind legislation and regulation can be broken down into the concrete changes that are sought, other actions may be found to be more effective in achieving each of the changes.

5. FOR WHAT CHANGES IN EFFECTIVE ACTIONS (E.G., IN STRATEGY, TIMING, OR LEVEL OF EFFORT) DO THE RESULTS OF THE TESTS CALL?

We begin this phase with one or more alternative actions that are successful enough to justify the effort and cost of adapting them to work better. Evaluators of experimental programs distinguish between formative and summative evaluation. The former guides the adaptation of an effective action, the latter brings in a verdict of "continue" or "discontinue" at a future time when an action is held accountable by government agencies, legislatures, etc.

Formative and summative evaluation are equally important in an "experimenting society," but they are not equally important in evaluating the same action. An apparently effective action benefits from formative evaluation; it is adapted to work better. Summative evaluation of an apparently effective action will, barring surprises, only confirm its effectiveness. When summative evaluations of such actions are required by government agencies and legislatures, they may have a ceremonial aspect.

Actions that are not going to succeed often provide early warnings of their failure, and formative evaluation is applied to the diagnostic problem of what went wrong. In such cases the role of summative evaluation is to conclude the trial, to say "discontinue" authoritatively.

6. WHAT ARE THE LONG-TERM EFFECTS OF ACTIONS?

The challenge of this phase is to measure the long-term effects of actions as well as side effects that enhance the actions or undermine them. Evaluators are sensitive to the different time periods in which the desired effects and the side effects become apparent. Side effects often develop slowly and cannot be measured immediately after an action is taken. Actions that disturb the *status quo* (including most actions to overcome media sexism) are met by resistance that usually becomes more skillful and organized over time. Change that seems to represent genuine progress in the early period after an action is taken later proves to have been token change; that is, the trend levels off at a "compliance criterion" instead of building on the early change.

RESEARCH INTO ACTION

Why does this chapter emphasize research when direct action against media sexism is possible and timely? We are moving into a period when real gains for women will result only from hard-fought litigation and well-informed action. Expert testimony and rigorous evidence will be needed to sustain suits against media corporations. Where findings of sexism are the basis of an action, the evidence must be rigorous or the action will be dismissed. Research is the means by which we "show cause" in the courts and regulatory agencies.

We are well into the age of the FW2 ("First woman to . . ."). Veronica Geng writes that she has a portfolio of FW2 clippings from the *New York Times* that are "boring because they falsify the reader's experience."[11] By patronizing the continuing struggle of women and by minimizing the distance from FW2 to HW2 ("hundredth woman to . . ."), these newspaper articles create an illusion of progress.

How do we achieve real progress? Wilma Scott Heide states the need for:

> . . . monitoring, license challenges, employment complaints and lawsuits, picketing, educational consciousness-raising, letter writing, meetings, caucus actions, alternate media and programming. . . .[12]

Mallica Vajrathon suggests practical steps that can be taken at the individual, community, national, and international levels to bring about change. Some media-related actions include:

> Collect facts and figures illustrating the differences (and similarities) between the current status of men and women . . . teach young people to be on the alert against sexism . . . set up a community task force on the status of women . . . meet with community leaders to demand changes in the social structure to give equal representation to men and women . . . organize group discussions on radio . . . monitor the media for sexist, stereotyped advertising and program content and organize protest to the use of such programs and advertising by the local papers or radio and television stations . . . write articles in newspapers about women's contributions to all fields of development and arts . . . urge large corporations to examine their hiring policies and working conditions for women . . . meet with journalists to arrange coverage of women leaders in order to create "role models" for other women. . . . [13]

There are many ways to bring about change, but we should remember that usually it is the functioning of organizations and bureaucracies that needs to be changed. According to Edgar Schein, organizational change is brought about by "unfreezing" an existing condition, changing that condition, and then "refreezing" the changed condition. Refreezing should not be confused with "rigidifying." Schein defines refreezing as the process of stabilizing and integrating changes so that the organization can function normally.[14]

Change legislation or advocacy sometimes leads only to the psychological process that Herbert Kelman calls "compliance." Compliance is fairly easy to achieve and does not represent an enduring change. Federal laws require change in employment practices in most media organizations. The organizations change, but only to comply with the law. When it is possible to circumvent the law, they do so. "Identification," the second phase, is a more durable form of change in which individuals indentify with the needs of other persons or groups. This kind of change occurs in the media when managers identify with the needs of women. As long as the needs of women remain salient to the managers, change will continue. However, other groups or events can upset the process of identification. Only in the third phase, "internalization," is there support for enduring change. Internalization is the psychological process by which change is integrated into an individual's own beliefs. For example, if a manager believes in equity and open-mindedness, then she or he may perceive that fair employment policies are corollaries of these existing beliefs. Such change is unlikely to regress.[15]

Change theorists distinguish among several change strategies, including the "power-coercive strategy" and the "empirical-rational strategy." The power-coercive strategy achieves rapid compliance, but the empirical-rational strategy builds cognitive support that causes the change to persist after pressure is removed.[16]

Confronting sexism, research is not an end in itself but a means to action. Linda Jean Busby outlined an approach to research that provides action data.[17] Busby's five research steps were reformulated by Matilda Butler for a limited testing of this research mode. Action is facilitated by:

1. Knowledge of the image of women portrayed by advertisers as well as the image of women portrayed in the programs they sponsor.
2. Knowledge of the functions that sexism serves.
3. Knowledge of who controls the image of women seen in advertising and programs as well as how the control is exercised.
4. Knowledge of the audience of advertisements and programs.
5. Knowledge of the effects of sexist advertising and programming on children and adults.[18]

The first step calls for *content* analysis and the second step for *cultural and social* analysis. That is, why are particular definitions of maleness and femaleness used in advertising and programming? What functions are served by putting women down, keeping them in their place, ignoring them, etc., for producers and viewers of the messages?

The third step calls for *control* analysis. This includes investigating who makes content and presentation decisions, to what extent company or network policies are responsible, how much influence advertisers have, etc.

The fourth step calls for *audience* analysis. In addition to knowing the demographics of the viewing audience for particular advertisements or programs, we compare the profiles of men and women as presented on media with profiles of media audiences, using census and other available data to reflect on real people and data from content analyses to reflect on "media" people. For example, women represent more than 40 percent of the current work force. Are women more than 40 percent of workers on television? Studies of attitudes toward occupational and family roles should be conducted for audience samples and compared with projected attitudes expressed by "television" people.

The fifth step calls for *effects* analysis. Each of us in the media audience is influenced by many forces, including our family, friends, and co-workers. These forces have different effects on each of us, depending on personal factors such as our sex, age, self-concept, beliefs, etc.

Two frameworks for research have been described in this chapter to indicate the types of coherent research programs that need to be established. These frameworks help us to see that *ad hoc* research projects are helpful in supplying data for action, but they are not comprehensive enough to meet the objections of critics. After we prove the case of media sexism, we must be ready to answer the questions, "All right, how would you handle the content differently?", and "How would you staff and manage the organization?" We must be ready to suggest and test alternative content as well as alternative organizational practices.

To use a metaphor that is supposed to separate "the men from the girls," without research we could lose the game in the bottom of the ninth.

THREE TYPES OF ACTION

Back where the ads are made, small wars occur daily. Unfortunately, women aren't winning many of them.[1]

Legal, economic, and social action can be brought to bear on sexism in media programming, advertising, employment, and training. This chapter reviews recent actions and emerging strategies and arguments on which future actions will be based.

LEGAL ACTION

The legal argument against sexism is based on antidiscrimination laws such as Title VII of the Civil Rights Act of 1964, Executive Orders 11478 and 11246 (as amended by Executive Order 11375 for Federal Contract Compliance), Title IX of the Education Amendments of 1972, the Equal Pay Act of 1963 (as amended by the Education Amendments of 1972), etc. Antidiscrimination provisions also exist in FCC regulations governing broadcast licenses.

This "due process" attack on sexism, as used by NOW and

other feminist groups, has been documented by Jinnet Fowles.[2] She reviewed the landmark cases, including NOW's 1972 petition to the FCC to deny the license renewals of WABC-TV in New York and WRC-TV in Washington, D.C. Other cases, involving programming and advertising as well as hiring and assignment, are mentioned elsewhere in this book (see Chapters 6, 7, and 12).

Due process is a difficult and doubtful strategy. Statistically, the odds are heavily against the complainant or petitioner. Bradley Canon, after reviewing more than 2000 fairness complaints, reported that only two "even achieved formal recognition (i.e., an adjudicatory hearing) from the Commission...." He added that between 1948 and 1968 no broadcaster lost a license or was reprimanded by the FCC for violation of the fairness doctrine.[3]

FCC actions regarding petitions to deny license renewals have been studied by Oscar Gandy, Ernest Ballesteros, Timothy Haight, and George Schement. They found that the outcome of a petition was affected by the specificity of the petition, its sponsorship, and the size of the broadcast market served. It also became clear in their study that the FCC routinely dismisses complaints that do not adequately document the case against the broadcaster. Ample monitoring data or other documentation must be supplied in the petition, because petitioners are not allowed to supply additional data through amendments, although broadcasters are allowed to amend their renewal applications.

In general, the larger and more prominent the group sponsoring the petition, the greater its chances of success.[4] Canon found that 75 percent of the complaints in his sample were originated by private citizens, while more than 75 percent of the successful complaints were originated by organized groups.[5] On the other side of the power balance, small stations lose more judgments than large ones. Large stations have powerful connections, and the FCC is unlikely to move against them unless the issue is politically important and might otherwise draw unfavorable attention to the FCC and its decision-making process.[6]

Gandy et al. analyzed 230 petitions to deny filed with the FCC between 1963 and 1973. Cases were chosen in which the petitioners were not part of the broadcast industry and in which factors of "presumed importance to minority groups" were cited, including public service, past performance, civic activities, programming, and community ascertainment. They found that:

> ... 60 percent of the cases were rejected because petitioners failed to provide sufficient evidence to support their charges, 11 percent of the cases were seen to fail because the petitioners missed an important deadline for the submission of legal documents, and 25 percent of the cases were seriously flawed because they requested Commission action in areas which were beyond the FCC's jurisdiction.[7]

Gandy et al. also found that national media organizations and national coalitions were more likely to be successful than local groups or private citizens. Previous evidence was supported by their finding that the larger the market and the higher the advertising rate, the lower the probability of a successful petition to deny.[8]

A recent stategy of feminists is to file an *informal objection* to a license renewal rather than a *petition to deny*. Both are provided by FCC regulations as means for the public to express complaints against broadcasters. Specifically, the *Procedure Manual* for the FCC says:

> You may raise any public interest question relating to the application or the applicant. Allegations have been made in the past, for example, that the station's programming does not serve the needs and interests of the community or that the station has engaged in discriminatory employment practices. . . . Your purpose in participating could properly be to effect a change in the station's policies or practices, by negotiation or by Commission direction, rather than to have the application denied.[9]

For the past decade, women's groups have used petitions to deny as their means of drawing attention to sexist policies, practices, and programming among FCC licensees. However, as the work of Gandy et al. and others shows, a petition to deny is difficult to prepare and rarely leads to change.

The FCC further describes the alternative.

> If you have information which you believe should be considered by the Commission . . . you may file an "informal objection." . . . Such objections may be filed in writing with the Secretary of the Commission, Washington, D.C. 20554, at any time prior to action on the application and must be signed by the person making them. There are no other requirements.[10]

The informal objection may also be effective during the present time when multimedia owners are being required to divest their holdings in certain markets to reduce concentrations of multimedia ownership. Instead of selling off their holdings, owners are trading with owners in other markets. By filing informal objections, women's groups may get owners to negotiate agreements during this period of transition. Over time the informal objection may prove to be a more useful strategy than the petition to deny, since it is easier to file and implies a desire to change policies, practices, or programming without removing the license.

The Federal Trade Commission (FTC) also makes decisions that can affect the presentation of women and men in the media. NOW, for example, petitioned the FTC to require National Airlines to substantiate its claim: "I'm going to fly you like you've never been flown before." NOW argued that such advertisements are:

> . . . deceptive because most of the ads refer to *stewardesses* who say *they* are going to fly passengers, when clearly they do not perform any of the duties entailed in navigating the aircraft. . . . Unless National Airlines can substantiate its claim that they are flying their passengers in a different method than the way a

passengers has been previously transported by an other commercial airline carrier, we respectfully urge the FTC to issue a cease and desist order to National for unfair and deceptive advertising claims.[11]

In a similar vein, Fowles discusses the complaint made by the Media Action Group of the Vancouver Status of Women to the Canadian Radio and Television Commision.

> As a result, Benson and Hedges withdrew its advertisement, "the longer the better," that featured a man emerging out of a manhole to gawk at a woman's legs. The Media Action Group suggested that the slogan might be an equally appropriate caption for a picture of a woman staring at a man's crotch.[12]

David Axelrad has proposed a system for monitoring sex-role stereotyping in television advertising that places responsibility on the individual station. His argument, based on legal precedents, is that advertising has always been subject to regulation and has not had unrestricted latitude under the First Amendment.[13] A recent decision, *Virginia State Board of Pharmacy* v. *Virginia Citizens Consumer Council, Inc.,*[14] reduces the amount of regulation that advertising is subject to. However, Axelrad contends that there is ample legislative and judical authority to make it clear:

> . . . that a reasonable regulation of the manner in which women are portrayed in television product advertising would withstand a first amendment challenge based on either consumers', advertisers', or broadcasters' rights to receive or disseminate stereotyped images of women. . . . Moreover, this type of regulation need not unconstitutionally restrict the flow of commercial information which is now considered vital to advertisers' and consumers' effective participation in our market economy.[15]

Axelrad proposes that each licensee's programming and advertising logs be adapted "to the task of monitoring the image of women in product commercials."[16] Although *no single* sexist advertisement could be the basis for a complaint to the FCC, the *overall pattern* of advertisements could be. This proposal extends the principle of a broadcaster's public-interest obligation in stating that national policy (e.g., federal and state laws against discrimination) sets the stage to require broadcasters to "meet adequately the interest of the community in eradicating sex-role stereotypes in product advertising."[17] Assuming that each station keeps logs of the portrayal of women and men in advertisements, upon receipt of a petition, the FCC would be required to examine the station's logs.

Axelrad argues that his proposal is not idealistic.

> . . . a regulatory scheme which would impose responsibility on the individual licensee is in most respects realistic. Even licensees affiliated with national networks retain control over the sale of advertising for locally produced and non-network programming; time slots between network programs are also sold directly by local stations . . .
>
> . . . If local television stations were held responsible by the FCC for balancing the image of women in television product advertising, the networks would have a vested interest in listening to their affiliates' demands for a change in advertising diet.[18]

Other legal strategies focus on discrimination in media employment and training. Discrimination in these areas can be challenged under Title VII of the Civil Rights Act of 1964 as amended by the Equal Employment Opportunity Act of 1972 and Executive Order 11478, under Executive Order 11246 as amended by Executive Order 11375 concerning Federal Contract Compliance, under the Equal Pay Act of 1963 as amended by the Education Amendments of 1972, and under Title IX of the Education Amendments of 1972. These and other federal laws against sex discrimination as well as complaint procedures are documented in *A Guide to Federal Laws Prohibiting Sex Discrimination* by the Commission on Civil Rights,[19] *Complaint Filing Guide* by the Department of Labor,[20] and *Affirma-*

tive Action and Equal Employment, by the Equal Employment Opportunity Commission.[21] Susan Ross's *The Rights of Women: The Basic ACLU Guide to a Woman's Rights*[22] contains chapters on employment and education discrimination and a chapter describing FCC regulations as they relate to women's rights. NOW has developed a *Broadcast Media Kit* that provides much-needed information concerning station monitoring, application of the fairness doctrine, license challenges, and license renewal application dates, and forms for recording employment statistics and for analyzing programs.

On August 31, 1977, a settlement was reached between NBC and its female employees who had filed a sex-discrimination suit on February 7, 1973, under Title VII of the Civil Rights Act of 1964. The settlement provided for payment of $2 million by NBC to those who were discriminated against on the basis of sex. Included in the settlement is an affirmative action program that gives goals and timetables for bringing women into managerial positions and technical positions that were previously closed.[23] The NBC case represents one of the successful outcomes of a legal strategy. Legal strategies against sexism, although necessary, may create only limited change.

The force of law can mean that salaries are upgraded or that more women are hired. However, after hiring, they must deal with sexism on the job. Maureen Callan interviewed five women copywriters, each of whom described problems in influencing advertising campaigns, in working with men who believe "sexism sells," and in having no role models. Ideas for nonstereotypic portrayals of women are ignored; campaigns showing equality in relationships are changed so that the woman becomes sexy but passive and the man becomes adventurous; reactions are gathered from male, never female, creative supervisors.[24] Callan concluded that it is difficult for women to change sexist advertising if they are not in decision-making positions.

Training of media personnel is another area where legal action can have impact through the enforcement of fair employment practice laws, although years may pass before we see significant change. A 1976 study showed that men continue to dominate the faculties of college-level journalism. A 1978 update indicates a lack of progress for some levels and a retrogression for other levels. Only data from the 1976 study was available at press time.

- Two percent of the professors were women.
- Eight percent of the associate professors were women.
- Fifteen percent of the assistant professors were women.
- Nineteen percent of the lecturers/instructors/others were women.[25]

At the 12 largest journalism schools, 96 percent of the faculty were men. Only 3 of the 12 schools had any women on the faculty.[26]

What of the students in journalism and communication? Paul Peterson reports that 51 percent of the undergraduates are women, 43 percent of the master's students are women, and 34 percent of the doctoral students are women. Data on degrees show a larger discrepancy between the percentage of women earning an M.A. and the percentage earning a Ph.D. Women receive 42 percent of the master's degrees and 23 percent of the doctorates.[27]

In a reanalysis of Steven Chaffee's and Peter Clarke's data on the training and employment of journalism/communication doctorates,[28] Matilda Butler, Suzanne Pingree, and William Paisley found that women were 10 percent of the doctoral graduates between 1968 and 1972. Fifty-seven percent of these women versus 70 percent of the men found positions in universities. Women were as likely as men to be appointed to the faculty of communication departments (10 percent of the women and 11 percent of the men). Journalism departments were another story. Forty-one percent of the women versus 67 percent of the men took those jobs.[29]

ECONOMIC STRATEGIES

An alternative to legal action against advertisers and broadcasters is a boycott of products that portray women offensively. Franchellie Cadwell, an advertising agency president, has stated that women must boycott products that do not present women as they are.[30] In individual and group actions, large numbers of women have chosen to boycott advertisers such as Wisk and National Airlines to protest their "Ring around the collar" and "Fly me" campaigns. The group approach is preferable, even if the effect on sales is the same, because advertisers may otherwise be misled about the reasons behind a campaign's failure in particular "markets."

Boycotts can also be effective in protesting employment discrimination. NOW organized a boycott of Sear's products because of that company's history of discrimination against women in technical and management positions. Sears eventually responded to the economic pressure with a program to recruit and promote women into these positions. The program's advertising campaign ("We don't separate the women from the men.". . . "At Sears Equal Opportunity = Action") was a symbolic reward for those who organized and followed the boycott.

Corporate interests may join public interests in economic action. The history of research and action concerning television violence, which led eventually to corporate boycotts of violent programming, offers an instructive parallel. Studies of the late 1960s linking television violence to children's antisocial behavior led Senator John Pastore, chairperson of the Senate Subcommittee on Communication, to request that HEW Secretary Robert Finch appoint:

> . . . a committee comprised of distinguished men and women to conduct a study under his supervision using those techniques which will establish scientifically insofar as possible what harmful effects, if any, these programs have on children.[31]

In the following 3 years more than $1 million were spent on television violence research; a five-volume report was issued by the government; newspapers carried feature stores; and the Pastore committee held hearings on the research findings. The circumstances surrounding these events are documented by Matilda Butler.[32] Of interest to the parallel between media violence and media sexism is that, prior to 1972, there was little awareness of the impact of television violence on children. By 1976, advertisers' violence consciousness was high enough that some were discontinuing their sponsorship of violent programs. *Better Radio and Television,* newsletter of the National Association for Better Broadcasting, reported that General Foods, the fourth largest national advertiser, "avoids programming that is dependent on the portrayal of graphic violence."[33] General Food's reasoning is based partly on awareness of the impact of violence and partly on economic self-interest. Archa Knowlton, media director for General Foods, said: "It is entirely possible that a commercial works harder in a program that reflects positive social interaction as opposed to one dealing with blood and guts."[34]

J. Walter Thompson, the nation's largest advertising agency, interviewed 1000 adults to find out what they thought about violent television programming and its sponsors. The Thompson report stated: ". . . enough viewers seem to be ready to take out their anger on advertisers to make the airing of commercials within violent programs a risky business indeed."[35] Thirty-five percent of those interviewed said they do not watch violence on television. For this reason, advertisers may find it unwise to sponsor those programs. And, although only 1.4 percent of the adults said they do not purchase products that sponsor violence, Thompson executives felt that advertisers are taking an unacceptable risk in continuing to sponsor certain programs. As one company official said:

> Even worse . . . advertisers who take the risk increasingly face nasty publicity and possible boycotts from anti-violence pressure groups.[36]

Thompson is showing a 40-minute, multimedia presentation of its findings to clients. Never before has the industry's truism, "Don't put a ketchup commercial in a Western," found so many believers.

Eric Levin reported in *TV Guide* about additional advertisers who have switched away from violent programs. In addition to General Foods, the list now includes Proctor and Gamble (the nation's largest television advertiser), McDonald's, Hunt-Wesson, Pfizer, Toyota, Ralston Purina, Clorox, Johnson & Johnson, Gillette, Bristol-Myers, Kraft, General Mills, Best Foods, and Samsonite.[37]

What will cause advertisers to switch away from sexist programming and to change their own presentation of women and men? Well-organized *boycotts* of products, supported by letters and posters saying why purchases are not being made, can influence advertisers who compete in the consumer marketplace. However, other advertisers operate regulated monopolies (e.g., telephone, utility, and transportation companies); their services and products cannot feasibly be boycotted. In such cases, *research* on the extent of their sexist practices, resulting in findings that are widely disseminated to government agencies and the public, can be influential.

SOCIAL ACTION

Advertisers' consciousness of sexism has been raised by history and by effective protest. In recent years some advertisers have created new campaigns that present women positively. The United Airlines' "You're the Boss" campaign has featured one commercial in which the traveler is a businesswoman. A Boeing Aircraft advertisement has shown a businesswoman working late in the evening in her airplane seat. Under the caption, "A woman's work is never done," the advertisement states that "Women are playing a new role in American business. And we at Boeing say . . . 'it's about time.' "

Jane Hall reported in *TV Guide* that Benton and Bowles

is one advertising agency that believes, "We can no longer afford the patronizing error of stereotyping a woman as a check-bouncing financial lost sheep."[38] According to Hall, change is coming slowly and large agencies such as J.Walter Thompson are just beginning to reconsider their presentation of women. Hall quoted Rena Bartos, who has conducted research on women for Thompson, saying that advertisers need to acknowledge the diverse roles that women play and create advertisements that reflect these roles. Predicting that the new advertisements will be quite different from the old ones, Bartos commented:

> But if we are pragmatic about the facts of the marketplace, there is no way we can write ads that show women as competitive housewives, simple-minded slobs or simpering idiots. That type of woman doesn't live here any more; and, what's more, she probably never did.[39]

Social action can be taken by *insiders* as well as *outsiders*. As media women create their own products, they can see to it that the program and advertisements present women positively. Feminist magazines, newspapers, newsletters, and television programs that now exist are good examples. *Media Report to Women* began its fifth year of publishing with a statement of journalistic principles. In the January 1, 1976 issue, the editor proposed three criteria for female journalism: "no attacks on people," "more factual information," and "people should speak for themselves."[40]

In 1976 CBS announced new training programs for its employees that included three seminars for women (Career Planning Seminar, Career Management Seminar, and Management and its Behavioral Implications), a seminar for men (Women in Management Seminar for Male Managers), and counseling services for women.[41]

Also in 1976, Women in Communications and the Alfred I. DuPont-Columbia University Survey and Awards Program jointly sponsored a research project on women in broadcast journalism. The survey obtained nominations of outstanding programs produced, directed, or reported by women and programs that focused on women. Information was compiled on affirmative action programs, employment of women, training of women, assignment of women, salaries of women, programming for women, and reporting of women's news. The results were published as part of a continuing survey of the broadcast media, and the volumes are now used by broadcasters, educators, and others concerned with media. These efforts by insiders create a climate for change.[42]

The effect of creating a climate for change is exemplified by recent events at the Corporation for Public Broadcasting, whose Board of Directors established The Task Force on Women in Public Broadcasting in November 1974. The report of that Task Force, coauthored by Caroline Isber and Muriel Cantor (see Chapters 6 and 12 for selected findings), was submitted to the CPB Board in October 1975. One month later the Board accepted the report and began to call for changes, including a Women's Training Grant Program. By mid-1978, the Board voted to double the amount of money for these training grants. It felt that the program represented "a viable mechanism for the advancement of women and minorities in public broadcasting."[43]

Inside action to create an awareness of media portrayals of women took place at WXYZ, the ABC affiliate in Detroit, in late 1976. The station produced a panel program that brought together the different viewpoints of advertisers, media staff, and women's action groups. "Womantime and Co." (now "Turnabout") a series produced by KQED, the public-broadcasting station in San Francisco, included a 1977 segment on "Images in the Media." This segment examined the presentation of women in programming and in commercials. In 1978, it produced a segment entitled "What Ever Happened to Dick and Jane?" that focused on sex-role stereotyping in elementary and secondary readers. KQED also produced an excellent program for its Documentary Showcase series entitled "Going Past Go: An Essay on Sexism."

Significant efforts to eliminate sexism from advertising have been undertaken by the National Advertising Review Board and the National Association of Broadcasters in the guidelines each has prepared. NARB's checklist asks 11 questions concerning *destructive portrayals*.[44]

- Am I implying in my promotional campaign that creative, athletic, and mind-enriching toys and games are not for girls as much as for boys? . . .
- Are sexual stereotypes perpetuated in my ad? . . .
- Are the women portrayed in my ad stupid? . . .
- Does my ad use belittling language? . . .
- Does my ad make use of contemptuous phrases? . . .
- Do my ads consistently show women waiting on men? . . .
- Is there a gratuitous message in my ads that a woman's most important role in life is a supportive one? . . .
- Do my ads portray women as more neurotic than men? . . .
- Do my ads feature women who appear to be basically unpleasant? . . .
- Do my ads portray women in situations that tend to confirm the view that women are the property of men? . . .
- Is there double entendre in my ads? Particularly about sex or women's bodies?"[45]

Seven questions are asked concerning *constructive portrayals.*

- Are the attitudes and behavior of the women in my ads suitable models for my own daughter to copy? . . .
- Do my ads reflect the fact that girls may aspire to careers in business and the professions? . . .
- Do my ads portray women and men (and children) sharing in the chores of family living? . . .
- Do the women in my ads make decisions . . . about the purchase of high-priced items and major family investments? . . .
- Do my ads portray women actually driving cars and showing an intelligent interest in mechanical features? . . .
- Are two-income families portrayed in my ads? . . .
- Are the women in my ads doing creative or exciting things? . . .[46]

The checklist concludes with two question concerning *positive appeals.*

- Is the product presented as a means for a woman to enhance her own self-esteem . . . to realize her full potential? . . .
- Does my advertisement promise women realistic rewards for using the product? . . .[47]

The National Association of Broadcaster's statement of principles is also directed to advertisers and emphasizes the need to portray both women and men as intelligent and informed, as people who share both occupational and family responsibilities. NAB calls for a balanced portrayal that reflects the roles that women and men actually play today.

Inside action can improve opportunities for women in academic employment related to media. Hiring in schools and departments of journalism/communication has traditionally relied on the "old boy network" of referrals, with discriminatory outcomes. To make deans and chairpersons aware of qualified women and minority men who should be considered for faculty openings, the Committee on the Status of Women of the Association for Education in Journalism (AEJ) compiled a *Directory of Women and Minority Men in Academic Journalism/Communication.*[48] Edited by Matilda Butler, Sheridan Crawford, and M. Violet Lofgren at Stanford University, the directory was published and distributed to all schools and departments of journalism/communication by AEJ, the American Association of Schools and Departments of Journalism, and the American Society of Journalism School Administrators.

Awards to outstanding women is another inside effort to highlight the achievements of women. *New Directions for Women* established a "Positive Image of Women" award in 1976. The winners for that year were Jacqueline Caballos, founder of a public relations firm, Ellen Cohn, journalist, Janice LaRouche, career counselor, Barbara Ringer, Register of Copyrights of the Library of Congress, Phyllis Sanders, producer and radio/television host, and Sally Wecksler, businesswoman and consultant in international book publishing.[49] At the 1978 meeting of the Annual Broadcast Industry Conference, Broadcast Preceptor Awards were given to women and men who had made contributions to the excellence of the media. The three women who received the award were Geraldine Lange, host of "Turnabout," Isabelle Lemon, radio advertising and promotion manager, and Donna Allen, editor of *Media Report to Women.* At the same meeting, Mady Werner received the Victoria St. Clair Award for the outstanding female student.[50] American Women in Radio and Television presented awards to 18 television programs "for enhancing the image, education and professionalism of women." Among those receiving the award in June 1978 were "Feminine Footprints," "Turnabout," "Edith's 50th Birthday" ("All in the Family"), "Woman of Valor," and "Women: A Celebration."[51]

One of the most unique inside efforts in recent years was an agreement among the editors of more than 30 women's magazines to provide coverage of the Equal Rights Amendment in the summer of the bicentennial year, 1976. Our content analysis of these articles is found in Chapter 7.

Social action strategies can also be used by outsiders. The International Women's Year (IWY) Committee on Media and the United Nations Commission on the Status of Women have recently developed questions and recommendations concerning media portrayal of women. The IWY questions include:

1. Are the women you portray shown as whole people or as weak and confused . . . ?
2. Do you look for ways to show women in roles that are not stereotypically defined . . . ?
3. Are you writing leading parts for women?
4. Is the exploitative "Woman as Victim" theme the main entertainment value of your piece . . . ?
5. If a rape is shown, is it dealt with as a basically sexual experience . . . or a physical assault . . . ?
6. Are women presented as appealing because they are "cute" . . . ?
7. Do you show men responding positively to strong independent women . . . ?

8. In a scene involving men and women, who does all the talking . . . ?
9. Are the women in a crisis portrayed as emotional and/or irrational . . . ?
10. If a woman has an idea, plan, solution or proposal, does she apologize first . . . ?
11. Are unmarried women usually presented as incomplete . . . ?
12. Does your work reflect the fact that some women occasionally rescue men . . . ?
13. When a woman takes action that reflects self-esteem, does she do so as a result of her own insight . . . ?
14. Do the women you portray have good, open friendships with other women . . . ?
15. Are the women excessively concerned with clothes and appearance . . . ?
16. Are the women you portray . . . obsessive about shiny floors, clean ovens . . . [52]

The United Nations' recommended measures can be taken by the media, by government, and by international organizations. Some of these measures are:

1. [Those in control of the media] should cease to project and should gradually eliminate commercialized, tasteless, and stereotyped images of women. . . .
2. They should depict the roles and achievement of women from all walks of life. . . .
3. They should avoid language that reinforces inequality. . . .
4. The concept of what is newsworthy should be defined to include more coverage of women's activities. . . .
5. Issues concerning women should . . . be treated as regular news. . . .
6. The media should co-operate . . . in establishing a regular service of news . . . on women's issues. . . .
7. They should publicize outstanding contributions by women in public life. . . .
8. Women should be given opportunities for employment in all systems of mass communication media at all levels. . . .
9. Women should be given a more decisive role in the planning and conception of publications and broadcasts for both men and women . . .
10. Training opportunities for qualified women should be increased, and more women should be appointed to positions on the faculties of communication training institutions. . . .

11. . . . the criteria for public service performance for periodic license reviews should include the projection of nondiscriminatory and positive roles for women. . . .

12. A network should be developed for the international exchange of information of special interest to women. . . .

13. Symposia, seminars, workshops or other types of international meetings and briefings should be organized for media authorities, with the participation of governments. . . .

14. Seminars should be organized for writers, journalists . . . producers on the treatment of news relating to and production of programmes on women. . . .[53]

Other projects that work effectively against media sexism are exemplified by the Citizen's Advisory Council on the Status of Women (sex discrimination in public schools, including research on textbooks, library books, and other curriculum aids), the Women's Action Alliance (nonsexist child development), the Kalamazoo Committee for Children's Television (monitoring), and the Project on Equal Education Rights (monitoring of investigations of federal complaints).

Efforts of those inside and outside the media are beginning to be supplemented by joint efforts. For instance, the Portland, Oregon, chapter of National Organization for Women has negotiated an agreement with KOIN-TV in which they will provide continuing input on women and minorities in employment and programming.[54] And CBS has agreed to meet regularly with the United Methodist Women's Division and the Sisters of Charity of St. Vincent de Paul of New York.[55]

More social action is underway than we can cover in this book, and more innovative strategies are needed than we can suggest. Many strategies can be facilitated by available resources for research and action, some of which are listed in the appendix.

CONCLUSION

Although all media and forms of content have been discussed, this book has emphasized sexism in advertising and television. These are the most powerful shapers of what can be called our "collective daydreams." Marshall McLuhan wrote in the *Mechanical Bride* that advertising agencies express for the society as a whole what dreams express for the individual. He continued:

> The advertising agencies and Hollywood, in their different ways, are always trying to get inside the public mind in order to impose their collective dreams on that inner stage. . . . One dream opens into another until reality and fantasy are made interchangeable.[56]

McLuhan's insight is as valid in the media culture of the late 1970s as it was 25 years ago. Arthur Asa Berger has stated:

> These collective daydreams contain hidden ideologies—a hidden curriculum—affecting our feelings and behavior. . . . Most people are blind to the power and effects of television programs. Their illusions about the sovereignty of their minds and their control of themselves make them all the more susceptible to the collective daydreams upon which they feed.[57]

The media set agendas that we all follow. They tell us how we should look, how we should act, what we should own, and what we should be concerned about. Efforts to reduce sexism in media portrayals of women have had some success. However, as Winston Churchill said, we have not reached the beginning of the end, only the end of the beginning. Children born this year will see uncountable thousands of sexist images during the 25,000 hours of television that they will watch before they make life choices in high school and college.

It is unlikely that media products can become less sexist than the media organizations where they are produced. If women lack respect and authority in the newsroom and studio, media products cannot confer that respect and authority on them elsewhere.

For how many years in the future will we see more symbols of change than substance of change in media treatment of women? The recommendations cited in this chapter are one basis for optimism. Women will receive better treatment in the media if these recommendations are adopted by media managers and advertisers.

At worst, change is patient. In the nineteenth and early twentieth centuries, suffragists did not always defeat their adversaries, but they almost always survived them. Sexist beliefs will follow antisuffrage beliefs into history. As Max Planck said of a new scientific theory:

> [It] does not triumph by convincing its opponents and making them see the light, but rather because its opponents eventually die, and a new generation grows up that is familiar with it.[58]

ADDITIONAL RESOURCES FOR RESEARCH AND ACTION

This appendix suggests some additional resources for research and action. It indicates what is available, and it is not comprehensive. Within the range of suggestions, we mention both print sources and people sources. We include examples of newsletters/presses, action groups, federal agencies, professional associations, advertising agencies, networks/film companies/ magazines, and advertisers. We urge the reader, whether researcher, activist, or concerned observer, to use these resources to help bring about nonstereotypic presentations of women and men in the mass media. Each resource can be used to locate additional sources.

NEWSLETTERS/PRESSES

An excellent example of a resource that enumerates other sources is *Media Report to Women.* The monthly newsletter contains reports of research and action projects. It provides information for obtaining full documentation of most articles.

Its yearly index/directory includes women's media groups and individual media women. Newsletters of interest include:

The Executive Woman
747 Third Avenue
New York, New York 10017

The Spokeswoman
5464 South Shore Drive
Chicago, Illinois 60615

Media Report to Women
3306 Ross Place N.W.
Washington, D.C. 20008

Although there are many feminist presses, two are of particular interest here. KNOW, Inc. has an extensive catalog of reprints as well as a few relevant original works, such as *Image, Myth and Beyond,* edited by Betty E. Chmaj, Judith Gustafson, and Joseph Baunoch. The Feminist Press has published books concerning the media and maintains extensive files for their Women's Studies Clearinghouse.

The Feminist Press
Box 334
Old Westbury, New York
11568

KNOW, Inc.
P.O. Box 86031
Pittsburgh, Pennsylvania
15221

ACTION/INFORMATION GROUPS

The Office of Communication of the United Church of Christ is both a source of printed information and a source of people concerned with the media. Each year, they publish a report of the employment practices of public and commercial television stations. They have also sponsored petitions to deny broadcast licenses. Action information groups include:

Action for Children's
Television
46 Austin Street
Newtonville, Massachusetts
02160

American Association of
University Women
2401 Virginia Avenue N.W.
Washington, D.C. 20037

American Women in Radio
and Television, Inc.
1321 Connecticut Avenue
N.W.
Washington, D.C. 20036

Journalists for Professional
Equality
Toni House, *Washington
Star-News*
225 Virginia Avenue S.E.
Washington, D.C. 20003

Media Women in Action
2722 Connecticut Avenue
N.W.
Washington, D.C. 20008

National Federation of Press
Women
5246 106th Avenue S.E.
Kent, Washington 98031

National Media Task Force
National Organization for
Women
427 13th Street N.W., Suite
1001
Washington, D.C. 20004

National Organization
Against Sexism in Media
1200 West Alabama
Houston, Texas 77006

NOW Legal Defense and
Education Fund
127 East 59th Street
New York, New York 10022

United Church of Christ
Office of Communication
289 Park Avenue South
New York, New York 10010

Women in Communications,
Inc.
8305-A Shoal Creek
Boulevard
Austin, Texas 78758

Women for Media Change
4898 Sharon Avenue
Columbus, Ohio 43214

Women's Action Alliance
370 Lexington Avenue
New York, New York 10017

Women's Educational Equity
Communications Network
1855 Folsom Street
San Francisco, California
94103

Women's Equity Action
League
538 National Press Building
Washington, D.C. 20004

Women's National Book
Association
124 Church Street
New Brunswick, New Jersey
08901

PROFESSIONAL ASSOCIATIONS

There are many relevant professional associations. Few, if any, consider media sexism a priority topic. Most, however, would be more active in eliminating media sexism if pressure for change were evident. The following associations cover advertising agency personnel, advertisers, educational television personnel, and academicians.

American Association of
Advertising Agencies
200 Park Avenue
New York, New York 10017

Association for Education in
Journalism
201 Murphy Hall
University of Minnesota
Minneapolis, Minnesota
55455

Association of National
Advertisers
155 East 44th Street
New York, New York 10017

International Communication Association
P.O. Box 7728
University Station
Austin, Texas 78712

National Association for
Educational Broadcasters
1771 N Street N.W.
Washington, D.C. 20036

FEDERAL AGENCIES

Most legal actions to end discrimination in employment and in the presentation of women involve one or more of the following federal agencies.

Equal Employment
Opportunity Commission
1800 G Street N.W.
Washington, D.C. 20506

Federal Communications
Commission
Complaints and Compliance
Division
1919 M Street N.W.
Washington, D.C. 20554

Federal Trade Commission
Pennsylvania Avenue at 6th
Street N.W.
Washington, D.C. 20580

Office of Civil Rights
Department of Health,
Education and Welfare
330 Independence Avenue
S.W.
Washington, D.C. 20201

NETWORKS/FILM COMPANIES/MAGAZINES

The media carry the message that women are sex objects and that women belong at home. They share in the responsibility for the creation of the message as well as for the dissemination of it. Here are the three commercial networks, the noncommercial network, film companies, and 18 magazines that have a circulation of more than 2 million per issue.

Television

American Broadcasting
  Corporation
1330 Avenue of the
  Americas
New York, New York 10019

Columbia Broadcasting
  System
51 West 52nd Street
New York, New York 10019

National Broadcasting
  Corporation
30 Rockefeller Plaza
New York, New York 10020

Public Broadcasting Service
304 West 58th Street
New York, New York 10019

Film

Allied Artists Pictures
  Corporation
15 Columbus Circle
New York, New York 10023

Avco Embassy Pictures
  Corporation
1301 Avenue of the
  Americas
New York, New York 10023

Columbia Pictures
  Industries, Inc.
711 Fifth Avenue
New York, New York 10022

Metro-Goldwyn-Mayer, Inc.
10200 West Washington
  Boulevard
Culver City, California
  90230

Paramount Pictures
  Corporation
1 Gulf & Western Plaza
New York, New York 10023

RKO General, Inc.
1440 Broadway
New York, New York 10018

Twentieth Century-Fox
Box 900
Beverly Hills, California
  90213

United Artists Corporation
729 Seventh Avenue
New York, New York 10019

Universal Pictures
445 Park Avenue
New York, New York 10022

Walt Disney Productions
500 South Buena Vista
  Street
Burbank, California 91521

Warner Bros., Inc.
75 Rockefeller Plaza
New York, New York 10019

Magazines

American Home
641 Lexington Avenue
New York, New York 10022

Better Homes & Gardens
1716 Locust Street
Des Moines, Iowa 50336

Cosmopolitan
224 West 57th Street
New York, New York 10019

Family Circle
488 Madison Avenue
New York, New York 10022

Good Housekeeping
959 Eighth Avenue
New York, New York 10019

Ladies' Home Journal
641 Lexington Avenue
New York, New York 10022

McCall's
230 Park Avenue
New York, New York 10017

Newsweek
444 Madison Avenue
New York, New York 10022

Penthouse
909 Third Avenue
New York, New York 10022

Playboy
919 North Michigan Avenue
Chicago, Illinois 60611

Reader's Digest
Pleasantville, New York
10570

Redbook
230 Park Avenue
New York, New York 10017

Sports Illustrated
Time and Life Building
Rockefeller Center
New York, New York 10020

Time
Time and Life Building
Rockefeller Center
New York, New York 10020

True Story
205 East 42nd Street
New York, New York 10017

TV Guide
Radnor, Pennsylvania 19088

U.S. News and World Report
2300 N Street N.W.
Washington, D.C. 20037

Woman's Day
1515 Broadway
New York, New York 10036

ADVERTISING AGENCIES

A handful of advertising agencies create most of the commercials we see and read. The following are the agencies with annual billings of more than $385,000,000. All agencies and the products they represent are reported in *Standard Directory of Advertising Agencies, 1976.*

Ted Bates and Company
1515 Broadway
New York, New York 10036
Annual Billings:
 $600,000,000
Sample Products/Clients:
 Marx Toys, Maybelline
 Co., Prudential Insurance
 Co. of America

Batten, Barton, Durstin and
 Osborn
383 Madison Avenue
New York, New York 10017
Annual Billings:
 $520,126,000
Sample Products/Clients:
 Breck Shampoo, Puss and
 Boots Cat Foods, Soft and
 Dri, Right Guard, Lucky
 Cigarettes

Leo Burnett Company, Inc.
Prudential Plaza
Chicago, Illinois 60601
Annual Billings:
    $623,000,000
Sample Products/Clients:
    Cheer Detergent, United
    Airlines, Secret
    Deodorant, Era Laundry
    Soap, Lava Soap, Maytag
    Co.

Grey Advertising, Inc.
777 Third Avenue
New York, New York 10017
Annual Billings:
    $399,300,000
Sample Products/Clients:
    Kool-Aid, Post Raisin
    Bran, Stove Top Stuffing
    Mix, Dristan, Freezone,
    Sleep-Eze

D'Arcy-Macmanus and
    Masius
437 Madison Avenue
New York, New York 10022
Annual Billings:
    $425,500,000
Sample Products/Clients:
    Gerber Products, Aetna
    Life and Casualty,
    Colgate-Palmolive Co.,
    Rawlings Sporting Goods

McCann-Erickson, Inc.
485 Lexington Avenue
New York, New York 10017
Annual Billings:
    $775,100,000
Sample Products/Clients:
    Laura Scudder Snack
    Foods, Keds and
    Grasshoppers Footwear,
    Airways Rent-A-Car,
    Tampax

Foote, Cone and Belding
200 Park Avenue
New York, New York 10017
Annual Billings:
    $385,438,000
Sample Products/Clients:
    Campbell Soup, Clairol
    Inc., Frito-Lay, Kraft
    Foods, Levi Strauss and
    Co.

Ogilvy and Mather, Inc.
2 East 48th Street
New York, New York 10017
Annual Billings:
    $582,000,000
Sample Products/Clients:
    Dove for Dishes, Gaines
    Meal Burgers, Aim,
    Imperial Margarine,
    Mattel, Swanson Products

SSC&B
One Dag Hammerskjold
Plaza
New York, New York 10017
Annual Billings:
$556,000,000
Sample Products/Clients:
Cover Girl Make-up,
Lipton Cup-A-Soup,
Hydrox Cookies, Lifebuoy,
Monster's Children
Vitamins

J. Walter Thompson
420 Lexington Avenue
New York, New York 10017
Annual Billings:
$897,500,000
Sample Products/Clients:
Close-Up Toothpaste,
Scott Paper Co., Deep
Magic Moisturizer,
Listerine Antiseptic, Uncle
Ben's Foods

Young and Rubicam
International
285 Madison Avenue
New York, New York 10017
Annual Billings:
$800,900,000
Sample Products/Clients:
Holiday Inns,
Metropolitan Life
Insurance Company,
American Home Foods,
Dr. Pepper Co.

ADVERTISERS

Magazines, radio, television, and newspapers all rely on advertising to help cover expenses. By letting the advertisers know we will not purchase products that show or sponsor sexist presentations of women and men, we can help to determine future characterizations of all people. A complete listing of advertisers can be found in *Standard Directory of Advertisers, 1976.*

American Home Products
685 Third Avenue
New York, New York 10017
Sample Products: Chef
   Boyardee

Bristol-Myers Company
345 Park Avenue
New York, New York 10022
Sample Products: Bufferin,
   Excedrin, Ultra Ban

Colgate-Palmolive Company
300 Park Avenue
New York, New York 10022
Sample Products: Ajax, Fab,
   Ultra-Brite Toothpaste,
   Colgate Toothpaste

Ford Motor Company
The American Road
Dearborn, Michigan 48120
Sample Products: Ford,
   Mercury, Lincoln

General Foods Corporation
250 North
White Plains, New York
   10605
Sample Products: Jello,
   Birds Eye, Kool-Aid,
   Gravy Train

General Motors Corporation
General Motors Building
Detroit, Michigan 48202
Sample Products: Chevrolet,
   Pontiac, Buick,
   Oldsmobile

Lever Brothers
390 Park Avenue
New York, New York 10022
Sample Products: Dove,
   Lux, Pepsodent, Aim,
   Imperial Margarine

Procter & Gamble Company
301 East Sixth Street
Cincinnati, Ohio 45202
Sample Products: Downy,
   Cheer, Ivory, Gain,
   Crisco, Duncan Hines,
   Charmin

Sears, Roebuck and
   Company
925 Smith Homan
Chicago, Illinois 60607

Sterling Drug, Inc.
90 Park Avenue
New York, New York 10022
Sample Products: Bayer
   Aspirin, Cope, Vanquish

NOTES

In many cases, these notes supplement findings reported in the text, but methodological details are generally omitted.

PART 1

1. Boorstin, D. *The image: A guide to pseudo-events in America.* New York: Harper & Row, 1961, p. 9.
2. Schroder, H., Driver, M., & Streufert, S. *Human information processing.* New York: Holt, Rinehart and Winston, 1967.

CHAPTER 1

1. Grimke, S. *Letters on the equality of the sexes and the condition of women.* Boston: Isaac Knapp, 1838, p. 10.
2. Ibid.
3. Stanton, E., Anthony, S., & Gage, M. (Eds.) *History of woman suffrage.* Vol. 1. Rochester, N.Y.: Charles Mann, 1889, p. 59.
4. Ibid., pp. 680–681.
5. Foner, P. (Ed.) *Life and writings of Frederick Douglass.* Vol. 4. New York: International Publishers, 1950, p. 212.

6. Flexner, E. *Century of struggle.* Cambridge, Mass.: Harvard University Press, 1959, p. 153.

7. Boorstin, D. *The Americans: The democratic experience.* New York: Random House, 1973, p. 3.

8. Tremain, R. *The fight for freedom for women.* New York: Ballantine Books, 1973, p. 100.

9. Ibid., pp. 122, 125.

10. Ibid., pp. 137, 141.

11. Ibid., p. 109.

12. Friedan, B. *The feminine mystique.* New York: W. W. Norton, 1963.

13. Myrdal, G. *An American dilemma: The Negro problem and modern democracy.* New York: Harper & Row, 1944, p. 1073.

14. Hacker, H. Women as a minority group. *Social Forces,* 1951, *30,* 62.

15. Ibid., p. 65. An indication of the relative progress of blacks and women is the applicability in 1978 of these lists of attributes. The black stereotype of 1944 is clearly out of date now, while the female stereotype persists almost unchanged.

16. Ibid., p. 67.

17. Hacker, H. Women as a minority group: Twenty years later. *International Journal of Group Tensions,* 1974, *4,* 126.

18. Lazarsfeld, P., & Merton, R. Mass communication, popular taste, and organized social action. In W. Schramm and D. Roberts (Eds.), *The process and effects of mass communication.* (Rev. ed.) Urbana: University of Illinois Press, 1971, pp. 554–578.

19. United Nations. *Influence of mass communication media on the formation of a new attitude towards the role of women in present-day society.* New York: United Nations, Economic and Social Council, Commission on the Status of Women, 1974, p. 15.

20. Ibid.

21. Bird, C. *Born female.* New York: Pocket Books, 1969, p. 125.

CHAPTER 2

1. *Webster's new world dictionary.* New York: American Book Company, 1961.

2. Whorf, B. *Language, thought, and reality.* New York: Wiley, 1956.

3. Association for Education in Journalism. *Newsletter,* July 1974.

4. Advertisement for Ximedia Systems, Inc., 1977.

5. Jesperson, O. *Growth and structure of the English language.* (4th ed.) New York: D. Appleton, 1955, p. 2.

6. Copperud, R. Editorial workshop. *Editor and Publisher,* June 8, 1974, p. 32.

7. Spock, B. *Baby and child care.* (Rev. ed.) New York: Pocket Books, 1976, p. xix.

8. Evans, R., & Meyer, E. Consequences of sexism in journalism texts. Paper presented at the Women in Journalism Seminar, University of Michigan, Ann Arbor, 1973.

9. Advertisement for Mutual Benefit Life Insurance Company, 1974.

10. Lakoff, R. *Language and woman's place.* New York: Harper & Row, 1975, p. 4.

11. Saporta, S. Language in a sexist society. Paper presented at the Annual Convention of the Modern Language Association of America, New York, 1974.

12. Bate, B. *Generic man, invisible woman: Language, thought, and social change.* Eugene, Ore.: University of Oregon, 1975.

13. Gershuny, H. Sexist semantics: An investigation of masculine and feminine nouns and pronouns in dictionary sentences that illustrate word usage as a reflection of sex-role. Unpublished doctoral dissertation, New York University, 1973.

14. Graham, A. The making of a non-sexist dictionary. *Ms.,* December 1973, pp. 12–16.

15. Martyna, W. What does "he" mean—use of the generic masculine. *Journal of Communication,* 1978, *28,* 131–138.

16. Ibid.

17. Schneider, J., & Hacker, S. Sex role imagery and use of the generic "man" in introductory texts: A case in the sociology of sociology. *The American Sociologist,* 1973, *8,* 12–18.

Although there is no "final word" on the effects of gendered pronouns on thought or action, evidence of various kinds tells us that the generic masculine inhibits reference to girls and women. For example, Joseph Turow reports the following exchange in an interview with a television casting agent.

Interviewer: Under what conditions would you suggest a woman if the breakdown [list of dramatic characters] said "banker?"

Agent: I wouldn't, because it would say "he."

Interviewer: Do you see "he" as necessarily denoting a male?

Agent: Oh, sure. I even look down [the breakdown page] for the "he" or "she" to see which [part] starts with "he" or "she."

(See Turow, J. Casting for TV parts: The anatomy of social typing. *Journal of Communication,* 1978, *28,* 22.

18. Bate, B. Nonsexist language use in transition. *Journal of Communication,* 1978, *28,* 139–149. (Also, an extensive review of alternative terms appears in Blaubergs, M. Changing the sexist language: The theory behind the practice. *Psychology of Women Quarterly,* 1978, *2,* 244–261.

19. Lakoff, op. cit., pp. 53–56.

20. Kramer, C. Women's rhetoric in *"New Yorker"* cartoons: Patterns for a Mildred Milquetoast. Paper presented at the Annual Convention of the Speech Communication Association, New York, 1973.

21. Zimbardo, P., & Meadow, W. Sexism springs eternal—in the Reader's Digest. Paper presented at the Annual Convention of the Western Psychological Association, San Francisco, 1974.

22. Saporta, op. cit.

CHAPTER 3

1. Boulding, K. *The image: Knowledge in life and society.* Ann Arbor: University of Michigan Press, 1956, p. 6.

2. Ibid., pp. 3–6.

3. Ibid., pp. 6–7.

4. McLuhan, M. *Understanding media: The extensions of man.* New York: New American Library, 1966.

5. Cantril, H., Gaudet, H., & Herzog, H. *The invasion from Mars.* Princeton, N.J.: Princeton University Press, 1940.

6. Boorstin, D. *The image: A guide to pseudo-events in America.* New York: Harper & Row, 1972, pp. 39–49.

7. Bruner, J., Goodnow, J., & Austin, G. *A study of thinking.* New York: Wiley, 1956, pp. 182–230.

8. Miller, G., Galanter, E., & Pribram, K. *Plans and the structure of behavior.* New York: Holt, Rinehart and Winston, 1960, p. 18.

9. Berger, P., & Luckmann, T. *The social construction of reality: A treatise on the sociology of knowledge.* Garden City, N.Y.: Doubleday, 1966.

CHAPTER 4

1. Schramm, W. *Men, messages, and media: A look at human communication.* New York: Harper & Row, 1973, pp. 16–17.

2. Ibid., p. 173. There was a much-publicized decrease in adult viewing hours during the 1977 to 1978 season. Nielsen's data for November 1977 show that only women in the 55+ age group were viewing as much as 5 hours per day on the average, followed by men in the 55+ age group with 4.5 hours. In contrast, women in the 18 to 54 age group averaged 4.2 hours and men in the 18 to 54 age group averaged 3.2 hours. (*Nielsen television '78.* Northbrook, Ill.: A. C. Nielsen Co., 1977, pp. 10–11.)

3. These historical and current data on the media are derived and often computed by us from a variety of sources, including the Audit Bureau of Circulation, National Association of Broadcasters, Electronic Industries Association, Federal Communications Commission, Bureau of the Census, and journals such as *Advertising Age* and *Editor and Publisher.*

4. McLuhan, M. *Understanding Media: The extensions of man.* New York: New American Library, 1966.

5. The $400 estimate is derived simply by dividing the 74 million American households (circa 1977) into the 30+ billion revenues of media and related industries (also circa 1977). The actual expenditures of a sample of households in a given year would have a high variance because of expensive equipment (e.g., videotape recorders, stereo phonograph systems) that some fraction of all households acquire or replace during the year. A 5-year average expenditure per household would be more valid because equipment costs of 1 year would be amortized across the other years.

6. Television Bureau of Advertising, Inc.

PART 2

CHAPTER 5

1. Berelson, B. *Content analysis in communication research.* New York: Free Press, 1952, p. 13.

2. Katz, D., McClintock, C., & Sarnoff, I. The measurement of ego defense as related to attitude change. *Journal of Personality,* 1957, *25,* 465–474.

   Rokeach, M. *The open and closed mind.* New York: Basic Books, 1960.

3. Gerbner, G. Communication and social environment. In *Communication, a Scientific American book.* San Francisco: W. H. Freeman, 1972, p. 114.

4. Berelson, op. cit., p. 18.

5. Lippmann, W., & Merz, C. A test of the news. *New Republic,* Supplement to issue of August 4, 1920.

6. Efron, E. *The news twisters.* New York: Manor Books, 1972.
    National Organization for Women. *Women in the wasteland fight back.* Washington, D.C.: NOW, National Capital Area Chapter, 1972.

7. Kingsbury, S., & Hart, H. *Newspapers and the news.* New York: Putnam, 1937.

8. Friedan, B. *The feminine mystique.* New York: W. W. Norton, 1963, pp. 28–61.

9. Saunders, D. Social ideas in the McGuffey Readers. *Public Opinion Quarterly,* 1941, *5,* 579–589.

10. Paisley, W. Introduction to Part III. In G. Gerbner, O. Holsti, K. Krippendorff, W. Paisley, and P. Stone (Eds.), *The analysis of communication content.* New York: Wiley, 1969, pp. 283–284.

11. Hall, E. *The silent language.* New York: Doubleday, 1959.

12. See, for example, Ekman, P., Friesen, W., & Taussig, T. VID-R and SCAN: Tools and methods for the automated analysis of visual records. In G. Gerbner, O. Holsti, K. Krippendorff, W. Paisley, and P. Stone (Eds.), *The analysis of communication content.* New York: Wiley, 1969, pp. 297–312.

13. Goffman, E. Gender advertisements. *Studies in the Anthropology of Visual Communication,* 1976, *3,* 65–154.

14. Ibid., p. 91.

15. The pioneering theoretical work on "kinesics" or body motion communication by Birdwhistell illustrates one framework in which analyses of visual media could be conducted. See Birdwhistell, R. *Kinesics and context: Essays on body motion communication.* Philadelphia: University of Pennsylvania Press, 1970. Some kinesic expressions of gender differences are discussed in Chapter 6, Masculinity and femininity as display.

16. Recommended book-length treatments are: Berelson, op. cit.; Holsti, O., *Content analysis for the social sciences and humanities.* Reading, Mass.: Addison-Wesley, 1969; Gerbner et al., op. cit.

17. Stevenson, R., Eisinger, R., Feinberg, B., & Kotok, A. Untwisting the

news twisters: A replication of Efron's study. *Journalism Quarterly,* 1973, *50,* 218–219.

18. Lukenbill, W. Who writes children's books? *Journal of Communication,* 1976, *26,* 97–100.

19. Schramm, W. *One day in the world's press.* Palo Alto, Calif.: Stanford University Press, 1959.

20. Berelson, op. cit., p. 198.

CHAPTER 6

1. U.S. Commission on Civil Rights. *Window dressing on the set: Women and minorities in television.* Washington, D.C.: U.S. Government Printing Office, 1977, p. 40.

2. National Organization for Women. *Women in the wasteland fight back.* Washington, D.C.: NOW, National Capital Area Chapter, 1972.

3. Hennessee, J., & Nicholson, J. NOW Says: TV commercials insult women. *The New York Times Magazine,* May 28, 1972, p. 48.

   Dominick, J., & Rauch, G. The image of women in network TV commercials. *Journal of Broadcasting,* 1972, *16,* 259–265.

   American Association of University Women. *The image of women in television.* Sacramento, Calif.: AAUW, Sacramento Branch, 1974.

   Silverstein, A., & Silverstein, R. The portrayal of women in television advertising. *Federal Communications Bar Journal,* 1974, *27,* 71–98.

   Culley, J., & Bennett, R. *The status of women in mass media advertising: An empirical study.* Newark: University of Delaware, Bureau of Economic and Business Research, 1974.

   Women on Words and Images. *Channeling children: Sex stereotyping in prime-time TV.* Princeton, N.J.: Women on Words and Images, 1975.

   Fox, H. Sex stereotypes in advertisements. *Business and Society,* 1976, *11,* 24–30.

   Cirksena, K., & Butler, M. *Sex bias in advertisements: Are we making progress?* San Francisco: Far West Laboratory for Educational Research and Development, 1978.

   O'Donnell, W., & O'Donnell, K. Update: Sex-role messages in TV commercials. *Journal of Communication,* 1978, *28,* 156–158.

   Maracek, J., Piliavin, J., Fitzsimmons, E., Krogh, E., Leader, E., & Trudell, B. Women as TV experts: The voice of authority? *Journal of Communication,* 1978, *28,* 159–168.

The ratios of female to male voice-overs reported in these studies were 11 percent to 89 percent (Hennessee and Nicholson); 6 percent to 94 percent (Dominick and Rauch); 6 percent to 94 percent (AAUW); 4 percent to 96 percent (Silverstein and Silverstein); 16 percent to 84 percent (Culley and Bennett); 4 percent to 96 percent (Women on Words and Images); 5 percent to 95 percent (Fox); 8 percent to 92 percent (Cirksena and Butler); 7 percent to 93 percent (O'Donnell and O'Donnell); and 6 percent to 94 percent (Maracek et al.).

4. Screen Actors Guild. *The relative roles of men and women in television commercials.* New York: Screen Actors Guild, New York Branch Women's Conference Committee, 1974.

5. Dominick & Rauch, op. cit.

6. Women on Words and Images, op. cit.

7. National Organization for Women, op. cit. Among product representatives, 87 percent of the women and 5 percent of the men were shown in family roles. Among characters other than product representatives, 77 percent of the women and 34 percent of the men were shown in family roles.

Courtney, A., & Lockeretz, S. A woman's place: An analysis of the roles portrayed by women in magazine advertisements. *Journal of Marketing Research,* 1971, *8,* 92–95.

Dominick and Rauch, op. cit.

Culley & Bennett, op. cit. Family roles were portrayed by 45 percent of the women and 15 percent of the men shown.

Fox, op. cit. Family roles were portrayed by 42 percent of the women and 27 percent of the men shown.

8. Women on Words and Images, op. cit.

Fox, op. cit. Among those shown employed, 32 percent were women and 68 percent were men.

9. National Organization for Women, op. cit.

Fox, op. cit. Defining high-status positions as business management and the professions (including entertainment professions), Fox found that 43 percent of the women and 63 percent of the men were shown in such positions.

10. National Organization for Women, op. cit.

Women on Words and Images, op. cit.

11. Women on Words and Images, op. cit.

12. Ibid.

13. Hennessee & Nicholson, op. cit.

    Women on Words and Images, op. cit.

14. Dominick & Rauch, op. cit.

    Culley and Bennett, op. cit. Characters shown in the home account for 34 percent of the women and 21 percent of the men.

    O'Donnell & O'Donnell, op. cit. Product representatives shown in the home account for 56 percent of the women and 18 percent of the men.

15. National Organization for Women, op. cit. Among the women shown, 82 percent seem to be under 40; among men shown, 56 percent seem to be under 40.

    Courtney & Whipple, op. cit.

    Culley & Bennett, op. cit. Among the women shown, 58 percent seem to be under 35; among men shown, 44 percent seem to be under 35.

16. Courtney & Whipple, op. cit.

17. National Organization for Women, op. cit.

18. Hennessee & Nicholson, op. cit.

19. Dominick & Rauch, op. cit.

20. Courtney & Whipple, op. cit.

21. Screen Actors Guild, op. cit.

22. Women on Words and Images, op. cit.

23. O'Donnell & O'Donnell, op. cit.

24. Maracek et al., op. cit.

25. Ibid.

26. Cirksena & Butler, op. cit.

27. Busby, L. Defining the sex-role standard in network children's programs. *Journalism Quarterly*, 1974, *51*, 690–696. Among characters shown in Saturday morning cartoons, 34 percent were girls/women; 66 percent were boys/men.

    O'Kelly, C. Sexism in children's television. *Journalism Quarterly*, 1974, *51*, 722–724. Girls/women were 33 percent of the characters shown; boys/men were 67 percent.

28. Chulay, C., & Francis, S. The image of the female child on Saturday morning television commercials. Paper presented at the Annual Convention of the International Communication Association, New Orleans, 1974.

    Barcus, E. *Saturday children's television.* Boston: Boston University,

School of Public Communication, 1971.

29. Barcus, op. cit.

30. O'Kelly, op. cit.

31. Chulay & Francis, op. cit.

32. Valdez, A. The socialization influence of television commercials on pre-school age children.. Unpublished doctoral dissertation, Stanford University, 1978.

33. Smythe, D. Reality as presented by television. *The Public Opinion Quarterly,* 1954, *18,* 143–156.

34. Northcutt, H., Seggar, J., & Hinton, J. Trends in TV portrayal of blacks and women. *Journalism Quarterly,* 1975, *52,* 741–744.

35. Head, S. Content analysis of television drama programs. *Quarterly of Film, Radio, and Television,* 1954, *9,* 175–194. Among major characters, 32 percent were women and 68 percent were men.

Gerbner, G. Violence in television drama: Trends and symbolic functions. In G. Comstock and E. Rubinstein (Eds.), *Television and social behavior.* Vol. 1: *Media content and control.* Washington, D.C.: U.S. Government Printing Office, 1972, pp. 28–187.

National Organization for Women, op. cit. Women were 30 percent of the characters shown; men were 70 percent.

Seggar, J., & Wheeler, P. World of work on TV: Ethnic and sex representation in TV drama. *Journal of Broadcasting,* 1973, *17,* 201–214. Among the white Americans, 19 percent were women and 81 percent were men. Among the black Americans, 17 percent were women and 83 percent were men.

Tedesco, N. Patterns in prime time. *Journal of Communication,* 1974, *24,* 119–124. Women were 28 percent of the characters shown; men were 72 percent.

Turow, J. Advising and ordering: Daytime, prime time. *Journal of Communication,* 1974, *24,* 138–141. Women were 30 percent of the characters shown; men were 70 percent.

McNeil, J. The reverse prism: A study of the images of women on television. Unpublished manuscript, University of Illinois at Urbana-Champaign 1974. A later version appeared as Feminism, femininity, and the television series: A content analysis. *Journal of Broadcasting,* 1975, *19,* 259–271.

Screen Actors Guild, op. cit. Women were 28 percent of the characters shown; men were 72 percent.

Women on Words and Images, op. cit. Women were 40 percent of the characters shown; men were 60 percent.

Kalamazoo Committee for Children's Television. KCCT's monitoring study results released. *KCCT Newsletter,* January 1975, pp. 1–2, 4.

Isber, C., & Cantor, M. *Report of the task force on women in public broadcasting.* Washington, D.C.: Corporation for Public Broadcasting, 1975. In general programming for adults, 15 percent of the characters were women and 85 percent were men.

36. National Organization for Women, op. cit. Among the soap opera characters, 46 percent were women and 54 percent were men.

Downing, M. Heroine of the daytime serial. *Journal of Communication,* 1974, *24,* 130–137. Among the soap opera characters, 50 percent were women and 50 percent were men.

Turow, op. cit. Among the soap opera characters, 46 percent were women and 54 percent were men.

37. DeFleur, M. Occupational roles as portrayed on television. *Public Opinion Quarterly,* 1964, *28,* 57–74. Among those shown employed, 16 percent were women and 84 percent were men.

National Organization for Women, op. cit. Among those shown employed, 21 percent were women and 79 percent were men.

Women on Words and Images, op. cit. Among those shown employed, 25 percent were women and 75 percent were men.

38. National Organization for Women, op. cit.

Tedesco, op. cit.

McNeil, op. cit.

39. DeFleur, op. cit.

Seggar & Wheeler, op. cit.

Downing, op. cit.

Tedesco, op. cit.

McNeil, op. cit.

40. DeFleur, op. cit.

Downing, op. cit.

41. Tedesco, op. cit. Marital status was known for 51 percent of the women and 32 percent of the men.

McNeil, op. cit. Marital status was known for 89 percent of the women and 54 percent of the men.

42. Downing, op. cit.

43. Smythe, op. cit.

44. DeFleur, op. cit.

45. Gerbner, op. cit.

46. Gerbner, G., & Gross, L. Living with television: The violence profile. *Journal of Communication,* 1976, *26,* 198.

47. National Organization for Women, op. cit.

48. Katzman, N. Television soap operas: What's been going on anyway? *Public Opinion Quarterly,* 1972, *35,* 200–212.

49. Downing, op. cit.

50. Tedesco, op. cit.

51. Turow, op. cit.

52. McNeil, op. cit.

53. Screen Actors Guild, op. cit.

54. AAUW, op. cit.

55. Women on Words and Images, op. cit.

56. Lemon, J. Dominant or dominated? Women on prime-time television. In G. Tuchman, A. Daniels, and J. Benet (Eds.), *Hearth and home: Images of women in the mass media.* New York: Oxford University Press, 1978, pp. 3–38.

57. Isber & Cantor, op. cit.

58. Seggar & Wheeler, op. cit.

59. Northcott, Seggar, & Hinton, op. cit.

60. Finz, S., & Waters, J. An analysis of sex role stereotyping in daytime television serials. Paper presented at the Annual Convention of the American Psychological Association, Washington, D.C., 1976.

61. Waiting for Freddie: Part 2. *Time,* May 29, 1978, p. 90.

62. *Media Report to Women,* June 1978.

63. Waiting for Freddie: Part 1. *Time,* May 15, 1978, p. 82.

64. Cathey-Calvert, C. *Sexism on Sesame Street: Outdated concepts in a "progressive" program.* Pittsburgh: KNOW, Inc., no date.

Hoffman, H. Monitoring of children's television programming aired by WRC-TV: A comparison of male and female roles. In National Organization for Women, op. cit., p. 103. Among all characters in the children's programs, 29 percent were girls/women and 71 percent were boys/men.

Busby, op. cit. Among all characters in the children's programs, 29 percent of major characters and 20 percent of minor characters were girls/women; 71 percent of major characters and 80 percent of minor characters were boys/men.

O'Kelly, op. cit. Among all characters in the children's programs, 15 percent were girls/women and 85 percent were boys/men.

Isber & Cantor, op. cit. Among all characters in the children's programs, 31 percent were girls/women and 69 percent were boys/men.

Hale, S. Children's programming. Unpublished manuscript, Stanford University, 1977.

Media Report to Women, August 1977. The Monitoring and Survey Committee of the Washington Association for Television and Children (WATCH) reported that 28 percent of the characters in the sampled program were girls/women and 72 percent were boys/men.

65. Busby, op. cit.

O'Kelly, op. cit. Women were shown in 5 roles, men in 56 roles.

66. O'Kelly, op. cit. Among women, 25 percent were shown in family roles; among men, 6 percent were shown in family roles.

67. Cathey-Calvert, op. cit.

Gardner, J. Sesame Street and sex-role stereotypes. *Women, a Journal of Liberation,* 1970, *1,* 41.

Isber & Cantor, op. cit.

68. Cathey-Calvert, op. cit.

69. Isber & Cantor, op. cit.

70. Hoffman, op. cit.

71. Busby, op. cit.

72. Long, M., & Simon, R. The roles and statuses of women on children and family TV programs. *Journalism Quarterly,* 1974, *51,* 107–110.

73. Ibid.

74. Sternglanz, S., & Servin, L. Sex role stereotyping in children's television programs. *Developmental Psychology,* 1974, *10,* 710–715.

75. Isber & Cantor, op. cit.

76. Women on Words and Images. *Products and dissemination strategies.* Washington, D.C.: National Advisory Council on Women's Educational Programs, 1977, pp. 15–16.

77. Arnheim, R. The world of the daytime serial. In P. Lazarsfeld and F. Stanton (Eds.), *Radio research, 1942–1943.* New York: Duell, Sloan, and Pearce, 1944, pp. 34–85.

78. Ibid.

CHAPTER 7

1. Van Gelder, L. Women's pages: You can't make news out of a silk purse. *MS.,* November 1974, pp. 112–116.

2. Courtney, A., & Lockeretz, S. A woman's place: An analysis of the roles portrayed by women in magazine advertisements. *Journal of Marketing Research,* 1971, 8, 92–95.

3. Wagner, L., & Banos, J. A woman's place: A follow-up analysis of the roles portrayed by women in magazine advertisements. *Journal of Marketing Research,* 1973, 10, 213–214.

   Culley, J., & Bennett, R. *The status of women in mass media advertising: An empirical study.* Newark: University of Delaware, Bureau of Economic and Business Research, 1974.

4. Courtney & Lockeretz, op. cit. Characters shown employed included 9 percent of the women and 45 percent of the men.

   Wagner & Banos, op. cit. Characters shown employed included 21 percent of the women.

   Culley & Bennett, op. cit. In the 1970 advertisements, 24 percent of the women and 48 percent of the men were shown employed. In the 1974 advertisements, 33 percent of the women and 54 percent of the men were shown employed.

   Courtney & Lockeretz, op. cit. None of the employed women and 19 percent of the employed men were shown in executive or professional roles.

   Wagner & Banos, op. cit. Among the employed women, 4 percent were shown in executive or professional roles.

   Culley & Bennett, op. cit. In the 1970 advertisements, none of the employed women and 13 percent of the employed men were shown in executive or professional roles. In the 1974 advertisements, 13 percent of the women and 30 percent of the men were shown in executive or professional roles.

   Courtney & Lockeretz, op. cit. Among those shown employed, 58 percent of the women and 20 percent of the men were shown as entertainers or athletes.

Wagner & Banos, op. cit. Among the employed women, 23 percent were shown as entertainers or athletes.

Culley & Bennett, op. cit. In the 1970 advertisements, 61 percent of the employed women and 26 percent of the employed men were shown as entertainers or athletes. In the 1974 advertisements, 42 percent of the employed women and 16 percent of the employed men were shown as entertainers or athletes.

5. Belkaoui, A., & Belkaoui, J., A comparative analysis of the roles portrayed by women in print advertisements: 1958, 1970, 1972. *Journal of Marketing Research,* 1976, *13* 168-172.

Fox, H. Sex stereotypes in advertisements. *Business and Society,* 1976, *11* 24–30.

6. Courtney & Lockeretz, op. cit. Among those in nonworking roles, 31 percent of the women and 22 percent of the men were shown in decorative roles.

Wagner & Banos, op. cit. Among those in nonworking roles, 56 percent of the women were shown in decorative roles.

Culley & Bennett, op. cit. Among those in nonworking roles in the 1970 advertisements, 29 percent of the women and 19 percent of the men were shown in decorative roles. Among those in nonworking roles in the 1974 advertisements, 11 percent of the women and 7 percent of the men were shown in decorative roles.

Fox, op. cit. Among those in nonworking roles, 40 percent of the women and 19 percent of the men were shown in decorative roles.

Venkatesan, M., & Losco, J., Women in magazine ads: 1959–1971. *Journal of Advertising Research,* 1975, *15,* 49–54. Although there was some decrease over time, women were frequently shown as sex objects or decoration.

Courtney & Lockeretz, op. cit. Among those in nonworking roles, 46 percent of the women and 56 percent of the men were shown in recreational roles.

Wagner & Banos, op. cit. Among those in nonworking roles, 36 percent of the women were shown in recreational roles.

Culley & Bennett, op. cit. Among those in nonworking roles in the 1970 advertisements, 42 percent of the women and 60 percent of the men were shown in recreational roles. Among those in nonworking roles in the 1974 advertisements, 53 percent of the women and 65 percent of the men were shown in recreational roles.

Fox, op. cit. Among those in nonworking roles, 31 percent of the women and 53 percent of the men were shown in recreational roles.

7. Courtney & Lockeretz, op. cit.

8. Ibid.

9. Wagner & Banos, op. cit.

10. McGinley, op. cit.

11. Ibid.

12. Sexton, D., & Haberman, P., Women in magazine advertisements. *Journal of Advertising Research,* 1974, *14,* 41–46.

13. Culley & Bennett, op. cit.

14. Ibid.

15 Fox, op cit. Fox sampled advertisements from *American Girl, American Home, Better Homes & Gardens, Business Week, Chicago, Forbes, Harper's, Ladies Home Journal, Modern Photography, Motor Trend, New York Magazine, Outdoor Life, Playboy, Psychology Today,* and *Time.*

16. Ibid.

17. Franzwa, H. Working women in fact and fiction. *Journal of Communication,* 1974, *24,* 104–109.

18. Bailey, M. The women's magazine short-story heroine in 1957 and 1967. *Journalism Quarterly,* 1969, *46,* 364–366.

19. Morelock, J., & Kurth, S. Giving women what they want? The representation of trends in the roles of women in women's magazines, 1956–1970. Unpublished paper, Pennsylvania State University, 1975.

20. Hatch, M., & Hatch, D. Problems of married and working women as presented by three popular working women's magazines. *Social Forces,* 1958, *37,* 148–153.

21. Flora, C. The passive female: Her comparative image by class and culture in women's magazine fiction. *Journal of Marriage and the Family,* 1971, *33,* 435–444.

22. Johns-Heine, P., & Gerth, H. Values in mass periodical fiction, 1921–1940. *Public Opinion Quarterly,* 1949, *13,* 105–113.

23. Hatch & Hatch, op. cit.

24. Clarke, P., & Esposito, V. A study of occupational advice for women in magazines. *Journalism Quarterly,* 1966, *43,* 477–485.

25. Bailey, op. cit.

26. Morelock & Kurth, op. cit.

27. Ibid.

28. Ibid.

29. Flora, op. cit.

30. Ibid.

31. Franzwa, op. cit.

32. Ibid.

33. Stolz, G., et al. *The occupational roles of women in magazines and books.* Chicago: Loyola University, no date.

34. Smith, M., & Matre, M. Social norms and sex roles in romance and adventure magazines. *Journalism Quarterly,* 1975, *52,* 309–315.

35. Ibid.

36. Newkirk, C. Female roles in non-fiction of three women's magazines. *Journalism Quarterly,* 1977, *54,* 780–781.

37. Lazer, C., & Dier, S. The labor force in fiction. *Journal of Communication,* 1978, *28,* 175.

38. Ibid., p. 176.

39. Ibid., p. 177.

40. Fisher, J., & Janus, N. Women and heart disease: Images in popular media from 1959–1974. Paper presented at the Annual Convention of the International Communication Association, Chicago, 1978.

41. White, D., Albert, R., & Seeger, R. Hollywood's newspaper advertising: Stereotype of a nation's taste. In B. Rosenberg and D. White (Eds.), *Mass culture: The popular arts in America.* Glencoe, Ill.: Free Press, 1957, pp. 443–456.

42. Miller, S. Changes in women's lifestyle sections. *Journalism Quarterly,* 1976, *53,* 641–647.

43. National Organization for Women, Northern Virginia chapter. *Newspaper Monitoring Project.* Arlington, Va.: NOW, Northern Virginia chapter, 1973.

44. Miller, S. The content of news photos: Women's and men's roles. *Journalism Quarterly,* 1975, *52,* 70–75.

45. Guenin, Z. Women's pages in American newspapers: Missing out on contemporary content. *Journalism Quarterly,* 1975, *52,* 66–69, 75.

    Miller, 1976, op. cit.

46. National Organization for Women, op. cit.

47. Miller, 1975, op. cit.

48. Ibid.

49. Guenin, op. cit.

50. Miller, 1976, op. cit.

51. Ibid.

52. Ibid.

53. Bogart, L. How the public gets its news. Address to the Associated Press Managing Editors, New Orleans, October 27, 1977, p. 16.

CHAPTER 8

1. Women on Words and Images. Dick and Jane as victims: Sex stereotyping in prime-time TV. Princeton, N.J.: Women on Words and Images, 1972, p. 30.

2. Shainess, N. Images of women: Past and present, overt and obscured. *American Journal of Psychotherapy,* 1969, *23,* 77–97.

3. Millett, K. *Sexual Politics.* Garden City, N.Y.: Doubleday, 1970.

4. Martin, W. Seduced and abandoned in the new world: The image of woman in American fiction. In V. Gornick and B. Moran (Eds.), *Woman in sexist society: Studies in power and powerlessness.* New York: Basic Books, 1971, pp. 328–346.

5. Schmidt, D. The great American bitch. *College English,* 1971, *32,* 900–905.

6. Gustafson, J. Stereotypes of women in American literature: Will the real great American bitch please stand up. In B. Chmaj (Ed.), *Image, myth and beyond.* Pittsburgh: KNOW, Inc., 1972, pp. 253–274.

7. Cornillon, S. (Ed.) *Images of women in fiction: Feminist perspectives.* Bowling Green, Ohio: Bowling Green University Popular Press, 1972.

8. Murray, M. (Ed.) *A house of good proportion: Images of women in literature.* New York: Simon and Schuster, 1973.

9. Schwartz, L. The image of women in the novels of Mme. de Souza. *The University of Michigan Papers in Women's Studies,* 1974, *1,* 142–148.

10. Holtzman, N. And they lived happily ever after??? Unpublished paper, Sepulveda, Calif., 1975.

11. Goodman, C. Images of American rural women in the novel. *The University of Michigan Papers in Women's Studies,* 1974, *1,* 57–70.

12. Smith, D. The social content of pornography. *Journal of Communication,* 1976, *26,* 16–24.

13. Kirschner, B. Introducing students to women's place in society. *American Journal of Sociology,* 1973, *78,* 1051–1054.

14. Scully, D., & Bart, P. A funny thing happened on the way to the orifice. Women in gynecology textbooks. In J. Huber (Ed.), *Changing women in a changing society.* Chicago: University of Chicago Press, 1973, pp. 283–288.

15. Birk, J., Brooks, L., Juhasz, J., Barbanel, L., Herman, M., Seltzer, R. & Tangri, S. A content analysis of sexual bias in commonly used psychology textbooks. Abstracted in JSAS Catalog of Selected Documents in Psychology, 1974, *4,* 107.

16. U'Ren, M. The image of women in textbooks. In V. Gornick and B. Moran (Eds.), *Woman in sexist society: Studies in power and powerlessness.* New York: Basic Books, 1971, pp. 318–328.

Feminists on Children's Literature. A feminist looks at children's books. *School Library Journal,* 1971, *17,* 19–24. A 1969 sample of books winning the Newbery Award and the Notable Books Award showed percentages of boys/men to be 75 percent and 66 percent, respectively.

Trumpeter, M., & Crowe, L. Sexism in picture books. *Illinois Libraries,* 1971, *53,* 499–502. Boys/men comprised 70 percent of the characters in Caldecott Award winners and runners-up from 1950 to 1970.

Graebner, D. A decade of sexism in readers. *The Reading Teacher,* 1972, *6,* 52–58.

Czaplinski, S. *Sexism in award winning picture books.* Pittsburgh: KNOW, Inc., 1972. Boys/men comprised 63 percent of characters in Caldecott winners from 1941 to 1972, 82 percent of characters in Lewis Carroll Book Shelf books from 1958 to 1972, and 91 percent of characters in picture books on the best-seller list of the *New York Times Review of Children's Books* in 1971.

Weitzman, L., Eifler, D., Hokada, E., & Ross, C. Sex-role socialization in picture books for preschool children. *American Journal of Sociology,* 1972, *77,* 1125–1149. Boys/men comprised 66 percent of characters in post-1967 Caldecott Award books.

Burton, G. *Sex-role stereotyping in elementary school primers.* Pittsburgh: KNOW, Inc., no date. Boys comprised 60 percent of the children shown in kindergarten books used in Prince George County (Maryland) public schools and 75 percent of the children shown in sixth-grade books. Men comprised 70 percent of the adults in kindergarten books and 90 percent of the adults in sixth-grade books.

Wiik, S. The sexual bias of textbook literature. *English Journal,* 1973, *62,* 224–229. Boys/men comprised 82 percent of characters in junior high school literature anthologies published between 1963 and 1971.

Begus, S., Berndt, R., Lupton, J., Lupton, M., & Mitzer, K. *Report on sexism and racism in elementary school readers.* Baltimore: Baltimore Feminist Project, 1973. Boys/men comprised 70 percent of the central characters in five series of textbooks used in the Baltimore public schools.

17. Czaplinski, op. cit.

18. Britton, G., & Lumpkin, M. *A consumer's guide to sex, race and career bias in public school textbooks.* Corvallis, Ore.: Britton and Associates, 1977.

19. Frisof, J. Textbooks and channeling. *Women: A Journal of Liberation,* 1969, *1,* 26–28. In a sample of social studies textbooks published between 1962 and 1969 for first through sixth grades, 72 percent of all pictures showed men alone, 9 percent showed women alone, and 19 percent showed both sexes.

    Fisher, E. The second sex, junior division. *New York Times Book Review, Part II,* May 24, 1970, pp. 5, 44. In a sample of children's books displayed in bookstores and libraries, 80 percent of the pictures showed boys/men.

    Nilson, A. Women in children's literature. *College English,* 1971, *32,* 918–926.

    U'Ren, op. cit.

    Graebner, op. cit. In 1961 to 1963 and 1969 to 1971 samples of elementary reading textbooks, 58 percent of the pictures in the earlier books and 68 percent of the pictures in the later books showed boys, while 63 percent of the pictures in both periods showed men.

    Scardina, F. *Sexism in textbooks in Pittsburgh public schools grades K–5.* Pittsburgh: KNOW, Inc., 1972. Boys/men were featured in 62 percent of pictures in language texts, 70 percent of pictures in teading texts, and 66 percent of pictures in science texts used in the Pittsburgh public schools.

    Czaplinski, op. cit.

    Weitzman, op. cit. Boys/men comprised 92 percent of the characters illustrated in post-1967 Caldecott Award books.

20. Fisher, op. cit.

21. Nilson, op. cit.

22. Fisher, op. cit. Boys/men were featured in 80 percent of the titles.

    Nilson, op. cit. Boys/men were cited by name in 78 percent of the titles.

    Weitzman, op. cit.

23. Weitzman, op. cit.

24. Graebner, op. cit.

25. Weitzman, op. cit.

26. Wiik, op. cit.

27. Lukenbill, W. Who writes children's books? *Journal of Communication*, 1976, *26*, 97–100.

28. Weitzman, op. cit.

    Wiik, op. cit.

29. Frisof, op. cit.

    Graebner, op. cit. For the period 1961 to 1963, men were shown in 38 occupations versus 5 for women; for the period 1969 to 1971, men were shown in 73 occupations versus 26 for women.

    Women on Words and Images, op. cit.

30. Women on Words and Images, op. cit.

31. Britton & Lumpkin, op. cit. In the 1976 Ginn Reading Series 720, men were shown in 249 occupations versus 49 for women.

32. Child, I., Potter, E., & Levine, E. Children's textbooks and personality development. *Social Psychology of Education Monographs*, 1946, *60*, 1–54.

    Graebner, op. cit.

    Women on Words and Images, op. cit.

33. Child et al., op. cit.

34. Frisof, op. cit.

35. Stefflre, B. Run, mamma, run: Women workers in elementary readers. *Vocational Guidance Quarterly*, 1969, *18*, 99–102.

36. Nilson, op. cit.

37. U'Ren, op. cit.

38. DeCrow, K. What the "helping" professions tell you about being a woman. In *The young woman's guide to liberation*. Indianapolis: Pegasus, 1971, pp. 128–137.

39. Lieberman, M. Someday my prince will come: Female acculturation through fairy tales. *College English*, 1972, *34*, 383–389.

40. Graebner, op. cit.

41. Czaplinski, op. cit.

42. Women on Words and Images, op. cit.

43. MacLeod, J., & Silverman, S. "You won't do": What textbooks on U.S. government teach high school girls. Pittsburgh: KNOW, Inc., 1973.

44. Pottker, J. Psychological and occupational sex stereotypes in elementary-school readers. In J. Pottker and A. Fishel (Eds.), *Sex bias in the schools: The research evidence.* London, England: Associated University Presses, 1977, pp. 111–125.

45. Jay, W. Sex stereotyping in elementary-school mathematics textbooks. In J. Pottker and A. Fishel (Eds.), *Sex bias in the schools: The research evidence.* London, England: Associated University Presses, 1977, pp. 126–145.

46. Trecker, J. Women in U.S. history high-school textbooks. In J. Pottker and A. Fishel (Eds.), *Sex bias in the schools: The research evidence.* London, England: Associated University Presses, 1977, pp. 146–161.

47. Brown, T. Sex stereotyping in primary reading textbooks. Unpublished manuscript, Santa Barbara, California, 1977.

48. Brown notes that Iowa, Massachusetts, New Jersey, and Pennsylvania have similar legislation and that the boards of education of Colorado, Maryland, Michigan, New York, South Dakota, and West Virginia have passed or proposed similar resolutions.

49. Saario, T., Jacklin, C., & Tittle, C. Sex role stereotyping in the public schools. *Harvard Educational Review,* 1973, *43,* 386–416.

50. Saenger, G. Male and female relations in the American comic strip. *Public Opinion Quarterly,* 1955, *19,* 195–205.

51. Ibid.

52. Steinem, G. Introduction. In *Wonder woman.* New York: Holt, Rinehart and Winston, 1972.

53. Chmaj, B. Fantasizing women's lib: Stereotypes of women in comic books. In B. Chmaj (Ed.) *Image, myth and beyond.* Pittsburth: KNOW, Inc., 1972, pp. 311–327.

54. Boyle, C., & Wahlstrom, B. Cultural analysis: Unmasking the makings of oppression. *University of Michigan Papers in Women's Studies,* 1974, *1,* 10–43.

CHAPTER 9

1. Haskell, M. *From reverence to rape: The treatment of women in the movies.* New York: Holt, Rinehart and Winston, 1973, p. 370.

2. Dale, E. *The content of motion pictures.* New York: Macmillan, 1935.

Jones, D. Quantitative Analysis of Motion Picture Content. *Public Opinion Quarterly,* 1942, *6*, 411–428.

3. Haskell, op. cit.

Mellen, J. *Women and their sexuality in the new film.* New York: Horizon Press, 1973.

Rosen, M. How the movies have made women smaller than life. *Journal of the University Film Association,* 1974, *26*, 6–10.

4. Gustafson, J. The decline of women among the top ten box office stars. In B. Chmaj (Ed.), *Image, myth and beyond.* Pittsburgh: KNOW, Inc., 1972, pp. 284–290.

Israel, L. Saving an endangered species. *MS.,* February 1975, pp. 51–57, 104.

Kovacs, M., reported in *Media Report to Women,* February 1976.

5. Griffith, R., & Mayer, A. *The movies.* New York: Bonanza Books, 1957.

6. Dale, op. cit.

7. Jones, op. cit.

8. Haskell, op. cit.

9. Ibid.

10. Dale, op. cit.

11. Jones, op. cit.

12. Wolfenstein, M., & Leites, N. The good-bad girl. In B. Rosenberg and D. White (Eds.), *Mass culture: The popular arts in America.* Glencoe, Ill.: Free Press, 1957, pp. 294–307.

13. Baunoch, J., with B. Chmaj. Film stereotypes of American women: An outline of star roles from the thirties to the present. In B. Chmaj (Ed.), *Image, myth, and beyond.* Pittsburgh: KNOW, Inc., 1972, pp. 275–284.

14. Gustafson, op. cit.

15. Mellen, op. cit., p. 26.

16. Haskell, op. cit.

17. Rosen, op. cit.

18. Haymes, H. Movies in the 1950's: Sexism from A to Zapata. *Journal of the American Film Association,* 1974, *26*, 12, 22.

19. Israel, op. cit.

20. Kovacs, op. cit.

21. The "endangered species" concept comes from Israel, op. cit.

CHAPTER 10

1. Komisar, L. The image of woman in advertising. In V. Gornick and B. Moran (Eds.), *Woman in sexist society: Studies in power and powerlessness.* New York: Basic Books, 1971, p. 304.

2. Ibid, p. 309.

3. *Advertising Age,* December 23, 1968, p. 23.

4. *Time,* February 11, 1974, p. 10.

5. Chulay, C., & Francis, S. The image of the female child on Saturday morning television commercials. Paper presented at the Annual Convention of the International Communication Association, New Orleans, 1974, p. 5.

6. Courtney, A., & Lockeretz, S. A woman's place: An analysis of the roles portrayed by women in magazine advertisements. *Journal of Marketing Research,* 1971, *8,* 92–95.

7. Standard Rate and Data Service. *Consumer magazine and farm publication: Rates and data.* Skokie, Ill.: Standard Rate and Data Service, Inc., 1975, p. 197.

8. Ibid., p. 196.

9. Ibid., p. 198.

10. McKnight, D. Sexism in advertising: What's a nice girl like you. . . . *Technology Review,* 1974, *76,* 20.

11. Rosen, M. How the movies have made women smaller than life. *Journal of the University Film Association,* 1974, *26,* 6.

12. Israel, L. Saving an endangered species. *MS.,* February 1975, pp. 51–57, 104.

13. Smith, S. The image of women in film. In B. Stanford (Ed.), *On being female.* New York: Pocket Books, 1974, p. 43.

14. Haskell, M. *From reverence to rape: The treatment of women in the movies.* New York: Holt, Rinehart and Winston, 1973, pp. 327–328.

15. Haskell, M. What is Hollywood trying to tell us? *MS.,* April 1977, pp. 49–50.

16. Hart, L., & Rodgers, R. *Isn't it romantic.* Copyright Famous Music Corporation, New York, 1932.

17. Asimov, I. Uncertain, coy, and hard to please. In I. Asimov, *The solar system and back.* New York: Doubleday, 1970, p. 243.

18. Komisar, op. cit., p. 307.

19. Survey of the "average housewife" conducted by Haug Associates. Quoted by V. Gornick and B. Moran (Eds.), *Woman in sexist society: Studies in power and powerlessness.* New York: Basic Books, 1971, p. 311.

20. *Editor and Publisher,* June 8, 1974, p. 31.

21. Kinzer, G. Soapy sin in the afternoon. *Psychology Today,* August 1973, p. 48.

22. Chulay and Francis, op. cit., pp. 3–4.

23. Courtney, A., & Whipple, J. W. Women in TV commercials. *Journal of Communication,* 1974, *24,* p. 116.

    See also Fisher, C., & Dean, D. *The realism of marital and parental roles on television.* Canton, N.Y.: Saint Lawrence University, 1976.

24. Cheles-Miller, P. An investigation of whether the stereotypes of husbands and wives presented in television commercials can influence a child's perception of the role of husband and wife. Unpublished doctoral dissertation, University of Ohio, 1974.

    Cheles-Miller, P. Reactions to marital roles in commercials. *Journal of Advertising Research,* 1975, *15,* 45–49.

25. Peck, E. Television's romance with reproduction. In E. Peck and J. Senderowitz (Eds.), *Pronatalism: The myth of mom and apple pie.* New York: Thomas Y. Crowell, 1974, p. 78.

26. Kinzer, op. cit., p. 48.

27. Advertisement for TDK Electronics Corporation, 1974.

28. Standard Rate and Data Service, op. cit., p. 365.

29. Advertisement for Healthknit Underwear, 1974.

30. Barry Goldwater, statement to press, 1974.

31. Campbell, R. Women's life styles in the 70's. Address on Stanford University Alumni Day, Stanford University, 1971, p. 3.

32. Advertisement for International Correspondence Schools, 1975.

33. Questionnaire in *McCall's,* February 1974, p. 45.

34. Standard Rate and Data Service. *Consumer magazine and farm publication: Rates and data.* Skokie, Ill.: Standard Rate and Data Service, 1974.

35. Morrow, L. Goodbye to "Our Mary." *Time,* March 14, 1977, p. 35.

36. Smith, J. Talking want ad. Copyright Bella Roma Music Company, New York, 1972.

37. Pingree, S., Hawkins, R. Butler, M., & Paisley, W. A scale for sexism. *Journal of Communication,* Autumn 1976, *26,* p. 197.

38. Pingree, S., Hawkins, R. & Waldinger, M. An analysis of sexism in TV advertising. Paper presented at Annual Convention of Pacific Chapter, American Association for Public Opinion Research, Asilomar, California, 1975.

PART 3

1. Stanton, E., Anthony, S., & Gage, M. (Eds.) *History of women suffrage.* Vol. 4. Rochester, N.Y.: Charles Mann, 1889, p. 312.

CHAPTER 11

1. Schramm, W. Media as communication institutions. In W. Schramm and D. Roberts (Eds.), *The process and effects of mass communication.* (Rev. Ed.) Urbana: University of Illinois Press, 1971, p. 57.

2. Gerbner, G. An institutional approach to mass communications research. In L. Thayer (Ed.), *Communication theory and research.* Springfield, Ill.: Charles C Thomas, 1967, p. 432.

3. Ibid., pp. 443–444.

4. Siebert, F., Peterson, T., & Schramm, W. *Four theories of the press.* Urbana: University of Illinois Press, 1956.

5. Talese, G. *The kingdom and the power.* New York: World, 1969.

   Metz, R. *CBS: Reflections in a bloodshot eye.* New York: New American Library, 1975.

6. Rivers, W. *The opinionmakers.* Boston: Beacon Press, 1965.

7. Bagdikian, B. *The information machines: Their impact on men and the media.* New York: Harper & Row, 1971.

8. Breed, W. Social control in the newsroom: A descriptive study. *Social Forces,* 1955, *33,* 326–335.

9. Garvey, D. Social control in the television newsroom. Unpublished doctoral dissertation, Stanford University, 1971.

10. White, D. The "gate keeper": A case study in the selection of news. *Journalism Quarterly,* 1950, *27,* 383–390.

11. Friendly, F. *Due to circumstances beyond our control.* New York: Vintage Books, 1968.

12. Nixon, R. The problem of newspaper monopoly. In W. Schramm (Ed.), *Mass communications.* Urbana: University of Illinois Press, 1960, pp. 241–250.

13. Howard, H. Cross-media ownership of newspapers and TV stations. *Journalism Quarterly,* 1974, *51,* 715–718.

14. Ibid.

15. Jennings, R., & Jefferson, V. *Television station employment practices, 1975: The status of minorities and women.* New York: United Church of Christ, Office of Communication, 1976.

16. Strainchamps, E. (Ed.) *Rooms with no view.* New York: Harper & Row, 1974.

CHAPTER 12

1. U.S. Commission on Civil Rights. *A guide to federal laws and regulations prohibiting sex discrimination.* Washington, D.C.: U.S. Government Printing Office, 1974, p. 11.

2. Letter to public radio and television stations from Jeanna Tulley, Special Assistant to the Director of the Office of Civil Rights, 1974.

3. Jennings, R. *Television station employment practices: The status of minorities and women, 1972.* New York: United Church of Christ, Office of Communication, 1972.

   Jennings, R., & Tillyer, D. *Television station employment practices: The status of women and minorities, 1973.* New York: United Church of Christ, Office of Communication, 1973.

   Jennings, R., & Jefferson, V. *Television station employment practices: The status of women and minorities, 1974.* New York: United Church of Christ, Office of Communication, 1974.

   Jennings, R., & Jefferson, V. *Television station employment practices: The status of women and minorities, 1975.* New York: United Church of Christ, Office of Communication, 1975.

   Jennings, R., & Walters, A. *Television station employment practices: The status of women and minorities, 1976.* New York: United Church of Christ, Office of Communication, 1977.

4. *Media Report to Women,* December 1972.

   Media Report to Women, June 1975.

   Isber, C., & Cantor, M. *Report of the task force on women in public broadcasting.* Washington, D.C.: Corporation for Public Broadcasting, 1975.

5. Komisar, L. Women in the media. In Professional Women's Caucus, New York University Law School, *Sixteen reports on the status of women in the professions.* Pittsburgh: KNOW, Inc., 1970.

    Strainchamps, E. (Ed.) *Rooms with no view.* New York: Harper & Row, 1974.

    Unpublished study by Sarah Seaver reported in *Media Report to Women,* March 1974.

    Additional data are available in the following unpublished studies conducted in the 1977 session of the course Women and the Media, taught by M. Butler at Stanford University: Durham, J. Low-down on the High-brows: Women and the analytic journals; Ellwood, C. Keeping women in their places: An examination of the hiring practices of nine magazines over time; Flores, J. News magazines; Levin, E. Business magazines, 1945–1977.

6. Komisar, op. cit., pp. 3–4.

    Data for four newspapers were reported in *Time,* March 20, 1972, pp. 48–53.

    National Organization for Women, Northern Virginia chapter. *Newspaper monitoring project.* Arlington: NOW, northern Virginia chapter, 1973.

    Data for the *Washington Post* were reported in *Media Report to Women,* September 1972.

    EEOC findings on the Washington Post complaint were reported in *Media Report to Women,* August 1974.

    Dorothy Jurney, executive director of The Woman's Network, compiled data for newspapers with daily circulations of 40,000 or more. Her data were reported in *Media Report to Women,* May 1977.

    EEOC findings on the *Newsday* (Long Island) complaint were reported in *Media Report to Women,* January 1977.

    Data compiled by Mark Killingsworth, professor of economics at Barnard College, in connection with litigation against the *New York Times,* reported in *Media Report to Women,* April 1978.

7. Membership data for the Producers Guild, the Directors Guild, and the Writers Guild were reported in *Media Report to Women,* September 1974.

    Membership data for the Motion Picture Academy of Arts and Sciences were reported in *Media Report to Women,* December 1975.

8. Komisar, op. cit., p. 7.

Strainchamps, op. cit., pp. 139–198.

9. Lichty, L., & Ripley, J. Size and composition of broadcasting stations' staffs. *Journal of Broadcasting,* 1967, *11,* 139–151.

10. Komisar, op. cit., pp. 1–2.

11. FCC Guidelines reproduced in *Media Report to Women,* December 1972.

12. Jennings, op. cit.

13. Jennings & Tillyer, op. cit.

14. Jennings & Jefferson, 1974, op. cit.

15. Jennings & Jefferson, 1976, op. cit.

16. Ibid., p. ii.

17. Jennings & Walters, op. cit.

18. Ibid.

19. U.S. Commission on Civil Rights. *Window dressing on the set: Women and minorities in television.* Washington, D.C.: U.S. Government Printing Office, 1977, pp. 88–97.

20. Isber & Cantor, op. cit.

21. CBC Task Force on the Status of Women. *Women in the CBC.* Ottawa, Ontario: Canadian Broadcasting Corporation, 1975.

22. Downing, M. Heroine of the daytime serial. *Journal of Communication,* 1974, *24,* pp. 130–137.

23. Strainchamps, op. cit.

24. *Media Report to Women,* October 1977.

25. Ibid.

26. *Media Report to Women,* December 1972.

27. *Media Report to Women,* June 1975.

28. Isber & Cantor, op. cit.

29. Komisar, op. cit., p. 7.

30. Strainchamps, op. cit.

31. Seaver, op. cit.

32. Hole, J., & Levine, E. *Rebirth of feminism.* New York: Quadrangle Books, 1971, p. 259.

33. Ibid.

34. *Media Report to Women,* January 1974.

35.   Ibid.

36.   Levin, op. cit.

37.   Flores, op. cit.

38.   Durham, op. cit.

39.   Ellwood, op. cit.

40.   Komisar, op. cit., pp. 3–4.

41.   *Time,* March 20, 1972, p. 53.

42.   National Organization for Women, op. cit., p. 8.

43.   *Media Report to Women,* September 1972.

44.   *Media Report to Women,* August 1974.

45.   *Media Report to Women,* June 1974.

46.   *Media Report to Women,* February 1975.

47.   Ibid.

48.   *Media Report to Women,* January 1977.

49.   *Media Report to Women,* April 1978.

50.   Jurney, op. cit.

51.   Komisar, op. cit., p. 4.

52.   *Time,* March 20, 1972, p. 53.

53.   Strainchamps, op. cit.

54.   Ibid.

55.   *Media Report to Women,* June 1978.

56.   *Media Report to Women,* May 1978.

57.   *Media Report to Women,* December 1975.

58.   *Media Report to Women,* September 1974.

59.   *Media Report to Women,* May 1976.

60.   Association of Cinematograph and Television Technicians. *Patterns of discrimination against women in the film and television industries.* London, England: ACTT, 1975, pp. 36–37.

61.   Komisar, op. cit., p. 7.

62.   Women's National Book Association. *The status of women in publishing.* New York: Women's National Book Association, New York chapter, 1971.

63.   Strainchamps, op. cit.

64.   Gorney, S. Status of women in public relations. *Public Relations Journal,* 1975, *31,* 11–12.

65.   U.S. Department of Labor, Bureau of Labor Statistics. *Directory of*

national unions and employee associations, 1973, Supplement 2. Washington, D.C.: U.S. Government Printing Office, 1975.

66. *Media Report to Women,* October 1974.

    Isber & Cantor, op. cit.

67. Endres, K. Capitol Hill newswomen: A descriptive study. *Journalism Quarterly,* 1976, *53,* 132–135.

68. Merritt, S., & Gross, H. *Women's page/lifestyle editors: Does sex make a difference?* Park Forest South, Ill.: Governors State University, 1977.

69. *Media Report to Women,* April 1978.

70. *Media Report to Women,* October 1974.

71. Isber & Cantor, op. cit.

72. Ibid.

73. CBC Task Force on the Status of Women, op. cit.

74. Isber & Cantor, op. cit.

75. Schuler, S. Women in journalism work twice as hard: Get only half as far. *Grassroots Editor,* 1973, *14,* 24–27.

76. *Media Report to Women,* January 1974.

77. *Media Report to Women,* May 1974.

78. Ibid.

79. *Media Report to Women,* April 1978.

80. Ibid.

81. *Media Report to Women,* August 1974.

82. *The Guild Reporter,* March 8, 1974, p. 6.

83. Ibid.

84. Chang, W. Characteristics and self-perceptions of women's page editors. *Journalism Quarterly,* 1975, *52,* 61–65.

85. Ibid.

86. Merritt & Gross, op. cit., p. 18.

87. Endres, op. cit.

88. Women's National Book Association, op. cit.

89. Isber & Cantor, op. cit.

90. Ibid.

91. Ibid.

92. Ibid.

93. Ibid., p. 44

94. CBC Task Force on the Status of Women, op. cit.

95. Ibid.

96. Isber & Cantor, op. cit.

97. *Media Report to Women,* August 1974.

98. *Media Report to Women,* January 1978.

99. John Abowd, lecturer in econometrics, Princeton University, reported in *Media Report to Women,* April 1978.

100. Isber & Cantor, op. cit.

101. Ibid.

102. Ibid.

103. Stone, V. More women reporting news on the air. *RTNDA Communicator,* February 1977, pp. 7–10.

104. Isber & Cantor, op. cit.

105. Ibid.

106. Stone, op. cit.

107. Strainchamps, op. cit.

108. Farley, J. Women's magazines and the ERA: Friend or foe? *Journal of Communication,* 1978, *28,* 187–192.

109. *Boston Globe,* July 18, 1972, p. 16.

110. *Media Report to Women,* September 1972.

111. *Media Report to Women,* August 1974.

112. Ibid.

113. *Media Report to Women,* February 1975.

114. Isber & Cantor, op. cit., p. 49.

115. CBC Task Force on the Status of Women, op. cit., pp. 41–46.

116. Ibid., pp. 46–53.

117. Ibid., pp. 53–54.

118. Ibid., p. 54.

119. *Broadcasting,* September 16, 1974, p. 36.

CHAPTER 13

1. *New York Times Magazine,* June 18, 1972, p. 4.

2. Breed, W. Social control in the newsroom: A descriptive study. *Social Forces,* 1955, *33,* 326–335.

3. Friendly, F. *Due to circumstances beyond our control.* New York: Vintage Books, 1968.

4. Orwant, J., & Cantor, M. How sex stereotyping affects perceptions of news preferences. *Journalism Quarterly,* 1977, *54,* 99–108.

5. Whitlow, S. How male and female gatekeepers respond to news stories of women. *Journalism Quarterly,* 1977, *54,* 573–579, 609.

6. Merritt, S., & Gross, H. *Women's page/lifestyle editors: Does sex make a difference:* Park Forest South, Ill.: Governors State University, 1977.

7. Ibid., p. 8.

8. Morris, M. Newspapers and the new feminists: Black out as social control? *Journalism Quarterly,* 1973, *50,* 37–42.

9. *New York Times,* December 9, 1974, p. 6.

10. *Writer's Yearbook,* 1975, p. 120.

11. Ibid., p. 110.

12. Ibid., p. 74.

13. *Editor and Publisher,* May 11, 1974, pp. 15, 71.

14. *New York Times Magazine,* June 18, 1972, p. 4.

15. Crawford, S. Purposes and functions of advertising agencies. In M. Butler (Ed.), *Image of women in advertisements: A preliminary study of avenues for change.* Palo Alto, Calif.: Stanford University, Institute for Communication Research, 1975, section V.

16. Ibid., pp. V.5–V.6.

17. Ibid., p. V.6

18. *Time,* January 12, 1976, p. 47

Chapter 14

1. Butler, M., Paisley, W., & Pingree, S. Professional concerns of women in the International Communication Association: Results of a survey. Paper presented at the Annual Convention of the International Communication Association, Portland, Oregon, 1976, p. 20.

2. Leifer, A. When are undergraduate admissions sexist? The case of Stanford University. Paper presented at the Annual Convention of the International Communication Association, New Orleans, 1974.

3. Baker, C., & Wells, A. *Earned degrees conferred: 1972–73 and 1973–74.* Washington, D.C.: U.S. Government Printing Office, 1976.

4. Ibid.

5. Butler, M., Pingree, S., & Paisley, W. Writers decry percentage of women doctoral students. *Journalism Educator,* 1977, *31,* 49–51, 104.

6. Applegate, R. Women as journalism educators. *The Matrix,* 1965, *50,* p. 5.

7. Ibid.

8. Rush, R. Women in academe: Journalism education viewed from the literature and other memorabilia. Report to the Association for Education in Journalism, Ad Hoc Committee on the Status of Women in Journalism Education, Fort Collins, Colorado, 1973.

9. Analysis conducted for this book by Kenneth Rees, Palo Alto, California, 1977.

10. Hansen, J. Women in journalism history textbooks. Paper presented at the Women in Journalism Seminar, University of Michigan, 1973.

11. Marzolf, M. *Up from the footnote: A history of women journalists.* New York: Hastings House, 1977.

12. Evans, R., & Meyer, E. Consequences of sexism in journalism texts. Paper presented at the Women in Journalism Seminar, University of Michigan, 1973.

13. Ibid.

14. Butler et al., op. cit., pp. 13–16.

15. Rush, op. cit., p. 20.

16. Resolution passed at the Annual Convention of the International Communication Association, Portland, Oregon, 1976.

17. Sargent, A. *Beyond sex roles.* St. Paul: West Publishing Co., 1976.

    Miller, J. *Toward a new psychology of women.* Boston: Beacon Press, 1976.

CHAPTER 15

1. Webb, E., Campbell, D., Schwartz, R., & Sechrest, L. *Unobtrusive measures: Nonreactive research in the social sciences.* Chicago: Rand McNally, 1966.

2. Charters, W. *Motion pictures and youth: A summary.* New York: Macmillan, 1933.

3. Lazarsfeld, P., & Kendall, P. *Radio listening in America.* New York: Prentice-Hall, 1948.

4. Lazarsfeld, P., & Wyant, R. Magazines in 90 cities—who reads what? *Public Opinion Quarterly,* 1937, *1,* 29–41.

5. Lazarsfeld, P. *Radio and the Printed Page.* New York: Duell, Sloan and Pearce, 1940.

6. Lazarsfeld & Kendall, op. cit.

7. Schramm, W., & White, D. Age, education, and economic status as factors in newspaper reading. In W. Schramm (Ed.), *Mass communication.* Urbana: University of Illinois Press, 1960, pp. 438–456.

   Axiom Market Research Bureau, Inc. *Target group index.* New York: Axiom Market Research Bureau, annual.

9. Israel, H., & Robinson, J. Demographic characteristics of viewers of television violence and news programs. In E. Rubinstein, G. Comstock, & J. Murray (Eds.), Television and social behavior. *Volume IV: Television in day-to-day life: Patterns of use.* Washington, D.C.: U.S. Government Printing Office, 1972, pp. 87–128.

10. Ibid.

11. Schramm, W., Lyle, J., & Parker, E. *Television in the lives of our children.* Palo Alto, Calif.: Stanford University Press, 1961.

12. Steiner, G. *The people look at television: A Study of Audience Attitudes.* New York: Alfred Knopf, 1963.

13. Rees, M., & Paisley, W. *Social and psychological predictors of information seeking and media use: A multivariate re-analysis.* Palo Alto, Calif.: Stanford University, Institute for Communication Research, 1967.

14. Berelson, B. What missing the newspaper means. In P. Lazarsfeld and F. Stanton (eds.), *Communications research 1948–1949.* New York: Harper, 1949, pp. 111–129.

15. Ibid.

16. Steiner, op. cit.

17. Webb et al., op. cit.

18. Ibid.

19. See, for example, Sikorski, L., Roberts, D., & Paisley, W., Letters in mass magazines as "outcroppings" of public concern. *Journalism Quarterly,* 1969, *46,* 743–752.

20. Steiner, op. cit.

PART 4

CHAPTER 16

1. Steiner, G. *The people look at television: A study of audience attitudes.* New York: Alfred Knopf, 1963.

2. A. C. Nielsen Company, *Nielsen television '78.* Northbrook, Ill. A. C. Nielsen Co., 1977, pp. 10–11.

3. Ibid.

4. *Broadcasting,* June 7, 1976, p. 40.

5. A. C. Nielsen Company, op. cit., pp. 10–11.

6. Ibid.

7. Ibid.

8. A. C. Nielsen Company. *Nielsen television '76.* Northbrook, Ill.: A. C. Nielsen Co., 1976.

9. Bower, R. *Television and the public.* New York: Holt, Rinehart and Winston, 1973.

10. Ibid.

11. Ibid.

12. Ibid.

13. A. C. Nielsen Company, op. cit., 1977, p. 18.

14. Bower, op. cit.

15. Ibid.

16. Ibid.

17. Katzman, N. Television soap operas: What's been going on anyway? *Public Opinion Quarterly,* 1972, *35,* 200–212.

18. Ibid.

19. Goldsen, R. Throwaway husbands, wives and lovers. *Human Behavior,* December 1975, pp. 64–69.

20. Israel, H., & Robinson, J., Demographic characteristics of viewers of television violence and news programs. In E. Rubinstein, G. Comstock, and J. Murray (Eds.), *Television and Social Behavior Volume IV: Television in day-to-day life: Patterns of use.* Washington, D.C.: U.S. Government Printing Office, 1972, pp. 87–128.

21. Ibid.

22. Ibid.

23. Steiner, op. cit.

24. Bower, op. cit.

25. Ibid.

26. *Good Housekeeping,* May 1971, p. 68.

27. Ibid.

28. Screen Actors Guild. *SAG documents use of women and minorities in prime-time TV shows.* Press Release. Hollywood, Calif.: Screen Actors Guild, October 31, 1974.

29. Ibid.

30. Ibid.

31. *Time,* May 31, 1976, p. 52.

32. Axiom Market Research Bureau, Inc. *Target group index 1977, D-2 and D-3.* New York: Axiom Market Research Bureau, Inc., 1977, pp. 4–6.

33. Ibid., p. 19.

34. Axiom Market Research Bureau, Inc. *Target group index 1975, D-2 and D-3.* New York: Axiom Market Research Bureau, Inc., 1975. pp. 4–6.

35. Axiom Market Research Bureau, Inc., 1977, op. cit., p. 7.

36. Ibid.

37. Parker, E., & Paisley, W., *Patterns of adult information seeking.* Palo Alto, Calif.: Stanford University, Institute for Communication Research, 1966.

CHAPTER 17

1. Mother Goose nursery rhyme.

2. Bem, S. Probing the promise of androgyny. In A. Kaplan and J. Bean (Eds.), *Beyond sex-role stereotypes: Readings toward a psychology of androgyny.* Boston: Little, Brown, 1976, pp. 47–62.

3. Maccoby, E., & Jacklin, C. *The psychology of sex differences.* Palo Alto, Calif.: Stanford University Press, 1974.

4. Slaby, R., & Frey, K. Development of gender constancy and selective attention to same-sex models. *Child Development,* 1975, *46,* 849–856.

5. Williams, J., Bennett, S., & Best, D. Awareness and expression of sex stereotypes in young children. *Developmental Psychology,* 1975, *11,* 635–642.

Best, D., & Williams, J. Development of sex-trait stereotypes among young children in the United States, England, and Ireland. *Child Development,* 1977, *48,* 1375–1384.

6. Maccoby and Jacklin, op. cit.

At college age, male and female students differ markedly in ascribing traits and values to the "average" male or female of their own age and to themselves. Bergum and Bergum gathered self-perceptions and normative perceptions from 891 students (34 percent female). On most traits and values, male self-perceptions were closer to the male stereotypes than female self-perceptions were to the female stereotype. For example, on the question of whether they enjoyed fishing, sailing, and hiking, male self-perceptions were 3 percent below the male stereotype and female self-perceptions were 52 percent above the female stereotype. On the question of whether their parents influence(d) their career choice, male self-perceptions were 9 percent below the male stereotype and female self-perceptions were 42 percent below the female stereotype.

See Bergum, B., & Bergum, J. Sex-role self-perceptions and sex-role stereotypes. *Perceptual and Motor Skills,* 1978, *46,* 303–307.

7. Bem, op. cit.

8. Block, J. Conceptions of sex roles: Some cross-cultural and longitudinal perspectives. *American Psychologist,* 1973, *28,* 512–526.

9. Bandura, A. Social-learning theory of identificatory processes. In D. Goslin (Ed.), *Handbook of socialization theory and research.* Chicago: Rand McNally, 1969, pp. 213–262.

10. Piaget, J. Piaget's theory. In P. Mussen (Ed.), *Carmichael's manual of child psychology.* Vol. 1. New York: Wiley, 1970, pp. 703–732.

11. Maccoby & Jacklin, op. cit.

12. Slaby & Frey, op. cit.

Bryan, J., & Luria, Z. Sex-role learning: A test of the selective attention hypothesis. *Child Development,* 1978, *49,* 13–23. This study of 5-year-olds and 9-year-olds suggests that the selectivity may occur in memory and performance rather than attention. No differences were found in alpha brain waves (whose lack indicates visual attention) for slides of male or female models performing sex-appropriate or sex-inappropriate tasks. However, both girls and boys recalled and preferred same-sex tasks more and preferred the same-sex model.

13. Perry, D., & Perry, L. Observational learning in children: Effects of sex model and subject's sex-role behavior. *Journal of Personality and Social Psychology,* 1975, *31,* 1084–1088.

A study of children's casual imitation of television characters indicates the same ambivalence among girls in choosing male or female models. All of the boys imitated male models (e.g., Fonzie, Six Million Dollar Man, Batman); 57 percent of the girls imitated female models (e.g., Wonder Woman, Bionic Woman) and 43 percent imitated male models.

See Epstein, R., & Bozler, D. *A Study of preschool children's television viewing behavior and circumstances.* Los Angeles: University of Southern California, Annenberg School of Communications, 1976.

14. Plost, M., & Rosen, M. Effect of sex of career models on occupational preferences of adolescents. *Audio-Visual Communication Review,* 1974, *22,* 41–49.

15. Lyle, J., & Hoffman, H. Children's use of television and other media. In E. Rubinstein, G. Comstock, and J. Murray (Eds.), *Television and social behavior. Volume IV: Television in day-to-day life: Patterns of use.* Washington, D.C.: U.S. Government Printing Office, 1972, pp. 129–256.

16. *Broadcasting Yearbook,* 1976, p. 213.

17. Ibid.

18. Lyle & Hoffman, op. cit.

19. Liebert, R., Neale, J., & Davidson, E., *The early window: Effects of television on children and youth.* New York: Pergamon, 1973.

20. Beuf, A. Doctor, lawyer, household drudge. *Journal of Communication,* 1974, *24,* 142–145.

21. Freuh, R., & McGhee, P. Traditional sex-role development and amount of time spent watching television. *Developmental Psychology,* 1975, *11,* p. 109.

22. Fischer, P., Torney, J. Influence of children's stories on dependency: A sex-typed behavior. *Developmental Psychology,* 1976, *12,* 489–490.

23. McArthur, L., & Eisen, S. Achievements of male and female storybook characters as determinants of achievement behavior by boys and girls. *Journal of Personality and Social Psychology,* 1976, *33,* 467–473.

24. Atkin, C., & Miller, M. The effects of TV advertising on children: Experimental evidence. Paper presented at the Annual Convention of the International Communication Association, Chicago, 1975.

25. Pingree, S. The effects of nonsexist television commercials and perceptions of reality on children's attitudes about women. *Psychology of Women Quarterly,* 1978, *2,* 262–277.

26. Flerx, V., Fidler, D., & Rogers, R. Sex-role stereotypes: Developmental aspects and early intervention. *Child Development,* 1976, *47,* 998–1007.

27. Pingree, op. cit.

28. Atkin & Miller, op. cit.

29. McArthur & Eisen, op. cit.

30. Guttentag, M., & Bray, H. *Undoing sex stereotypes: Research and resources for education.* New York: McGraw-Hill, 1976.

    Garrett, C., Ein, P., & Tremaine, L. The development of gender stereotyping of adult occupations in elementary school children. *Child Development,* 1977, *48,* 507–512. Fifth graders held more flexible conceptions of appropriate jobs for men and women than did first graders or third graders. However, this does not necessarily mean "the older the better."

31. Drabman, R., Hammer, D., & Jarvie, G. *Children's perceptions of media-portrayed sex roles across ages.* Jackson: University of Mississippi Medical Center, Department of Psychiatry and Human Behavior, 1976.

32. Koblinsky, S., Cruse, D., & Sugawara, A. Sex role stereotypes and children's memory for story content. *Child Development,* 1978, *49,* 452–458.

33. Schramm, W. The nature of communication between humans. In W. Schramm and D. Roberts (Eds.), *The process and effects of mass communication.* (Rev. ed.) Urbana: University of Illinois Press, 1971, pp. 3–53.

CHAPTER 18

1. Johnson, N. *Test pattern for living.* New York: Bantam, 1972, pp. 85, 87.

2. Festinger, L. *A theory of cognitive dissonance.* Palo Alto, Calif.: Stanford University Press, 1957.

3. Ray, M. Psychological theories and interpretations of learning. In S. Ward and T. Robertson (Eds.), *Consumer behavior.* Englewood Cliffs, N.J.: Prentice-Hall, 1973, pp. 45–117.

4. Janis, I., & Field, P. Sex differences and personality factors related to persuasibility. In C. Hovland and I. Janis (Eds.), *Personality and persuasibility.* New Haven, Conn.: Yale University Press, 1959, pp. 55–68.

5. Comstock, G., Chaffee, S., McLeod, J., & Roberts, D. *Television and human behavior.* New York: Columbia University Press, 1978.

6. Adorno, T., Frenkel-Brunswik, E., Levinson, D., & Sanford, R. *The authoritarian personality.* New York: Harper, 1950.

7. Katz, D., McClintock, C., & Sarnoff, I. The measurement of ego defense as related to attitude change. *Journal of Personality,* 1957, *25,* 465–474.

8. Cohen, A. Some implications of self-esteem for social influence. In C. Hovland and I. Janis (Eds.), *Personality and persuasibility.* New Haven, Conn.: Yale University Press, 1959, pp. 102–120.

9. Allport, G., Postman, L. *The psychology of rumor.* New York: Holt, 1947.

10. Rokeach, M. *The open and closed mind.* New York: Basic Books, 1960.

11. Gross, L. The "real" world of television. *Today's Education,* 1974, *63,* 86, 89–92.

12. Bem, S., & Bem, D. Does sex-biased job advertising "aid and abet" sex discrimination? *Journal of Applied Social Psychology,* 1973, *3,* 6–7.

13. Ibid.

PART 5

CHAPTER 19

1. Likert, R., & Lippitt, R. The utilization of social science. In L. Festinger and D. Katz (Eds.), *Research methods in the behavioral sciences.* New York: Dryden Press, 1953, p. 618.

2. Campbell, D. *Methods for the experimenting society.* Evanston, Ill.: Northwestern University, Department of Psychology, 1969, p. 1.

3. Bauer, R. (Ed.) *Social indicators.* Cambridge, Mass.: MIT Press, 1967.

4. U.S. Department of Health, Education, and Welfare. *Toward a social report.* Washington, D.C.: U.S. Government Printing Office, 1969.

   U.S. Department of Commerce, Bureau of the Census. *Social indicators 1976.* Washington, D.C.: U.S. Government Printing Office, 1977.

5. Sheldon, E., & Moore, W. (Eds.) *Indicators of social change: Concepts and measurements.* New York: Russell Sage Foundation, 1968.

   Ferriss, A. *Indicators of trends in the status of American women.* New York: Russell Sage Foundation, 1971.

6. Ferriss, op. cit., p. 2.

7. Webb, E., Campbell, D., Schwartz, R., & Sechrest, L. *Unobtrusive measures: Nonreactive research in the social sciences.* Chicago: Rand McNally, 1966, p. 77.

8. Gerbner, G. Communication and social environment. In *Communication, a Scientific American book.* San Francisco: W. H. Freeman, 1972, pp. 111–118.

9. Jennings, R. *Television station employment practices: The status of minorities and women, 1972.* New York: United Church of Christ, Office of Communication, 1972.

Jennings, R., & Tillyer, D. *Television station employment practices: The status of women and minorities, 1973.* New York: United Church of Christ, Office of Communication, 1973.

Jennings, R., Jefferson, V. *Television station employment practices: The status of women and minorities, 1974.* New York: United Church of Christ, Office of Communication, 1974.

Jennings, R., & Jefferson, V. *Television station employment practices: The status of women and minorities, 1975.* New York: United Church of Christ, Office of Communication, 1975.

Jennings, R., & Walters, A. *Television station employment practices: The status of women and minorities, 1976.* New York: United Church of Christ, Office of Communication, 1977.

FCC Commissioner Margita White's proposal to evaluate Form 395, the broadcasters' employment reporting form, has been accepted. Pending final approval, the revisions will lead to the collection of less biased employment data. See Chapter 12 for a discussion of problems encountered with current form. See also *Media Report to Women,* January 1978.

10. *Media Report to Women,* June 1978.

11. Geng, V. Requiem for the women's movement: Empty voices in crowded rooms. *Harper's,* November 1976, p. 50.

12. *Media Report to Women,* December 1976.

13. Vajrathon, M. Toward liberating women: A communications perspective. In I. Tinker and M. Bramsen (Eds.), *Women and world development.* Washington, D.C.: Overseas Development Council, 1976, pp. 98–99.

14. Schein, E. The mechanisms of change. In W. Bennis, K. Benne, and R. Chin (Eds.), *The planning of change.* New York: Holt, Rinehart and Winston, 1969, pp. 98–107.

15. Kelman, H. Compliance identification, and internalization.: Three processes of attitude change. *Journal of Conflict Resolution,* 1958, *2,* 51–60.

16. Chin, R., & Benne, K. General strategies for effecting changes in human systems. In W. Bennis, K. Benne, and R. Chin (Eds.), *The planning of change.* New York: Holt, Rinehart and Winston, 1969, pp. 32–59.

17. Busby, L. Mass media research needs: A media target for feminists. *University of Michigan Papers in Women's Studies,* June 1974, *1,* 9–29.

18. Butler, M. (Ed.) *Image of women in advertisements: A preliminary study of avenues for change.* Palo Alto, Calif.: Stanford University, Institute for Communication Research, 1975, pp. I. 2–3.

CHAPTER 20

1. Statement by Maureen Callan, *Advertising Age,* October 4, 1976, p. 76.

2. Fowles, J. Some recent efforts to change the image of women. In M. Butler (Ed.), *Image of women in advertisements: A Preliminary study of avenues for change.* Palo Alto, Calif.: Stanford University, Institute for Communication Research, 1975, section III.

3. Canon, B. Clientele attitudes, perceptions and compliance with policy: Broadcasters and the "fairness doctrine". Paper presented at the Annual Convention of the Southern Political Science Association, Atlanta, 1968, p. 6.

4. Gandy, O., Ballesteros, E., Haight, T., & Schement, G. Citizen action and broadcasters' interests: The record of the FCC. Paper presented at the Annual Convention of the International Communication Association, Portland, Oregon, 1976.

5. Canon, op. cit.

6. Noll, R., Peck, M., & McGowan, J., Economic aspects of television regulation. Washington, D.C.: The Brookings Institution, 1973, pp. 124–125.

7. Gandy et al., op. cit., pp. 15–16.

8. Ibid.

9. U.S. Federal Communications Commission. Broadcast procedure manual. *Federal Register,* September 5, 1974, *39* (173), 32291.

10. Ibid.

11. *Media Report to Women,* March 1975.

12. Fowles, op. cit., p. III.2

13. Axelrad, D. Ring around the collar—chain around her neck: A proposal to monitor sex role stereotyping in television advertising. *Hastings Law Journal,* 1976 *8,* 149–190.

14. *Virginia State Board of Pharmacy* vs. *Virginia Citizens Consumer Council, Inc.,* 96 S.C. 1817, 1976.

15. Axelrad, op. cit., pp. 175–176.

16. Ibid., p. 179.

17. Ibid., p. 180.

18. Ibid., pp. 181–182.

19. U.S. Commission on Civil Rights. *A guide to federal laws and regulations prohibiting sex discrimination.* Washington, D.C.: U.S. Government Printing Office, 1974.

20. U.S. Department of Labor. *Complaint filing guide.* Washington, D.C.: U.S. Department of Labor, 1973.

21. Idelson, E. *Affirmative action and equal employment: A guidebook for employers.* Washington D.C.: U.S. Equal Employment Opportunity Commission, 1974.

22. Ross, S. *The rights of women.* New York: Avon, 1973.

23. *Media Report to Women,* August 1977.

24. Callan, op. cit.

25. *Journalism Educator,* 1976, *30,* 52–87. As this book goes to press, 1978 data are scheduled to appear in *Media Report to Women,* October 1978.

26. *Media Report to Women,* August 1976.

27. Peterson, P. J-enrollments continue to soar—Autumn 1975 total: 64,151. *Journalism Educator,* 1976, *30,* 3–8.

    Peterson, P., Journalism schools report record 65,962 enrollment. *Journalism Educator,* 1978, 32, 3–8.

    Data pertaining to undergraduates and doctoral students are reported from the 1978 article. Data for the masters' students were not reported in 1978; the text therefore reports 1976 data.

28. Chaffee, S., & Clarke P., Training and employment of Ph.D.'s in mass communication. *Journalism Monographs,* 1975, *42.*

29. Butler, M., Pingree, S., & Paisley, W., Writers decry percentage of women doctoral students. *Journalism Educator,* 1977, *31,* pp. 49–51, 104.

30. *Advertising Age,* October 18, 1976, p. 35.

31. U.S. Surgeon General's Scientific Advisory Committee on Television and Social Behavior. *Television and growing up: The impact of televised violence.* Washington D.C.: U.S. Government Printing Office, 1971, p. 1.

32. Butler, M. *Social policy research and the realities of the system: Violence done to TV research.* Palo Alto, Calif.: Stanford University, Institute for Communication Research, 1972.

33. *Better Radio and Television,* Winter 1976, p. 2.

34. Ibid.

35. *Advertising Age,* October 18, 1976, pp. 1, 112.

36. Ibid.

37. *TV Guide,* January 1, 1977, p. 13.

38. *TV Guide,* December 18, 1976, p. 8.

39. Ibid., p. 30.

40. *Media Report to Women,* January 1976.

41. *Media Report to Women,* March 1976.

42. *Dupont survey.* New York: Thomas Y. Crowell, 1977.

43. *Women Today,* August 21, 1978, *8* (17), 105.

44. National Advertising Review Board. *Advertising and women.* New York: National Advertising Review Board, 1975.

45. Ibid., pp. 15–17.

46. Ibid., pp. 18–19.

47. Ibid., p. 19.

48. Butler, M., Crawford, S., & Lofgren, M. *Directory of women and minority men in academic journalism/communication.* Palo Alto, Calif.: Stanford University, Institute for Communication Research, 1975.

49. *Media Report to Women,* January 1977.

50. *Media Report to Women,* May 1978.

51. *Media Report to Women,* July 1978.

52. National Commission on the Observance of International Women's Year. . . . *To form a more perfect union* . . . Washington, D.C.: U.S. Government Printing Office, 1976, pp. 252–253.

53. United Nations. *Influence of mass communication media on the formation of a new attitude towards the role of women in present-day society.* New York: United Nations, Economic and Social Council, Commission on the Status of Women, 1974, p. 15.

54. U.S. Commission on Civil Rights. *Window dressing on the set: Women and minorities in television* Washington, D.C.: U.S. Government Printing Office, 1977, pp. 150–152.

55. *Media Report to Women,* May 1977 and April 1978.

56. McLuhan, M. *The mechanical bride.* Boston: Beacon Press, 1951, p. 97.

57. *KQED Focus* (San Francisco), January 1977, p. 45.

58. Planck, M. *Scientific autobiography.* Translated by F. Gaynor. New York: Philosophical Library, 1949, p. 18.

BIBLIOGRAPHY

Adorno, T., Frenkel-Brunswik, E., Levinson, D., & Sanford, R. *The authoritarian personality.* New York: Harper, 1950.

Allport, G., & Postman, L. *The psychology of rumor.* New York: Holt, 1947.

American Association of University Women. *The image of women in television.* Sacramento, Calif.: AAUW, Sacramento Branch, 1974.

Applegate, R. Women as journalism educators. *The Matrix,* June 1965, *50,* 4–5, 10.

Arnheim, R. The world of the daytime serial. In P. Lazarsfeld and F. Stanton (Eds.), *Radio research, 1942–1943.* New York: Duell, Sloan, and Pearce, 1944, pp. 34–85.

Asimov, I. Uncertain, coy, and hard to please. In I. Asimov, *The solar system and back.* New York: Doubleday, 1970.

Association of Cinematograph and Television Technicians. *Patterns of discrimination against women in the film and television industries.* London, England: ACTT, 1975.

Atkin, C., & Miller, M. The effects of TV advertising on children: Experimental evidence. Paper presented at the Annual Convention of the International Communication Association, Chicago, 1975.

Axelrad, D. Ring around the collar—chain around her neck: A proposal to monitor sex role stereotyping in television advertising. *The Hastings Law Journal,* 1976, *28,* 149–190.

Axiom Market Research Bureau, Inc. *Target group index.* New York: Axiom Market Research Bureau, annual.

Bagdikian, B. *The information machines: Their impact on men and the media.* New York: Harper & Row, 1971.

Bailey, M. The women's magazine short-story heroine in 1957 and 1967. *Journalism Quarterly,* 1969, *46,* 364–366.

Baker, C., & Wells, A. *Earned degrees conferred: 1971–1972.* Washington, D.C.: U.S. Government Printing Office, 1975.

Bandura, A. Social-learning theory of identification processes. In D. Goslin (Ed.), *Handbook of socialization theory and research.* Chicago: Rand-McNally, 1969, pp. 213–262.

Barcus, E. *Weekend commercial children's television, 1975. A study of programming and advertising to children on five Boston stations.* Boston: Action for Children's Television, 1975.

Barcus, E. *Saturday children's television.* Boston: Boston University, School of Public Communication, 1971.

Barnouw, E. *Tube of plenty: The evolution of American television.* New York: Oxford University Press, 1975.

Bart, P. *Sexism and social science: From the gilded cage to the iron cage or the perils of Pauline.* Pittsburgh: KNOW, Inc., no date.

Bate, B. *Generic man, invisible woman: Language, thought, and social change.* Eugene: University of Oregon, 1975.

Bate, B. Nonsexist language use in transition. *Journal of Communication,* 1978, *28,* 139–149.

Bauer, R. (Ed.) *Social indicators.* Cambridge, Mass.: MIT Press, 1967.

Baunoch, J., with B. Chmaj. Film stereotypes of American women: An outline of star roles from the thirties to the present. In B. Chmaj (Ed.), *Image, myth and beyond.* Pittsburgh: KNOW, Inc., 1972, pp. 275–284.

Beasley, M., & Silver, S. *Women in media: A documentary source book.* Washington, D.C.: Women's Institute for Freedom of the Press, 1977.

Begus, S., Berndt, R., Lupton, J., Lupton, M., & Mitzner, K. *Report on sexism and racism in elementary school readers.* Baltimore: Baltimore Feminist Project, 1973.

Belkaoui, A., & Belkaoui, J. A comparative analysis of the roles portrayed by women in print advertisements: 1958, 1970, 1972. *Journal of Marketing Research,* 1976, *13,* 168–172.

Bem, S. Probing the promise of androgyny. In A. Kaplan and J. Bean (Eds.), *Beyond sex-role stereotypes: Readings toward a psychology of androgyny.* Boston: Little, Brown, 1976.

Bem, S., & Bem, D. Does sex-biased job advertising "aid and abet" sex discrimination? *Journal of Applied Social Psychology,* 1973, *3,* 6–18.

Berelson, B. *Content analysis in communication research.* New York: The Free Press, 1952.

Berelson, B. What missing the newspaper means. In W. Schramm (Ed.), *The *process and effects of mass communication.* Urbana: University of Illinois Press, 1961.

Berelson, B., & Salter, P. Majority and minority Americans: An analysis of magazine fiction. *Public Opinion Quarterly,* 1946, *10,* 168–197.

Berger, P., & Luckmann, T. *The social construction of reality: A treatise on the sociology of knowledge.* Garden City: Doubleday, 1966.

Bergum, B., & Bergum, J. Sex-role self-perceptions and sex-role stereotypes. *Perceptual and Motor Skills,* 1978, *46,* 303–307.

Best, D., & Williams, J. Development of sex-trait stereotypes among young children in the United States, England, and Ireland. *Child Development,* 1977, *48,* 1375–1384.

Better Radio and Television. General Foods leads effort to reduce advertising support for violence. *Better Radio and Television,* Winter 1976, p. 2.

Beuf, A. Doctor, lawyer, household drudge. *Journal of Communication,* 1974, *24,* 142–145.

Bird, C. *Born female.* New York: Pocket Books, 1969.

Birdwhistell, R. *Kinesics and context: Essays on body motion communication.* Philadelphia: University of Pennsylvania Press, 1970.

Birk, J., Brooks, L., Juhasz, J., Barbanel, L., Herman, M., Seltzer, R., & Tangri, S. A content analysis of sexual bias in commonly used psychology textbooks. *JSAS Catalog of Selected Documents in Psychology,* 1974, *4,* 107

Blaubergs, M. Changing the sexist language: The theory behind the practice. *Psychology of Women Quarterly,* 1978, *2,* 244–261.

Block, J. Conceptions of sex roles: Some cross-cultural and longitudinal perspectives. *American Psychologist,* 1973, *28,* 512–526.

Bogart, L. How the public gets its news. Address to the Associated Press Managing Editors, New Orleans, October 27, 1977.

Boorstin, D. *The Americans: The democratic experience.* New York: Random House, 1973.

Boorstin, D. *The image: A guide to pseudo-events in America.* New York: Harper & Row, 1961.

Boulding, K. *The image: Knowledge in life and society.* Ann Arbor: University of Michigan Press, 1956.

Boyle, C., & Wahlstrom, B. Cultural analysis: Unmasking the makings of oppression. *University of Michigan Papers in Women's Studies,* 1974, *1,* 10–43.

Bower, R. *Television and the public.* New York: Holt, Rinehart and Winston, 1973.

Breed, W. Social control in the newsroom: A descriptive study. *Social Forces,* 1955, *33,* 326–335.

Britton, G., & Lumpkin, M. *A consumer's guide to sex, race and career bias in public school textbooks.* Corvallis, Ore.: Britton and Associates, 1977.

Brown, T. Sex stereotyping in primary reading textbooks. Unpublished manuscript. Santa Barbara, Calif., 1977.

Bruner, J., Goodnow, J., & Austin, G. *A study of thinking.* New York: Wiley, 1956.

Bryan, J., & Luria, Z. Sex-role learning: A test of the selective attention hypothesis. *Child Development,* 1978, *49,* 13–23.

Burton, G. *Sex-role stereotyping in elementary school primers.* Pittsburgh: KNOW, Inc., no date.

Busby, L. Defining the sex-role standard in network children's programs. *Journalism Quarterly,* 1974, *51,* 690–696.

Busby, L. Mass media research needs: A media target for feminists. *University of Michigan Papers in Women's Studies,* 1974, *1,* 9–29.

Butler, M. (Ed.) *Image of women in advertisements: A preliminary study of avenues for change.* Palo Alto, Calif.: Stanford University, Institute for Communication Research, 1975.

Butler, M. *Social policy research and the realities of the system: Violence done to TV research.* Palo Alto, Calif.: Stanford University, Institute for Communication Research, 1972.

Butler, M., Crawford, S., & Lofgren, M. *Directory of women and minority men in academic journalism/communication.* Palo Alto, Calif. Stanford University, Institute for Communication Research, 1975.

Butler, M., & Paisley, W. Equal rights coverage in magazines, summer 1976. *Journalism Quarterly,* 1978, *55,* 157–160.

Butler, M., & Paisley, W. Magazine coverage of women's rights. *Journal of Communication,* 1978, *28,* 183–186.

Butler, M., Paisley, W., & Pingree, S. Professional concerns of women in the International Communication Association: Results of a survey. Paper presented at the Annual Convention of the International Communication Association, Portland, Oregon, 1976.

Butler, M., Pingree, S., & Paisley, W. Writers decry percentage of women doctoral students. *Journalism Educator,* 1977, *31,* 45–51, 104.

Campbell, D. *Methods for the experimenting society.* Evanston, Ill.: Northwestern University, Department of Psychology, 1969, p. 1.

Campbell, R. Women's life styles in the '70's. Address on Stanford Alumni Day, Stanford University, 1971.

Canon, B. Clientele attitudes, perceptions, and compliance with policy: Broadcasters and the "fairness doctrine." Paper presented at the Annual Convention of the Southern Political Science Association, 1968.

Cantril, H., Gaudet, H., & Herzog, H. *The invasion from Mars.* Princeton, N.J.: Princeton University Press, 1940.

Cathey-Calvert, C. Sexism on Sesame Street: Outdated concepts in a "progressive program." Pittsburgh: KNOW, Inc., no date.

CBC Task Force on the Status of Women. *Women in the CBC.* Ottawa, Canada: Canadian Broadcasting Corporation, 1975.

Chaffee, S., & Clarke, P. Training and employment of Ph.D.'s in mass communication. *Journalism Monographs,* 1975, *42,* 1–31.

Chang, W. Characteristics and self-perceptions of women's page editors. *Journalism Quarterly,* 1975, *52,* 61–65.

Charters, W. *Motion pictures and youth: A summary.* New York: Macmillan, 1933.

Cheles-Miller, P. An investigation of whether the stereotypes of husbands and wives presented in television commercials can influence a child's perception of the role of husband and wife. Unpublished doctoral dissertation, University of Ohio, 1974.

Cheles-Miller, P. Reactions to marital roles in commercials. *Journal of Advertising Research,* 1975, *15,* 45–49.

Child, I., Potter, E., & Levine, E. Children's textbooks and personality development. *Social Psychology of Education Monographs,* 1946, *60,* 1–54.

Chin, R., & Benne, K. General strategies for effecting change in human systems. In W. Bennis, K. Benne, and R. Chin (Eds.), *The planning of change.* New York: Holt, Rinehart and Winston, 1969, pp. 32–59.

Chmaj, B. Fantasizing women's lib: Stereotypes of women in comic books. In B. Chmaj (Ed.), *Image, myth and beyond.* Pittsburgh: KNOW, Inc., 1972, pp. 311–327.

Chulay, C., & Francis, S. The image of the female child on Saturday morning television commercials. Paper presented at the Annual Convention of the International Communication Association, New Orleans, 1974.

Cirksena, K., & Butler, M. *Sex bias in advertisements: Are we making progress?* San Francisco: Far West Laboratory for Educational Research and Development, 1978.

Clarke, P., & Esposito, V. A study of occupational advice for women in magazines. *Journalism Quarterly,* 1966, *43,* 477–485.

Cohen, A. Some implications of self-esteem for social influence. In C. Hovland and I. Janis (Eds.), *Personality and persuasibility.* New Haven, Conn.: Yale University Press, 1959, pp. 102–120.

Comstock, G., Chaffee, S., McLeod, J., & Roberts, D. *Television and human behavior.* New York: Columbia University Press, 1978.

Copperud, R. Editorial workshop. *Editor and Publisher,* June 8, 1974, p. 32.

Cornillon, S. (Ed.) *Images of women in fiction: Feminist perspectives.* Bowling Green, Ohio: Bowling Green University Popular Press, 1972.

Courtney, A., & Lockeretz, S. A woman's place: An analysis of the roles portrayed by women in magazine advertisements. *Journal of Marketing Research,* February 1971, *8,* 92–95.

Courtney, A., & Whipple, T. Women in TV commercials. *Journal of Communication,* 1974, *24,* 110–118.

Crawford, S. Purposes and functions of advertising agencies. In M. Butler (Ed.), *Image of women in advertisements: A preliminary study of avenues for change.* Palo Alto, Calif.: Stanford University, Institute for Communication Research, 1975.

Culley, J., & Bennett, R. *The status of women in mass media advertising: An empirical study.* Newark: University of Delaware, Bureau of Economic and Business Research, 1974.

Czaplinski, S. *Sexism in award winning picture books.* Pittsburgh: KNOW, Inc., 1972.

Dale, E. *The content of motion pictures.* New York: Macmillan, 1935.

DeCrow, K. What the "helping" professions tell you about being a woman. In K. DeCrow, *The young woman's guide to liberation.* Indianapolis: Pegasus, 1971, pp. 128–137.

DeFleur, M. Occupational roles as portrayed on television. *Public Opinion Quarterly,* 1964, *28,* 57–74.

DeFleur, M., & Ball-Rokeach, S. *Theories of mass communication.* New York: David McKay, 1975.

DiMaggio, E. *What's a nice girl like you doing in a place like this: Interviews with women journalists.* Palo Alto, Calif.: Stanford University, Institute for Communication Research, 1974–1975.

Dohrmann, R. A gender profile of children's educational TV. *Journal of Communication,* Autumn 1975, *25,* 56–65.

Dominick, J., & Pearce, M. Trends in network prime-time programming, 1953–1974. *Journal of Communication,* 1976, *26,* 70–80.

Dominick, J., & Rauch, G. The image of women in network TV commercials. *Journal of Broadcasting,* 1972, *16,* 259–265.

Downing, M. Heroine of the daytime serial. *Journal of Communication,* 1974, *24,* 130–137.

Drabman, R., Hammer, D., & Jarvie, G. *Children's perception of media-portrayed sex roles across ages.* Jackson: Department of Psychiatry and Human Behavior, University of Mississippi Medical Center, 1976.

Durham, J. Low-down on the high-brows: Women and the analytic journals. Unpublished manuscript, Stanford University, 1977.

Efron, E. *The news twisters.* New York: Manor Books, 1972.

Ekman, P., Friesen, W., & Taussig, T. VID-R and SCAN: Tools and methods for the automated analysis of visual records. In G. Gerbner, O. Holsti, K. Krippendorff, W. Paisley, and P. Stone (Eds.), *The analysis of communication content.* New York: Wiley, 1969, pp. 297–312.

Ellwood, C. Keeping women in their places: An examination of the hiring practices of magazines over time. Unpublished manuscript, Stanford University, 1977.

Embree, A. Media images 1: Madison Avenue brainwashing—the facts. In R. Morgan (Ed.) *Sisterhood is powerful: An anthology of writings from the women's liberation movement.* New York: Random House, 1970, pp. 175–190.

Endres, K. Capitol Hill newswomen: A descriptive study. *Journalism Quarterly,* 1976, *53,* 132–135.

Epstein, C. *Woman's place: Options and limits in professional careers.* Berkeley: University of California Press, 1970.

Epstein, R., & Bozler, D. *A study of preschool children's television viewing behavior and circumstances.* Los Angeles: University of Southern California, Annenberg School of Communications, 1976.

Evans, R., & Meyer, E. Consequences of sexism in journalism tests. Paper presented at the Women in Journalism Seminar, University of Michigan, 1973.

Farley, J. Women's magazines and the ERA: Friend or foe? *Journal of Communication,* 1978, *28,* 187–192.

Feminists on Children's Literature. A feminist look at children's books. *School Library Journal,* 1971, *17,* 19–24.

Ferriss, A. *Indicators of trends in the status of American women.* New York: The Russell Sage Foundation, 1971.

Festinger, L. *A theory of cognitive dissonance.* Palo Alto, Calif.: Stanford University Press, 1957.

Finz, S., & Waters, J. An analysis of sex role stereotyping in daytime television serials. Paper presented at the Annual Convention of the American Psychological Association, Washington, D.C., 1976.

Fischer, P., & Torney, J. Influence of children's stories on dependency: A sex-typed behavior. *Developmental Psychology,* 1976, *12,* 489–490.

Fisher, C., & Dean, D. *The realism of marital and parental roles on television.* Canton, N.Y.: Saint Lawrence University, 1976.

Fisher, E. The second sex, junior division. *New York Times Book Review,* Part II, May 24, 1970, pp. 5, 44.

Fisher, J., & Janus, N. Women and heart disease: Images in popular media from 1959–1974. Paper presented at the Annual Convention of the International Communication Association, Chicago, 1978.

Flerx, V., Fidler, D., & Rogers, R. Sex-role stereotypes: Developmental aspects and early intervention. *Child Development,* 1976, *47,* 998–1007.

Flexner, E. *Century of struggle.* Cambridge, Mass.: Harvard University Press, 1959.

Flora, C. The passive female: Her comparative image by class and culture in women's magazine fiction. *Journal of Marriage and the Family,* 1971, *33,* 435–444.

Flores, J. Employment of women in news magazines. Unpublished manuscript, Stanford University, 1977.

Foner, P. (Ed.) *Life and writings of Frederick Douglass.* Vol. 4. New York: International Publishers, 1950.

Fox, H. Sex stereotypes in advertisements. *Business and Society,* 1976, *11,* 24–30.

Fowles, J. Some recent efforts to change the image of women. In M. Butler (Ed.), *Image of women in advertisements: A preliminary study of avenues for change.* Palo Alto, Calif.: Institute for Communication Research, Stanford University, 1975.

Franzwa, H. Working women in fact and fiction. *Journal of Communication,* 1974, *24,* pp. 104–109.

Freuh, R., & McGhee, P. Traditional sex-role development and amount of time spent watching television. *Developmental Psychology,* 1975, *11,* 109.

Friedan, B. *The feminine mystique.* New York: W. W. Norton, 1963.

Friedman, L. *Sex role stereotyping in the mass media: An annotated bibliography.* New York: Garland Publishing, 1977.

Friendly, F. *Due to circumstances beyond our control.* New York: Random House, 1967.

Frisof, J. Textbooks and channeling. *Women: A Journal of Liberation,* 1969, 1, 26–28.

Gandy, O., Haight, T., Schement, J., Soriano, E., & Gutierrez, F. Citizen action and broadcasters, interests: The record of the FCC. Paper presented at the Annual Convention of the International Communication Association, Portland, Oregon, 1976.

Gardner, J. Sesame Street and sex-role stereotypes. *Women: A Journal of Liberation,* 1970, 1, 42.

Garrett, C., & Ein, P., Tremaine, L. The development of gender stereotyping of adult occupations in elementary school children. *Child Development,* 1977, *48,* 507–512.

Garvey, D. Social control in the television newsroom. Unpublished doctoral dissertation. Stanford University, 1971.

Geng, V. Requiem for the women's movement: Empty voices in crowded rooms. *Harper's Magazine,* November 1976, pp. 49–68.

George, A. *Propaganda analysis: A study of inferences made from Nazi propaganda in World War II.* Evanston, Ill.: Row, Peterson, 1959.

Gerbner, G. Communication and social environment. In *Communication, A Scientific American Book.* San Francisco: W. H. Freeman, 1972, pp. 111–118.

Gerbner, G. An institutional approach to mass communications research. In L. Thayer (Ed.), *Communication theory and research.* Springfield, Ill.: Charles C Thomas, 1967, pp. 429–451.

Gerbner, G. Violence in television drama: Trends and symbolic functions. In G. Comstock and E. Rubinstein (Eds.), *Television and social behavior.*

Volume 1: Media content and control. Washington, D.C.: U.S. Government Printing Office, 1972, pp. 28–187

Gerbner, G., & Gross, L. Living with television: The violence profile. *Journal of Communication,* 1976, *26,* 173–199.

Gerbner, C., Holsti, O., Krippendorff, K., Paisley, W., & Stone, P. (Eds.) *The analysis of communication content.* New York: Wiley, 1969.

Gershuny, H. Sexist semantics: An investigation of masculine and feminine nouns and pronouns in dictionary sentences to illustrate word usage as a reflection of sex-role. Unpublished doctoral dissertation, New York University, 1972.

Goffman, E. Gender advertisements. *Studies in the Anthropology of Visual Communication,* 1976, *3,* 65–154.

Goldsen, R. Throwaway husbands, wives and lovers. *Human Behavior,* December 1975, pp. 64–69.

Gordon, F., & Strober, M. *Bringing women into management.* New York: McGraw-Hill, 1975.

Goodman, C. Images of American rural women in the novel. *University of Michigan Papers in Women's Studies,* 1975, *1,* 57–70.

Gorney, S. Status of women in public relations. *Public Relations Journal,* 1975, *31,* 10–13

Gornick, V., & Moran, B. (Eds.) *Woman in sexist society: Studies in power and powerlessness.* New York: Basic Books, 1971.

Graebner, D. A decade of sexism in readers. *The Reading Teacher,* 1972. *6,* 52–58.

Graham, A. The making of a non-sexist dictionary. *MS.,* December 1973, pp. 12–16.

Griffith, R., & Mayer, A. *The movies.* New York: Bonanza Books, 1957.

Grimke, S. *Letters on the equality of the sexes and the condition of women.* Boston: Isaac Knapp, 1838.

Gross, L. The "real" world of television. *Today's Education,* 1974, *63,* 86, 89–92.

Guenin, Z. Women's pages in American newspapers: Missing out on contemporary content. *Journalism Quarterly,* 1975, *52,* 66–69, 75.

Gustafson, J. The decline of women among the top ten box office stars. In B. Chmaj (Ed.), *Image, myth and beyond.* Pittsburgh: KNOW, Inc., 1972, pp. 284–290.

Gustafson, J. Stereotypes of women in American literature: Will the real great American bitch please stand up. In B. Chmaj (Ed.), *Image, myth and beyond.* Pittsburgh: KNOW, Inc., 1972, pp. 253–274.

Guttentag, M., & Bray, H. *Undoing sex stereotypes: Research and resources for education.* New York: McGraw-Hill, 1976.

Hacker, H. Women as a minority group. *Social Forces,* 1951, *30,* 60–69.

Hacker, H. Women as a minority group: Twenty years later. *International Journal of Group Tensions,* 1974, *4,* 122–132.

Hale, S. Children's Programming. Unpublished manuscript, Stanford University, 1977.

Hall, E. *The silent language.* New York: Doubleday, 1959.

Hansen, J. Women in journalism history textbooks. Paper presented at the Women in Journalism Seminar, University of Michigan, 1973.

Haskell, M. *From reverence to rape: The treatment of women in the movies.* New York: Holt, Rinehart and Winston, 1973.

Haskell, M. What is Hollywood trying to tell us? *MS.,* April 1977, pp. 49–50.

Hatch, M., & Hatch, D. Problems of married and working women as presented by three popular working women's magazines. *Social Forces,* 1958, *37,* 148–153.

Haymes, H. Movies in the 1950's: Sexism from A to Zapata. *Journal of the University Film Association,* 1974, *26,* 12, 22.

Head, S. Content analysis of television drama programs. *Quarterly of Film, Radio, and Television,* 1954, *9,* 175–194.

Henley, N. *Body politics: Power, sex, and nonverbal communication.* Englewood Cliffs, N.J.: Prentice-Hall, 1977.

Hennessee, J., & Nicholson, J. NOW says: TV commercials insult women. *New York Times Magazine,* May 28, 1972, pp. 13, 48–51.

Herzog, H. Motivations and gratifications of daily serial listeners. In W. Schramm (Ed.), *The process and effects of mass communication.* Urbana: University of Illinois Press, 1961, 50–55.

Hoffman, H. Monitoring of children's television programming aired by WRC-TV: A comparison of male and female roles. In National Organization for Women, *Women in the wasteland fight back.* Washington, D.C.: NOW, National Capital Area chapter, 1972.

Holcomb, M. *Legislation affecting the rights of women enacted by, or pending in the 93rd Congress.* Washington, D.C.: Library of Congress, Congressional Research Service, 1974.

Hole, J., & Levine, E. *Rebirth of feminism.* New York: Quadrangle Books, 1971.

Holsti, O. *Content analysis for the social science and humanities.* Reading, Mass.: Addison-Wesley, 1969.

Holtzman, N. *And they lived happily ever after???* Unpublished manuscript, Sepulveda, Calif., 1975.

Howard, H. The contemporary status of television group ownership. *Journalism Quarterly,* 1976, *53,* 399–405.

Howard, H. Cross-media ownership of newspapers and TV stations. *Journalism Quarterly,* 1974, *51,* 715–718.

Idelson, E. *Affirmative action and equal employment: A guidebook for employ-*

ers. Washington, D.C.: Equal Employment Opportunity Commission, 1974.

Isber, C., & Cantor, M. *Report of the task force on women in public broadcasting.* Washington, D.C.: Corporation for Public Broadcasting, 1975.

Israel, H., & Robinson, J. Demographic characteristics of viewers of television violence and news programs. In E. Rubinstein, G. Comstock, and J. Murray (Eds.), *Television and Social Behavior. Volume 4: Television in day-to-day life: Patterns of use.* Washington, D.C.: U.S. Government Printing Office, 1972, pp. 87–128.

Israel, L. Saving an endangered species. *MS.,* February 1975, pp. 51–57, 104.

Janis, I., & Field, P. Sex differences and personality factors related to persuasibility. In C. Hovland and I. Janis (Eds.), *Personality and persuasibility.* New Haven, Conn.: Yale University Press, 1959, pp. 55–68.

Jay, W. Sex stereotyping in elementary-school mathematics textbooks. In J. Pottker and A. Fishel (Eds.), *Sex bias in the schools: The research evidence.* London, England: Associated University Presses, 1977, pp. 126–145.

Jennings, R. *Television station employment practices: The status of minorities and women, 1972.* New York: United Church of Christ, Office of Communication, 1972.

Jennings, R., & Jefferson, V. *Television station employment practices: The status of minorities and women, 1974.* New York: United Church of Christ, Office of Communication, 1974.

Jennings, R., & Jefferson, V. *Television station employment practices: The status of minorities and women, 1975.* New York: United Church of Christ, Office of Communication, 1976.

Jennings, R., Tillyer, D. *Television station employment practices: The status of minorities and women, 1973.* New York: United Church of Christ, Office of Communication, 1973.

Jennings, R., & Walters, A. *Television station employment practices: The status of women and minorities, 1976.* New York: United Church of Christ, Office of Communication, 1977.

Jesperson, O. *Growth and structure of the English language.* (4th ed.) New York: D. Appleton, 1955.

Johns-Heine, P., & Gerth, H. Values in mass periodical fiction, 1921–1940. *Public Opinion Quarterly,* 1949, *13,* 105–113.

Johnson, N. *Test pattern for living.* New York: Bantam, 1972.

Johnstone, J. Organizational constraints on newswork. *Journalism Quarterly,* 1976, *53,* 5–13.

Johnstone, J., Slawski, E., & Bowman, W. The professional values of American newsmen. *Public Opinion Quarterly,* 1972–1973, *26,* 522–540.

Jones, D. Quantitative analysis of motion picture content. *Public Opinion Quarterly,* 1942, *6,* 411–428.

Jones, B., & Brown, J. *Toward a female liberation movement.* Boston: New England Free Press, 1968.

Kalamazoo Committee for Children's Television. KCCT's monitoring study results released. *KCCT Newsletter,* January 1975, pp. 1–2, 4.

Katz, D. The functional approach to the study of attitudes. *Public Opinion Quarterly,* 1960, *24,* 163–176.

Katz, D., McClintock, C., & Sarnoff, I. The measurement of ego defense as related to attitude change. *Journal of Personality,* 1957, *25,* 465–474.

Katzman, N. Television soap operas: What's been going on anyway? *Public Opinion Quarterly,* 1972, *35,* 200–212.

Kay, H. Notes on a Sunday newspaper readership survey technique. *Journalism Quarterly,* 1955, *32,* 76–77, 118.

Kelman, H. Compliance, identification, and internalization: Three processes of attitude change. *Journal of Conflict Resolution,* 1958, *2,* 51–60.

Key, M. *Male/female language.* Metuchen, N.J.: Scarecrow Press, 1975.

KDKA-TV, Women's Advisory Council. *Women in TV: Reflections in a funhouse mirror.* Pittsburgh: KDKA-TV, 1976.

Kingsbury, S., & Hart, H. *Newspapers and the news.* New York: Putnam, 1937.

Kinzer, G. Soapy sin in the afternoon. *Psychology Today,* August 1973, pp. 46–48.

Kirschner, B. Introducing students to women's place in society. *American Journal of Sociology,* 1973, *78,* 1051–1054.

Klagsbrun, R. (Ed.) *Free to be . . . you and me.* New York: McGraw-Hill, 1974.

Klapper, J. *The effects of mass communication.* New York: The Free Press, 1960.

Koblinsky, S., Cruse, D., & Sugawara, A. Sex role stereotypes and children's memory for story content. *Child Development,* 1978, *49,* 452–458.

Komisar, L. The image of woman in advertising. In Gornick and B. Moran (Eds.), *Woman in sexist society: Studies in power and powerlessness.* New York: Basic Books, 1971, pp. 302–317.

Komisar, L. Women in the media. In Professional Woman's Caucus, New York University Law School, *Sixteen reports on the status of women in the professions.* Pittsburgh: KNOW, Inc., 1970.

Kramer, C. Women's rhetoric in *New Yorker* cartoons: Patterns for a Mildred Milquetoast. Paper presented at the Annual Convention of the Speech Communication Association, New York, 1973.

Lakoff, R. *Language and woman's place.* New York: Harper & Row, 1975.

Lasswell, H., Leites, N., Fadner, R., Goldsen, J., Grey, A., Janis, I., Kaplan, A., Kaplan, D., Mintz, A., Pool, I., Yakobson, S. *Language of politics: Studies in quantitative semantics.* New York: Stewart, 1949.

Lazarsfeld, P. *Radio and the printed page.* New York: Duell, Sloan and Pearce, 1940.

Lazarsfeld, P., & Kendall, P. *Radio listening in America.* New York: Prentice-Hall, 1948.

Lazarsfeld, P., & Merton, R. Mass communication, popular taste, and organized social action. In W. Schramm and D. Roberts (Eds.), *The process and effects of mass communication.* (Rev. ed.) Urbana: University of Illinois Press, 1971, pp. 554–578.

Lazarsfeld, P., & Wyant, R. Magazines in 90 cities—who reads what? *Public Opinion Quarterly,* 1937, *1,* 29–41.

Lazer, C., & Dier, S. The labor force in fiction. *Journal of Communication,* 1978, *28,* 174–182.

Leifer, A. When are undergraduate admissions sexist? The case of Stanford University. Paper presented at the Annual Convention of the International Communication Association, New Orleans, 1974.

Lemon, J. Dominant or dominated? Women on prime-time television. In G. Tuchman, A. Daniels, and J. Benet (Eds.), *Hearth and home: Images of women in the mass media.* New York: Oxford University Press, 1978, pp. 3–38.

Levin, E. Employment of women in business magazines, 1945–1977. Unpublished manuscript, Stanford University, 1977.

Lichty, L., & Ripley, J. Size and composition of broadcasting stations' staffs. *Journal of Broadcasting,* 1967, *11,* 139–151.

Lieberman, M. Someday my prince will come: Female acculturation through fairy tales. *College English,* 1972, *34,* 383–389.

Liebert, R., Neale, J., & Davidson, E. *The early window: Effects of television on children and youth.* New York: Pergamon, 1973.

Likert, R., & Lippitt, R. The utilization of social science. In L. Festinger and D. Katz (Eds.), *Research methods in the behavioral sciences.* New York: Dryden Press, 1953, pp. 581–646.

Lippmann, W. *Public opinion.* New York: Macmillan, 1922.

Lippmann, W., & Merz, C. A test of the news. *New Republic,* Supplement to issue of August 4, 1920.

Logan, B. (Ed.) *Television awareness training.* New York: Media Action Research Center, 1977.

Long, M., & Simon, R. The roles and statuses of women on children and family TV programs. *Journalism Quarterly,* 1974, *51,* 107–110.

Lukenbill, W. Who writes children's books? *Journal of Communication,* 1976, *26,* pp. 97–100.

Lyle, J., & Hoffman, H. Children's use of television and other media. In E. Rubinstein, G. Comstock, and J. Murray (Eds.), *Television and social behavior. Volume 4: Television in day-to-day life: Patterns of use.* Washington, D.C.: U.S. Government Printing Office, 1972, pp. 129–256.

McArthur, L., & Eisen, S. Achievements of male and female storybook characters as determinants of achievement behavior by boys and girls. *Journal of Personality and Social Psychology,* 1976, *33,* 467–473.

McGinley, E. *The image of the American woman in advertising, 1962–1972.* West Liberty, W. Va.: West Liberty State College, 1973.

McGraw-Hill Book Company. *Guidelines for equal treatment of the sexes in McGraw-Hill Book Company publications.* New York: McGraw-Hill, 1974.

McKnight, D. Sexism in advertising: What's a nice girl like you. . . . *Technology Review,* May 1974, pp. 20–21.

McLuhan, M. *Understanding media: The extensions of man.* New York: New American Library, 1966.

McNeil, J. *The reverse prism: A study of the images of women on television.* Urbana: University of Illinois, Department of Radio and Television, 1974.

McNeil, J. Feminism, femininity, and the television series: A content analysis. *Journal of Broadcasting,* 1975, *19,* 259–271.

Maccoby, E., & Jacklin, C. *The psychology of sex differences.* Palo Alto, Calif.: Stanford University Press, 1974.

Macleod, J., & Silverman, S. *"You won't do": What textbooks on U.S. government teach high school girls.* Pittsburgh: KNOW, Inc., 1973.

Maracek, J., Piliavin, J., Fitzsimmons, E., Krogh, E., Leader, E., & Trudell, B. Women as TV experts: The voice of authority? *Journal of Communication,* 1978, *28,* 159–168.

Martin, W. Seduced and abandoned in the new world: The image of woman in American fiction. In V. Gornick and B. Moran (Eds.), *Woman in sexist society: Studies in power and powerlessness.* New York: Basic Books, 1971, pp. 328–346.

Martyna, W. What does "he" mean—Use of the generic masculine. *Journal of Communication,* 1978, *28,* 131–138.

Marzolf, M. *Up from the footnote: A history of women journalists.* New York: Hastings House, 1977.

Mellen, J. *Women and their sexuality in the new film.* New York: Horizon Press, 1973.

Merriam, E. Sex and semantics: Some notes on BOMFOG. *New York University Education Quarterly,* 1974, *5,* 22–27.

Merritt, S., & Gross, H. *Women's page/lifestyle editors: Does sex make a difference?* Park Forest South, Ill.: Governors State University, 1977.

Metz, R. *CBS: Reflections in a bloodshot eye.* New York: New American Library, 1975.

Miller, C., & Swift, K. *Words and women: New language in new times.* New York: Doubleday, 1975.

Miller, G., Galanter, E., & Pribram, K. *Plans and the structure of behavior.* New York: Holt, 1960.

Miller, J. *Toward a new psychology of women.* Boston: Beacon Press, 1976.

Miller, S. Changes in women's lifestyle sections. *Journalism Quarterly,* 1976, *53,* 641–647.

Miller, S. The content of news photos: Women's and men's roles. *Journalism Quarterly,* 1975, *52,* 70–75.

Millett, K. *Sexual politics.* Garden City, N.Y.: Doubleday, 1970.

Mills, K. Fighting sexism on the airwaves. *Journal of Communication,* 1974, *24,* 150–155.

Morelock, J., & Kurth, S. Giving women what they want? The representation of trends in the roles of women in women's magazines, 1956–1970. Unpublished paper, Pennsylvania State University, 1975.

Morris, M. Newspapers and the new feminists: Black out as social control? *Journalism Quarterly,* 1973, *50,* 37–42.

Murray, M. (Ed.) *A house of good proportion: Images of women in literature.* New York: Simon and Schuster, 1973.

Myrdal, G. *An American dilemma: The Negro problem and modern democracy.* New York: Harper & Row, 1944.

National Advertising Review Board. *Advertising and women.* New York: NARB, 1975.

National Commission on the Observance of International Women's Year. . . . *To form a more perfect union.* . . . Washington, D.C.: U.S. Government Printing Office, 1976, pp. 252–253.

National Organization for Women, National Capital Area chapter. *Women in the wasteland fight back.* Washington, D.C.: NOW, National Capital Area chapter, 1972.

National Organization for Women, Northern Virginia chapter. *Newspaper monitoring project.* Arlington: NOW, Northern Virginia chapter, 1973.

Newkirk, C. Female roles in non-fiction of three women's magazines. *Journalism Quarterly,* 1977, *54,* 780–781.

A. C. Nielsen Company. *Nielsen television '76.* Northbrook, Ill.: A. C. Nielsen Co., 1976.

A. C. Nielsen Company. *Nielsen television '78.* Northbrook, Ill.: A. C. Nielsen Co., 1977.

Nilsen, A. Women in children's literature. *College English,* 1971, *32,* 918–926.

Nixon, R. The problem of newspaper monopoly. In W. Schramm (Ed.), *Mass communications.* Urbana: University of Illinois Press, 1960, pp. 241–250.

Noll, R., Peck, M., & McGowan, J. *Economic aspects of television regulation.* Washington, D.C.: The Brookings Institution, 1973.

Northcott, H., Seggar, J., & Hinton, J. Trends in TV portrayal of blacks and women. *Journalism Quarterly,* 1975, *52,* 741–744.

O'Donnell, W., O'Donnell, K. Update: Sex-role messages in TV commercials. *Journal of Communication,* 1978, *28,* 156–158.

O'Kelly, C. Sexism in children's television. *Journalism Quarterly,* 1974, *51,* 722–724.

Orwant, J., & Cantor, M. How sex stereotyping affects perceptions of news preferences. *Journalism Quarterly,* 1977, *54,* 99–108.

Paisley, W. Introduction to Part III. In G. Gerbner, O. Holsti, K. Krippendorff, W. Paisley, and P. Stone (Eds.), *The analysis of communication content.* New York: Wiley, 1969, pp. 283–284.

Parker, E., & Paisley, W. *Patterns of adult information seeking.* Palo Alto, Calif.: Stanford University, Institute for Communication Research, 1966.

Peck, E. Television's romance with reproduction. In E. Peck and J. Senderowitz (Eds.), *Pronatalism: The myth of mom and apple pie.* New York: Thomas Y. Crowell, 1974, pp. 78–97.

Peck, E., & Senderowitz, J. (Eds.) *Pronatalism: The myth of mom and apple pie.* New York: Thomas Y. Crowell, 1974.

Perry, D., & Perry, L. Observational learning in children: Effects of sex of model and subject's sex-role behavior. *Journal of Personality and Social Psychology,* 1975, *31,* 1084–1088.

Peterson, P. J-enrollments continue to soar—Autumn 1975 total: 64,151. *Journalism Educator,* 1976, *30,* 3–8.

Peterson, P. Journalism schools report record 65, 962 enrollment. *Journalism Educator,* 1978, *32,* 3–8.

Piaget, J. Piaget's theory. In P. Mussen (Ed.), *Carmichael's manual of child psychology.* Vol. 1. New York: Wiley, 1970.

Pingree, S. The effects of nonsexist television commercials and perceptions of reality on children's attitudes about women. *Psychology of Women Quarterly,* 1978, *2,* 262–277

Pingree, S., & Butler, M. Attitudes toward hiring professional couples in schools and departments of journalism. *Journalism Educator,* 1978, *33,* 61–63.

Pingree, S., Butler, M., Paisley, W., & Hawkins, R. Anti-nepotism's ghost: Attitudes of administrators toward hiring professional couples. *Psychology of Women Quarterly,* 1978, *3,* 22–29.

Pingree, S., Hawkins, R., Butler, M., & Paisley, W. A scale for sexism. *Journal of Communication,* 1976, *26,* 193–200.

Pingree, S., Hawkins, R., & Waldinger, M. An analysis of sexism in TV advertising. Paper presented at Annual Convention of Pacific Chapter, American Association for Public Opinion Research, Asilomar, California, 1975.

Planck, M. *Scientific autobiography.* Translated by F. Gaynor. New York: Philosophical Library, 1949.

Plost, M., & Rosen, M. Effect of sex of career models on occupational preferences of adolescents. *Audio-Visual Communication Review,* 1974, *22,* 41–49.

Pottker, J. Psychological and occupational sex stereotypes in elementary-school readers. In J. Pottker and A. Fishel (Eds.), *Sex bias in the schools: The research evidence.* London, England: Associated University Presses, 1977, pp. 111–125.

Ray, M. Psychological theories and interpretations of learning. In S. Ward and T. Robertson (Eds.), *Consumer behavior.* Englewood Cliffs, N.J.: Prentice-Hall, 1973, pp. 45–117.

Rees, M. Achievement motivation and media content preferences. *Journalism Quarterly,* 1967, *44,* 688–692.

Rees, M., & Paisley, W. *Social and psychological predictors of information seeking and media use: A multivariate re-analysis.* Palo Alto, Calif.: Stanford University, Institute for Communication Research, 1967.

Rees, M., & Paisley, W. Social and psychological predictors of adult information seeking and media use. *Adult Education,* 1968, *19,* 11–29.

Rivers, W. *The opinionmakers.* Boston: Beacon Press, 1965.

Rivers, W., Thompson, W., & Nyhan, M. (Eds.) *The Aspen handbook on the media: 1977–1979 edition.* New York: Praeger, 1977.

Rokeach, M. *The open and closed mind.* New York: Basic Books, 1960.

Rosen, M. How the movies have made women smaller than life. *Journal of the University Film Association,* 1974, *26,* 6–10.

Ross, S. *The rights of women.* New York: Avon, 1973.

Rush, R. Women in academe: Journalism education viewed from the literature and other memorabilia. Report to the Ad Hoc Committee on the Status of Women in Journalism Education, Association for Education in Journalism, Fort Collins, Colorado, 1973.

Saario, T., Jacklin, C., & Tittle, C. Sex role stereotyping in the public schools. *Harvard Educational Review,* 1973, *43,* 386–416.

Saenger, G. Male and female relations in the American comic strip. *Public Opinion Quarterly,* 1955, *19,* 195–205.

Saporta, S. Language in a sexist society. Paper presented at the Annual Convention of the Modern Language Association of America, New York, 1974.

Sargent, A. *Beyond sex roles.* St. Paul: West Publishing Co., 1976.

Saunders, D. Social ideas in the McGuffey Readers. *Public Opinion Quarterly,* 1941, *5,* 579–589.

Scardina, F. *Sexism in textbooks in Pittsburgh public schools grades K-5.* Pittsburgh: KNOW, Inc., 1972.

Schein, E. The mechanisms of change. In W. Bennis, K. Benne, and R. Chin (Eds.), *The planning of change.* New York: Holt, Rinehart and Winston, 1969, pp. 98–107.

Schiller, H. *Mass communications and American empire.* Boston: Beacon, 1971.

Schmidt, D. The great American bitch. *College English,* 1971, *32,* 900–905.

Schneider, J., & Hacker, S. Sex role imagery and use of the generic man in introductory texts: A case in the sociology of sociology? *The American Sociologist,* 1973, *8,* 12–18.

Schramm, W. Media as communication institutions. In W. Schramm and D. Roberts (Eds.), *The process and effects of mass communication.* (Rev. ed.) Urbana: University of Illinois Press, 1971, pp. 57–61.

Schramm, W. *Men, messages, and media: A look at human communication.* New York: Harper & Row, 1973.

Schramm, W. The nature of communication between humans. In W. Schramm and D. Roberts (Eds.), *The process and effects of mass communication.* (Rev. ed.) Urbana: University of Illinois Press, 1971, pp. 3–53.

Schramm, W. *One day in the world's press.* Palo Alto, Calif.: Stanford University Press, 1959.

Schramm, W., Lyle, J. & Parker, E. *Television in the lives of our children.* Palo Alto, Calif.: Stanford University Press, 1961.

Schramm, W., & White, D. Age, education, and economic status as factors in newspaper reading. *Journalism Quarterly,* 1949, *26,* 149–159.

Schroder, H., Driver, M., & Streufert, S. *Human information processing.* New York: Holt, Rinehart and Winston, 1967.

Schuler, S. Women in journalism work twice as hard: Get only half as far. *Grassroots Editor,* 1973, *14,* 24–27.

Schwartz, L. The image of women in the novels of Mme. de Souza. *The University of Michigan Papers in Women's Studies,* 1974, *1,* 142–148.

Screen Actors Guild. *SAG documents use of women and minorities in prime-time TV shows.* Press Release. Hollywood, Calif.: Screen Actors Guild, October 31, 1974.

Screen Actors Guild. *The relative roles of men and women in television commercials.* New York: Women's Conference Committee, New York Branch, Screen Actors Guild, 1974.

Scully, D., & Bart, P. A funny thing happened on the way to the orifice: Women in gynecology textbooks. In J. Huber (Ed.), *Changing women in a changing society.* Chicago: University of Chicago Press, 1973, pp. 283–288.

Sears, D., Freedman, J. Selective exposure to information: A critical review. In W. Schramm and D. Roberts (Eds.), *Process and effects of mass communication.* (Rev. ed.) Urbana: University of Illinois Press, pp. 209–234.

Seggar, J., & Wheeler, P. World of work on TV: Ethnic and sex representation in TV drama. *Journal of Broadcasting,* 1973, *17,* 201–214.

Sexton, D., & Haberman, P. Women in magazine advertisements. *Journal of Advertising Research,* 1974, *14,* 41–46.

Shainess, N. Images of woman: Past and present, overt and obscured. *American Journal of Psychotherapy*, 1969, *23*, 77–97.

Sheldon, E., & Moore, W. (Eds.) *Indicators of social change: Concepts and measurements*. New York: Russell Sage Foundation, 1968.

Sherif, M., & Hovland, C. *Social judgment*. New Haven, Conn.: Yale University Press, 1961.

Siebert, F., Peterson, T., & Schramm, W. *Four theories of the press*. Urbana: University of Illinois Press, 1956.

Sikorski, L., Roberts, D., & Paisley, W. Letters in mass magazines as "outcroppings" of public concern. *Journalism Quarterly*, 1969, *46*, 743–752.

Silverstein, A., & Silverstein, R. The portrayal of women in television advertising. *Federal Communications Bar Journal*, 1974, *27*, 71–98.

Skornia, H. *Television and society*. New York: McGraw-Hill, 1965.

Slaby, R., & Frey, K. Development of gender constancy and selective attention to same-sex models. *Child Development*, 1975, *46*, 849–856.

Slaby, R., Quarforth, G., & McConnachie, G. Television violence and its sponsors. *Journal of Communication*, 1976, *26*, 88–96.

Smith, D. The social content of pornography. *Journal of Communication*, 1976, *26*, 16–24.

Smith, M., & Matre, M. Social norms and sex roles in romance and adventure magazines. *Journalism Quarterly*, 1975, *52*, 309–315.

Smith, S. The image of women in film. In B. Stanford (Ed.), *On being female*. New York: Pocket Books, 1974, pp. 43–52.

Smuts, R. *Women and work in America*. New York: Columbia University Press, 1959.

Smythe, D. Reality as presented by television. *Public Opinion Quarterly*, 1954, *18*, 143–156.

Snider, P. "Mr. Gates" revisited: A 1966 version of the 1949 case study. *Journalism Quarterly*, 1967, *44*, 419–427.

Spock, B. *Baby and child care*. (Rev. ed.) New York: Pocket Books, 1976.

Standard directory of advertisers. Skokie, Ill.: National Register Publishing Co., annual.

Standard directory of advertising agencies. Skokie, Ill.: National Register Publishing Co., annual.

Standard Rate and Data Service. *Consumer magazine and farm publication: Rates and data*. Skokie, Ill.: Standard Rate and Data Service, Inc., annual.

Stanford, B. *On being female*. New York: Pocket Books, 1974.

Stapton, E., Anthony, S., & Gage, M. (Eds.) *History of women suffrage*. Vol. 1–4. Rochester, N.Y.: Charles Mann, 1889.

Stefflre, B. Run, mamma, run: Women workers in elementary readers. *Vocational Guidance Quarterly*, 1969, *18*, 99–102.

Steinem, G. Introduction. In *Wonder woman.* New York: Holt, Rinehart and Winston, 1972.

Steiner, G. *The people look at television: A study of audience attitudes.* New York: Alfred Knopf, 1963.

Sterling, C., & Haight, T. *The mass media: Aspen Institute guide to communication industry trends.* New York: Praeger, 1978.

Sternglanz, S., & Servin, L. Sex role stereotyping in children's television programs. *Developmental Psychology,* 1974, *10,* 710–715.

Stevenson, R., Eisinger, R., Feinberg, B., & Kotok, A. Untwisting the news twisters: A replication of Efron's study. *Journalism Quarterly,* 1973, *50,* 211–219.

Stolz, G., et al. *The occupational roles of women in magazines and books.* Chicago: Loyola University, no date.

Stone, P., Dunphy, D., Smith, M., & Olgilvie, D. *The general inquirer: A computer approach to content analysis.* Cambridge, Mass.: The MIT Press, 1966.

Stone, V. More women reporting news on the air. *RTNDA Communicator,* February 1977, 7–10.

Strainchamps, E. (Ed.) *Rooms with no view.* New York: Harper & Row, 1974.

Talese, G. *The Kingdom and the power.* New York: World, 1969.

Tedesco, N. Patterns in prime time. *Journal of Communication,* 1974, *24,* 119–124.

Thorne, B., & Henley, N. (Eds.) *Language and sex: Difference and dominance.* Rowley, Mass.: Newbury House, 1975.

Tremain, R. *The fight for freedom for women.* New York: Ballantine Books, 1973.

Trecker, J. Women in U.S. history high-school textbooks. In J. Pottker and A. Fishel (Eds.), *Sex bias in the schools: The research evidence.* London, England: Associated University Presses, 1977, 146–161.

Trumpeter, M., & Crowe, L. Sexism in picture books. *Illinois Libraries,* 1971, *53,* 499–502.

Tuchman, G. The symbolic annihilation of women by the mass media. In G. Tuchman, A. Daniels, and J. Benet (Eds.), *Hearth and home: Images of women in the mass media.* New York: Oxford University Press, 1978, pp. 51–68.

Turow, J. Advising and ordering: Daytime, prime time. *Journal of Communication,* 1974, *24,* 138–141.

Turow, J. Casting for TV parts: The anatomy of social typing. *Journal of Communication,* 1978, *28,* 18–24.

United Nations. *Statistical Yearbook.* New York: United Nations, Department of Economic and Social Affairs, annual.

United Nations. *Influence of Mass Communication Media on the formation of a new attitude towards the role of women in present-day society.* New

York: United Nations, Economic and Social Council, Commission on the Status of Women, 1974.

U.S. Bureau of the Census. *Statistical Abstract of the United States.* Washington, D.C.: U.S. Government Printing Office, annual.

U.S. Commission on Civil Rights. *A guide to federal laws and regulations prohibiting sex discrimination.* Washington D.C.: U.S. Government Printing Office, 1974.

U.S. Commission on Civil Rights. *Window dressing on the set: Women and minorities in television.* Washington, D.C.: U.S. Government Printing Office, 1977.

U.S. Department of Health, Education, and Welfare. *Toward a social report.* Washington, D.C.: U.S. Government Printing Office, 1969.

U.S. Department of Labor. *Complaint filing guide.* Washington, D.C.: U.S. Department of Labor, 1973.

U.S. Department of Labor. *Directory of national unions and employee associations, 1973, Supplement 2.* Washington, D.C.: U.S. Government Printing Office, 1975.

U.S. Federal Communications Commission. Broadcast procedure manual. *Federal Register,* September 5, 1974, *39* (173).

U.S. Office of Management and Budget. *Social indicators 1976.* Washington, D.C.: U.S. Government Printing Office, 1977.

U.S. Surgeon General's Scientific Advisory Committee on Television and Social Behavior. *Television and growing up: The impact of televised violence.* Washington, D.C.: U.S. Government Printing Office, 1971.

U'Ren, M. The image of women in textbooks. In V. Gornick and B. Moran (Eds.), *Woman in sexist society: Studies in power and powerlessness.* New York: Basic Books, 1971, 318–328.

Vajrathon, M. Toward liberating women: A communications perspective. In I. Tinker and M. Bramsen (Eds.), *Women and world development.* Washington, D.C.: Overseas Development Council, 1976, 95–104.

Valdez, A. The socialization influence of television commercials on pre-school age children. Unpublished doctoral dissertation, Stanford University, 1978.

Van Gelder, L. Women's pages: You can't make news out of a silk purse. *MS.,* November 1974, pp. 112–116.

Venkatesan, M., & Losco, J. Women in magazine ads: 1959–1971. *Journal of Advertising Research,* 1975, *15,* 49–54.

Wagner, L., & Banos, J. A woman's place: A follow-up analysis of the roles portrayed by women in magazine advertisements. *Journal of Marketing Research* 1973, *10,* 213–214.

Webb, E., & Roberts, K. Unconventional uses of content analysis in the social sciences. In G. Gerbner, O. Holsti, K. Krippendorff, W. Paisley, and P.

Stone (Eds.), *The analysis of communication content.* New York: Wiley, 1969, pp. 319–332.

Webb, E., Campbell, D., Schwartz, R., & Sechrest, L. *Unobtrusive measures: Nonreactive research in the social sciences.* Chicago: Rand McNally, 1966.

Webster's new world dictionary. New York: American Book Company, 1961.

Weingast, D. Walter Lippmann: A content analysis. *Public Opinion Quarterly,* 1950, *14,* 296–302.

Weisstein, N. Woman as nigger. *Psychology Today,* October 1969, pp. 20, 22, 58.

Weitzman, L., Eifler, D., Hokada, E., & Ross, C. Sex role socialization in picture books for preschool children. *American Journal of Sociology,* 1972, *77,* 1125–1149.

White, D. The "gatekeeper:" A case study in the selection of news. *Journalism Quarterly,* 1950, *27,* 383–390.

White, D., Albert, R., & Seeger, R. Hollywood's newspaper advertising: Stereotype of a nation's taste. In B. Rosenberg and D. White (Eds.), *Mass culture: The popular arts in America.* Glencoe, Ill.: The Free Press, 1957, pp. 443–456.

Whitlow, S. How male and female gatekeepers respond to news stories of women. *Journalism Quarterly,* 1977, *54,* 573–579, 609.

Whorf, B. *Language, thought, and reality.* New York: Wiley, 1956.

Wiik, S. The sexual bias of textbook literature. *English Journal,* 1973, *62,* 224–229.

Williams, J., Bennett, S., & Best, D. Awareness and expression of sex stereotypes in young children. *Developmental Psychology,* 1975, *11,* 635–642.

Wolfenstein, M., & Leites, N. The good-bad girl. In B. Rosenberg and D. White (Eds.), *Mass culture: The popular arts in America.* Glencoe, Ill.: The Free Press, 1957, pp. 294–307.

Women on Words and Images. *Channeling children: Sex stereotyping in prime-time TV.* Princeton, N.J.: Women on Words and Images, 1975.

Women on Words and Images. *Dick and Jane as victims: Sex stereotyping in children's readers.* Princeton, N.J.: Women on Words and Images, 1972.

Women on Words and Images. *Products and dissemination strategies.* Washington, D.C.: National Advisory Council on Women's Educational Programs, 1977.

Women's National Book Association. *The status of women in publishing.* New York: Women's National Book Association, New York chapter, 1971.

Zimbardo, P., & Meadow, W. Sexism springs eternal—in the *Reader's Digest.* Paper presented at the Annual Convention of the Western Psychological Association, San Francisco, 1974.

Name Index

Burton, G., 371
Busby, L., 89, 321, 365
Butler, M., 75, 167, 244, 258, 321, 330, 332, 337

Cadwell, F., 272, 331
Callan, M., 329, 395
Campbell, D., 261, 312, 314, 386
Campbell, R., 159
Canon, B., 324
Cantor, M., 85, 89, 91, 190, 194, 211, 218–219, 221–223, 227, 232, 335
Cantril, H., 356
Cathey-Calvert, C., 89, 364
Chaffee, S., 330, 392
Chang, W., 216
Charters, W., 253
Cheles-Miller, P., 155
Child, I., 128
Chin, R., 394
Chmaj, B., 136, 141
Chulay, C., 77, 150
Churchill, W., 322
Cirksena, K., 75
Clarke, P., 105–106, 108, 330
Cohen, A., 303
Comstock, G., 392
Copperud, R., 37
Cornellion, S., 122
Courtney, A., 71, 96–98, 101–102, 155
Covington, J., 154
Crawford, S., 236–237, 337
Crowe, L., 371
Cruse, D., 298
Culley, J., 96, 101–102
Czaplinski, S., 126, 131, 371

DaCosta, J., 154
Dale, E., 138, 140
Davidson, E., 392
DeCrow, K., 130
DeFleur, M., 80
Dier, S., 110
Dominick, J., 70, 73, 99
Douglass, F., 26
Downing, M., 82, 191
Drabman, R., 297
Driver, M., 353
Durham, J., 197, 380

Efron, E., 64
Eifler, D., 126–127, 371
Eisen, S., 294, 296
Eisinger, R., 358
Ekman, P., 358

Ellwood, C., 197–198, 380
Endres, K., 216–217, 383
Epstein, R., 391
Esposito, V., 105–106, 108
Evans, R., 246, 355

Farley, J., 224
Feinberg, B., 358
Ferriss, A., 313
Festinger, L., 392
Fidler, D., 296
Field, P., 392
Finz, S., 87
Fischer, P., 294
Fisher, E., 372
Fisher, J., 113–114
Fitzsimmons, E., 359
Flerx, V., 296
Flexner, E., 354
Flora, C., 104, 107–108
Flores, J., 197, 380
Foner, P., 354
Fowles, J., 324, 327
Fox, H., 96–97, 102
Francis, S., 77, 150
Franzwa, H., 103–104, 108
Frenkel-Brunswik, E., 303
Freuh, T., 293
Frey, K., 286, 389
Friedan, B., 354, 358
Friendly, F., 179, 232
Friesen, W., 358
Frisof, J., 129, 372

Gage, M., 353, 378
Galanter, E., 49
Gandy, O., 324–326
Gardner, J., 365
Garvey, D., 178
Gaudet, H., 356
Geng, V., 319
Gerbner, G., 80–81, 176, 314
Gershuny, H., 355
Gerth, H., 104
Goffman, E., 63
Goldsen, R., 270
Goldwater, B., 377
Goodman, C., 122
Goodman, E., 225
Goodnow, J., 356
Gorney, S., 208
Gornick, V., 377
Graebner, D., 127–128, 130–131, 371
Graham, A., 355
Grimke, S., 25, 353
Gross, H., 216, 233–234, 383

Subject Index